Winning Strategies, Recommenda[...]
Resources, Ethics and Ongoing C[...]
for Lobbyists and Washington Ad[...]
The Best of Everything Lo[...]
and Washington Advocacy

Lobbying
and
Advocacy

Deanna R. Gelak

TheCapitol.Net
Alexandria, VA 2008

TheCapitol.Net, Inc. is a non-partisan firm that annually provides continuing professional education and information for thousands of government and business leaders that strengthens representative government and the rule of law.

Our publications and courses, written and taught by *current* Washington insiders who are all independent subject matter experts, show how Washington works.™ Our products and services can be found on our web site at *<www.TheCapitol.Net>*.

Additional copies of *Lobbying and Advocacy* can be ordered online: *<www.LobbyingAndAdvocacy.com>*.

Citation Form—URLs: We use a standard style for all web addresses, also known as Uniform Resource Locators (URLs). URLs appear in text next to the first mention of the resource being described, and are surrounded with open and close angle brackets.

For URLs that have the standard web addressing form at the beginning of the URL of "http://www." we show only the initial "www." For example, the URL "http://www.domainname.com" will appear in text and tables as "*<www.domainname.com>*".

For URLs that begin with anything other than "www.", such as "http://thomas.loc.gov", the URL will appear in text and tables as "*<http://thomas.loc.gov>*". For example, the URL "http://www3.domain.gov" will appear in text and tables as "*<http://www3.domain.gov>*".

Design and production by Zaccarine Design, Inc., Evanston, IL; 847-864-3994.

v 1.0

Lobbying and Advocacy, hardbound: *Lobbying and Advocacy*, softbound:
ISBN: 1587331047   ISBN: 1587331004
ISBN 13: 978-1-58733-104-6   ISBN 13: 978-1-58733-100-8

Summary Table of Contents

Table of Contents

Chapter 4: Understanding Government
Institutions and Processes 115

Chapter 10: Media Engagement and Testimony: Perfect Your Public Presence 297

Chapter 11: Managing and Maintaining a
High-Performance Government Affairs Program 343

Deanna R. Gelak has worked in the legislative branch, executive branch, and private/nonprofit sector arenas since 1984. She is founder and president of Working for the Future, LLC, a public policy firm that advises organizational spokespersons and citizen leaders on effective political involvement and communication strategies.

Ms. Gelak served two terms as the president of the American League of Lobbyists, the national professional association for lobbyists. In that capacity, she served as chair of the board and the national spokesperson for the advocacy profession.

She has promoted the importance of effective and ethical lobbying in such venues as C–SPAN's *Washington Journal*, National Public Radio's *Talk of the Nation*, and the National Press Club. Her press interviews have also included: NBC Nightly News, MSNBC, Associated Press, Scarborough Country, Fox News, several National Public Radio shows, The Tavis Smiley Show, America's Voice, *Wall Street Journal*, *Time* magazine, *Wall Street Journal* Talk, The Mary Matalin Show, National Press Club, Monitor Radio, Bloomberg, Family News in Focus, *National Journal*, United Press International, *Washington Post*, *Washington Times*, *Roll Call*, *USA Today*, *Investors Business Daily*, CBS Marketwatch.com, *Chicago Tribune*, *San Francisco Chronicle*, Knight Ridder/Tribune, Strategic Finance, *Christian Science Monitor*, *Boston Globe*, *Boston Herald*, *Baltimore Sun*, *Austin Statesman*, *Orlando Sentinel*, *Miami Herald*, *Business Insurance*, *Business Week*, *Parenting*, *Parents*, *Glamour*, and *Working Woman*.

She is a faculty member for TheCapitol.Net, the exclusive provider of Congressional Quarterly Executive Conferences and a certificate trainer for the American League of Lobbyists' Lobbying Certificate Program.

Ms. Gelak assists leaders to more effectively influence public policy. Her communications training method has been used in Afghanistan, Jordan, Morocco, and Iraq. For more than a decade, she has provided congressional briefings, political involvement training programs and consulting to thousands of organizations and individuals, including congressional leadership and committees, the U.S. Coast Guard, the U.S. Department of Veterans Affairs, and the U.S. Department of Labor. She designed the "mock Congress" for National 4–H to educate high school students from across the nation on how Congress works.

Ms. Gelak has led numerous congressional coalitions. For example, she chaired the national Congressional Coverage Coalition, the successful effort to make labor and civil rights laws applicable to members of Congress and their staffs for the first time in history. Previously, members of Congress were exempt from the labor and civil rights laws that they had passed for the rest of the country.

Ms. Gelak achieved certification as a Senior Professional in Human Resources, which reflects her expertise in human resource policy issues. She is the former director of governmental affairs for the Society for Human Resource Management, a professional society with more than 175,000 professional members, and has authored numerous articles and publications on various workplace public policy issues. She has achieved significant expertise on work-life balance policy issues and served on a Bureau of National Affairs advisory committee in the area. Ms. Gelak also has worked for the Committee on Education and Labor of the U.S. House of Representatives and as a congressional liaison officer in the executive branch (U.S. Department of Labor).

Originally from Niceville, FL, Ms. Gelak is a graduate of the University of Florida.

Preface

"Everything in the world that deals with human relations, in one way or another passes through the halls of Congress. Everything eventually ends up somewhere in the legislative thinking of Congress."

Mike Michaelson, former C–SPAN executive vice president
and former staffer for five House speakers

Source: Exploring the Capitol: A Self-Guided Tour through the Halls of Congress (C-SPAN)

Former President Dwight D. Eisenhower once suggested that "Politics ought to be the part-time profession of every citizen who would protect the rights and privileges of free people and who would preserve what is good and fruitful in our national heritage." He understood that laws touch the lives of ordinary people.

Members of Congress continually cast consequential votes and make decisions that can directly influence issues as personal to us as the air we breathe, the products we buy, the services we use, the policies where we work, the health care that we receive, the benefits we will receive upon retirement, and the defense of our country. Whether aware of it or not, Americans do not go through a day without being affected in some way by a federal, state, or local law.

Indeed, legislative decisions are increasingly complex. First, the sheer volume of legislative activity is enormous. For example, in 2005 alone, 8,321 measures were introduced in Congress, 728 recorded votes were cast in the full House of Representatives and Senate, and 169 public bills were enacted into law. Approximately 7,553 witnesses testified before Congress in 1,546 congressional hearings. In the April 25, 2007, article, "What You Know Washington," a guest columnist for *The Hill* newspaper documented the increase in legislative and executive branch activity:

"The 109th Congress introduced 64 percent more pieces of legislation than the 104th Congress (13,074 pieces of legislation, up from 7,991) while the Federal Register last year published more than 75,000 pages of rules and regulations."

According to the July 2002 edition of *The American Prospect* magazine, approximately 150,000 bills are considered annually by the fifty state legislators and about 25 percent of them become law. Lobbyists at all levels are frequently evaluating and refining their strategies and tools for tracking and shaping state and local legislation and regulations. According to Paul W. Hallman, president of MultiState Associates, Inc.: "Given the nearly 200,000 bills introduced per biennium in the states, this amounts to the enactment of some 40,000 to 50,000 new laws every two years."

Federal, state, and local lobbying activities are an important part of the deliberative process. These activities represent thousands of hours of research and preparation by government affairs professionals. Lobbyists—whether paid professionals who advocate for a particular issue or concerned citizens who express their voices through the power of the ballot box as individual lobbyists—must be well-equipped for today's complex and challenging environment. Lobbyists are challenged to excel strategically, technically, ethically, and interactively.

Strategically: Effective lobbyists are continually building their expertise, refining their strategies, and adapting their plans. In an increasingly competitive and complicated field, lobbyists need to develop, refine, and adjust effective approaches if they want to succeed with their issues and the groups they represent. This book presents the top strategies for winning as an effective lobbyist. Winning strategies, resources, and tips relevant to congressional, executive branch, and state and local lobbying are included.

Technically: Legislators are constantly addressing a variety of complex issues. Many legislative decisions are extremely complicated. In her July 13, 2006, *Wall Street Journal* column on "The Complexity Crisis," Peggy Noonan dubbed this legislative era "the increasing complexity of everything." Frequently, today's legislators are not painting on a clean palette. Bills often amend existing laws, and policymakers are making decisions in a complicated legal environment. Often, practical ramifications or long-term implications of proposals are not readily apparent. In this complex environment, well-intentioned legislators may pass a law with unintended consequences.

Ethically: Today's lobbyists must respect not only the laws, but the professional standards governing advocacy in order to earn a positive reputation, to maintain credible contacts, and to avoid public and political embarrassment, the kiss of death for a lobbyist. The attributes for achieving lobbying success include integrity, reputation, and adherence to professional values.

It has been said that "In Washington, you are allowed to make one mistake . . . Maybe." Politics can be a ruthless business, and lobbying, especially in our nation's capitol, can be brutal. This harsh reality led former President Harry S. Truman to say, "If you want a friend in Washington, get a dog." John F. Kennedy described Washington as "a city of Southern efficiency and Northern charm." Actions can be scrutinized by both the opposition and the press. Mistakes made by a lobbying group on an issue that would go unnoticed in most organizations can appear on the front page of *The Washington Post*.

In lobbying, like life, the one thing that is constant is change. As governments at all levels continue to respond to specific situations and aim to win positive public approval, legal and ethical lobbying requirements have become increasingly complex and have presented new liabilities. Lobbying scandals, changes in the political environment, and compliance problems with new requirements will continue to prompt revisions to lobbying rules. While this book should not take the place of appropriate legal counsel, it does provide practical resources and methods for maintaining compliance and staying abreast of ethical and legal requirements.

Interactively: It's not just what you say, but how you say it. It's not just your information or your position, but how you present it. Lobbyists must think proactively and creatively about all of their communications. This book includes practical tips, research-based methods, and step-by-step guides for communicating with policymakers in every venue most effectively, including telephone calls, emails, congressional meetings, testifying before Congress, building coalitions, and working with the press.

Despite the scandals and cynicism that regularly appear in the daily news cycle, lobbying remains an essential part of the American political process. *Political involvement is not merely a right of an informed citizenry, it is a responsibility.* Our government does not function properly without an engaged and involved electorate. The role of professional lobbyists is to assist with citizen engagement and involvement.

During his tribute to those who died at the battle of Gettysburg, President Abraham Lincoln admonished Americans to be dedicated to the cause of freedom, the unfinished work of those who had given their lives for it:

> *"It is for us the living, rather, to be dedicated here to the unfinished work which they who fought here have thus far so nobly advanced. . . . for us to be dedicated to the great task remaining before us—that from these honored dead we take increased devotion to that cause for which they gave the last full measure of devotion—that we here highly resolve that these dead shall not have died in vain—that this nation, under God, shall have a new birth of freedom—and that government of the people, by the people, and for the people, shall not perish from the earth."*

It is my hope this book will be a useful tool for citizen leaders and organizational spokespersons, and that it will help them to effectively exercise their rights and responsibilities as they honor the trust placed in them by the interests they represent.

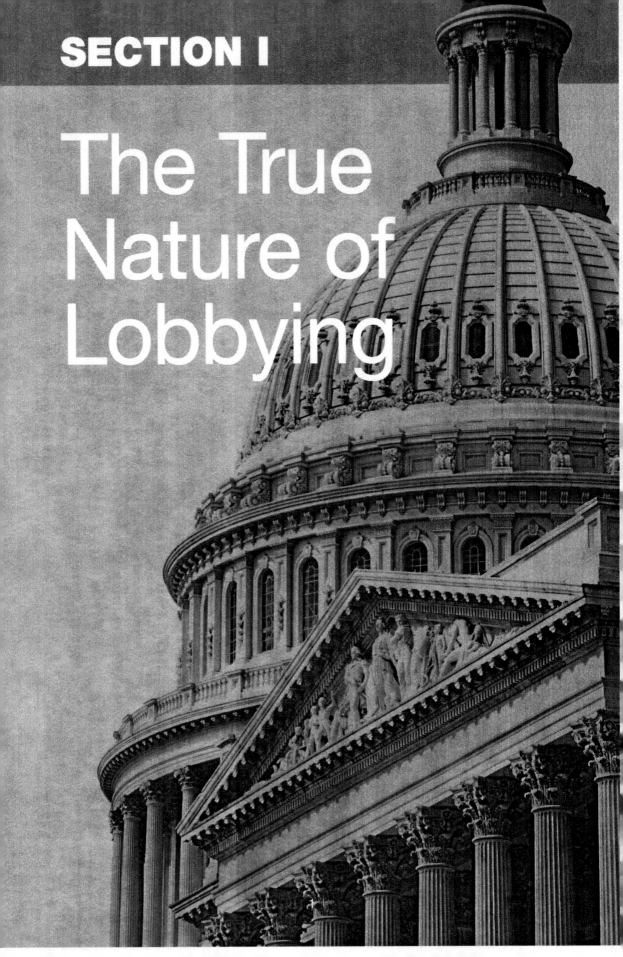

The True Nature of Lobbying

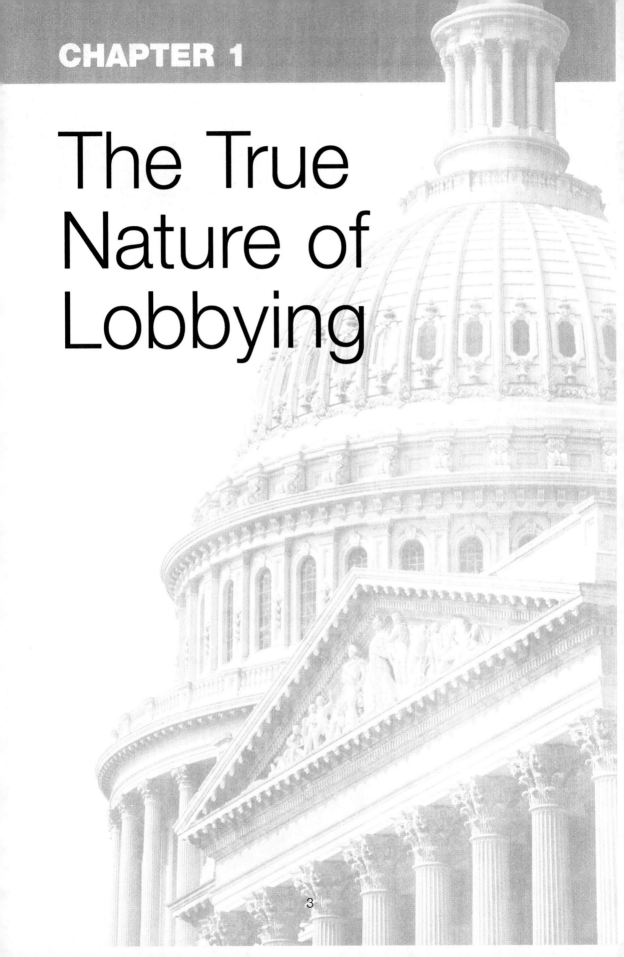

CHAPTER 1

The True Nature of Lobbying

Chapter 1: The True Nature of Lobbying

§1.1 **Introduction**

Nearly every legislative day, thousands of lobbyists are watching, monitoring, and working to influence the outcome of legislation at the federal level. Simultaneously, lobbyists are presenting hundreds of testimonies and briefings in state legislatures, municipalities, and local governments. The constitutional basis and role of lobbying as an essential part of our governmental process are discussed in this chapter.

Lobbyists frequently find themselves in a position of defending their profession. Chapter One provides a brief overview of the development of the practice of lobbying in the United States, which reveals the profession's honorable birth. This chapter also includes a discussion of the basis for lobbying, an overview of types of lobbying, and profiles lobbyists and the nature of their work.

§1.2 **The Textbook Definition of Lobbying**

According to the *2007 Merriam-Webster Online Dictionary*, lobbying means "to conduct activities aimed at influencing public officials and especially members of a legislative body." *Encyclopedia Britannica Online* defines lobbying as "any attempt by individuals or private interest groups to influence the decisions of government."

These definitions serve as a brief, general description. However, a fuller appreciation for the meaning of lobbying can only be gained by understanding the constitutional basis and the early history of lobbying, which are covered briefly in §§ 1.3 and 1.5.

§1.3 **The Constitutional Basis for Lobbying**

The fundamental right to lobby is grounded and protected in the First Amendment to the U.S. Constitution, the cornerstone of our freedoms:

> ". . . *Congress shall make no law . . . or abridging the freedom of speech, or of the press; or the right of the people peaceably to assemble, and to **petition the Government for a redress of grievances.**"* [emphasis added]

This book's companion, *Lobbying and Advocacy Sourcebook*, contains the text of the U.S. Constitution.

§1.4 **What Are Special Interests?**

> *"Ambition must be made to counter ambition."*
> James Madison, Federalist 51

Our founding fathers understood human nature. They recognized that it leads individuals to represent their own interests, rather than the greater public interest. They also understood that "factions" were inevitable, so they viewed "factions" as a necessary part of a competitive system of checks and balances.

The regulation of these various and interfering interests forms the principal task of modern legislation, and involves the spirit of party and faction in the necessary and ordinary operations of the government.

> *"No man is allowed to be a judge in his own cause, because his interest would certainly bias his judgment, and, not improbably, corrupt his integrity. With equal, nay with greater reason, a body of men are unfit to be both judges and parties at the same time; yet what are many of the most important acts of legislation, but so many judicial determinations, not indeed concerning the rights of single persons, but concerning the rights of large bodies of citizens? And what are the different classes of legislators but advocates and parties to the causes which they determine?"*
>
> James Madison, The Federalist Papers: No. 10

Our nation's founders constructed a system of checks and balances that depends on government accountability by a plurality of interests, not just the select voices of a few. Our nation was built on a system of a plurality of citizen special interests all expected to participate in the American political system.

However, to many people, the mere mention of the term "special interests" has almost become a curse term. It is frequently used as a derogatory descriptor in the press for unsavory influence on the political or policy process. How did this term become so sinister? What is a "special interest"? Is our nation not a plurality of interests? After all, special interests naturally express the views of those on whose behalf they petition. Veterans, disabled, teachers, and students are all examples of special interests. I recall reading about a public contest for a motto for the U.S. Congress several decades ago. The winning entry was, "Congress: Because there's no interest as special as your own." This drives home the fact that all citizens have special interests. The nation was built on citizens participating in the political system, and effective legislating depends on it.

Lobbying is an integral part of the American political process. It is no wonder the right to petition the government was included in the First Amendment to the U.S. Constitution.

§1.5 A Brief History: The Origin and Development of the Term "Lobbyist"

While persuading government officials has occurred since the origins of government itself, three major accounts have been circulated in discussions on the origin of the term "lobbying":

1. Ask any federal lobbyist how the term lobbyist originated and you will probably hear that the phrase was coined to describe individuals frequenting the Willard Hotel lobby in Washington, DC, to seek an audience with President Ulysses S. Grant, since Grant was often found there after work, enjoying a cigar and brandy.

§1.6 What's in a Name?

Professional lobbyists in the United States frequently find themselves in professional and social situations where they attempt to explain the credibility of their profession to people who have negative views of the term. A brief look at the development of the practice of American lobbying reveals the profession's honorable birth.

Colonial Agents and Petitioners: Paid "colonial agents" influenced British leaders and gave them information about the colonies. Colonial agents represented the needs of the colonies. According to Dr. John P. Kaminski, director, Center for the Study of the American Constitution, all of our paid colonial agents were lobbyists:

> *"The job of paid colonial agents was to influence the King and Parliament and give them information about the Colonies. For example, Ben Franklin was a 'colonial agent' and spent much of his time in England making contacts to get the best possible deal for the colonies. When Franklin discovered nasty letters from the British government, he sent them to the Colonists whom he represented."*

American lobbying actually originated with the birth of our country. Our nation was born from brave acts of individuals holding the government accountable. Our very first lobbyists were our nation's founders, who petitioned King George for redress. They stood on principle and held the government accountable, even at great risk and personal cost. In 1774, as a commoner, Thomas Jefferson wrote the draft petition, "A Summary View of the Rights of British America," which appealed to the king regarding his duty to the colonies. The document was published as a pamphlet without Jefferson's knowledge or approval, yet it earned him the respect of the colonists and with it, the opportunity to author the Declaration of Independence.

Lobby "Agent": One of the first American lobbyists, William Hull, worked to build a coalition of "agents" representing veterans' groups in his effort to get congressional approval for compensation for soldiers who fought in the American Revolution:

> *"In 1792, [William] Hull wrote to other veterans' groups, recommending that they have their "agent or agents" cooperate with him during the next session to pass a compensation bill."*

Source: Senate Majority Leader Robert C. Byrd's Essay on "Lobbyists" September 28, 1987 (updated 1989), found at <www.senate.gov/legislative/common/briefing/Byrd_History_Lobbying.htm>.

"Lobby": The evolution of the term is implied as early as 1808 during the U.S. House floor debate on moving the seat of government. More from the lively debate is at § 1.8.

HISTORY OF CONGRESS.	1536
Removal of the Seat of Government	FEBRUARY, 1808.

We have heard it said that if we move to Philadelphia we shall have a commanding lobby; we shall learn the sentiments of the population!

1536

Source: Annals of Congress

(Continued on page 8)

§1.6 What's in a Name? (continued)

"Lobbying": Usage of the term can be traced to U.S. senators lobbying their House colleagues in 1820:

> *"Other letters from Washington affirm, **that members of the Senate**, when the compromise question was to be taken in the House, were not only "**lobbying about the Representatives' Chamber,**" but were active in endeavoring to intimidate certain weak representatives by insulting threats to dissolve the Union."* [emphasis added]
> Source: *New Hampshire Sentinel,* April 1, 1820 (America's Historical Newspapers)

According to Fred R. Shapiro, editor, *Yale Book of Quotations,* and associate librarian for Collections and Access and lecturer in Legal Research at Yale Law School:

> *"This citation of lobbying seems not to be referring to the Senators themselves, but Senators in the capacity of influencing other legislators (Representatives)."*

This is quite fitting since James Madison had earlier discussed legislators as advocates of special interests themselves: "And what are the different classes of legislators but advocates and parties to the causes which they determine?" (Source: The Federalist Papers: No. 10) As indicated by their usage of the phrase, "We the People" in the preamble of the Constitution, our first leaders viewed themselves as part of the citizenry and considered our government as emanating from the people.

"Lobby Member": By 1856, the term "lobby member" was in use, along with the expression "third house." A whimsical *New York Herald* report from its "Washington Correspondence" column (briefly excerpted below and reprinted from the original image in § 1.7) provides an amusing commentary on the remarkable influence of "female lobby members," who are described as influencing every bill passed by Congress in 1856, even though women were denied the right to vote until 1920. The column is a classic depiction of the media's longstanding tradition for scrutinizing lobbyists:

> *"In classifying the lobby members of Congress the female representatives of the 'third house' occupy no unimportant position. Indeed, I may say that one experienced female lobbyist is equal to any three schemers of the other sex with whom I am acquainted. . . . and not a great measure comes before Congress that they do not have an important, if not a conspicuous, "finger in the pie." Their interest is secured for all schemes, private and public, for lobbying through private bills and public acts, for the extension of a patent or granting of an indefinite number of acres of public lands for private speculative purposes. . . . Be sure the female lobby members deserve consideration while treating upon the system which affords her a stage to act upon.*

> *"The female lobby member is of no particular age. Age is not a consideration; but she must have tact, talent, and a thorough contempt for the conventionalities of society. She must be easy, affable and accommodating in her disposition . . . Sometimes the female lobby member is a strong-minded woman, an advocate for woman's rights; again, she is a literary celebrity, a poetess, perhaps or a tyro in literature . . . But whether strong-minded or gifted, the female lobby member has a good share of strong practical common sense and a keen perception of human nature."*

> The *New York Herald,* Morning Edition, December 17, 1856. See § 1.8 for the fuller 1956 *New York Herald* column image, "Our Washington Correspondence."

2. A second account has the origin of the term deriving first from "lobby-agents" to designate those petitioners in the lobby of the New York State Capitol waiting to address legislators.

3. Yet a third account has the term originating as early as the 1840s in the United Kingdom, where members of the British public would gather in the Central Lobby of the Parliament Building to meet with their representatives.

It does not appear that any of these traditional accounts can be authenticated. In fact, the usage of the term "lobbying" to pertain to persuading public officials can be traced back to 1820, two years before Ulysses S. Grant was even born (April 27, 1822). The evolution of the term "lobbying" by members of Congress themselves is implied as early as 1808 on the House floor (see §§ 1.6 and 1.8). Also, there is evidence of the terms "lobbying" or "lobbyists" being used to pertain to persuading public officials before Grant became president in 1869. Therefore, the term could not have been first coined in the Willard Hotel lobby. The New York historians I contacted were not able to validate the account of the term originating in the New York State Capitol. Similarly, although the word was used as early as the 1840s in the United Kingdom, the UK House of Commons is unable to prove the term originated there. In addition, the *Oxford-English Dictionary* credits the United States with the word's origin. See § 1.6 for a brief summary of the development of the term and practice of lobbying in the United States.

§1.7 **The Profession's Forefathers**

Regardless of the origin of the term, lobbying by "humbly" petitioning the government was a hallmark of our nation's birth. The first American lobbyists were the colonial agents, including some of our nation's founders.

Some of the First Lobbyists

1. Thomas Jefferson

> "*In every state of these Oppressions* **We have Petitioned for Redress in the most humble terms:** *Our repeated Petitions have been answered only by repeated injury.*" [emphasis added]
> The Declaration of Independence, July 4, 1776

2. William Hull

William Hull, a Revolutionary War hero, was hired by the Continental Army's Virginia veterans to help the soldiers receive compensation. After serving as governor of Michigan, he fought in the War of 1812, was court-martialed and barely escaped being hanged for treason after allegedly surrendering Fort Detroit to the British without firing a shot. He said that he was misunderstood and spent the rest of his life trying to clear his name.

§1.8 Lobby Facts

Historical Quotes

Despite what most lobbyists believe, the term lobbyist or lobbying did not first originate as visitors frequented the well-known Washington, DC, Willard Hotel to seek an audience with President Ulysses S. Grant. Grant was born on April 27, 1822, and was president from 1869-1877. In fact, the evolution of the term is implied as early as 1808, during the following House debate on moving the seat of government back to Philadelphia. The Willard brothers bought the hotel in 1850. There are at least seven documented instances of the use of the term lobbying or lobbyist before Grant was president and one before he was even born:

1535	HISTORY OF CONGRESS.	1536
H. OF R.	*Removal of the Seat of Government.*	FEBRUARY, 1808.

To that gentleman I shall make some reply, though I shall be very brief. He has undertaken to suppose that the large majority of this House in favor of consideration of the motion, was not from a belief of the propriety of passing it; I hope he will be convinced that the decision proceeded from a sense of duty and a firm conviction of the propriety of the measure. I shall never call anything extravagant which the interest of my country calls for—a removal of the seat of Government from a place which has everything against it and nothing in its favor—which is exposed to sickness and to death.

The gentleman from Virginia has mentioned the danger of division. I am as much in favor of unity as that gentleman or any other on the floor, and shall always aim at it. Members of this House who are at least of equal standing with him and myself, consider it essentially necessary that this should not interfere; it is not our desire to call it up to interfere; we wish to progress with harmony—to give our aid to every measure.

The gentleman supposes I have not read the Constitution. I may not possess the ability or nice discernment of that gentleman; but plain common sense will show to every observer, as that gentleman and some others want to stifle discussion on the subject and to prevent us from showing it by fair reasoning, that the contract is unconstitutional. This is what we wish to show at a future day, and what we shall show if we are not prevented. I will submit it to the good sense of this House, of the citizens in the galleries, and to the impartial determination of all the people of the United States, whether those who feel themselves laboring under a great national grievance, and have brought it before the National Legislature, and declared that they do not mean to urge it, but will give a full and fair opportunity for discussion, and every opportunity for argument—whether these, the friends of the resolution, act fairly and impartially, or those the opponents of it, who wish to smother the investigation of it.

I will now barely observe that that gentleman may think as he pleases, and on a future day I will enlarge upon the subject, and show that it is the duty of this House, and I hope to God we shall fulfil it, to remove the seat of Government.

Mr. LYON said the gentleman from New Jersey had endeavored to have it understood that this was a subject of great importance. Mr. L. believed it was all-important to that gentleman; he appeared to think of nothing else. The matter was growing too serious now to talk of hobbyhorses. It seemed that gentlemen who had helped him on his hobby-horse found it necessary to adhere to him too closely. He was in hopes they would have left him and his hobby-horse together. The gentleman, said Mr. L. has talked about eating and drinking; everybody knows what is his profession—but I will drop all this sort of talking. It looks serious—twenty-one in a majority, by yeas and nays to consider this resolution. I will say that I am one of those who was dragged here against my will by a Federal majority. I then thought it was not time to come this far South; but having been brought here, I looked about me, like a farmer about a new farm; I endeavored to dress it up, to build improvements on it, and make it better, and I have acted in that way ever since. What has happened since then? We have acquired a new world to the Southward and Westward of this place. If it was then proper to fix the seat of Government here, what is it now? I cannot see how Federal gentlemen can look or talk of the subject without blushing. What can they think of their predecessors for bringing us here when we had not that country! Kentucky too, which now sends six and which at the next census may send ten members to this House, then only sent two.

While I am up I will tell gentlemen a story. A question similar to this is now pending in Kentucky. The seat of Government is now at Frankfort. The people in the Southern and Western part of the State have joined to move it Eastward; and why, do you suppose? In order that they may hereafter carry it Westward. It is now immoveable except by a majority of two-thirds; and in order to carry the seat of Government Westward by and by, they agree to carry it Eastward now. The Kentucky policy prevails here; no kind of doubt of it. Gentlemen from the Southward and Westward intend to humor those Eastward, that they may move it Westward hereafter. Carry it to Philadelphia—how long will it stay there? The next census will give us ten or fifteen additional members from the Westward. Will they be willing to retain it at Philadelphia, or will they carry it to Pittsburg or farther West? It is mere trifling to suppose it will be fixed at Philadelphia. The only object is to destroy this place, on which so much money has been expended. Now I have been obliged to come here, very reluctantly I must say; but when I got here, the more I looked at it, the more I thought this was the proper site. It is one hundred miles nearer to the Western country than Philadelphia, with a water communication upon which improvements are daily making. It has been said that the merchants from the Western country can manage their business much better at Philadelphia. I know that, if I were sent to Congress for myself alone, I should wish to go to Philadelphia; but I have constituents, friends, children; and it is much better for the country that we should be here, and aid the improvement of the place. Bring here the Bank of the United States; we shall soon have a large city; no doubt of it. The reason why you have not now a large population or great improvements, is, that you are always talking about moving. I wish it to stand at least sixty or one hundred years as it is; I am convinced that this of all places in the Union is the best. It is said we ought to be near the seashore, near the water. Here is water. Some say we should go to New York. Here is a good place. Some sneer at the navy yard, and why? Because they refuse to do what they ought towards clothing it, and then laugh at its nakedness.

We have heard it said that if we move to Philadelphia we shall have a commanding lobby; we

Source: *Annals of Congress*, pages 1536–1537, February, 1808.

1537	HISTORY OF CONGRESS.	1538
FEBRUARY, 1808.	*Removal of the Seat of Government.*	H. OF R.

shall learn the sentiments of the population! The only inducement which influenced me to be a little satisfied at moving from Philadelphia, was, because Congress were almost overawed by the population of that city; measures were dictated by that city. I had rather move into a wilderness; I do not want to go among these people; I have seen too much of them, I have seen the time when members of this House could not walk the streets in safety. I have seen the time when men with cockades in their hats would say "there goes one of the d——d minority." I can never forget the insults I received in Philadelphia whilst in the minority.

Here too is a Constitutional provision with regard to the seat of Government, whether held in this or any other place—a feature in the Constitution, and on that feature a contract is built; on which subject the gentleman from Virginia (Mr. LOVE) has dwelt very ably. I will not answer the observation of the gentleman from New Jersey (Mr. SLOAN) about contracts; he knows how to make a contract about a cow or an ox; but as to any other contract he knows nothing. [Mr. LYON was here called to order.] I do not mean to be disorderly, I assure you. One word more as to the health of this place. The gentleman from New Jersey has unfortunately compared it with Philadelphia. Have we not been compelled to suspend business and leave Philadelphia on account of the yellow fever? I have been a little sick here; and so I should perhaps any where else. Has any member of Congress lost his life here in consequence of the unhealthiness of the place? They have died of consumption or other diseases brought with them from home. I have seen or heard nothing of the unhealthiness of this place. It is really unfortunate to compare the two places together. In Philadelphia Congress sat one year till July, and would not then have adjourned but for the yellow fever; and it is a ridiculous story to talk of changing the seat of Government from this place to Philadelphia, on account of its superiority in healthiness. I have gone through the observations I mean to make.

Mr. GARDENIER said he should not indulge himself at this time in following gentlemen in any remarks they had made. He could easily conceive that there were members in the House to whom the proposition of the gentleman from New Jersey must be disagreeable, and who were impelled to oppose it more by their feelings than their reason. A very considerable and respectable portion of the House had manifested a disposition to hold the question open to discussion—not that they were determined on removal, but that it was a case in which discussion might enlighten and could not do harm. The present motion was designed to stifle discussion; he would submit to his friend from Virginia (Mr. LEWIS) whether he could calculate upon any permanent good to result from this procedure. Would they not prosper their cause infinitely more by reasoning with those gentlemen who were doubtful, than by telling them that they would give no opportunity to satisfy their minds on the subject?

10th CON. 1st SESS.—49

Could gentlemen expect that a treatment of this kind will be submitted to hereafter, or that any session of Congress would pass by without agitating this question? He submitted to the opponents of the motion whether it would not be better to enter fairly into the discussion—to govern gentlemen who wished for removal by argument and not by force of numbers. He trusted there were very few gentlemen on the floor who were not open to conviction, even against their own wishes. It struck him that, if they were forced into silence, it would only be making discontent worse; if put down by fair argument, they would have nothing to complain of. The proper and regular course of debate would then be pursued. This question once fairly agitated and negatived, if that should be the result, would have the effect of putting the question more permanently at rest, and more substantially answer the purpose of the gentleman from Virginia (Mr. LEWIS) than the mode now pursued by that gentleman, who he had no doubt was actuated by honest motives, and Mr. G. honored him for it. He again repeated, would it not be better to promote discussion than thus to force them to silence—to smother the matter? He did not say this was the intention, for he believed the gentleman was influenced by better motives.

He had avoided making any observations on the main question, because he did not consider this the time for them. If the House were so perfectly satisfied on this subject, and thought so little was due to those who wished a discussion, he must submit; but this procedure would not satisfy the minority or the public. Without committing himself on the question one way or the other, because the vote which had already been taken did not commit any one, he wished to have the matter discussed, that those for it and those against it might have an opportunity to offer arguments. In his own mind, he felt a difficulty in declaring how he should vote, and therefore wished a discussion.

Mr. LEWIS assured his friend from New York that he had no intention to stifle investigation. The subject was now before the House, and as perfectly open to discussion as if before a Committee of the Whole House. My object, said Mr. L., in making this motion, was to invite discussion, but to invite it at this moment; because every moment that the subject is pending is death to the interest of the District. I wish it to be ascertained at once whether a majority is in favor of removal or not. I wish this investigation, and was in hopes that the gentleman from New York, or some other, would offer some reasons for bringing forward this measure, so fraught with mischief and distraction to the District. It is no reason with me to remove to Philadelphia because I and others can be better accommodated there than at this place; it is no reason that beef or any other article sells cheaper than at this place, or that we can get information from the lobby at Philadelphia which we cannot get here. If members of this House should ever become so dependent that they must be indebted to persons out

(Continued on page 12)

§1.8 Lobby Facts (Continued)

NEWHAMPSHIRE SENTINEL.

"I WILL SPEAK OF THE THINGS ... SEEN, AND TOUCH UPON THOSE REPORTED, THAT THE PEOPLE MAY CONSIDER THE *WHOLE MATTER*."

SENTINEL—PUBLISHED EVERY SATURDAY, BY JOHN & GEORGE W. PRENTISS—APPOINTED TO PUBLISH THE LAWS OF THE UNITED STATES.

Vol. XXII.—No. 1095.]   SATURDAY, APRIL 1, 1820.   [1 Doll. 75 cts. per ann.

April 1, 1820, *New Hampshire Sentinel* (America's Historical Newspapers) Concerning the Missouri Compromise Vote:

"Other letters from Washington affirm, that members of the Senate, when the compromise question was to be taken in the House, were not only 'lobbying about the Representatives' Chamber,' but were active in endeavoring to intimidate certain weak representatives by insulting threats to dissolve the Union."

N. H. SENTINEL.

SLAVERY.

The following is the most particular account we have seen, of the manner in which the *compromise*, as it is called, was effected. If there be any one who can read the account here given, of this disgraceful procedure, and not feel his cheeks glow with indignation, he can have but little regard for the honor and reputation of his country—and so little for his own rights as a freeman as to be almost unworthy of that character. Other letters from Washington affirm, that members of the Senate, when the compromise question was to be taken in the House, were not only " lobbying about the Representatives' Chamber," but were active in endeavoring to intimidate certain *weak* representatives by insulting threats *to dissolve the Union ;* and openly declaring, that unless the compromise was acceded to, they would immediately dissolve the Senate and go home. And, shame to tell it, their threats had the desired effect. May the truckling spirits who were thus influenced, never again be the representatives of freemen.

Courtesy of the New Hampshire Historical Society

October 2, 1825, *Ballston Spa* (NY), *Gazette* 4 (America's Historical Newspapers):

"It is gratifying to the FREEMEN of this district, that the only charge which the Regency papers have alledged against Mr. Viele, is, that in former times he differed with them in opinion. But no Bank Agency, no Lobbying, has ever been laid at his door. How is it with Cramer?—Has he never been engaged in procuring BANK charters?"

May 1826, *Reformer*, Philadelphia, PA (America's Historical Newspapers):

"Rumour says that several of these self-styled reverend divines have been guilty of 'lobbying' for funds, as will seem to appear by the following extract from the New York Courier of 1st April. More than half a million of dollars has been paid into the treasury of New York from lotteries, since 1801, and been appropriated to the endowment of colleges, charitable and pious institutions, the education of children, and public improvements."

January 26, 1829, *New-Hampshire Patriot* (America's Historical Newspapers):

"Some of the Sabbath Day memorialists are here lobbying Congress on the subject."

January 15, 1830, *New-York Spectator* (19th Century U.S. Newspapers):

"We learn from Albany that Col. Stone is lobbying for the Federal papers in this city, against the law providing that one copy of the legal notices shall be published in this paper."

October 6, 1837, *Cleveland Herald*:

"Gen. Bronson . . . spent a considerable portion of the last winter in Columbus, lobbying to procure the establishment of a Bank at Ohio City."

§1.8 Lobby Facts (Continued)

July 2, 1849, *New Hampshire Gazette* (America's Historical Newspapers and The Oxford English Dictionary Online):

"This interest and this feeling were taken advantage of and subjected to a constant stimulation by a score of indefatigable lobbyists, who kept up an untiring attack upon the members."

December 17, 1856, *New York Herald*, Morning Edition:

Despite the fact that women were decades from securing the right to vote, this whimsical column (see § 1.6) illustrates that female lobbyists were extremely influential on Capitol Hill:

THE NEW YORK HERALD.

WHOLE NO. 7414. MORNING EDITION—WEDNESDAY, DECEMBER 17, 1856. PRICE TWO CENTS.

Our Washington Correspondence.

WASHINGTON, Dec. 18, 1856.

The Herald and the Lobby System—Female Members of the "Third House"—New Ocean Mail Contracts.

Your evident determination to expose and ultimately explode the present detestable lobby system is producing its effect here. Those who have in hand gigantic schemes for plundering the public treasury are becoming more sly in their movements, and go about the House with a cat-like action, decidedly in keeping with their general characteristics and the plots which they have concocted. Even the Chevalier Webb and Thurlow Weed, the boldest operators against the purity of our national legislation, are acting more cautiously in view of the position assumed by the HERALD, and appear as mild and sanctimonious as cyprians at a christening. The great question, and that which creates the most attention and excitement in all circles just now, is, will the list desired by you be furnished? This problem will probably be solved somewhere about the close of the holidays; it will take some time to make it full and fair to all parties. The document must prove a pen picture worth the looking at.

In classifying the lobby members of Congress the female representatives of the "third house" occupy no unimportant position. Indeed, I may say that one experienced female lobbyist is equal in point of influence to any three schemers of the other sex with whom I am acquainted. Every session draws to Washington a number of those feminine birds of passage, as well as prey, and you will find their names at Willard's, Brown's, the National, or wherever members most do congregate; and not a great measure comes before Congress that they do not have an important, if not a conspicuous, "finger in the pie." Their interest is secured for all schemes, private and public, for lobbying through private bills and public acts, for the extension of a patent or the granting of an indefinite number of acres of public lands for private speculative purposes. Woman's influence has often secured the attendance of a member when his vote was sure and needed, and her fascinations has been exerted when it was necessary that an opposition vote should be absent from the House. Many a poor member has braved the censure of his constituents and neglected his duty for the poor recompense of an hour's tete a tete with an empty smile from a pretty, persevering, fast and fascinating woman. Be sure the female lobby member deserves consideration while treating upon the system which affords her a stage to act upon.

The female lobby member is of no particular age. Age is not a consideration; but she must have tact, talent and a thorough contempt for the conventionalities of society. She must be easy, affable and accommodating in her disposition, and it matters not whether she be sweet sixteen "or fat, fair and forty," a maid, wife or widow. Sometimes the female lobby member is a strong-minded woman, an advocate for woman's rights; again, she is a literary celebrity, a poetess, perhaps, or a tyro in literature, whose incipient effort is stowed away upon the shelves of some prudent friend from sheer regard for the public, whose taste is too crude for the delectable food furnished through the travail of the spirit's medium. I know of such. But whether strong-minded or gifted, the female lobby member has a good share of strong practical common sense and a keen perception of human nature. Without these qualities she would be naught. Widows form the majority of the class of which I am treating. Why this is so I am not able to say; but that it is so is the fact. Perhaps they understand better, from previous trial, the springs by which the male animal is actuated, and can manage the machine to more advantage from knowing its complications. Be that as it may, the widow is the most powerful of the tribe to which she belongs, and many a member has an abiding regret that he has neglected Sam Weller's caution to "beware of the vidders." Now and then a belle finds herself in the ranks of the lobbyists, but does not stay there long. She goes the way of womankind generally, and probably marries a good deal of money attached to an official of some grade nearly twice her age. But all play their part alike, which is to mystify and perplex the people's servants, and the end is accomplished most perfectly and to the entire satisfaction of all concerned. In a subsequent letter I will give some rich developements in regard to the management of the female lobby members.

Commodore Vanderbilt is after the mail contract again. The prospects of the Commodore have been jeopardized by the meagre show which he made of his steamer last summer. Some of the members of the House got drunk on the Commodore's champagne, but the entertainment was generally too shabby to have any influence. An attempt will be made during the session to drive through Congress another mail contract, and for the establishment of a steamship line to India via the Sandwich Islands. The scheme had its conception in New York but I don't know who is to be midwife to the bantling yet. The session will be a short but a merry one. The lobby force is well organized, and only waiting the signal to act.

From the collection of The New-York Historical Society, negative 81048d.

Sources: *Oxford English Dictionary Online*, *Annals of Congress*, and Fred R. Shapiro, editor, *Yale Book of Quotations* and associate librarian for Collections and Access and Lecturer in Legal Research, Yale Law School

§1.9 Recommended Resources

Historical Documents

- The complete text online of the U.S. Constitution, The Bill of Rights, the Declaration of Independence, and a topical index to the Constitution may be viewed through links on the U.S. Government Printing Office (GPO) web site at *<www.gpoaccess.gov>*.

- Bulk copies of the pocket edition of the Constitution of the United States of America may also be ordered from the GPO site.

- See also *Lobbying and Advocacy Sourcebook*, 24, for the U.S. Constitution.

- *The U.S. Constitution and Fascinating Facts About It* (pocket edition with useful index to the U.S. Constitution and Amendments), ISBN-13: 978-1891743009. This pocket edition may also be ordered at *<www.constitutionfacts.com>*.

- Neil H. Cogan, *The Complete Bill of Rights: The Drafts, Debates, Sources and Origins*. ISBN-13: 978-0195103229.

- See § 2.34 for historical quotations on congressional ethics. Browse congressional debate archives online at the Library of Congress, *<www.loc.gov>*.

3. Daniel Webster

With low pay for members of Congress and few perks, and years before ethics rules governing conflicts of interests between policymakers and lobbyists, Daniel Webster, a renowned orator, served as a member of Congress and as a lobbyist simultaneously. He wrote to one client because his retainer had not been renewed or refreshed:

> *"Since I have arrived here [in Washington], I have had an application to be concerned, professionally, against the bank, which I have declined, of course, although I believe my retainer has not been renewed or refreshed as usual. If it be wished that my relation to the Bank should be continued, it may be well to send me the usual retainers."*

So when we look at early lobbyists, whether Thomas Jefferson, William Hull, or Daniel Webster, we see that since the beginning, lobbyists have been ignored, misunderstood, and underpaid!

§1.10 Federal, State, and Local Lobbying

Professional lobbying takes place in both chambers of the U.S. Congress, the federal executive branch agencies, state legislatures, state executive branches, and local governments, including mayors' offices. Lobbyists are engaged in not only legislative practices, but also in regulations and executive branch policies, actions, and decisions. They are also interested in reviewing and tracking court decisions at all levels that may drive legislation and shape public policy. In essence, lobbyists are involved wherever public policy decisions are made that impact the citizen concerns that they represent.

§1.11 The Two Major Parts of Lobbying Work

There are two primary aspects of lobby work: informing and communicating with those you represent, and advocacy with policymakers. Lobbyists are frequently challenged to achieve the right balance between them, since both functions are important.

Informing and Communicating with Those Whom You Represent	Advocacy with Policymakers
Examples of Representation Tasks:	**Examples of Advocacy Tasks:**
• Survey members to determine public policy positions, update legislative positions and priorities, and gather timely information (for example, practical effects of legislation) relevant to public policy discussions.	• Send letter to Congress on behalf of the organization.
	• Testify before Congress.
• Answer phone calls and emails from members on the status and outlook of legislative and regulatory proposals.	• Work within a coalition to advance your organization's legislative goals.
	• Make direct contact with congressional staff and members.
• Draft legislative publications to keep members informed on legislative status changes.	• Develop public relations plan to communicate positions on key legislation.
• Send alerts to members/clients when specific action is needed.	• Obtain or prepare legislative and legal analysis of proposals.
• Provide speeches to members, clients, or corporate staff on legislative activity that will affect them or their organization.	• Track legislation and monitor legislative activity; provide input, including technical expertise to policymakers; research long-term ramifications of proposals; determine the practical ramifications of proposals; prepare analysis of complex proposals; bring attention to provisions that are buried within larger legislative packages or regulatory proposals; evaluate interactions with existing laws.
• Update web page.	
• Write articles for the magazine; provide information and statements to internal and external reporters.	
• Recruit and train grassroots members/seek clarification from client or organization.	

§1.12 Lobby Facts

Benefits of Lobbying

Lobbying plays a critical role in our democratic process. Here are several examples of lobbying's key role:

- Provides policy expertise on complex legislation;
- Provides practical insight on technical, practical, and long-term ramifications of legislation and public policy;
- Connects and communicates citizen concerns to public officials and lawmakers;
- Informs citizens of impending legislation and public policy developments, raises public awareness of legislation and public policy changes;
- Holds lawmakers and other public officials accountable for their actions and votes; and
- Unites citizens with like concerns.

The necessity and benefits of lobbying may be best showcased by reviewing situations where it has been excluded. For example, in 1986, members of Congress hastily added an unexamined tax provision (which amended Section 89 of the tax code) without the benefit of public hearings or debate. The complicated provision required companies to provide equivalent benefits to all employees. Something that looked good on paper behind closed doors in a conference meeting, but had not been examined by interested parties, ended up not working in the real world. The measure led to the cancellation of many health plans. In 1989, members of Congress realized their mistake and repealed the hastily passed provision.

§1.13 How Do Lobbyists Divide Their Work Time?

While the old lobbying stereotype depicts lobbyists slapping backs in smoke-filled back rooms or circling fundraisers, lobbyists actually spend more time writing, analyzing, and interacting with those they represent. For example, the American League of Lobbyists' (ALL) 1998 Membership Survey found:

- Lobbyists spend more time "writing or communicating with their own members, clients or companies" than on any other function (20 percent);
- 10 percent of the responding lobbyists indicated that they spend most of their time on stereotypical lobbying activity—directly contacting representatives and officials;
- 15 percent indicated that they spend more time on internal management of employees than on any other function;
- 15 percent indicated that they spend most of their time on internal administrative/office issues;

- Only 5 percent indicated that they spent most of their time on campaign or fundraising activities; and
- 20 percent did not respond to the question.

While the survey is dated, the results likely hold true today. These findings do not square with the old stereotype where wining and dining, or a pat on the back and a campaign check get you everything you need. See Chapter Eleven for a discussion of organizing tasks and maintaining priorities within a governmental affairs office. See Appendix 1 for a detailed list of various lobbying activities.

§1.14 **Stereotypes**

What is the profile of a typical lobbyist? Is it the old stereotype of a portly cigar-smoking man carrying a cash-filled briefcase and cutting deals in smoke-filled back rooms? Profiling today's lobbyist is not an easy task because lobbyists are as diverse as the interests that they represent. Additionally, some bad actors receive significant media and public attention. Cartoonists frequently portray negative lobbyist stereotypes:

Copyright ©2005 Mark Wilson. Used with permission.

§1.15 Three Major Types of Lobbyists

There are three major types of registered lobbyists: 1. association/non-profit, 2. corporate, and 3. contract/consultants. The first type of lobbyist represents members of an association or non-profit organization, such as the American Association of Retired Persons (AARP) or the National Federation of Independent Business (NFIB). Corporate lobbyists work on issues that concern their companies. Contract or self-employed (consultant) lobbyists work on a contractual basis for client organizations who hire them with a contract or retainer.

According to a Government Accountability Office (GAO) report on Lobbyists' Registrations, approximately 20 percent of federal registered lobbyists are hired lobbyists within their organizations and 80 percent work at firms with outside clients (contract lobbyists). (Source: Government Accountability Office GAO/GGD–98–105R, Lobbyists' Registrations, April 28, 1998.)

§1.16 Number of Federal Registered Lobbyists per Subject Area

A breakdown of the number of lobbyists per general subject area (in parentheses next to each subject area title) is presented below. The average number of issue areas lobbied by each of the approximately 11,778 federal lobbyists is five out of 77 subject areas. The average does not change whether considering in-house or consultant lobbyists. (Source: Information extracted on July 2, 2007, from "Washington's Power Tool Database," produced by Columbia Books, <*www.lobbyists.info*>.)

Number of Federal Registered Lobbyists Per Subject Area

- Accounting (100)
- Agriculture (492)
- Apparel/Clothing Industry/Textiles (89)
- Aviation/Aircraft/Airlines (337)
- Beverage Industry (72)
- Civil Rights/Civil Liberties (179)
- Communications/Broadcasting/ Radio/TV (333)
- Consumer Issues/Safety/ Protection (357)
- Disaster Planning/Emergencies (235)
- Education (731)
- Family Issues/Abortion/Adoption (135)
- Food Industry (231)
- Gaming/Gambling/Casino (126)
- Homeland Security (592)
- Indian/Native American Affairs (191)
- Law Enforcement/Crime/Criminal Justice (356)
- Media (Information/Publishing) (96)
- Minting/Money/Gold Standard (20)
- Postal (109)
- Advertising (63)
- Alcohol and Drug Abuse (91)
- Arts/Entertainment (124)
- Banking (359)
- Budget/Appropriations (1434)
- Clean Air and Water (Quality) (442)
- Computer Industry (254)
- Copyright/Patent/Trademark (344)
- District of Columbia (44)
- Energy/Nuclear (783)
- Financial Institutions/Investments/ Securities (445)

- Foreign Relations (355)
- Government Issues (719)
- Housing (340)
- Insurance (332)
- Manufacturing (261)
- Medical/Disease Research/Clinical (432)
- Natural Resources (367)
- Railroads (154)
- Aerospace (144)
- Animals (89)
- Automotive Industry (131)
- Bankruptcy (125)
- Chemicals/Chemical Industry (124)
- Commodities (Big Ticket) (27)
- Constitution (92)
- Defense (822)
- Economics/Economic Development) (349)
- Environmental/Superfund (790)
- Firearms/Guns/Ammunition (52)
- Fuel/Gas/Oil (271)
- Health Issues (1214)
- Immigration (347)
- Labor Issues/Antitrust/Workplace (571)
- Marine/Maritime/Boating (270)

- Medicare/Medicaid (627)
- Pharmacy (250)
- Real Estate/Land Use/ Conservation (261)
- Religion (45)
- Science/Technology (519)
- Taxation/Internal Revenue (1127)
- Torts (249)
- Travel/Tourism (106)
- Urban Development/ Municipalities (164)
- Waste (Hazardous/Solid/Nuclear) (174)
- Retirement (256)
- Small Business (257)
- Telecommunications (490)
- Trade (Foreign and Domestic) (785)
- Trucking/Shipping (121)
- Utilities (247)
- Welfare (115)
- Roads/Highway (206)
- Sports/Athletics (46)
- Tobacco (133)
- Transportation (826)
- Unemployment (38)
- Veterans (165)

(Note: Lobbyists may select more than one subject area.)
Source: <www.lobbyists.info>, produced by Columbia Books Inc. Extracted July 2, 2007.

§1.17 Work Experience

Generally, federal registered lobbyists have job experience working on Capitol Hill as a member of Congress or a congressional staffer. Also, some lobbyists have worked on political campaigns and some have experience in other government agencies, state legislatures, or governors' offices. The 1998 American League of Lobbyists' Membership Survey documented that most lobbyists had congressional experience, but only 38 percent had previous executive branch experience and 25 percent had experience working for a state or local government.

Although the majority of federal lobbyists have not had experience working in the executive branch, most of them end up with at least some responsibilities for lobbying federal agencies. Chapter Eight describes strategies and resources for lobbying the federal executive branch. Similarly, federal lobbyists are frequently engaged in state, multistate, or local level lobbying. Chapter Three recommends resources for monitoring and shaping public policies at the state and local levels.

§1.19 Gender Breakdown of Federal Registered Lobbyists
In-House vs. Consultant Lobbyists*

Gender	In-house		Consultant		All	
	Count	% of Known	Count	% of Known	Count	% of Known
M	2287	64%	4362	75%	6508	71%
F	1266	36%	1437	25%	2672	29%
Known	3553		5799		9180	
Unknown	1317		938		2234	

*Where gender is discernable by analysis of lobbying reports.
Source: <www.lobbyists.info>, August 23, 2006, Columbia Books Inc.

§1.18 Education

Almost all lobbyists have a college degree and many have a law degree, according to the American League of Lobbyists' 1998 Membership Survey. The survey revealed that federal lobbyists most typically earned their undergraduate degree in the related areas of political science, government, or history. The next most frequently cited undergraduate degree areas included English and journalism (12 percent of respondents).

While advanced degrees are not a requirement, most lobbyists do develop specific areas of expertise. For example, a lobbyist may initially work on the Senate Banking Committee, leave Capitol Hill after a couple of years to work for a banking association, and then later take a position with a contract lobbying firm representing banking clients.

§1.20 Lobbyists' Compensation

Compensation for lobbyists varies widely, depending on the resources of the employing client, association, or company. Recruiting talent includes qualitative considerations such as an individual's reputation and political connections, as well as the knowledge, skills, and abilities necessary for lobbying. Generally, associations do not pay their lobbyists as much as corporate or contract lobbyists pay their employees, but their benefits packages may be more generous. Considerations for compensating lobbyists and a list of resources on lobbying compensation is included in Chapter Eleven (§§ 11.7 and 11.8).

§1.21 Lobby Tips

Personal Qualities Helpful for Lobbying

"Nothing in the world can take the place of persistence. Talent will not; nothing is more common than unsuccessful men with talent. Genius will not; unrewarded genius is almost a proverb. Education will not; the world is full of educated derelicts. Persistence and determination alone are omnipotent. The slogan "Press On" has solved and will always solve the problems of the human race."

—Calvin Coolidge

"I never could have done what I have done without the habits of punctuality, order, and diligence, without the determination to concentrate myself on one subject at a time . . ."

—Charles Dickens

Personal qualities and abilities helpful for lobbying include: diligence, excellent written and oral communication skills, public speaking experience, diplomacy, savvy, judgment from experience, and good research skills. Lobbyists may also obtain special training, education, or certification in the field they represent. For example, an accounting firm may hire a Certified Public Accountant as a lobbyist or an association for engineers may hire a civil engineer.

§1.22 How Many Federal Lobbyists Are There?

While accounts vary somewhat, depending on how and when the data are compiled, a good estimate of the number of federal registered lobbyists is approximately 12,000. According to <*www.lobbyists.info*>, 11,778 lobbyists were registered under the Lobbying Disclosure Act in 2007. (Source: <*www.lobbyists.info*> Columbia Books Inc., July 2, 2007.)

As of June 23, 2008, 2,237 lobbying organizations were registered under the Lobbying Disclosure Act to lobby executive branch agencies. Two hundred and eighty-seven of the executive branch lobbying organizations were registered to lobby the White House. (Source: Senate 2008 Filings extracted by Columbia Books Inc.)

§1.23 How Many State Lobbyists Are There?

Approximately 47,000 lobbyists are registered to lobby at the state level, according to figures compiled from material found in *The COGEL Blue Book: 2005 Lobbying Update on Legislation and Litigation, U.S. & Canada*, Council on Governmental Ethics Laws.

Number of Registered Lobbyists at the State Level

State	Number of Registered Lobbyists	Number of Registered Employers (Organizations)
AL	659	648
AK	130	377
AZ	4629 (average 4500) (public and lobbyists' employees included)	961 (average 975)
ARK	352 (as of September 30, 2005)	
CA	1089	1965
CO	493 (2003-2004)	
CT	728 individuals (in 2004) (including 482 in-house communicators and 246 contract communicators registered a total of 2511 times)	3383 registrations
DE	243 (as of October 17, 2005)	441 (as of October 17, 2005)
DC	Approximately 230 (as of November 11, 2005)	Approximately 200 (as of November 11, 2005)
FL	1342 (executive branch) 2041 (legislative branch) (in 2004)	2285
GA	1333	4600
HI	269	282
ID	318 (in 2005)	387 (in 2005) (see note)
IL	2251 (in 2004)	1687 (in 2004)
IN	Approximately 1400	Not available
IA	514 (executive branch)	522 (executive branch)
KS	567	1365
KY	689 (executive agency) 633 (legislative)	384 (executive agency) 569 (legislative)
LA	509 (legislative) 88 (executive)	981 principals
ME	202 individuals and individual associates	417
MD	755 (as of October 31, 2004)	1059 (number of registrations is 2555)
MA	639 (as of July 1, 1997)	885 (as of July 1, 1997)
MI	Approximately 1250 at any given time	Approximately 1100 at any given time
MN	1230	1240
MS	418 (2005)	537 (in 2005) (number of registered certificates is 829)

State	Number of Registered Lobbyists	Number of Registered Employers (Organizations)
MO	Approximately 1200	Approximately 1195
MT	483	411
NE	353	505
NV	807	970
NH	655	Not available
NJ	582	1392 lobbyist organizations
NM	Approximately 900	
NY	Approximately 6000	
NC	Approximately 611 with 1261 registrations	706
ND	688 in session	Not applicable
OH	1640 (as of October 31, 2005)	1525 (as of October 31, 2005)
OK	392	652
OR	844 (as of November 1, 2005)	848 (as of November 1, 2005)
PA	999 (as of July 2, 2007)	86 (as of July 2, 2007)
RI	815 (includes duplicate and government lobbyists)	
SC	387 as of November 18, 2005	531 (as of November 18, 2005)
SD	592	592
TN	560	Not available
TX	1683 (as of November 10, 2005) (includes those who registered but later terminated)	
UT	495	505
VT	Approximately 300	Approximately 300
VA	867 (May 1, 2004 to April 30, 2005)	
WA	951 (for Fiscal Year 2005) (for Fiscal Year 2002)	1002 lobbyist employers
WI	800	700
WY	Approximately 500	
Total (approx.)	**47,099**	**37,626**

Source: Figures compiled from COGEL Blue Book: 2005 Lobbying Update on Legislation and Litigation, U.S. & Canada, Council on Governmental Ethics Laws at <www.cogel.org/story_topics/documents/blue_books> (purchase required) with the exception of Pennsylvania and Wyoming figures, which were obtained from those states' web sites. Where states provided separate numbers for legislative and executive branch lobbying, only the highest figure was counted in order to avoid double counting.

§1.24 **How Many Foreign Agents Are There?**

Registration is also required under the Foreign Agents Registration Act, 22 U.S.C. § 611 *et seq.*, for those who lobby the U.S. Congress on behalf of a foreign government or political party, but those lobbying for foreign companies (not foreign governments or political parties) may register under the Lobbying Disclosure Act instead. As of July 2, 2007, there were approximately 1,433 registered foreign agents.

§1.25 Types of Registered Lobbyists and Agents (2007)*

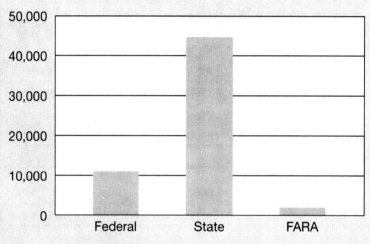

* Does not include registered local lobbyists.

 ## §1.26 Lobby Facts

Number of Lobbyists
per Legislator and per Citizen

- Number of federal registered lobbyists: Approximately 12,000
- Number of state registered lobbyists: Approximately 47,000
- Number of total registered state and federal lobbyists: Approximately 59,000
- Number of federal lobbyists per U.S. Senator: Approximately 120
- Number of federal lobbyists per U.S. House member: Approximately 28
- Number of state lobbyists per state legislator: Approximately 6 (but it varies considerably from state to state)
- Number of U.S. citizens per lobbyist: Approximately one lobbyist per 25,000 citizens at the federal level, one lobbyist per 6,400 citizens at the state level

(Based on more than 300 million citizens.)

§1.27 Recommended Resources

Databases, Directories, and Reports

Searchable Lobbyist Database: *Washington Representatives*, the preeminent lobbying directory by Columbia Books Inc. for more than 30 years is now available online at *<www.lobbyists.info>*. The site profiles federal lobbyists searchable by individual lobbyist, name of organization or lobbying firm, subject matter lobbied, and state. The database is helpful for building coalitions, checking on competing interests, and monitoring those who represent you. Subscription required.

Lobbyist Directory: The hard-copy *Washington Representatives* directory, similar to a telephone book, is helpful for building coalitions, checking on competing interests, and monitoring those who represent you. The directory is produced by Columbia Books twice yearly and may be ordered via *<www.lobbyists.info>*. Every lobbyist should have this directory on his or her bookshelf. Subscription required.

Lobby Reports: View actual (pdf) files of federal lobbyist registrations by state, name, subject area, and executive branch agency lobbied at *<www.disclosure.senate.gov>*. The U.S. Secretary of the Senate prepares these reports. Monitor the site for new database features pursuant to lobbying reform legislation.

Foreign Agents Databases: FARA registrations searchable by country. The database is regularly updated. The database at *<www.lobbyists.info>*, produced by Columbia Books Inc., is updated regularly. Subscription required. The U.S. Department of Justice Foreign Agents Registration Act database at *<www.usdoj.gov>* provides some information and is being enhanced.

§1.28 Keep Current

Congressional Databases

The Secretary of the Senate and the Clerk of the House web sites have searchable congressional databases of lobbyists. Per lobbying reform legislation, the databases include information required on lobbying registrations and reports. See the Lobbying Disclosure Database on the Senate web site, *<www.disclosure.senate.gov>*, and the Lobbying Disclosure Filing Search on the House web site, *<http://lobbyingdisclosure. house.gov>*.

§1.99 **Chapter Summary**

- Lobbying is grounded in the First Amendment to the U.S. Constitution. (§ 1.3)
- While the term "special interests" has become a modern-day derogatory term for many people, our founders expected the participation of "special interests" or "factions" to be an essential part of our governmental system of checks and balances. (§ 1.4)
- Our nation's founders understood human nature. They understood that personal ambition and political conflicts were facts of life. Accordingly, they designed a system where special interests would compete against each other as an integral part of our government's checks and balances. (§ 1.4)
- Competing factions are an essential part of a system designed to consider and reflect a plurality of interests, not just individual or select interests. (§ 1.4)
- An examination of the development of the practice of lobbying in the United States reveals that traditional accounts pertaining to the origin of the term "lobbying" cannot be authenticated (§ 1.5). Research into the origin of the term defies the conventional knowledge that the term was first coined in the lobby of the Willard Hotel in Washington, DC (§ 1.8).
- The first U.S. lobbyists were the colonial agents, some of our nation's founders. (§§ 1.6 and 1.7)
- Forefathers of the profession include Thomas Jefferson, William Hull, and Daniel Webster. (§ 1.7)
- The act of lobbying by petitioning the British government was a hallmark of our nation's birth. (§ 1.8)
- Electronic and bulk copies of the pocket version of the Constitution and the Bill of Rights are available and recommended. (§ 1.9)
- The two major parts of lobbying work are (§ 1.11):
    1. Advocacy with policymakers; and
    2. Communicating with the represented interest.
- Basic benefits of lobbying include (§ 1.12):
    1. Provides policy expertise on complex legislation;
    2. Provides insight on technical, practical, and long-term ramifications of legislation and public policy;
    3. Connects and communicates citizen concerns to public officials and lawmakers;
    4. Informs citizens of impending legislation and public policy developments, raises public awareness of legislation and public policy changes, and holds lawmakers and other public officials accountable for their actions and votes; and
    5. Unites citizens with like concerns.
- A look at the true nature of lobbying work defies traditional stereotypes, where a pat on the back and a campaign check gets you legislative favors. For example,

lobbyists spend more time writing or communicating with those they represent than on any other function. (§ 1.13)

- There are three major types of registered lobbyists (§ 1.15):
    1. Association or non-profit lobbyists represent members of an association or non-profit organization;
    2. Corporate lobbyists work on issues that concern their companies; and
    3. Contract or self-employed (consultant) lobbyists work on a contractual basis for client organizations who hire them with a contract or retainer.
- Approximately 20 percent of federal registered lobbyists are from organizations that hire lobbyists within their organizations (associations or companies) and 80 percent are firms with outside clients (contract or consultant lobbyists). (§ 1.15)
- Lobbyists frequently specialize according to issue areas. Lobbyists may obtain special training, education, or certification in the field they represent. The average number of issue areas lobbied is 5 out of 77 subject areas. (§ 1.16)
- Most federal lobbyists have had experience working in the U.S. Congress and some have had experience working in a state government or in the federal executive branch. Many lobbyists have experience working on political campaigns. (§ 1.17)
- Most federal lobbyists have some responsibility for lobbying executive branch agencies even though most lobbyists do not have work experience in the federal agencies. (§ 1.17)
- Most federal lobbyists have a college degree and some have law degrees. Political science, government, history, English, and journalism are common majors for lobbyists. (§ 1.18)
- The gender breakdown for lobbyists is approximately 71 percent male and 29 percent female. (§ 1.19)
- Personal qualities helpful for lobbying include: diligence, excellent written and oral communication skills, public speaking experience, diplomacy, savvy, and good research skills. (§ 1.21)
- Approximately 2,200 organizations are registered with Congress to lobby the various executive branch agencies. (§ 1.22)
- According to 2007 data, there are approximately 12,000 federal registered lobbyists (§ 1.22), 47,000 state registered lobbyists (§ 1.23), and approximately 1,400 registered foreign agents (§ 1.24).
- A lobbyist directory and databases are useful tools for expanding coalitions and monitoring competition. Lobbyist directories can provide contact information for federal lobbyists according to state, name, organization, subject matter lobbied, and governmental organization lobbied. (§ 1.27)

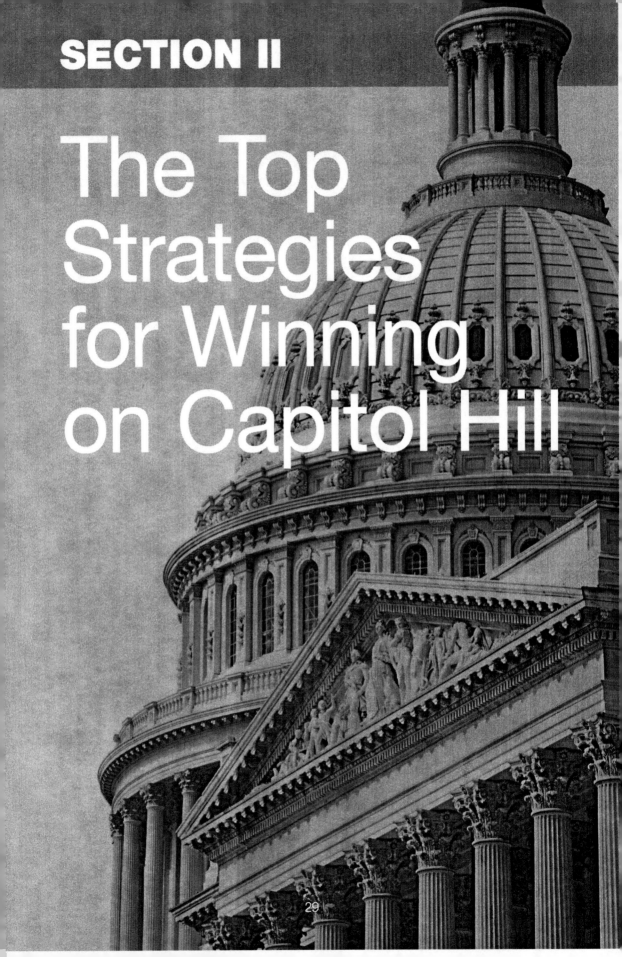

The Top Strategies for Winning on Capitol Hill

Legal and Ethical Considerations

"Character is more easily kept than recovered."

Thomas Paine

Chapter 2: Legal and Ethical Considerations

§2.1 **Introduction**

Legal compliance and ethical conduct are the essential foundations for successful lobbying. Without building and maintaining these foundations, the other strategies provided in this book will become compromised over time. As Thomas Jefferson observed, "Honesty is the first chapter in the book of wisdom."

Chapter Two provides a brief overview of references useful for determining and maintaining compliance with professional ethics and regulations at the federal, state, and local levels as the foundation for a successful lobbying strategy. The chapter includes tips for designing and maintaining a system for effective compliance as well as recommended resources for determining and maintaining compliance as requirements change. The processes for registering as a lobbyist at the federal, state, and local levels are discussed and registration and reporting tips are provided.

Regard this information as a resource guide and not as a substitute for professional advice from legal or other professionals. Keep in mind that many of the specific rules change over time and you should check with authoritative sources regularly for the most current information.

§2.2 **The Ethics Imperative**

"Ethics is not a 90 percent thing, nor a 95 percent thing, you either have it or you don't."

Peter Scotese, former President/CEO of Springs Industries

One of the most vital lobbying strategies is to protect your reputation and maintain your integrity. What has taken years to build up can be torn down overnight by one incident of carelessness or lapse in judgment. No lobbying strategy, no matter how brilliant, can undo the irreparable damage caused by national headlines charging one's organization with unethical activities, such as lobbying law violations or unethical actions with elected officials.

Laws are not a ceiling, but a floor for ethical conduct for lobbyists. To contribute positively to the profession's reputation and the reputation of individual lobbyists, as well as to defy the negative stereotypes that are unfortunately reinforced periodically by a few bad actors, lobbyists must uphold the law and avoid even the slightest appearance of impropriety or conflict of interest.

§2.3 Recommended Resources: Determining Compliance with Key Lobbying and Ethics Requirements

"A lobbyist should seek to comply fully with all laws, regulations and rules applicable to the lobbyist. A lobbyist should be familiar with laws, regulations and rules applicable to the lobbying profession and should not engage in any violation of such laws, regulations and rules."

Lobbyists' Code of Ethics, American League of Lobbyists, Article II and Section 2.1

A variety of governmental agencies at the federal, state, and local level enforce an array of laws that apply to lobbying and political activity. Violating even one of these requirements can result in not only legal penalties, but also in negative media exposure:

"At the federal level and in most states we have laws against bribery, extortion, and gratuities; we have ethics rules governing elected officials; we have ethics committees or commissions; and, perhaps as important as our laws and official overseers, we have a vigilant media fixed on exposing public wrongdoing. States and the federal government also have laws and rules governing lobbyists, including registration, disclosure, and routine reporting."

Remarks of Thomas M. Susman (partner, Ropes & Gray LLP, and chair, American League of Lobbyists' Ethics Committee), Forum on Lobbying Ethics, Woodstock Theological Center, October 24, 2002

The following chart lists potential resources for determining and maintaining compliance with key governmental lobbying and ethics requirements.

Requirement:

Federal Lobbying Registration and Periodic Reporting on Congressional and Executive Branch Lobbying

(The Lobbying Disclosure Act of 1995, Pub. L. No. 104-65, as amended in 1998 and 2007), 109 STAT. 691, 2 U.S.C. § 1601 et seq.
(Available in Lobbying and Advocacy Sourcebook, 2 and 3.)

Summary:

1. Requires registration as a federal lobbyist for individuals who are paid or otherwise compensated to lobby Congress or the executive branch. Registration is required within 45 days of meeting threshold requirements (detailed in § 2.9).
2. Requires registered lobbyists to file periodic reports on lobbying activity according to deadlines established, and occasionally revised, by Congress.
3. Reports are filed with the House (Clerk of the House) and the Senate (Secretary of the Senate) and include information such as the amount spent on or received for legislative or executive branch action lobbying.
4. Clerk of the House and Secretary of the Senate receive and process registrations and refer potential violations to the Department of Justice.

See <www.LobbyingAndAdvocacy.com> for updates.

5. Congress periodically considers changes to the Lobbying Disclosure Act of 1995 and associated penalties, deadlines, thresholds, and Congressional disclosure databases.

Determine and Maintain Compliance:

Federal lobbyists register with the House and the Senate. The following House and Senate offices may be contacted with questions regarding the Lobbying Disclosure Act of 1995 (LDA) filings:

The Clerk of the House, Legislative Resource Center
202–226–5200, <*http://lobbyingdisclosure.house.gov*>.

The web site provides the full text of the Lobbying Disclosure Act of 1995 and the Technical Amendments Act of 1998 as well as a Guide to the Lobbying Disclosure Act and Reporting Deadlines.

The Secretary of the Senate, Office of Public Records
202–224–2115, <*www.disclosure.senate.gov*>.

Always check with each office before filing, because submission and delivery procedures can vary based on technological changes, security concerns, and lobbying reforms.

See § 2.9 for thresholds that trigger registration; §§ 2.14–2.19 for deadline and form information; § 2.7 for tips for maintaining ongoing compliance as requirements continue to change; and §§ 2.4 and 2.5 for designing and maintaining an effective compliance system.

Every federal lobbyist should read the full text of The Honest Leadership and Open Government Act of 2007 (HLOGA) (Pub. L. 110-81), included in the *Lobbying and Advocacy Sourcebook*, 20. The landmark legislation bans congressional gifts and trip sponsorship from lobbyists and organizations that employ them; subjects federal lobbyists and their organizations to congressional travel and event sponsorship restrictions; and requires lobbyists to attest that they did not unlawfully provide gifts to legislative or executive branch policymakers. The law presents significant potential liabilities (civil and criminal) for lobbying organizations; requires lobbyists to file a quarterly report with the House and Senate on political contributions and activities; requires disclosure of coalition activity; changes periodic Lobbying Disclosure Act reporting from semi-annual to quarterly; and raises considerations for negotiating and employing certain congressional officials as lobbyists.

Senior managers of government affairs offices and executives with governmental affairs oversight should ensure that all employees involved in government affairs in their organization are familiar with the requirements of HLOGA and verify that a system is in place to maintain ongoing compliance. Compliance and oversight procedures should be adjusted, and competent legal counsel should be consulted as appropriate.

See Appendix 7 for the LDA as amended by HLOGA and this book's companion volume, *Lobbying and Advocacy Sourcebook*, 3, 5, and 20, for LDA guidance.

See <www.LobbyingAndAdvocacy.com> *for updates.*   *(Continued on page 36)*

Requirement:

State (or Local) Involvement in Lobbying:
Registration, Reporting, and Ethics

Summary:

Requirements vary from state to state. Federal lobbyists who occasionally become engaged in advocacy at the state or local levels need to check the pertinent registration requirements as well as other ethical or legal restrictions, such as gift or sponsorship of activities that may apply.

Organizations with a state presence (chapters, office, members, or a corporate facility) should verify that the state entities are in compliance with state and local requirements for registration, reporting, and ethics (as well as pertinent national requirements).

Determine and Maintain Compliance:

Federal, state, local, and multi-state lobbyists should maintain systems to monitor changing state and local reporting, disclosure and ethics requirements, and restrictions.

Federal lobbyists should check relevant state or local registration and ethics requirements before becoming involved in state and local advocacy efforts, such as testifying before a state legislature or sponsoring an event.

National organizations with state and local facilities, clients, chapters, or employees should also be aware of all relevant state and local registration, reporting and ethics requirements at all levels of government.

Requirement:

Congressional Ethics Rules

Rules include Senate Rule 35 and House Rule 25
(Available in Lobbying and Advocacy Sourcebook, *6 and 8.)*

Summary:

The House and Senate establish and periodically revise rules governing members of Congress, congressional officers, and congressional employees.

The Honest Leadership and Open Government Act of 2007 (HLOGA) (Pub. L. 110-81, 121 Stat. 735) provides restrictions and prohibitions in areas such as sponsored trips, events, meals, and gifts. As discussed in § 2.19, lobbyists must file periodic attestations on gift and travel rule compliance. Criminal penalties can apply.

Determine and Maintain Compliance:

Every federal lobbyist and those with oversight responsibility for government affairs should periodically review the current House and Senate ethics rules, which may be obtained from the House and Senate Ethics Committees:

See <www.LobbyingAndAdvocacy.com> for updates.

U.S. House of Representatives Committee on Standards of Official Conduct
Office of Advice and Education, 202-225-7103, <*http://ethics.house.gov*>.

U.S. Senate Select Committee on Ethics
220 Hart Building, United States Senate, Washington, DC 20510. Telephone:
202- 224-2981. Fax: 202-224-7416. See the Senate Ethics Manual (which is
searchable): <*http://ethics.senate.gov*>. An overview of the Senate Code of
Conduct and Related Laws is also available at this site.

Address Uncertainties
Before acting, you may benefit from contacting the House or Senate Ethics
Committees to get clarification in an area that might involve congressional ethics.

Complaints
While the House Committee does not accept official complaints from outside of
Congress, both the House and Senate Committees state that they accept and review
credible information on a confidential basis from third parties who believe that ethics
rules have been violated. For example, the Senate's Rules of Procedure allow the
committee to act upon allegations from credible information from a variety of sources,
including anonymous or informal complaints. See § 2.37 Filing Complaints Regarding
Public Officials, and see the Senate Ethics Manual's Appendix C, Rule 2, p. 371 at
<*http://ethics.senate.gov*>.

Standards of Ethical Conduct for Employees of the Executive Branch,
(5 C.F.R. Part 2635), published by the Office of Government Ethics (OGE), details
ethics rules for government employees, <*www.usoge.gov*>, some of which apply to
congressional employees.

See §§ 2.35–2.39 for additional information and resources.

This book's companion volume, *Lobbying and Advocacy Sourcebook*, 6, 7, 8, 9, and 17
contains the text and summaries of House and Senate gift rules.

Requirement:

The Federal Gratuity Statute

18 U.S.C. § 201(c)

Summary:

Lobbyists may be subject to criminal prosecution for giving, offering, or promising
illegal gratuities to legislators "for or because of an official act performed or to be
performed by that public official."

The prohibition includes "anything of value" given, offered, or promised to a
public official.

See also the gift restrictions and gift disclosure requirements applicable
to lobbyists under the Honest Leadership and Open Government Act of 2007
(Pub. L. 110-81, 121 Stat. 735), and included in *Lobbying and Advocacy Sourcebook*.

See <www.LobbyingAndAdvocacy.com> *for updates.*   *(Continued on page 38)*

Determine and Maintain Compliance:

In the executive branch, each federal agency head is responsible for insuring compliance with standards relating to gifts and ethical conduct. The relevant federal agency officials are the best place to start with questions since federal regulations are in some cases supplemented by specific agency regulations. A list of designated Agency Ethics Officials (DAEOs) is available at *<www.usoge.gov>*.

General information on federal government standards that cover all executive branch agencies is available from the Office of Government Ethics (OGE): *<www.usoge.gov>*, 202-482-9300, 1201 New York Avenue, NW, Suite 500, Washington, DC 20005, email: ContactOGE@oge.gov

(*Note:* Do not send confidential or sensitive information via email. Include your mailing address, email address, and a daytime telephone number.)

See this book's companion volume, *Lobbying and Advocacy Sourcebook*, 11, for an OGE brochure and federal employee crossword puzzle on accepting gifts.

Standards of Ethical Conduct for Employees of the Executive Branch, (5 C.F.R. Part 2635), published by OGE, details ethics rules for government employees.

Requirement:
Bribery
18 U.S.C. § 201(b)

Summary:

Soliciting or receiving bribes is a criminal statute. Lobbyists should avoid quid pro quo (one thing in return for another).

Additionally, campaign contributions could give rise to criminal prosecution if given in exchange for political favors.

Determine and Maintain Compliance:

Bribery is prosecuted by the U.S. Department of Justice. Agency inspectors general may review complaints.

See 5 C.F.R. § 2635.902 (Related statutes of the Standards of Ethical Conduct for Employees of the Executive Branch).

Requirement:
Honest Services Fraud
18 U.S.C. § 1346

Summary:

Based on the concept that the public has a right to honest government, a scheme to deprive the public of honest services is punishable as wire or mail fraud. Prosecutors use this statute in a variety of public corruption cases; the use of mail or wire does not need to be an essential element of the scheme.

See <www.LobbyingAndAdvocacy.com> for updates.

Determine and Maintain Compliance:

The U.S. Department of Justice handles criminal prosecutions: <*www.usdoj.gov*>. See the *Lobbying and Advocacy Sourcebook*, 14, for federal employee crossword puzzles on misuse of position and gifts, and *Sourcebook*, 17, for a report on congressional gifts.

See the Criminal Resources Portion of the **U.S. Attorneys' Manual**, Section 950. <*www.usdoj.gov/usao/eousa/foia_reading_room/usam*>

Requirement:

False Statements Act

18 U.S.C. § 1001

Summary:

Criminal penalties for:
1. "Knowingly and willfully" falsifying, concealing or covering up a material fact; or
2. Making any materially false, fictitious, or fraudulent statement or representation; or
3. Making or using any false writing or document knowing that it has a false, fictitious, or fraudulent statement or entry.
   Applies to anyone "in any matter within the jurisdiction of the executive, legislative, or judicial branch" of the government.

Legislative branch jurisdiction includes information submitted during or for congressional hearings or commissions:
1. A document required by law, rule, or regulation to be submitted to the Congress or any office or officer within the legislative branch; or
2. Any investigation or review, conducted pursuant to the authority of any committee, subcommittee, commission, or office of the Congress, consistent with applicable rules of the House or Senate.

Determine and Maintain Compliance:

The U.S. Department of Justice handles criminal prosecutions: <*www.usdoj.gov*>. See *Lobbying and Advocacy Sourcebook*, 10, for the False Claims Act.

See the Criminal Resources Portion of the **U.S. Attorneys' Manual**, Section 815, Elements of Offense of False Statements. <*www.usdoj.gov/usao/eousa/foia_reading_room/usam*>

Requirement:

Election and Campaign Activity

Summary:

Financial participation in the political process is regulated through laws addressing contribution limits, expenditure prohibitions, and disclosure requirements such as:

The Federal Election Campaign Act of 1971 (FECA) as amended; Pub. L. No. 92-225, 86 Stat. 3 (1972) (codified as amended at 2 U.S.C. §§ 431 *et seq.*);

The Bipartisan Campaign Reform Act of 2002 (BCRA, Pub. L. 107-155, 116 Stat. 81) (also known as McCain-Feingold);

Various regulations issued by the Federal Election Commission (FEC); and
Various state and local election laws.

Soliciting or receiving a donation on federal property is unlawful, 18 U.S.C. § 607 (a)(1).

Even though protected by the First Amendment to the U.S. Constitution as political speech, campaign contributions could give rise to criminal prosecution if given in exchange for political favors. Freedom of speech doesn't prevent perjury convictions.

The Honest Leadership and Open Government Act of 2007 (HLOGA) (Pub. L. 110-81, 121 Stat. 735) requires all federal lobbyists to submit a new report quarterly to the Senate and House clerks with information on federal campaign contributions and activity. This is separate from any reporting to the Federal Election Commission.

HLOGA also requires reporting and disclosure of quarterly and certain "bundled" campaign contributions (contributions that lobbyists arranged or facilitated).

Determine and Maintain Compliance:

Laws and regulations governing election activity are subject to change. All federal lobbyists, even those working for organizations without Political Action Committees (PACs), should be familiar with the potential implications that election laws have on their organizations, association members, clients, or employees. Changes to laws and regulations governing campaign and election activity should be monitored.

Federal Election Commission
<*www.FEC.gov*> 999 E Street, NW, Washington, DC 20463, 800-424-9530; in Washington: 202-694-1100

Familiarize yourself with FEC rules that may be applicable to you, your organization, your members, your employees, or your clients. The FEC's *Campaign Guide for Corporations and Labor Organizations* may be found at <*www.fec.gov*>.

Use the confidential FEC hotline (800-424–9530) if you have any questions about your compliance. (*Note:* If you are concerned about caller identification, simply use a caller block code that can be obtained from your telephone operator.)

You may also contact the FEC's Information Division email at <*info@fec.gov*>.

For help with reporting and compliance, including filing information, deadlines, publications, educational outreach, and tips for treasurers, go to <*www.fec.gov*>.

See the **Bipartisan Campaign Reform Act (BCRA/McCain-Feingold)** (Pub. L. 107-155, 116 Stat. 81).

FEC Donor Database: View the disclosure database to look up political contributions by individuals, candidates, and PAC/Party (from the last two congressional election cycles), and committees, at <*www.fec.gov*>.

See <www.LobbyingAndAdvocacy.com> for updates.

View reports filed by organizations organized under Section 527 of the Internal Revenue Code: *<www.irs.gov>*, and link provided at *<www.LobbyingandAdvocacy.com>*.

Money in Politics Database by *Congressional Quarterly*: *<www.fecinfo.com>*.

Search the **Open Secrets** campaign contributions database: *<www.opensecrets.org>*.

State and Local Election Boards and General Election Information: *<http://usgovinfo.about.com>*.

This book's companion volume, *Lobbying and Advocacy Sourcebook*, 15, FEC Special Notices on Political Ads and Solicitation.

This book's companion volume, *Lobbying and Advocacy Sourcebook*, 21, Congressional Research Service Report on Campaign Finance Legislation.

Money in State Politics: *<www.followthemoney.org>*.

The New Campaign Finance Sourcebook, Anthony Corrado, Daniel R. Ortiz, Thomas E. Mann and Trevor Potter, Brookings Institution Press 2005.

See also the nonprofit political involvement restrictions and IRS resources in this chart.

Requirement:

Revolving Door Restrictions for Former Congressional and Executive Branch Employees Negotiating and Accepting Non-Government Employment (Post-Employment Conflict of Interest Restrictions)

18 U.S.C. § 207; 41 U.S.C. § 423(c) (Also Senate Rule 37)

Summary:

High-ranking U.S. House and executive branch officials must abide by conflict of interest restrictions that prohibit lobbying their former employer for one year (or longer in some cases). High-ranking Senate officials cannot lobby their former employer for two years.

Highly compensated executive branch and congressional employees must also abide by restrictions as they negotiate or accept an offer of new employment.

For example, highly compensated officials are required to notify the relevant ethics office upon contact by a potential employer and to exclude themselves from matters that could present a conflict of interest while negotiating or after accepting an offer of employment.

Many states have established similar measures.

The Honest Leadership and Open Government Act of 2007 (HLOGA), (Pub. L. 110-81, 121 Stat. 735), available in the *Lobbying and Advocacy Sourcebook*, 2, prohibits House members from accepting employment until the member's replacement has been elected.

See <www.LobbyingAndAdvocacy.com> for updates.   *(Continued on page 42)*

Determine and Maintain Compliance:

Lobbying organizations should be aware of conflict of interest restrictions relating to job negotiations and lobbying restrictions as well as potential public disclosure of employment negotiations with House members that may apply to the congressional and executive branch employees they recruit and hire.

U.S. Office of Government Ethics (OGE) provides information on current executive branch revolving door restrictions: *<www.usoge.gov>*.

Standards of Ethical Conduct for Employees of the Executive Branch: 5 C.F.R. § 2635, published by OGE, details ethics rules for government employees.

Compilation of Federal Ethics Laws linked to at *<www.usoge.gov>*.

Lobbying and Advocacy Sourcebook, 12, OGE revolving door brochure.

Lobbying and Advocacy Sourcebook, 13, OGE's Rules for the Road.

Lobbying and Advocacy Sourcebook, 14, OGE Federal Employee Crossword Puzzles.

Revolving Door Database by the Center for Responsive Politics: *<www.opensecrets.org/revolving>*.

State Revolving Door restrictions: *<www.ncsl.org>*.

Requirement:

Foreign Agents Registration Act (FARA)

22 U.S.C. § 611-621, 28 C.F.R. Ch.1 Part 5
As amended in 1995 and 1998 as part of the Lobbying Disclosure Act.

Summary:

Requires "agents" of "foreign principals" to register with the U.S. Department of Justice within ten days of agreeing to be an agent and before performing any services.
 Requires periodic disclosures about activities, income, and expenses.

A "foreign principal" is defined as:
 1. Foreign governments,
 2. Foreign political parties,
 3. Foreign individuals,
 4. Foreign non-governmental organizations, or
 5. Foreign businesses.

An "agent" is anyone who acts within the United States for, or in the interests of, a foreign principal:
 1. On political activities or as a political consultant;
 2. As a public relations counsel or a publicity agent;
 3. To solicit or disburse funding; or,
 4. To represent the interest before any U.S. government official or agency.

See <www.LobbyingAndAdvocacy.com> for updates.

Agents appearing before a congressional committee must provide the committee with their most recent registration statement. Exemptions include:

1. Legal representation (within a judicial or administrative proceeding and where a law degree is required to do the work);
2. Commercial activities (with no arising public policy, foreign policy, or spending issues); and
3. Agents of foreign principals registered under the Lobbying Disclosure Act of 1995 (who are *not* working on behalf of a foreign government or a foreign political party). The LDA, 2 U.S.C. § 1601, focuses on those engaged in lobbying activities on behalf of domestic *and foreign* interests. FARA exempts those agents of foreign principals, other than agents of foreign governments and foreign political parties, who engage in lobbying activities and who register under the LDA.

Contingent fee lobbying is prohibited under FARA.

Determine and Maintain Compliance:

The FARA Registration Unit within the National Security Division of the U.S. Department of Justice enforces FARA and may be contacted at: <*www.fara.gov*> 1400 New York Avenue, NW, Suite 100, Washington, DC 20005, Public Office: 202-514-1145, Main Office: 202-514-1216. (*Note:* These are not toll-free numbers; but are equipped with voice mail for after-hours calls.)

Public Research office hours of operation: Monday–Friday, 11:30 a.m.–3:00 p.m. (You must pay a per page fee to copy documents.)

FARA Disclosure Databases: <*www.lobbyists.info*>, by Columbia Books Inc. provides a searchable database of FARA foreign agents by lobbyist, organization, and country, and is regularly updated.

The U.S. Department of Justice FARA database: <*www.fara.gov*>.

See Appendix 7 for the text of FARA as amended by HLOGA.

Requirement:

Nonprofits/Associations

Restrictions on campaign and political participation;
non-deductibility of dues income

Summary:

Limitations on Lobbying

Generally, Section 501 (c)(3) organizations may not engage in significant lobbying activities, subject to the "election" exemption. Specifically, nonprofits that receive significant public support may file an "election" with the IRS that permits more substantial lobbying activities. Election requires substantial record-keeping, but may be well worth it nonetheless.

Section 501 (c)(4) organizations are permitted to lobby without the restrictions placed on 501 (c)(3) organizations.

See <www.LobbyingAndAdvocacy.com> *for updates.*   (*Continued on page 44*)

Prohibitions from Certain Political Activities

Limitations on legislative activities and political activities apply to tax-exempt organizations. Section 501 (c)(3) organizations are prohibited from participating or intervening in political campaigns on behalf of a candidate.

Certain political activities, such as voter registration drives and voter guides, are not prohibited as long as they are conducted in a non-partisan manner and do not contain bias that would favor or oppose individual candidates. Informing on issues is acceptable, but showing bias for or against specific candidates or parties is not.

Reporting and coordination with the Lobbying Disclosure Act of 1995

Lobbyists should coordinate LDA and Internal Revenue Code (IRC) reporting closely with their legal and financial staff since the LDA and the IRC are inter-related in certain provisions beyond the scope of this book. For example, the IRC has limitations on deductibility of lobbying expenses by businesses and trade associations as well as by tax-exempt organizations. Lobbying restrictions on and reporting requirements for tax-exempt organizations are governed by the Internal Revenue Code, while registration and reporting requirements to Congress are stipulated by the LDA.

Entities required to report lobbying expenses to the IRS (under Title 26 U.S.C. § 6033(b)(8) of the IRC or subject to § 162(e) of the IRC) may plug in the amount that is ultimately reportable to the IRS in the expense section of LDA forms (for purposes of LDA Sections (4)(a)(3) and 5(b)(4)). This option is permitted under Section 15 of the LDA (2 U.S.C. § 1610).

Determine and Maintain Compliance:

You may have technical assistance e-mailed to you from the IRS and view published and planned guidance for nonprofits at *<www.irs.gov>*.

To learn more about compliance and enforcement information for political organizations, go to *<www.irs.gov>*.

IRS Revenue Ruling 2007-41, 2007-25 I.R.B. (June 18, 2007), provides guidance for exempt organizations on the scope of the tax law prohibition of campaign activities by 501(c)(3) tax-exempt organizations. The guidance discusses 21 factual situations involving 501(c)(3) organizations, including churches, and activities that may prohibit campaign intervention. In each situation, the ruling applies tax law and regulations and concludes that prohibited political activity has or has not occurred.

See *Lobbying and Advocacy Sourcebook*, 18, for a Congressional Research Service report on Tax-Exempt Organizations: Political Activity Restrictions and Disclosure Requirements.

See *Lobbying and Advocacy Sourcebook*, 16, for IRS descriptions of Political Activities and Lobbying Restrictions.

For a collection of links to state government web sites with useful information for tax-exempt organizations, go to *<www.irs.gov>* or *<www.LobbyingAndAdvocacy.com>*.

The Lobbying Manual, by William V. Luneburg and Thomas M. Susman (ABA 2005). See "Special Considerations for Lobbying by Nonprofit Corporations" (Chapter 19) and Chapter 15, "Office of Management and Budget Regulations Governing Lobbying Costs Incurred by Nonprofit Organizations." Chapter 15 includes tips for nonprofits for compliance with both the IRC and the LDA.

Lobbying and Advocacy Sourcebook, 3, provides the LDA text (refer to LDA Section 15).

Requirement:
Conflicts of Interest

Summary:

Lobbyists must take care to avoid conflicts of interests.

Conflict of interest rules applicable in various venues may be applicable to lobbyists. For example, leaders involved in association governance have certain fiduciary responsibilities, including a legal duty of loyalty to further the interests of the association and to avoid conflicts of interest. Additionally, lobbyists have an obligation to avoid conflicts of interests with their clients.

Determine and Maintain Compliance:

American League of Lobbyists' Code of Ethics (Article IV) addresses conflicts of interest for lobbyists at Appendix 6: *<www.alldc.org>*.

Recommended article: "Updating Your Association's Board Conflict of Interest Policy" by Jeffrey S. Tenenbaum, Esq., Venable, Baetjer, Howard & Civiletti, Washington, DC, available online: *<www.venable.com>*.

Ethical guidance to the nonprofit that considers the Sarbanes-Oxley Act of 2002. "Corporate Responsibility: Avoiding Holes in Your SOX," Center Collection. Published: April 2005, ASAE and the Center for Association Leadership, available online: *<www.asaecenter.org>*.

Requirement:
Lobbying with Appropriated Moneys Act
(Commonly referred to as the Anti-Lobbying Act of 1919)
Pertains to executive branch employees' lobbying of Congress and other government officials.
18 U.S.C. § 1913

Summary:

The Anti-Lobbying Act aims to address concerns regarding the use of lobbying with appropriated funds. However, the Act's application is tempered by the rights grounded in the Constitution, for example, for the president and cabinet officers to speak on issues of public concern and to recommend measures. The restriction depends on whether a lobbying effort is or is not "necessary for the efficient conduct of public business," which, of course, may be debatable.

See <www.LobbyingAndAdvocacy.com> for updates. *(Continued on page 46)*

While official enforcement of the Anti-Lobbying Act is limited, it has been invoked periodically by members of Congress claiming that a federal agency has been inappropriately lobbying. Additionally, specific incidents may be cited by the GAO, and allegations are sporadically highlighted in the press.

The Act bars "gross solicitations" of grassroots (public) support, according to the U.S. Department of Justice. The measure was amended in 2002 to expand the law to apply to lobbying of any government official, not just members of Congress.

Determine and Maintain Compliance:

Standards of Ethical Conduct for Employees of the Executive Branch (5 C.F.R. Part 2635), published by OGE, details ethics rules for government employees, as well as a compilation of federal ethics laws is available at *<www.usoge.gov>*.

Questions concerning lobbying provisions applicable to federal grantees or contractors should be directed to the appropriate office or agency administering the award.

Requirement:

Antitrust Consent Decree Lobbying
(Commonly referred to as the Tunney Act after former U.S. Senator John Tunney (D-CA 1971-1976))
15 U.S.C. § 16(a)-16(i)(2000)

Summary:

Requires disclosure of lobbying contacts made for antitrust defendants within ten days of filing any proposal for a consent judgment.

The requirement was prompted by a controversy in 1972 regarding the settlement of an antitrust case against International Telephone & Telegraph (ITT). The Act's purpose is to provide transparency in settlements of antitrust claims by consent decree.

Determine and Maintain Compliance:

Contact the Federal Trade Commission (*<www.ftc.gov>*) or the Department of Justice (*<www.usdoj.gov>*) with questions.

The Lobbying Manual, by William V. Luneburg and Thomas M. Susman (ABA 2005). See Chapter 16, "Antitrust Consent Decree (Tunney Act) Lobbying."

Requirement:

Byrd Amendment
Pertains to federal contractors and other government awardees.

Summary:

Promoted by Senator Robert Byrd (D-WV) in response to a West Virginia university's hiring of a lobbying firm to seek federal funds.

See <www.LobbyingAndAdvocacy.com> for updates.

Prohibits lobbying with "appropriated" federal funds for any type of federal award (including any extension, continuation, renewal, amendment, or modification).

Requires disclosure for using nonappropriated funds to lobby for obtaining federal contracts, loans, grants, and cooperative agreements.

Applies to businesses, nonprofits, state and local governments, and sub-contractors/subgrantees.

Applies to lobbying the executive branch and Congress and contains specific exemptions.

Overlaps with the Federal Acquisition Regulation (FAR).

Determine and Maintain Compliance:

Questions concerning lobbying provisions applicable to federal grantees or contractors should be directed to the appropriate office or agency administering the grant or award.

For a discussion of uncertainties pertaining to the Byrd Amendment and a discussion of its current interpretation, see *The Lobbying Manual,* by William V. Luneburg and Thomas M. Susman (ABA 2005). See Chapter 13, "The Byrd Amendment."

Requirement:

Federal Acquisition Regulation (FAR) Governing Contractor Lobbying

48 C.F.R. § 31.205-22 (2003)

Summary:

Federal contractors are subject to certain restrictions, many of which involve ethical considerations and standards of conduct. These restrictions are provided by law or regulation, by contract, and often by contractors, themselves.

Reimbursement:

Details the types of lobbying costs that the federal government may reimburse federal contractors. Does not pertain to lobbying with nonfederal funds. Disallows reimbursement for improperly influencing "an employee or officer of the executive branch of the federal government to give consideration to or act on a regulatory or contract matter." (48 C.F.R. 31.205-22(a)(6)).

Reporting:

Requires reporting for total lobbying costs when a contractor seeks reimbursement for indirect costs. Records must be maintained. Department of Defense contractors with sole-source awards over $100,000 must certify FAR compliance.

The government has the authority to identify unallowable costs through organizations such as the Defense Contract Audit Agency.

The Byrd rule also addresses federal contracting.

The Honest Leadership and Open Government Act of 2007 (HLOGA) (Pub. L. 110-81, 121 Stat. 735) includes requirements for federal contractors that contract with the Congress.

See <www.LobbyingAndAdvocacy.com> for updates. *(Continued on page 48)*

Determine and Maintain Compliance:

The full text of **FAR** may be found at *<www.arnet.gov/far>*.

FAR is issued by the General Services Administration (GSA), the Department of Defense, and the National Aeronautics and Space Administration (NASA). Information is available at *<www.gsa.gov/far>*.

Additionally, each federal agency may have its own specific requirements beyond the FAR.

The Lobbying Manual, by William V. Luneburg and Thomas M. Susman (ABA 2005). See Chapter 14.

Lobbying and Advocacy Sourcebook, 3, (HLOGA).

Requirement:

Executive Branch Ethics Rules and Restrictions Applicable to Lobbying

Ethics in Government Act of 1978, Pub. L. 95-521, 92 Stat. 1824-1867
Ethics Reform Act of 1989, Pub. L. 101-194, 202, 103 Stat. 1716, at 1724

Summary:

See §§ 2.30 and 2.31 for a summary of major executive branch ethics rules and restrictions pertaining to lobbying.

Determine and Maintain Compliance:

See § 2.32 for Recommended Resources regarding executive branch lobbying rules.

Requirement:

Help America Vote Act of 2002

HAVA, PL 107-252, 42 U.S.C. § 15301 et seq.
(Election Assistance Commission)

Summary:

The Election Assistance Commission, created by the Help America Vote Act of 2002, provides information concerning the administration of federal elections.

Determine and Maintain Compliance:

Election Assistance Commission
<www.eac.gov>, 1225 New York Avenue NW, Suite 1100, Washington, DC 20005
Telephone 202-566-3100, Toll Free: 866-747-1471, Fax: 202-566-3127, email:
<HAVAinfo@eac.gov>.

See <www.LobbyingAndAdvocacy.com> for updates.

Requirement:
Professional Standards

Summary:

Successful lobbying in today's environment necessarily involves respect for, and compliance with, not only laws, but also with ethical standards. Lobbying is a highly visible activity subject to critique and criticism. Clients, association members, board members, stockholders, and employees are increasingly aware of the need for the organizations that represent them to be in full compliance with lobbying laws and to practice professional ethics.

The American League of Lobbyists designed a "Lobbyists' Code of Ethics" to serve as a guide for the professional conduct of lobbyists.

Lawyers who lobby are also responsible for complying with their state bar code of ethics.

Determine and Maintain Compliance:

Those with supervisory responsibility for government affairs and those hiring contract lobbyists should ensure that their lobbyists subscribe to the Lobbyists' Code of Ethics.

The American League of Lobbyists (ALL) "Lobbyists' Code of Ethics" is included in Appendix 6, and may be found at *<www.alldc.org>*.

All professional lobbyists joining the American League of Lobbyists must subscribe to the Code. The ALL Code has been used as a model ethics code for various governmental affairs organizations. The Code is applicable to federal, state, and local lobbying.

A list of state lobbying associations is available at *<www.alldc.org>*.

Information on codes and standards for lawyers on a state-by-state basis is available at *<www.law.cornell.edu/ethics>*.

The American Bar Association's **Directory of Lawyer Disciplinary Agencies** is found at *<www.abanet.org>*.

The American Bar Association also provides a Model Code of Judicial Conduct at *<www.abanet.org>*.

See <www.LobbyingAndAdvocacy.com> for updates.

§2.4 **Designing an Effective Compliance System**

"An ounce of prevention is worth a pound of cure."

Benjamin Franklin

Beyond registering and reporting as a lobbyist (addressed in §§ 2.8–2.24), effective compliance demands ongoing monitoring and diligence, because rules, submission requirements, or methods are occasionally modified pursuant to legislative reforms, changes in leadership, and the implementation of new technology.

The best rule of thumb is to prepare a proactive ethics compliance plan and to keep it updated. Periodically refresh yourself and your staff on the rules. While some lobbyists may deliberately ignore laws and ethics, more often, busy lobbyists with good intentions fail to check authoritative sources regarding their uncertainties, or neglect to seek qualified advice when questionable ethics situations arise. An effective government affairs compliance system will help to avoid these scenarios.

§2.5 **Seven Elements of an Effective Government Affairs Compliance System**

The text below is based on "A Government Affairs Compliance System: Effective Policies and Procedures Under the Sentencing Guidelines to Address Political and Lobbying Activity," January 2006, By Martha L. Cochran, Robert S. Litt, and Ronald A. Schechter, Arnold & Porter, LLP, Washington, DC. Reprinted with permission.

In summary:

1. Establish compliance standards and procedures to prevent and detect criminal conduct.
2. Provide appropriate oversight.
3. Exclude high-risk individuals from government affairs activity.
4. Periodically communicate the standards and procedures.
5. Monitor and audit for compliance, and provide and publicize a system for reporting potential or actual wrongdoing without fear of retaliation.
6. Provide incentives and discipline to promote compliance, including discipline of individuals responsible for the failure to take reasonable steps to prevent or detect an offense.
7. Respond appropriately to violations and take steps to prevent similar conduct, including making any necessary modifications to the program.

Excerpts from

A Government Affairs Compliance System

Effective Policies and Procedures Under the Sentencing Guidelines to Address Political and Lobbying Activity

January 2006

By Martha L. Cochran, Robert S. Litt, and Ronald A. Schechter,
Arnold & Porter, LLP, Washington, DC

This summary is intended to be a general summary of the law and does not constitute legal advice. You should consult with competent counsel to determine applicable legal requirements in a specific fact situation.

Organizations whose interests are affected by government action must engage with decision makers at all levels of government in the United States. It is a simple fact of doing business.

Large corporations often have Washington, D.C., and regional and state offices, staffed with government affairs employees and supported by large numbers of outside lobbyists. The government affairs operations of smaller companies are more modest. But, whatever their size and scope, an organization's government affairs activities are subject to strict and varying laws and rules at the Federal, state and local level, which dictate:

- Whether, how, and within what limits corporations and other organizations and individuals may contribute to candidates for public office;
- Whether, how, and within what limits a private party may confer meals, entertainment, or other benefits upon government officials; and
- Whether and how those who communicate with government officials with regard to legislation or executive action must disclose those communications and related expenditures.

Those who fail to follow the rules face potential civil and criminal consequences. The requirements are even more complex for companies that sell goods or services to the government, who risk losing existing government contracts and being barred from new ones if they fail to comply.

Until recently, some lawmakers, executive branch officials, lobbyists and business organizations have winked at the rules and assumed lax enforcement. But now, perhaps more than any time in recent memory, it is clear: The cops are on the beat. Federal prosecutors have shown that they will not hesitate to target those in the private sector, as well as those in government, who violate these rules. Government auditors, inspectors general, and debarment officials stand ready to act against government contractors

(Continued on page 52)

whose conduct may not rise to the level of a criminal offense but violates contractual or civil legal requirements. Federal prosecutors and enforcement officials are joined by increasing numbers of state prosecutors, who in recent years have targeted both government officials and private entities engaged in political corruption.

Although reform is in the air in Washington, and the rules may change, it is not too early for companies active in the public policy arena to reexamine existing compliance policies and procedures and ask:

- Do they cover all relevant risk areas of the company's government relations, political and procurement activity?
- Are they widely distributed or do they simply sit on the shelf?
- Are employees appropriately trained?
- Is it time to self-audit areas of significant risk?
- In the event of wrongdoing by a company's employees or agents, can the company demonstrate to a prosecutor or to other authorities that it exercised appropriate due diligence to prevent and detect wrongful conduct through the implementation of a reasonably designed, implemented, and enforced government affairs compliance program?

Importance of a Compliance Program to Reduce Potential Organizational Liability

The willingness of prosecutors and other enforcement officials to seek criminal, civil, and contractual penalties for violations of these laws should serve as a warning to any politically active company: A compliance program for government affairs is just as important as a program for insider trading, antitrust, environmental law or other areas of potential organizational liability.

In recent years, the establishment of effective corporate compliance programs has become particularly important as a way of minimizing the potential liabilities of a corporation and its officers and directors. The Department of Justice guidelines used by prosecutors in determining whether to bring criminal charges against corporations for the acts of their employees, known as the "Thompson Memorandum," cite "[t]he existence and adequacy of the corporation's compliance program" as an important factor in deciding whether to prosecute. Similarly, the Securities and Exchange Commission in its "Seaboard Report" and statements of policy has emphasized the importance of an effective corporate compliance system in the Commission's evaluation of whether to bring an enforcement action against, or seek substantial civil fines from, a corporation. The Federal Acquisition Regulation ("FAR"), which governs virtually all federal government procurements, identifies whether a contractor had "effective standards of conduct and internal control systems in place" as a key factor in deciding whether to suspend or debar the contractor based upon wrongdoing by its employees. A truly effective compliance program thus can help a company avoid criminal prosecution, civil penalties, and suspension or debarment for the acts of its employees. It can also help a corporation minimize the consequences of any such enforcement action.

The United States Sentencing Guidelines for organizations provide for a substantial reduction in a corporation's sentence if the corporation has an effective compliance and ethics program. The Guidelines emphasize the importance of commitment by senior management and the board of directors to the program. Although the Supreme Court last year held that the Guidelines were no longer mandatory, most federal judges continue to afford them great weight in sentencing, and the Guidelines' discussion of compliance programs remains extremely influential. The Thompson Memorandum, the Sentencing Guidelines, SEC policy statements, the FAR, and the specter of potential director liability for failure to assure the implementation of an effective compliance program, all offer powerful incentives to establish and implement policies and procedures to address all relevant legal requirements and a system of internal controls reasonably designed to assure compliance.

The Seven Elements of an Effective Compliance Program

No compliance program can be effective in all companies and all situations. A compliance program must be tailored to the needs of the individual company. However, the Sentencing Guidelines identify seven elements to determine whether a compliance program is sufficiently effective to justify mitigation of sentence. In the government affairs context, these criteria provide important guidance in developing a governmental affairs compliance program.

FIRST, establish standards and procedures to prevent and detect criminal conduct.

The first step in establishing such policies and procedures is to identify the legal requirements that govern the company's business. As discussed above, the key areas of law governing most organizations' government affairs activities in the U.S. are lobbying laws, ethics and gifts restrictions, and campaign finance laws. Government contractors also must comply with broad and detailed procurement-related laws and rules. The company should have written materials that set forth legal standards, as well as the company's own policies, in these key areas.

A policy statement typically would state—in strong and unambiguous language—the company's policy of complying with all relevant federal and state laws and regulations and would state company policy on key issues. It may address, among other things, corporate policy on activities that may be legal in some jurisdictions but prohibited under company policy (or permitted only with specified approval), such as whether corporate funds may be used to provide benefits or other gifts to government officials or to charities designated by them, and whether corporate funds may be used for campaign contributions in states where such contributions are legal.

The company should develop written procedures that employees must follow to comply with legal requirements and corporate policies. An informal "practice" is no substitute for written procedures. Such procedures might require written approval by specified individuals or require submission of a form confirming that appropriate legal review has been conducted in connection with any request for payment of expenses for an event attended by government officials. The procedures also might call for employee

(Continued on page 54)

"checklists" or other mechanisms to capture information required for filing accurate lobbying activity expenses with a government agency.

The size and formality of the government affairs compliance program may vary with the size of the organization, as well as with the nature of its business and any prior history of misconduct. What is important is that <u>some</u> program be designed to prevent violations, that it be implemented and followed, and that it be memorialized in writing.

SECOND, provide appropriate oversight.

The Sentencing Guidelines state that a company's board of directors should be knowledgeable about, and exercise oversight over, the organization's compliance program, and that high-level personnel must be assigned overall responsibility for it. Specified individuals must be delegated day-to-day responsibility and given adequate resources for the program, reporting periodically to high-level personnel and to the board.

The appropriate level of board and senior management oversight of the company's government affairs compliance program will differ, depending upon the scope of the company's government affairs activity and the risks it may present. However, someone must be accountable for day-to-day compliance responsibilities. Ideally, this should be someone who does not have line responsibility for the success of the government affairs efforts. The legal department constitutes an important component of the organization's government affairs compliance infrastructure.

Those with responsibility for supervision should identify all employees whose conduct or decision making potentially could lead to a violation of the laws discussed above. Typically, these will be employees who have lobbying or other government affairs responsibilities in the relevant jurisdictions. If the company is a government contractor, members of the company's sales force also should be included. Someone within the company should be assigned responsibility for ensuring compliance by outside consultants.

Procedures should be adopted to ensure that compliance directives are carried out. Supervisors should have explicit responsibility for compliance with the requirements of law and company policy, and someone should be tasked with disseminating compliance materials and monitoring compliance.

THIRD, exclude high-risk individuals from government affairs activity.

The Sentencing Guidelines state that a company must use reasonable efforts to ensure that individuals who have engaged in illegal activities or conduct inconsistent with effective compliance are not allowed to exercise substantial authority within the organization. While this guideline speaks to management of the corporation generally, it offers useful guidance to those responsible for staffing a government affairs operation.

In the areas of political and procurement law, this element may be most relevant in the selection of outside lobbyists and consultants, but it also applies to any employee who may be given discretion in the conduct of any government affairs effort. Some companies delegate substantial discretion to retained lobbyists or business development specialists, particularly at the state and local level where a national company may have inadequate knowledge of what "buttons to push," or otherwise may lack the connections to reach governmental decision makers. It is not satisfactory simply to hire lobbyists and consultants and send them on their way. Their activities should be monitored and their expense vouchers carefully reviewed. An "expense" submitted for payment may actually represent an illegal gift to a government official. Employees of the organization responsible for compliance should be alert to any "red flags" suggesting possible illegal activity.

FOURTH, periodically communicate the standards and procedures.

This may be done by requiring participation in training programs or by disseminating publications that explain in a practical manner what is required. Managers must receive training on the legal requirements applicable to their areas of responsibility. They, in turn, must ensure that their subordinates and the company's agents understand their compliance responsibilities.

Many companies have policies relating to gift-giving, political contributions and lobbying in their codes of conduct. However, a generalized code of conduct of a large corporation that speaks to a variety of subjects cannot include the specificity needed to address compliance in any one area, nor can it address the specific procedures necessary in each area of potential liability.

Policies and procedures specific to government relations and government sales should be disseminated to those who need to know. For example, a brief description of the legal requirements governing the use of corporate resources for political activity, as well as the company's own policies and procedures, could be sent to all employees who may be in a position to violate these requirements. The company may send a notice to all employees stating that no employee may engage in political activity during his or her working hours or use corporate resources to further such activity, unless specific approval has been given by a designated individual. There should be a flat statement that no employee can expect reimbursement from the company for any political contribution; such reimbursement likely will be found to be illegal, even in jurisdictions where corporate contributions are themselves legal.

Broadly disseminated materials need not contain the detail that may be required of materials designed for those with key responsibilities for the corporation's political or government sales activities. The company also may require employees and outside consultants with specific government affairs and marketing responsibilities to attend periodic compliance seminars. Moreover, employees, as well as outside lobbyists and consultants, should be asked to certify that they have ready the company's code of conduct and policy statements in this area and will abide by them.

(Continued on page 56)

FIFTH, monitor and audit for compliance, and provide and publicize a system for reporting potential or actual wrongdoing without fear of retaliation.

Monitoring and auditing should be tailored to the relevant activity. As noted earlier, lobbyist and sales consultant expense reports are, for many companies, a significant area of potential risk; the procedures for reviewing and approving these types of payments should be audited periodically. A number of organizations ask outside counsel to audit their political action committee, as well as other risk areas, such as their procedures for hosting candidates or government officials, capturing employee lobbying expenses, or approving corporate funding of venues or events to which government officials may be invited, such as stadium boxes or cultural events.

A key aspect of an effective reporting system lies in the company's assurance to potential whistle-blowers that they will face no retribution. Even if there is no fear of organizational retaliation, if the working environment fosters unofficial punishment for the individual encouraged to report violations by fellow workers, then the system will prove unworkable. There must be a tone at the top of the organization that encourages compliance and supports those who report improper or illegal conduct.

SIXTH, provide incentives and discipline to promote compliance, including discipline of individuals responsible for the failure to take reasonable steps to prevent or detect an offense.

This criterion is applied in the government affairs context in the same manner as it is in other areas of compliance. Employees and agents must understand in advance the consequences of noncompliance and appreciate that the same standard of justice will be applied to offenders regardless of their position within, or their perceived value to, the company.

SEVENTH, respond appropriately to violations and take steps to prevent similar conduct, including making any necessary modifications to the program.

The program itself should prescribe measures to be taken, if an offense occurs, to review the policies and procedures and to amend them if necessary to reduce the likelihood that the offense will be repeated. Outside counsel frequently is called in at this point and may evaluate the offense, the individual who committed it, and the programmatic measures that might have failed to prevent the commission or detection of the offense. Appropriate amendments to the program may be recommended.

Conclusion

This paper gives some examples of standards and procedures that might constitute elements of an effective compliance program in the areas of government relations and government sales and marketing. But as noted above, the program that will work for a particular company must be tailored to fit its organizational structure and the nature of the government relations and marketing activities in which it engages. What is important is that any politically active company have such a program, that management be fully committed to it, that high level personnel within the company be charged with responsibility for it, and that all employees and agents whose activities might lead to potential criminal liability for the organization be well informed of their responsibilities under the program and effectively supervised for compliance with it.

The key questions that a government agency will ask in assessing a compliance program that has failed to prevent a violation of law will be: Was this a genuine effort, to which top management was fully committed, to prevent and detect violations of law? Was it designed and implemented effectively? Or was it simply a paper program, pretending to encourage compliance but really condoning wrongdoing?

The development and implementation of an effective government affairs and marketing compliance program requires commitment by the top of the organization, hard work by management, the dedication of sufficient resources, and the acceptance of those employees whose conduct is addressed by the program. Nonetheless, the result is well worth the effort. It can help companies avoid problems, mitigate problems that occur and, in the final analysis, afford the corporation, its officers, and its directors substantial protection when they need it most. In the era of increased attention to political law violations, government affairs and marketing compliance should be a priority for all companies active in this area.

§2.6 **Recognize the Constancy of Change**

"[R]eform is very hard work. It is a constant work in progress. I was reminded by one of my staff members that I had said at one point as we moved ahead with a reform bill, which I am happy to say we passed in the last Congress, I said, when we are done with that reform, what we need to do is work on more reform. . . . And I believe it is part of our responsibility to constantly look at ways in which we can reform and improve the operations of this institution."

The Hon. David Dreier (R-CA), U.S. House of Representatives, Debate on the Rule for Consideration of Lobbying Reform Legislation, May 24, 2007.

In lobbying, like most of life, the one thing that is constant is change. Lobbying scandals, changes in the political environment, and problems or perceived problems with existing requirements will continue to prompt revisions to lobbying rules and methods of enforcement at all levels of government. Competing priorities, an increasingly feverish work pace, and changing lobbying laws can present ongoing challenges for insuring compliance and maintaining professional standards. Additionally, the methods for submitting required reports (for example, hardcopy via mail or electronic signature via the Internet) change periodically due to security concerns, the creation of new databases, and upgraded technological capabilities.

Periodic confirmation of requirements should be part of every lobbyist's action plan and calendar. See § 2.7, Maintaining Ongoing Compliance.

§2.7 Lobby Tips

Maintaining Ongoing Compliance

- Determine who in your organization is responsible for ensuring compliance for each statute/requirement;
- Determine who has back-up responsibility for oversight and what should happen in the case of staff absence or transition;
- Prepare information for and periodically update all staff members involved in government affairs activities and oversight, such as the general counsel, and finance and accounting departments;
- Provide orientation information and reference material for all new employees involved in government affairs;
- Seek appropriate counsel to determine the need for an internal legal review of your compliance process for all relevant lobbying, ethics, and political regulations;
- Note disclosure and reporting deadlines on internal calendars, legislative action plans, etc., prior to the start of the year. Establish an effective calendar/tickler system to ensure that you don't miss any dates. The calendar should include intermediate steps. Include steps such as:
  1. Compile required information (legislation lobbied, campaign contributions, meetings and contacts, etc.).
  2. Prepare draft.
  3. Review/address questions and answers.
  4. Approve/sign.
  5. Make copies.
  6. Mail/transmit electronically, taking care to submit all pages.
  7. Retain copy and proof of submission (for example, electronic submission receipt).
  8. Monitor forthcoming lobbying reform changes and develop proactive implementation plans for information gathering, compliance and oversight.
  9. Check government disclosure databases such as <www.disclosure.senate.gov> and <www.fec.gov> to verify that your report is included and correct.
  10. Ensure that your staff is fully trained and held accountable, with back-up plans for absences. Refresher information should be provided periodically and organizational meetings should be conducted regularly in light of any changes in reporting requirements or processes.
  11. Include language in your retainers with any contract lobbyists stating that they are responsible for compliance with appropriate federal, state, and local laws.
  12. Maintain a system to report violations or any pressure to violate rules or ethical standards.
  13. Verify any changes to the physical method of transmission/submission well before the deadline, for example, electronic submission via the web or postmarked in the mail, in light of ongoing security concerns and process changes.
- Join a professional association such as the American League of Lobbyists (<www.alldc.org>), the National Council of State Legislators (<www.ncsl.org>), The Council on Governmental Ethics Laws (<www.cogel.org>), or state lobbying organizations to assist you in staying abreast of ethical and legal changes and developments in the field.
- See the Lobbyists Annual Calendar: Key Dates and Activities Template in Appendix 5.

§2.8 **Overview: Registering as a Lobbyist**

*"The purpose of our lobbying laws is to tell the public
who is being paid how much to lobby whom on what."*
Sen. Carl Levin (D-MI), 1992

Federal lobbyists must register with the U.S. House of Representatives and the U.S. Senate. Some states and localities have additional restrictions on lobbying and campaign activity and require registration and disclosure. As you become involved in lobbying or take on a new lobbying contract or responsibility, one of the first questions to examine is whether you should register as a lobbyist at the federal level, the state level, or both.

The thresholds for registering as a federal lobbyist are explained in § 2.9; § 2.21 and § 2.22 explain how to determine state registration requirements; and §§ 2.23 and 2.24 provide tips for determining and maintaining compliance with local lobbying requirements.

The Lobbying Disclosure Act (LDA) provides that the Secretary of the Senate and the Clerk of the House may refer potential noncompliance situations to the U.S. Department of Justice (DOJ). In a February 8, 2006, Senate Rules Committee hearing on lobbying reform, it was revealed that as of January 1, 2003, the Secretary of the Senate had referred over 2,100 cases of potential noncompliance to DOJ.

The Clerk of the House and the Secretary of the Senate are required to review the forms submitted by lobbyists and send corrections notices in writing when they are needed. Those who knowingly fail to correct a problem within sixty days after receiving notice or to comply with any other provision of the Act may be subject to a civil fine for up to $100,000/$200,000 as well as *criminal penalties* enacted as part of the Honest Leadership and Open Government Act of 2007 (HLOGA) (Pub. L. 110-81, 121 Stat. 735), available in *Lobbying and Advocacy Sourcebook*, 2. Also, as a result of HLOGA, the Comptroller General conducts random audits of lobbyist filings annually.

It should also be noted that The False Statements Accountability Act of 1996 (18 U.S.C. § 1001, discussed in the chart at § 2.3) makes it a crime to willfully falsify or use information with respect to matters within the jurisdiction of the legislative, executive, or judicial branch.

Additionally, the LDA (as amended) requires the Clerk of the House and the Secretary of the Senate to make all registrations and reports available for public viewing online. Senate lobbying registration forms may be viewed online at *<www.disclosure. senate.gov>* and House reports are available at *<www.disclosure.house.gov>*. Private databases such as *<www.lobbyists.info>* and *CQ MoneyLine <www.cqmoneyline.com>* also provide searchable information based on federal lobbying registration filings.

The importance of accurate and timely filings is magnified with criminal penalties for noncompliance and public disclosure databases that will provide investigative reporters, competing lobbyists and even those whom you represent an enhanced ability to scrutinize lobbyists' filings.

§2.9 **Who Must Register as a Federal Lobbyist?**

The Lobbying Disclosure Act of 1995 (2 U.S.C. § 1603) maintains that paid or otherwise compensated federal lobbyists meeting certain thresholds must register and report on lobbying activities with the Clerk of the U.S. House of Representatives and the Secretary of the Senate (Office of Public Records). Lobbying activities include contacts with high-ranking executive branch officials. LDA registration and activity reports should not be taken lightly. There is no accommodation for reports received after the deadline. The enactment of The Honest Leadership and Open Government Act of 2007 (HLOGA) (Pub. L. 110-81) (available in *Lobbying and Advocacy Sourcebook*), which subjects lobbyists to new criminal penalties and potential audits, provides added impetus to correctly register and report as a federal lobbyist. Additional resources for determining and maintaining LDA compliance are included in the chart at § 2.3.

Criteria for eligibility for outside contract lobbyists (lobbying on behalf of clients for compensation) versus in-house lobbyists (employed by an organization to represent its interests) differ as follows (2 U.S.C. §§ 1602 and 1603):

Outside (Contract) Lobbyists

Contract lobbying organizations are required to register when their services are acquired or retained by a client for financial or other compensation and the following three tests are all met:

1. **The Contact Test:** The lobbyist makes more than one written, oral, or electronic lobbying contact (to the House or Senate or covered executive branch official) on behalf of the client;
2. **The Money Test:** The lobbyist earns $6,000 or more from the client during the quarter; and
3. **The Time Test:** Lobbying activities constitute at least 20 percent of his or her services on behalf of the client during the quarter (the "20 percent rule").

In-House Lobbyists
(Employed by the organization they are representing)

Organizations are required to register upon meeting all three of the following tests:

1. **The Contact Test:** The lobbyist makes more than one written, oral, or electronic lobbying contact (to the House or Senate or covered executive branch official);
2. **The Money Test:** The organization *spent or is expected to spend* $12,250 or more on lobbying-related expenses during the quarter;
3. **The Time Test:** At least one employee of that organization spends at least 20 percent of his or her time lobbying. Activities to examine in determining whether lobbying activities constitute 20 percent or more of an individual's time include:
   a. Lobbying contacts to legislative and executive branch officials and efforts in support of such contacts,

   b. Background work that is intended, at the time it was performed, for use in contacts, and

   c. Coordination with the lobbying activities of others.

If the intent of the work is to support ongoing and future lobbying, then the activity would fall within the definition of lobbying activities.

   (*Note:* The trigger amounts are adjusted every four years based on the Consumer Price Index and are scheduled to be adjusted again in 2009.)

§2.10 **What Must Be Reported?**

Pursuant to Section 4 of the Lobbying Disclosure Act, 2 U.S.C. § 1603, all organizations meeting the threshold requirements described in § 2.9 are required to register and periodically report on their activities by submitting filings electronically. Reports include information on the amount of money spent (in the case of organizations with in-house lobbyists) and information on the amount received (in the case of outside/contract lobbyists). The reports also require information on government entities contacted, lobbyists engaged, and specific legislation or action lobbied. The initial registration form (LD–1) and ongoing activity reports (LD–2) are identical for the House and the Senate even though the two chambers have separate review processes.

§2.11 **How to Report to the House**

Before each filing deadline, lobbyists should check for submission process and form updates via the office of the Clerk of the House at: <*http://lobbyingdisclosure.house.gov*>. This site also offers answers to frequently asked questions on filing electronically with the House.

   For additional assistance, contact: The Clerk of the House, Legislative Resource Center, 202–226–5200, <*http://lobbyingdisclosure.house.gov*>.

§2.12 **How to Report to the Senate**

Senate filing instructions and forms are available at: <*www.senate.gov/lobby*>. Pursuant to the "Honest Leadership and Open Government Act of 2007"(HLOGA) (Pub. L. 110-81), available in *Lobbying and Advocacy Sourcebook*, electronic filing is required for Senate reports filed after January 1, 2008. Senate reports may be filed electronically via the House electronic system at <*www.lobbyingdisclosure.house.gov*>. Updates to submission requirement updates are posted on the Senate web site at <*www.disclosure.senate.gov*> and should be verified long before each filing deadline.

   For additional assistance, contact: The Secretary of the Senate, Office of Public Records, 202–224–2115 or 202-224-0758, <*www.disclosure.senate.gov*>.

§2.13 Maintain Confirmation of Your Filings

Always keep a copy of your submitted reports and a transmission receipt for your files. If you do not receive a confirmation of receipt of your submission, contact the office and request one. Maintaining confirmation is especially important during periods when the House and Senate offices are making significant software changes pursuant to lobbying reform legislation, because technical problems with the new systems could arise.

§2.14 Report One: Initial Registration (LD-1 Form)

Timing: Within 45 days of meeting threshold requirements referenced in § 2.9.

Exercise due diligence as you approach the threshold:

> *"Once a quarter, sample the last week of your time. How much time was spent on lobbying, e.g., if it's two hours, you're not close yet. Once you reach 15 percent, it would be a good idea to develop a time table for compliance."*
> Source: Pamela Gavin, Office of the Secretary of the Senate

Form Used: LD–1

Links to these forms can be found at *<www.lobbyingdisclosure.house.gov>*, *<www.disclosure.senate.gov>*, and on this book's web site *<www.LobbyingAndAdvocacy.com>*.

Tips:

- Indicate that you are a new registrant.
- Leave the House and Senate identification number fields blank. Upon registering as a federal lobbyist, the House and Senate will each provide you with a registration identification number. Once you register, you need to keep your House and Senate filing numbers on file so that you can use them for your periodic filings, amendments, or in the case of a termination.
- The effective date for your initial lobbying registration is the date that you were retained or first made a lobbying contact for that client, whichever is earlier.
- Upon registering, mark your calendar with periodic reporting deadlines (see § 2.15 for deadline information). Once you are registered with the House and Senate (with LD-1 forms), you will need to file regular (LD-2) reports according to congressional deadlines until a termination report is filed. You must file an LD-2 report to capture activity upon registration. The initial registration (LD-1) does not replace the need for your first regular report (LD-2) on your first quarter of lobbying activity.
- Verify the proper delivery method and confirm that no process or delivery changes to the processes have been implemented via the Secretary of the Senate or the Clerk of the House before filing your initial registration and before each subsequent (periodic) filing.
- If you are a 501(c) organization, make sure that your Lobbying Disclosure Act information (under Section 15) and your Internal Revenue 990 filings are consistent and correct.
- *Always* keep a copy of all of the forms that you submit and an electronic confirmation.
- Also see "Lobbying Disclosure Act Guidance," online at *<http://lobbyingdisclosure.house.gov>* and in *Lobbying and Advocacy Sourcebook*.

§2.15 Report Two: Periodic Reports (LD-2)

Once you are registered as a federal lobbyist (with an LD-1 Form), you will need to file regular (LD-2) reports until a termination report is filed, even if you do not have any lobbying activity during that period. In that case, simply indicate "no lobbying activity" for question #11.

Timing: Reporting periods and deadlines for submitting forms are established by Congress and periodically changed pursuant to lobbying reform legislation. For example, the Honest Leadership and Open Government Act of 2007 (HLOGA) (Pub. L. 110-81) replaced semi-annual activity reporting with quarterly periods.

Report on the lobbying activity that occurred during the relevant quarter beginning on the following dates:

- January 1,
- April 1,
- July 1, and
- October 1.

Filing Deadlines: Quarterly reports are due within 20 days of the end of the quarter (or the first business day after the 20th day if that day is not a business day):

- January 20,
- April 20,
- July 20, and
- October 20.

Form Used: LD–2

Links to this form can be found at <*www.lobbyingdisclosure.house.gov*> and on this book's web site <*www.LobbyingAndAdvocacy.com*>.

Tips:
- The reports must be filed and received by both the Secretary of the Senate and the Clerk of the House on time. Late periodic reports are not counted.
- To verify current deadlines and transmission procedures, contact:

  The Clerk of the House, Legislative Resource Center, 202–226–5200, <*http://lobbyingdisclosure.house.gov*> and

  The Secretary of the Senate, Office of Public Records, 202–224–2115 or 202-224-0758 <*www.disclosure.senate.gov*>.

§2.16 Report Three: Amendment

Timing: As needed. An amendment may be made to correct or modify information provided in a previously filed LD-2 (periodic report).

Form Used: LD–2 (This is the same form that is used for periodic reports. Check "amendment" on question #9.)

Links to this form can be found at <www.lobbyingdisclosure.house.gov> and on this book's web site <www.LobbyingAndAdvocacy.com>.

§2.17 Report Four: New Client Registration

Timing: Upon adding a new client.

Form Used: LD–1

Links to this form can be found at <lobbyingdisclosure.house.gov> and on this book's web site <www.LobbyingAndAdvocacy.com>.

§2.18 Report Five: Termination

Timing: Upon termination of lobbying as an organization or upon termination of a client.

Form Used: LD–2 (Check termination for question #10.)

Links to this form can be found at <www.lobbyingdisclosure.house.gov> and on this book's web site <www.LobbyingAndAdvocacy.com>.

§2.19 Report Six:
Gift Rule Attestation and Campaign Contributions

Timing: The Honest Leadership and Open Government Act of 2007 (HLOGA) (Pub. L. 110-81) requires all federally registered lobbyists to submit a new report on campaign contributions and related activities for quarterly periods beginning on:

- January 1,
- April 1,
- July 1, and
- October 1.

Quarterly reports are due within twenty days of the end of the quarter (or the first business day after the twentieth day if that day is not a business day).

Form Used: Links to this form can be found at <www.lobbyingdisclosure.house.gov> and on this book's web site <www.LobbyingAndAdvocacy.com>.

§2.20 Recommended Resources

LDA Compliance

See the Chart at § 2.3 for LDA compliance resources and disclosure databases.

§2.21 Who Must Register as a State Lobbyist?

As indicated in § 1.23, numerous lobbyists are registered at the state level and must take care to ensure that they are in full compliance with relevant state laws and ethical standards. Additionally, federal and multi-state lobbyists must monitor their own involvement in state/local issues to determine whether certain registration and ethical requirements pertain to them. Those with oversight responsibility for government affairs should also be cognizant of the application of state and local requirements to their local affiliates.

Also, when an issue is hot, it can move at the federal and state levels simultaneously. State or local laws or legislation can drive federal legislative activity and attract national attention. Accordingly, federal lobbyists are frequently asked to provide policy or political expertise and may become highly engaged at the state and local levels. The chart at § 2.22 provides listings of state ethics and lobbying reporting and ethics resources that may be useful to your organization in this regard.

§2.22 Recommended Resources

State Lobbying and Ethics Compliance

Links to the following charts are provided at this book's web site
<*www.LobbyingAndAdvocacy.com*>:

- The National Conference of State Legislatures (NCSL) provides several excellent charts explaining laws for lobbyists in all fifty states <*www.ncsl.org*>.

- An excellent listing of summaries and links for state ethics and lobbying laws is provided by the Council on Governmental Ethics Laws <*www.cogel.org*>.

- A chart with links to the state agency lobbying disclosure and ethics web sites is provided by The Center for Public Integrity <*www.publicintegrity.org*>.

§2.24 Recommended Resources

Local Government Compliance and Ethics

Links to the following charts are provided at this book's web site
<*www.LobbyingAndAdvocacy.com*>:

- Links to each local government web site by state are provided by the International City/County Management Association <*www.icma.org*>.
- ICMA also provides local government ethics resources <*www.icma.org*>.

§2.23 Who Must Register as a Local Lobbyist?

Elizabeth Kellar, deputy executive director, International City/County Management Association and County Ethics Committee commissioner for eight years, gives the following tips for complying with local government lobbying disclosure and ethics requirements:

1. Go directly to the local government source (see the local government web site links at <*www.icma.org*>) to view current registration requirements, disclosure standards, and ethics rules.
2. While local governments are creatures of states and most local governments derive their skeleton disclosure and ethics requirements from state laws, some may go further. Additionally, formats, timing, or method of submission may vary.
3. Remember that local laws may change frequently. Check the local government sources periodically to capture any changes (for example, in the wake of changes in administration).

§2.25 The Financial Pressures of Political Campaigns

*"There are two things that are important in politics. The first
is money and I can't remember what the second one is."*
—United States Senator Mark Hanna (R-OH), 1895

Securing political contributions for expensive re-election campaigns has become a major focus for elected officials. At the federal level, expensive campaigns are launched essentially the day after members of Congress are elected as they seek funding for their re-election. Many members of Congress complain that the tremendous pressures to secure campaign financing detract significantly from their legislative work and they regularly discuss various approaches to reform the campaign finance system.

The mean cost for a 2006 Senate election campaign was more than $5 million (from approximately $3.2 million in 2004) and the mean cost for a 2006 House general election candidate was approximately $902,000 (from $640,000 in 2004). The Center for Responsive Politics brochure, "Who's Paying," reveals that approximately 80 percent of Americans gave nothing at all (at any governmental level). According to Ken Cooper at Political Moneyline (now CQ MoneyLine), "Less than one percent contributes financially into federal elections." While exact data are not available, the available data suggest meager political participation financially by the citizenry in view of the increased expenditures of political campaigns. Through polling, 13 percent of Americans claim that they gave money to a political campaign according to the American National Election Studies (2004), but given the bias that goes with self-reporting, that figure is likely to be lower than 13 percent. According to a February 9, 2005, letter to congressional leaders from former Federal Election Commissioners Michael Toner and Bradley Smith, the percentage of Americans choosing to contribute to the public financing system on their tax returns has also dropped significantly over the last twenty years:

> *"From the mid-1970s through the mid-1980s, the check-off percentage*
> *averaged between 25–30 percent, and never dropped below 23 percent. . . .*
> *For tax returns received in 2003, the check-off rate was 11.25 percent,*
> *which is only one out of nine of the nation's taxpayers participating."*

§2.26 The Campaign Compliance Imperative

Contributing financially to political campaigns is an important way for citizens to be engaged in the American political process. Campaign contributions are a necessary part of the political process and allow special interests and individuals to express support for their chosen candidates. However, contributing money to campaigns is an area where compliance is especially important. Federal, state, and local political campaign law violations can bring both civil and criminal penalties. Even though protected by the First Amendment to the U.S. Constitution as political speech, campaign contributions could give rise to criminal prosecution if given in exchange for political favors.

Lobbyists don't have to work with an organization that has a Political Action Committee (PAC) to inadvertently violate a political involvement law. Several important limitations need to be observed to avoid inadvertent violations. The chart at § 2.3 describes the applicable laws with citations and recommended compliance resources. Additionally, public interest groups and the media give significant attention to the activities of lobbyists in this area. See § 2.27 for a listing of common pitfalls to avoid and § 2.28 for campaign dos and don'ts, with references to particularly useful FEC resources and highlights of specific areas to watch out for as part of your ongoing efforts to avoid political campaign and contribution violations.

§2.27 Common Campaign Pitfalls to Avoid
Provided by the Hon. Michael Toner
2006 Chairman, Federal Election Commission

For Individuals:

- Exceeding the contribution limit.
- Making a contribution on a corporate account.
- Failing to observe the correct newspaper/advertising technical disclaimer requirements.

For Corporations:

- Using corporate facilities or subsidizing fundraising.
- Bringing pressure to bear on employees to give to a PAC.
- Failure to use corporate facilities properly or follow the rules on endorsements.

§2.28 Political Campaign Participation and Contribution Dos and Don'ts

DOs:

- Use the confidential FEC hotline 800–424–9530 if you have any questions about your compliance. (*Note:* If you are concerned about caller I.D., simply use your phone's caller I.D. block, which can be obtained from your operator.)
- Familiarize yourself with FEC rules that may be applicable to you or your organization. The FEC's *Campaign Guide for Corporations and Labor Organizations* may be found on the FEC website: *<www.fec.gov>* (134-page PDF).
- Contact the FEC's Information Division email at: *<info@fec.gov>*.
- Check the FEC homepage for FEC answers to frequently asked questions.
- Be aware of how much you can contribute (for 2008, individuals may give $2,300 per candidate or a candidate's committee per election). The limit is increased according to inflation in odd-numbered years. Future limits will be posted on *<www.fec.gov>* and published in the *Federal Register*.
- Mark the FEC reporting dates on your calendar.
- Bookmark *<www.fec.gov/law/law.shtml>*. The site links to all federal campaign finance laws, reviews current laws, provides instructions on requesting an advisory opinion (A.O.), and provides FEC policy statements and opinions.
- Understand the disclaimers that must appear in ads and mailings. See "Special Notices on Political Ads and Solicitations" on the FEC site *<www.fec.gov>*, and also available in *Lobbying and Advocacy Sourcebook*.

§2.29 Recommended Resources

Campaign Compliance

See the chart at § 2.3 for federal, state, and local campaign compliance resources and disclosure databases.

Also see documents from the Internal Revenue Service, Office of Government Ethics, Federal Election Commission, Office of Special Counsel, and Congressional Research Service, in *Lobbying and Advocacy Sourcebook.*

DON'TS:

• Exceed the contribution limit. For 2008, individuals may give $2,300 per candidate or a candidate's committee per election. The limit is inflation-indexed in odd-numbered years. Future limits will be posted on *<www.fec.gov>* and published in the *Federal Register.*

• Accept contributions from foreign nationals.

• Accept contributions from corporations.

• Fail to observe correct newspaper/advertising technical disclaimer requirements.

• Fail to observe corporation fund-raising prohibitions.

• Place pressure on employees to give to a PAC.

• Use corporate facilities incorrectly.

• Violate certain rules with endorsements.

§2.30 Executive Branch Lobbying Rules

Federal government ethics rules are important to federal employees involved in communicating with Congress, but they are also important for those who lobby the federal government.

Entities involved in interpreting and enforcing executive branch ethics rules include the Office of Government Ethics (policy and oversight); The Department of Justice, including U.S. Attorneys' Offices (criminal statutes); the Office of Personnel Management's Office of Special Counsel (personnel issues such as the Hatch Act); agency Inspectors General; and the pertinent federal agency involved. See § 2.32 for contact information.

§2.31 Highlights of Major Executive Branch Ethics Rules and Restrictions Applicable to Lobbying

The following chart provides some highlights of the ethics rules that may pertain to federal lobbying. However, federal employees as well as those involved with federal agencies or hiring government employees should read the entire statutory requirements and any associated regulations or rulings and seek guidance from the appropriate Designated Agency Ethics Official (DAEO). See § 2.32 for DAEO information.

The U.S. Office of Government Ethics (OGE) (<*www.usoge.gov*>) oversees federal agency ethics enforcement efforts and trains agency officials, but each federal agency head is responsible for insuring ethics compliance. Accordingly, each federal agency provides ethics training for its own employees, answers inquiries regarding agency requirements, and is responsible for taking appropriate administrative actions against employees. Information on useful OGE documents summarizing agency-wide requirements is also included in § 2.32.

Issue	General Description
Misuse of Position 5 C.F.R. §§ 2635.701-705	Employees may not use public office for private gain including coercion for any benefit:
	"Public service is a public trust. Each employee has a responsibility to the United States Government and its citizens to place loyalty to the Constitution, laws and ethical principles above private gain." (5 C.F.R. § 2635.101)
	See *Lobbying and Advocacy Sourcebook*, 14, for an Office of Government Ethics misuse of position crossword puzzle.

Issue	General Description
Gifts from Outside Sources 5 C.F.R. §§ 2635.201-205	*"Public officials may not seek or accept anything of value in return for performing official duties." (18 U.S.C. § 201 (b))*
	The emolument clause of the U.S. Constitution "prohibits anyone holding an office of trust or profit under the U.S. from accepting anything of value." (The U.S. Constitution, Art. I, Section 6)
	Generally, no federal employee shall "solicit or accept anything of value" from a person seeking official action from, doing business with, or (in the case of executive branch officers and employees) conducting activities regulated by, the individual's employing entity; or "whose interests may be substantially affected by the performance or nonperformance of the individual's official duties."

There are a number of exceptions to the ban on gifts from outside sources (5 C.F.R. § 2635.204). These allow an employee to accept—

- A gift valued at $20 or less (the $20 rule), provided that the total value of gifts from the same person is not more than $50 in a calendar year.
- A gift motivated solely by a family relationship or personal friendship.
- A gift based on an employee's or his spouse's outside business or employment relationships, including a gift customarily provided by a prospective employer as part of *bona fide* employment discussions.
- A gift provided in connection with certain political activities.
- Gifts of free attendance at certain widely attended gatherings, provided that the agency has determined that attendance is in the interest of the agency.
- Modest refreshments (such as coffee and donuts), greeting cards, plaques, and other items of little intrinsic value.
- Discounts available to the public or to all government employees, rewards, and prizes connected to competitions open to the general public.

In addition, an employee can never solicit or coerce the offering of a gift, or accept a gift in return for being influenced in the performance of an official act. An employee cannot accept gifts so frequently that a reasonable person might think that the employee was using public office for private gain.

An excellent pamphlet by the U.S. Office of Government Ethics titled, "Gifts from Outside Sources" explains exceptions including the $20 rule and is available at <*www.usoge.gov*> and in *Lobbying and Advocacy Sourcebook*, 11.

Issue	General Description
Seeking Future Employment *18 U.S.C. § 208; 5 C.F.R. §§ 2635.601–606*	*"Employees shall not engage in outside employment or activities, including seeking or negotiating for employment, that conflict with official Government duties and responsibilities." (5 C.F.R. §§ 2635.601–606)* Employees may not participate in matters that may directly affect the financial interests of an organization with whom they are arranging future employment. An employee may need to disqualify himself or herself from participation in an issue concerning potential or future employment. A waiver may be sought while seeking or negotiating employment. See *Lobbying and Advocacy Sourcebook*, 14, for an OGE crossword puzzle on job seeking.

(Continued on page 72)

Issue	General Description
Post-Employment Restrictions (Revolving Door Restrictions) *18 U.S.C. § 207, 41 U.S.C. § 423(c)*	*"Ninety-nine percent of governmental affairs professionals (lobbyists) believe that the general public is not aware of the current revolving door restrictions."* Source: American League of Lobbyists, 2004 Survey on Lobbyist Restrictions

Pursuant to 18 U.S.C. § 207 (c), senior executive personnel are prohibited from lobbying for at least one year after leaving their government position. In some cases the restrictions are greater (such as two years for very senior staff). Legislative changes in this area are important to track and regulations must be observed when hiring and employing government staff.

Recommended resources are provided in the chart in § 2.3.

See *Lobbying and Advocacy Sourcebook*, 12, for an OGE revolving door fact sheet and *Sourcebook*, 13, for OGE's Rules for the Road. |

Issue	General Description
Conflicts of Interest *18 U.S.C. § 208; 5 C.F.R. §§ 2635.401-403; 5 C.F.R. Part 2640*	*"Officials may not participate in any matter in which they can use their official position to directly improve financially."* (5 C.F.R. §§ 2635.401-403)

"Outside activities must not conflict with official duties. Prior approval may be obtained for participation on certain outside employment and activities." (5 C.F.R. §§ 2635.801-809)

Each federal agency sets rules for prior approval of employment or activities.

The Honest Leadership and Open Government Act of 2007 (HLOGA), reprinted in *Lobbying and Advocacy Sourcebook*, 2, requires the disclosure of post-congressional employment negotiations to the relevant House or Senate Ethics Committee. The legislator cannot vote on any bill that would impact his or her potential employer. |

Issue	General Description
Lobbying with Appropriated Moneys Act (Commonly referred to as the Anti-Lobbying Act of 1919) *Pertains to executive branch*	The Anti-Lobbying Act aims to address concerns regarding the use of lobbying with appropriated funds. However, the Act's application is tempered by the rights grounded in the Constitution, for example, for the president and cabinet officers to speak on issues of public concern and to recommend measures. The restriction depends on whether a lobbying effort is or is not "necessary for the efficient conduct of public business," which, of course, may be debatable.

While official enforcement of the Anti-lobbying Act is limited, it has been invoked periodically by members of Congress |

*employees'
lobbying of
Congress and
other government
officials.
18 U.S.C. § 1913*

claiming that a federal agency has been inappropriately lobbying. Additionally, specific incidents may be cited by the GAO, and allegations are sporadically highlighted in the press.

The Act bars "gross solicitations" of grassroots (public) support, according the U.S. Department of Justice. (See, for example, U.S. Dept. of Justice Office of Legal Counsel opinion, "Guidance on 18 U.S.C. § 1913," April 14, 1995.) The measure was amended in 2002 to expand the law to apply to lobbying of any government official, not just members of Congress.

| Issue | General Principles |

**Examples
of Other
Miscellaneous
Statutes
Involving
Government
Officials**

"Executive branch employees hold their positions as a public trust and the American people have a right to expect that all employees will place loyalty to the Constitution, laws, regulations, and ethical principles above private gain. Employees fulfill that trust by adhering to general principles of ethical conduct, as well as specific ethical standards."

Source: Common Ethics Issues,
Office of Government Ethics, General Principles

*Executive Order
(E.O.) 11222,
May 8, 1965;
E.O. 12674,
April 12, 1989,
as modified by
E.O. 12731,
October 17, 1990;
3 C.F.R. (1990);
5 C.F.R. § 2635.101;
18 U.S.C. § 202*

*See additional
statutory
references in
the Office of
Government
Ethic's
Compilation
of Federal Ethics
Laws at
<www.usoge.gov>.*

A number of criminal statutes involving government officials can pertain to lobbying activities, including:

1. The prohibition against solicitation or receipt of bribes (18 U.S.C. § 201(b)).
2. The prohibition against solicitation or receipt of illegal gratuities (18 U.S.C. § 201(c)).
3. The prohibition against seeking or receiving compensation for certain representational services before the government (18 U.S.C. § 203).
4. The prohibition against participating in matters affecting an employee's own financial interests or the financial interests of other specified persons or organizations (18 U.S.C. § 208).
5. The prohibition against receiving salary or any contribution to or supplementation of salary as compensation for government service from a source other than the United States (18 U.S.C. § 209).
6. The prohibition against solicitation or receipt of gifts from specified prohibited sources (5 U.S.C. § 7353).
7. The prohibition against certain political activities (5 U.S.C. §§ 7321-7326 and 18 U.S.C. §§ 602, 603, 606-607). For example, the Hatch Act of 1939 (5 U.S.C. § 7321 et seq.) prohibits federal employees from engaging in partisan political activity. The Act is named after former Sen. Carl Hatch of New Mexico.

See § 2.32 for Hatch Act recommended resources.

§2.32 Recommended Resources

Executive Branch Rules

Links to these websites can be found at book's website
<*www.LobbyingAndAdvocacy.com*>.

- Designated Agency Ethics Officials (DAEOs): Federal employees and those involved with federal agencies seeking specific agency information or interpretations should seek guidance from the appropriate Designated Agency Ethics Official (DAEO).

- U.S. government entities with ethics/conduct-related authority.

- Standards of Ethical Conduct for Employees of the Executive Branch (5 C.F.R. Part 2635) published by OGE, details ethics rules for government employees.

- The U.S. Department of Justice (criminal prosecutions).

- Department of Justice United States Attorneys' Manual, Title 9, Criminal Resource Manual linked to at the DOJ web site.

Federal Employee Rules regarding Gifts from Outside Sources:

- An excellent pamphlet by the U.S. Office of Government Ethics titled, "Gifts from Outside Sources," which provides Frequently Asked Questions on gift restrictions for federal employees, available in *Lobbying and Advocacy Sourcebook*, 11.

- Ethics Rules for Government Employees (Standards of Ethical Conduct for Employees of the Executive Branch, 5 C.F.R. Part 2635).

- Office of Government Ethics, Laws and Regulations: <*www.usoge.gov*>.

- Common ethics issues and a compilation of federal ethics laws are listed on the Office of Government Ethics webpage.

- *Lobbying and Advocacy Sourcebook*, 14: OGE federal employee crossword puzzle on gifts.

Hatch Act (Political Activity):

- See *Lobbying and Advocacy Sourcebook*, 22, for an Office of Special Counsel booklet.

Whistleblowers Statutes:

- Office of the Special Counsel: <*www.osc.gov*>.

- Information on whistleblower statutes applicable to federal employees is available from the National Whistleblower Center at <*www.whistleblowers.org*>. Individuals aware of illegal or unethical behavior of state officials can contact their state's ethics board. Additionally, information on private sector whistleblower protections, including those under the Sarbanes Oxley Act § 806 at 29 C.F.R. Part 1980 is available from the U.S. Department of Labor.

§2.32 Recommended Resources (Continued)

- Contact information for the Office of Government Ethics: U.S. Office of Government Ethics, 1201 New York Avenue, NW, Suite 500, Washington, DC 20005, <*www.usoge.gov*>, 202-482-9300, email: ContactOGE@oge.gov. (Do not send confidential or sensitive information via email since they do not have a secure email server.)

- A database of federal lobbyists by executive branch agency lobbied is found at <*www.lobbyists.info*> (fee).

- View lobbying registration and disclosure forms submitted by federal lobbyists who lobby executive branch agencies (by specific agency) at <*www.disclosure.senate.gov*>.

§2.33 Keep Current

Executive Branch Rules

Updates to federal ethics rules may occur at any time as a result of lobbying and ethics reforms, transitions in leadership, or in response to specific situations. Therefore, it is prudent to monitor the progress and status of potential changes via the relevant government agencies and the Office of Government Ethics web site at <*www.usoge.gov*>. Information on agency-wide rules can be found in several documents on this site.

Federal employees may also contact the agency at 202-482-9300, 1201 New York Avenue, NW, Suite 500, Washington, DC 20005, email: ContactOGE@oge.gov. Do not send confidential or sensitive information via email and include your mailing address, email address and a daytime telephone number.

See *Lobbying and Advocacy Sourcebook* for several Office of Government Ethics resources.

§2.34 Historical Observations on the Importance of Ethics for Members of Congress

Congress has struggled with congressional ethics, bribery, and foreign agent traitors since the infancy of our nation. George Washington was challenged by corrupt foreign agents, and Congress has addressed public official corruption since its early years. For example, on January 4, 1808, President Thomas Jefferson sent Congress information pursuant to a House resolution to provide Congress with a list of foreign agents for dismembering the Union from George Washington's term. In 1808, Congress set up an early legislative committee to draft Government ethics legislation:

". . . to punish any person holding an office or profit or trust, either civil or military, under the Government of the United States, who shall receive money, or accept any present, emolument, office or title, from any King, Prince or foreign State, without the consent of Congress . . ."
Source: House Journal Jan. 22, 1808, on the motion of Congressman Marmaduke Williams

Congressional debates throughout the centuries have included statements by representatives themselves on taking responsibility for their own conduct. For example, in 1808, Federalist Congressman William Milnor of Pennsylvania offered a bit of tongue-in-cheek banter in his clever commentary on the House floor concerning the importance of personal integrity for members of Congress:

"It has been said by the gentleman from Maryland that he should be at all times opposed to the seat of Government being fixed in any large city, and he has alluded to the influence which it might possess over members of Congress. I will ask the honorable member whether he feels that he should be influenced by considerations of that nature? I have put this question home to individual members who have made this suggestion, but have never yet found the man who himself should be influenced in that way. He has no suspicion of himself, but mistrusts his weaker friends. I cannot suppose that the Representatives of the nation can possibly be so weak or so wicked as to suffer considerations of this kind to influence their better judgment."
Source: *Annals of Congress*, U.S. House of Representatives, p. 1550, February 1808

Another timeless, insightful musing regarding personal responsibility for congressional conduct was delivered by Congressman Gardenier of New York on the House floor in 1808:

"We are not tied down here by any wizard spell—there is no enchanted castle here, from which, like some of the heroes of knight-errantry, we cannot escape. The charm is easily broken."
Source: *Annals of Congress*, U.S. House of Representatives, p. 1554, February 1808

§2.35 Congressional Ethics Rules at a Glance

This book does not attempt to provide details on the myriad of ever-changing rules that apply to congressional members and employees, but rather highlights the major rules with resources for determining and keeping current on the requirements.

However, lobbyists should both know the rules and comply with them because they cannot afford to be implicated in a scandal. Reputation is perhaps the most valuable attribute for a lobbyist. For these reasons the American League of Lobbyists' Code of Ethics requires lobbyists to know and respect the laws relevant to public officials:

"A lobbyist should not cause a public official to violate any law, regulation or rule applicable to such public official."
American League of Lobbyists' Code of Ethics, Article II, Section 2.2

Most officials and their staff members appreciate knowledgeable lobbyists who help them avoid problems. However, don't assume that policymakers know or remember the rules in the press of their daily work. One's acceptance of a meal or gift does not mean the meal or gift is legal or ethical.

An example of scrutiny that lobbying organizations can face relating to congressional gift and meal rules is found in a situation involving Bell South Corporation. A Bell South clerical employee provided *The Washington Post* with internal audit documents that listed numerous situations where the limit for taking Congressional members and staff to lunch had been exceeded under House and Senate gift rules. As reported by the Post, the 21-page spreadsheet provided to the reporters showed that, "More than 80 lawmakers and Capitol Hill aides are listed as having accepted entertainment from lobbyists for Bell South Corp. at levels that appear to exceed congressional gift limits. . ." (*The Washington Post* "Hill Gift Limits Often Exceeded, Lobbyists' Records Show," by Jeffrey H. Birnbaum and Thomas B. Edsall, January 1, 2006; p. A04.)

Members of Congress and staff may never solicit a gift, or accept a gift that is linked to any action they have taken or are being asked to take. Members of Congress, their staff, and congressional officers are generally not permitted to accept gifts or meals from lobbyists, foreign agents, or their employing organizations, with certain exceptions. See § 2.19 for the Honest Leadership and Open Government Act's lobbyist's gift and travel attestation. Do not offer any gifts or meals, plan congressional events, negotiate employment or arrange trips with policymakers unless you are absolutely certain that no rules are being violated. See § 2.38 for resources to determine current prohibitions.

Congressional members and staff may accept free attendance for only certain types of events and under very specific criteria, which was further restricted by the Honest Leadership and Open Government Act of 2007, for example, a bona fide constituent event without registered lobbyist sponsorship or participation.

To stay abreast of congressional reforms and ethics changes that may apply, lobbyists need to incorporate monitoring into their legislative action plans and monitor the changes in congressional rules via the congressional ethics committees' web sites (links provided at book's web page), as well as reources recommended in § 2.38, congressional publications and legislative tracking databases. You can also become a member of the American League of Lobbyists (<*www.alldc.org*>) to keep current on changing requirements.

§2.36 **Congressional Oath of Office**

Congressional ethics flow from the oath of office that all members of Congress are required to take when they are elected or reelected into their office. The tradition dates back to the first Congress in 1789 and was last revised in the 1860s:

> *"I do solemnly swear (or affirm) that I will support and defend the*
> *Constitution of the United States against all enemies, foreign and*
> *domestic; that I will bear true faith and allegiance to the same; that*
> *I take this obligation freely, without any mental reservation or purpose*
> *of evasion; and that I will well and faithfully discharge the duties of*
> *the office on which I am about to enter: So help me God."*
>
> Source: *<www.senate.gov/artandhistory/history/common/briefing/Oath_Office.htm>*

§2.37 **Filing Complaints Regarding Public Officials**

Individuals aware of evidence pertaining to illegal behavior of congressional members or staff have the right to provide information to the House or Senate Ethics Committees as identified in the chart at § 2.3. Citizens aware of evidence of illegal behavior of executive branch officials can contact the Office of Government Ethics *<www.usoge.gov>*, an agency's ethics official, or the U.S. Department of Justice *<www.usdoj.gov>* in the case of criminal statutes.

 # §2.38 Recommended Resources

Congressional Ethics Rules

The rules of the House and Senate are available on their web sites and linked to from this book's web site: *<www.LobbyingAndAdvocacy.com>*.

    This book's companion volume, *Lobbying and Advocacy Sourcebook*, 6, 7, 8, 9, 17, and 20 contains congressional gift rules and Congressional Research Service reports on ethics rules.

 # §2.39 Keep Current

Congressional Rules

Although the House of Representatives changes rules for members, officers, and staff at the beginning of each new Congress, keep in mind that both Senate and House rules can be revised at any time.

    See *<www.LobbyingAndAdvocacy.com>* for updates as rules and laws change.

§2.99 **Chapter Summary**

- Chapter Two explains the importance of recognizing "the ethics imperative" (§ 2.2), legal compliance and professional standards as the foundations of an effective lobbying strategy (§ 2.1).
- A chart provides highlights of each of the lobbying and ethics requirements with resources for determining and maintaining compliance in each area. (§ 2.3)
- Throughout the chapter, recommended resources and practical tips are provided for determining and maintaining compliance with various rules, professional standards, and registration requirements, at the federal, state, and local levels.
- Strategies are discussed for designing an effective compliance program including seven elements of an effective compliance system (§ 2.5) and practical tips for keeping current on an ongoing basis (§ 2.7).
- § 2.9 discusses the triggers for registering as a federal lobbyist: the contact test, the money test, and the time test.
- The chapter discusses the process for registering as a federal lobbyist including what must be reported (§ 2.10), and how to report to the House and Senate (§§ 2.11 and 2.12).
- A brief description with associated timeframes for using the federal lobbying registration and reporting forms is provided. (§§ 2.14–2.19)
- The chapter provides tips for determining and maintaining compliance with state (§§ 2.21 and 2.22) and local (§§ 2.23 and 2.24) lobbying and ethics requirements.
- In light of the "Campaign Compliance Imperative" (§ 2.26), Chapter two provides common campaign pitfalls to avoid (§ 2.27), campaign dos and don'ts (§ 2.28), and recommended resources for ongoing campaign compliance (§ 2.29).
- An overview of executive branch lobbying rules is provided at § 2.30, along with a chart of restrictions applicable to lobbying (§ 2.31). Recommended resources for keeping current on executive branch rules are also provided (§§ 2.32 and 2.33).
- Information is provided on congressional ethics history (§ 2.34) and on filing complaints regarding the illegal behavior of public officials (§ 2.37).
- Chapter Two explains why lobbyists should understand and keep current with rules relating to the conduct of members of Congress and their staffs. Resources are recommended for becoming familiar with congressional rules (§ 2.38) and keeping current as they change (§ 2.39). The text of the Congressional Oath of Office is provided (§ 2.36).

Position Drivers:
Forces That Shape Legislation

"Seek first to understand and then to be understood."

Stephen R. Covey, American speaker, trainer and author
(adapted from Saint Francis of Assisi)

Chapter 3: Position Drivers: Forces That Shape Legislation

§3.1 **Introduction**

"A week is a long time in politics."

Harold Wilson, United Kingdom Prime Minister

You should think about each of your issues in light of the broader context of the current political landscape, because policymakers will. Your issue will not be considered in a vacuum; numerous external factors will influence its dispensation. Therefore, understanding and responding appropriately to the broader political environment is essential. Chapter Three will help equip you to study and respond to the changing political environment and position drivers. This chapter aims to help you research and understand the determining influences (determinants) driving policymakers' positions. Your understanding of what drives a policymaker's perspective will enable you to put your best foot forward and maximize your opportunities during communication.

The outcome of legislation and policy issues is impacted by a number of factors outside the control of you and your organization. By studying and understanding these determining influences, you will improve your ability to forecast and shape legislation. In some cases you may be able to better influence these factors through your efforts and strategies. Most legislation passes Congress as part of other legislation. This chapter will help you to determine how your issue might fit into larger macro-political circumstances substantively, rhetorically, or even procedurally, as you identify potential legislative vehicles to which your issue could be attached as an amendment.

Finally, you will gain the ability to time your efforts for maximum impact, as the conditions of factors fluctuate over time. Much like a kite is best released when the wind is just right, you will have the ability to launch or expand your best efforts when the factors are most favorable.

§3.2 **Study the Legislative District's Demographics and Politics prior to Communicating with the Policymaker**

"The royal road to a man's heart is to talk to him about the things he treasures most."

Dale Carnegie

Where they stand depends on where they sit. Former House Speaker Tip O'Neill's timeless truth that "all politics is local" necessitates an examination of the political, economic, and cultural demographics of the district or state before initiating a lobbying contact with an elected official or the official's representative.

Due to full schedules and competing priorities, most lobbyists are challenged to spend significant time preparing for meetings with policymakers. More from circumstance than from lack of intent, lobbyists tend to target every policymaker with the same canned message. The lobbyist's natural inclination is to focus pre-contact time on preparing to discuss the issue at hand (discussed in Chapter Six) to the exclusion of other important considerations. Neglecting to research the unique attributes of a policymaker before contact typically results in using canned talking points, which do not optimize results. However, finding time to uncover the factors that will drive an official's decision-making process *before* attempting communication is time well invested. Researching the representative in advance will engender a more meaningful connection, enable efficient communications, and lessen the likelihood of making inappropriate or irrelevant comments. Advanced research will not only increase your chances of impacting the decision, but it will also enhance your ability to develop and maintain an ongoing relationship.

Failing to conduct advanced research is analogous to a person who plans a trip but focuses so much time on planned specific vacation activities that he fails to take the time to assess the conditions such as traffic, weather, roadblocks, and detours that could adversely influence the experience. It's more impressive and time-efficient to invest twenty minutes on the front side of the process before your initial communication than two hours in the wake of your conversation trying to address conditions that you discovered during your communication, but could have known in advance.

A good rule of thumb is to spend at least as much time researching the specific policymaker's background as you plan to spend communicating. For example, if you expect to have a thirty-minute meeting, you should spend at least thirty minutes researching the policymaker's background and constituency. This is beyond time spent researching the substance of a particular issue. (See Chapter Six for information on researching the substance of specific issues.)

§3.3 The Benefits of Studying "Position Drivers"

"Position drivers" are the driving forces that shape legislation. The key to deciphering position drivers is learning about the background and interests of specific elected officials, their staffs, and their constituencies. This knowledge will provide the following major benefits:

- Provides a knowledge base for building stronger and deeper relationships with representatives and staff.
- Helps you to identify and connect with members who may be champions for your cause or naturally inclined to have an interest in your issue.
- Helps to set priorities for your time and efforts on the policymakers whose vote you can most likely influence. See Chapter Eight for information on ranking members of Congress (§ 8.18) and establishing a target list (§ 8.16).
- Assists your efforts to communicate perspectives and requests in a manner that can be heard and agreed upon by legislative officials.
- Facilitates the process of selecting legislators who may be most inclined to respond favorably.

- Assists in predicting legislative scenarios, your chances for success, and the shape and ultimate outcome of legislation.
- Lessens the likelihood of making irrelevant, or even offensive, points or comments.

§3.4 Identifying "Position Drivers"

"You never know till you try to reach them how accessible men are; but you must approach each man by the right door."
Henry Ward Beecher

A variety of specific determinants, or position drivers, should be studied before making a lobbying contact. Researching key policymakers before the beginning of the congressional session should be incorporated into every lobbyist's legislative action plan. (See § 6.10 for a discussion of the content of legislative action plans.) Then, immediately before communications, more succinct research can be conducted to check for new developments.

Government affairs directors should encourage their lobbyists to proactively assess position drivers before communications, thereby linking advance research to staff goals and performance measures as appropriate. Directors can also set aside some staff time before the congressional session begins to plan a strategy for key policymakers, using the Seven Ps as discussed in §§ 3.5–3.12. As issues develop and specific lobbying opportunities emerge, make every effort to schedule an examination of the Seven Ps in time to tailor your message accordingly. Planning time to consider how a member's perspective is driven by his or her constituency, policies, and professional and personal background will make a tremendous difference.

§3.5 The Seven "Position Drivers" ("The Seven Ps")

"Really seeking to understand another person is probably one of the most important deposits you can make, and it is the key to every other deposit."
Stephen R. Covey

The seven factors (the seven position drivers, or the seven Ps, that determine policymakers' positions) are: **profile**, **previous experience**, **positions**, **press/public opinion**, **promoters**, **priorities**, and **personal experience**.

Consider and answer the sample questions in the following worksheet before communicating with a policymaker. Recommended resources are provided in the worksheet to help answer these questions.

Position Drivers (The Seven Ps)

§3.6 The Seven Ps	Questions to consider before communicating with policymakers:

§3.6
The Seven Ps

1. Profile
(Constituency
Represented)

Questions to consider before communicating with policymakers:

Examples of general questions to consider:

1. What are the demographics of the constituency (for example, urban or rural, traditional or progressive, level of prosperity, level of education, ethnicity, transient or stable)?
2. How much of the economy is agriculture, service, technology, or manufacturing-oriented?
3. For what products, attractions, annual events (such as traditional festivals), or services is the area known?
4. What is the history of the area (for example, how did the area develop, have there been natural disasters recently)?

Examples of questions relevant to your issue:

1. Does your interest, organization, or client have a presence in the area?
2. How significant is your issue in the district or state? (See Chapter Six for resources on researching your issue and Chapter Ten for strategies on presenting your issue effectively.)
3. Does the area have a law on the books related to your issue? If so, how is it being implemented, and what is the status of proposed changes?
4. Who are the other members of the state delegation in the House and Senate? Are other delegate members visible on the issue who could bring additional considerations or pressures, depending on upcoming election campaigns and the relationships of the players involved? Members of state delegations may compete against each other for higher office, work together, or lobby each other.
5. On what committees does the legislator serve, and why? For example, a senator may chair an agricultural committee because of the farming interests of his or her state. Even though a member's committee or subcommittee issues may not relate to your interest, it is important to recognize that the legislator's associated responsibilities are a major focus of his or her time and attention.
6. Does the legislator participate in informal coalitions or caucuses, and, if so, which ones?

See Chapter Six for information on ranking and targeting legislators.

Recommended resources for preparing to communicate with legislators:

Check a city, county, or state's official web page at <*www.statelocalgov.net*>, <*www.usa.gov*> (select State or Local under Government Agencies). More links are available under "State and Local" on this book's Resources page: <*www.LobbyingAndAdvocacy.com*>.

Obtain detailed information on state and congressional district demographics and characteristics through subscriptions and publications:
The Almanac of American Politics, by Michael Barone and Richard E. Cohen, National Journal Group, contains useful state and congressional district demographic information on members of Congress and governors, including state and district maps; profiles of the state or district based on census and political information; number of registered voters by political party; education level; industry or occupation; urban or rural population; percentage of white-collar, blue-collar, and gray-collar workers; percentage of the population that lives in urban or rural areas; unemployment; percentage of non-citizens; language, race, and ethnic origin; military veterans; and the district or state's Partisan Voting Index (PVI), as used by Charlie Cook, well-known Washington, DC, political election handicapper.

The Almanac of American Politics is published in odd-numbered years. Hard copy or online subscribers have access to more frequent updates via the *Almanac* web site.

CQ's Politics in America, by CQ Press, provides detailed state and district profile information. The online edition provides keyword search and the capability to browse by member, state, district, party, or chamber. The online version is searchable by keyword across the four most recent editions of *CQ's Politics in America* and includes the Your Profile feature, so that you can permanently save your favorite documents.

A **printable congressional district map** may be accessed at <*www.nationalatlas.gov*>, from the Dept. of the Interior.

Congressional salary information is available at <*www.legistorm.com*> and at <*www.congresspay.com*>.

The Council of State Government's web page at <*www.csg.org*>, provides the following useful publications with state-specific information:
1. *The Book of the States* provides information, answers, and comparisons for all 56 U.S. states and territories.

(Continued on page 88)

2. *State Directories* includes the names and contact information for key state government officials.
3. *State News Magazine* provides updates and analyses of state programs, policies, and trends in the executive, legislative, and judicial branches.

How to use the **USNewswire/PRNewswire** to search for state information:
1. Go to <*www.prnewswire.com*>.
2. Select "US State Policy News," or "Federal and State Legislation," or "Congressional, Senatorial, Gubernatorial, and Presidential Campaigns."
3. Search all releases using a particular state name, for example, go to the search box in the bottom left corner and enter the name of a state.

The full text of every **governor's annual state of the state speech** is linked to at <*www.stateline.org*>.

See the **Stateside Associates** web site for comprehensive state legislative monitoring and profiling (including information about existing state laws and regulations, and issues developing across states and localities): <*www.stateside.com*>.

<*www.fedspending.org*> by **OMBWatch** uses data from the Federal Procurement Data System and the Federal Assistance Award Data System to provide a free database of federal government contracting and spending. The database allows searches by congressional district, state, and contracting agency.

Recommended resources for preparing to communicate with executive branch officials:

1. Recognize that the demographics and politics of an agency's represented constituencies and the constituencies of political interest to the administration can shape policy positions. Consider the constituencies addressed, affected, or served by the agency's programs. This information is available on the agency's web page.
2. Every federal agency lobbyist should have a copy of the *Federal Yellow Book* for general agency descriptions and agency contact information. The online book allows you to see where an individual fits within the agency's programs and hierarchy. An annual subscription includes four hard-copy editions (produced quarterly). See <*www.leadership directories.com*> for subscription information.
3. Every four years (2008, 2012, 2016, etc.), Congress publishes the *Plum Book* (officially titled, the *United*

States Government Policy and Supporting Positions) listing the names and titles of all federal political appointees. The book covers positions such as agency heads and their reports, policy executives and advisors, and aides who report to these officials. The Plum Book may be obtained from the House Committee on Oversight and Government Reform at <*http://oversight.house.gov*> or the Government Printing Office bookstore at <*bookstore.gpo.gov*>.

4. While the U.S. Government Manual online contains very basic federal agency contact information and is updated annually, it is free and can be accessed at <*www.gpoaccess.gov/gmanual/index.html*>.

5. <*www.fedspending.org*> by OMBWatch uses data from the Federal Procurement Data System and the Federal Assistance Award Data System to provide a free database of federal government contracting and spending. The database allows searches by contracting agency, state, congressional district, contracting agency or type of award.

Links to all web resources are available on the Resources page for this book: <*www.LobbyingAndAdvocacy.com*>.

**§3.7
The Seven Ps**

**2. Previous
Experience**

Questions to consider before communicating with policymakers:

It is important to understand how previous experience and educational background can influence a policymaker's perspective. For example, a former governor may have strong views on the issue of states' rights. A lawyer may ask questions about the legal history of the issue and may point out that the legislation is drafted in a way that would encourage unnecessary litigation.

Examples of general questions to consider:
1. Where did the policymaker grow up and attend school?
2. What career path did the policymaker pursue before entering politics?
3. What political or policy-making positions did the official hold previously?
4. How might these positions shape the official's current views?
5. What other events or interests might have helped shape the official's views and approach to policy proposals?

Examples of questions to raise related to your issue:
1. Has the official had a personal experience relating to the issue which may affect his or her perspective? For example, a former small business owner may have implemented an employment law.

(Continued on page 90)

Recommended resources for preparing to communicate with legislators:

Project Vote Smart at: <*www.vote-smart.org*> provides biographical information on federal and state legislators.

Congressional members' official web sites:
Members of Congress post their official biographies for public viewing on their congressional web sites. The bio generally provides information on their background prior to serving in Congress, major congressional accomplishments and current committee and subcommittee assignments.

House member web sites: <*www.house.gov*>.

Senate web sites: <*www.senate.gov*>.

Free and very basic congressional bio information and an official photograph of every member of Congress is available at <*http://bioguide.congress.gov*>.

Tip: Be sure to indicate the year that you are looking for in the search. The bios are searchable by name, year, state, and party. Searching previous years allows you to see bios from former members of Congress who once served that particular area. This site does not contain some of the more interesting information provided by subscription services.

Subscription:
CQ's Politics in America, by CQ Press, provides detailed member state and district profile information. The online edition provides keyword search and the capability to browse by member, state, district, party, or chamber. The online version is searchable by keyword across the four most recent editions of *CQ's Politics in America* and includes the Your Profile feature so that you can permanently save your favorite documents.

The Almanac of American Politics, by Michael Barone and Richard E. Cohen, National Journal Group, contains useful political background information on members of Congress and governors, including date elected or appointed, date and place of birth, hometown, education and degrees conferred, religion, marital status, and spouse's name (if applicable).

You can have Congress, state legislature, and governors' contact information downloaded and updated automatically into your existing Microsoft Outlook Contacts folder or synched into your PDA or cellular phone at <*www.knowwho.com*>. A complete directory of members of Congress and staffs can be downloaded to your existing Microsoft Outlook contacts folder. Put your needed legislator data in the folder where you keep your important contact data. Also, you can synch the contact data to a PDA or a cellular phone and have mobile contact data at no extra charge.

Congressional Staff Biographies:
For bios of congressional staffers, see the *Almanac of the Unelected* at *<www.bernanpress.com>* and CQ Press's *Congressional Staff Directory*: *<http://csd.cq.com>*.

Recommended resources for preparing to communicate with executive branch officials:

Check the agency official's biographical information. Sources include:
1. The agency's web page and
2. *Congressional Quarterly's Federal Staff Directory* (print or online) *<www.cqpress.com>*.

Links to all web resources are available on the Resources page for this book: *<www.LobbyingAndAdvocacy.com>*.

---

§3.8
The Seven Ps

3. Positions

Questions to consider before communicating with policymakers:

1. What are the legislator's overall political philosophy and views?
2. How does the member typically respond to these types of proposals?
3. How familiar is the policymaker with your interest or concern?
4. What is the legislator's voting record on your issue of interest or on similar issues?
5. Has the legislator ever been approached by you, your organization, or client organization? If so, what was the response?
6. What statements has the member made regarding your organization, interest, client, or similar organizations?
7. How strongly held was any previous position? Was the vote unexpected with a decision made at the last minute, or did the legislator take a more deliberate stand months before the vote? Is he or she simply following the party leadership, or does the position come from a strongly held personal conviction?
8. What drove any existing position or previous vote on the topic, and how was it received by constituents and the press?
9. What is the member's history on your particular issue or similar issues? Knowing that policymakers are usually

(Continued on page 92)

criticized for changing their position on an issue, have they
ever cast a vote, issued a statement, or made a comment
on the issue (either from a currently held position or from
a past position)?

Much can be determined through your own research, but if
nothing can be found publicly, you can also ask the question
during conversation with the member's staff or former staff
or someone else whom you might know.

See Chapter Eight for strategies for asking a legislator to
change an established position.

Recommended resources for preparing to communicate with legislators:

Go to Project Vote Smart at *<www.vote-smart.org>* to view
interest group ratings, issue positions, and public statements
by federal and state legislators.

The government database, Thomas (*<www.thomas.gov>*), can
be used to search for a legislator's public positions and official
statements published in the *Congressional Record* (official
transcript of the full House's and the full Senate's proceedings)
on various bills and topics. The Thomas homepage allows the
user to:

1. Search for bills introduced or cosponsored by a legislator,
   and
2. Search the *Congressional Record* for statements made on a
   specific subject, bills, or amendments debated, and materials
   included in the record by a member of Congress:

Browse profiles for free at the Open Congress database:
<www.opencongress.org>. The database includes searchable
congressional profile information and bill information with RSS
feeds on all federal legislators and legislation.

CQ's Politics in America, by CQ Press, provides congressional
member profiles. The online edition provides keyword search
and the capability to browse by member, state, district, party,
or chamber. The online version is searchable by keyword
across the four most recent editions of *CQ's Politics in
America* and includes the Your Profile feature so that you
can permanently save your favorite documents.

The Almanac of American Politics contains *National Journal*
political ratings analyzing numerous congressional votes.
The *Almanac* also lists various interest-group ratings for every
member of Congress, including the American Civil Liberties

Union, the National Taxpayers Union, and the U.S. Chamber of Commerce. See above entry.

Numerous subscription databases provide advance searches of congressional committee activity and congressional communications beyond the general committee reports available on the free Thomas (<*www.thomas.gov*>) database.

The Gallerywatch database at <*www.gallerywatch.com*> provides extensive information and documentation including legislators' voting history, committee documents, and congressional committee reports and transcripts. Gallerywatch also provides customized information.

TheCapitol.Net's pocket *Congressional Directory* is available at <*www.CongressDirectory.com*>.

Many interest groups also publish and distribute lists of how all members of Congress voted on key issues. Often referred to as "How They Voted Guides," these organizational publications may be publicly available on interest-group web sites, or by searching for the publications through <*www.google.com*>, <*www.lexisnexis.com*>, or <*www.highbeam.com*>.

Much information about legislators' positions on issues can be collected through research, but if the legislators' positions have not been recorded publicly, you can ask the legislator or staffer for his or her position on the issue or a similar issue in the past. A former staff member or colleague may also make an excellent resource.

Recommended resources for preparing to communicate with executive branch officials:

Numerous administration positions and communications can drive individual agency priorities. Before communicating with agency officials, the following resources can be useful for determining current executive branch positions and priorities:

1. **Specific White House Policies and Initiatives**: Specific policies and initiatives are posted on <*www.whitehouse.gov*>. You can search the White House web site by any term of interest.

2. **The President's Annual State of the Union Address**: *"He shall from time to time give to the Congress Information of the State of the Union, and recommend to their Consideration such Measures as he shall judge necessary and expedient."* Article II, Sec. 3, U.S. Constitution

(Continued on page 94)

The annual State of the Union is provided, by law, to a joint session of Congress in January. The president's speech presents administration priorities, and the address is generally cleared in advance by, if not drafted by, the various cabinet agencies before it is delivered. The text of previous State of the Union Addresses is available at *<www.whitehouse.gov>*.

C-SPAN provides archives of previous state of the union addresses at *<www.cspan.org>*.

The remarks are also published in the *Congressional Record*, which is searchable at *<www.thomas.gov>*.

3. **The President's Weekly Radio Address**: The president's Saturday morning radio broadcast is carried weekly on C-SPAN radio at *<www.cspan.org>* and available in print and broadcast live via the White House web site at *<www.whitehouse.gov>*. This site also provides an index of previous radio address topics and texts.

4. **White House email updates**: You can sign-up to receive weekly Saturday morning email updates featuring speeches, events, and White House web site exclusives at *<www.whitehouse.gov>*.

5. **The Administration's Budget**: Information on the President's Budget, which is transmitted annually to Congress by the first Monday in February, reflects administration policies and is available at *<www.gpoaccess.gov/usbudget>* or *<www.budget.gov>*.

6. **Semiannual Regulatory Agenda (Unified Agenda)**: Published semiannually (usually in April and October) in the Federal Register (FR), the agenda summarizes the rules and proposed rules that each federal agency expects to issue during the next six months. The agenda is published by the Office of the Federal Register National Archives and Records Administration (NARA). Current and previous issues may be searched at *<www.gpoaccess.gov/ua>*.

   Additional information on the regulatory process is available in Chapter Four.

7. **Statements of Administration Policy**: For the administration's official statements on legislation, go to *<www.whitehouse.gov/omb/legislative/sap/index.html>*.

8. **Regulations under Review**: For current and past regulations under review (updated daily) as well as links to letters from the Office of Management and Budget

(OMB) to federal agencies with comments on specific regulations (for example, return letters responding to a draft rule, prompt letters, suggesting an issue worthy of agency priority and post review letters sent after an OMB review), go to *<www.whitehouse.gov/omb>*.

9. **Congressional Testimony**: Legislators on the following congressional committees tend to have heightened influence (positively and negatively) on federal agencies:

   a. **Appropriations Committees**: The House and Senate Appropriations Committees draft the legislation that allocates federal funds to the various government agencies yearly. Appropriations hearings can be a venue for members of Congress to raise concerns with an agency over a policy issue.

      You can check the relevant House and Senate appropriations subcommittees via the following links to obtain agency head testimony and hearing records (transcripts) regarding an agency's funding legislation at *<http://appropriations.house.gov>* and *<http://appropriations.senate.gov>*.

   b. **Committees and subcommittees with legislative jurisdiction over the agency's laws**: Related congressional hearings with jurisdiction over the laws administered by the agency.

   c. **Congressional oversight committees** can show a keen interest in agency activities through hearings, letters, meetings, and even investigations. Moreover, one committee used a "report card" system to rank agencies' compliance with performance and results measures.

   d. **Member Actions**: Any member of Congress can introduce legislation, make statements, or attempt to offer amendments regarding an issue of federal agency concern. Members of Congress write agency heads frequently expressing their concerns, and typically agencies are required to respond to congressional correspondence within a certain time period.

10. **Strategic Plans and Performance Reports**: Each agency has a long-term strategic plan and performance reports that are posted on the agency's web site. Each agency has a public affairs office that posts press releases and recent speeches or announcements.

(Continued on page 96)

11. **Government Accountability Office Reports on Specific Federal Agencies**: Locate reports conducted by the Government Accountability Office (GAO) on a federal agency at *<www.gao.gov>*.

12. **Executive Branch Lobbyists**: Check lobbyist databases to determine which lobbyists are contacting specific federal agencies (also searchable by state): *<www.lobbyists.info>*, or *<www.senate.gov/lobby>*.

13. **Media Coverage and Agency Press Releases**: Search for media coverage with subscription services, such as the Federal News Service at *<www.fnsg.com/>*, which monitors approximately 2,000 television news programs on network, cable, and local stations in more than 150 cities daily. Daily or weekly monitoring reports are available, and tapes or transcripts can be acquired.

    a. LexisNexis offers searches of print media, transcripts, and newswires at *<www.lexisnexis.com>* and is available by subscription or per usage basis. Titles can be retrieved without purchasing the text of the articles and may be sufficient in some cases for a cursory look at a person or agency.

    b. Highbeam offers searches of articles and includes some government documents at *<www.highbeam.com>*. (Titles can be retrieved without purchasing the text of the articles.)

    c. Google *<www.google.com>* is a free search engine. Select "news" and sort by date.

    d. Search for news releases about or posted by the federal agency with the USNewswire/PRNewswire at *<www.usnewswire.com>*. (Select the Federal Executive Branch Agency feature.)

    e. Use agency directories to contact agency press departments. (See § 3.11 for additional information.)

    f. Project Vote Smart (*<www.vote-smart.org>*) provides information including biographical information and public statements on executive branch agency heads.

Links to all web resources are available on the Resources page for this book: *<www.LobbyingAndAdvocacy.com>*.

**§3.9
The Seven Ps**

4. Press
   and Public
   Opinion

Questions to consider before communicating with policymakers:

1. What is the current and anticipated public opinion regarding your issue?
2. What has been the nature and extent of press coverage in the state or district (or nation, in the case of executive branch officials) on the issue?
3. What type of press coverage will the legislator likely receive upon publicly supporting your position?
4. Would the policymaker be criticized in the media for changing a previously established position?

Recommended resources for preparing to communicate with legislators:

1. Legislators track press coverage in their state or district very closely. Become aware of themes or criticisms that are playing in the state or local press.

2. Look at the legislator's **press release section of his or her web site** and find the accomplishments for which the legislator is especially proud. Congressional members' home pages can be found at <*www.house.gov*> or <*www.senate.gov*>.

   State legislators' home pages can be found at <*www.ncsl.org*> under "Legislatures," then "Web Sites."

3. Conduct your own **press searches** at <*www.lexisnexis.com*> or <*www.highbeam.com*> to determine recent press coverage.

   Search breaking online press at: <*www.google.com*>. Select "NEWS," and search using the name of the member of Congress, and then sort "BY DATE" for breaking news regarding that legislator. Select a "WEB" search to find out what other organizations are saying about the legislator.

   Search the newswire by region or state at <*www.usnewswire.com*>.

   To search the legislator or opponent's campaign ads by state, go to C-SPAN's database at <*www.campaignnetwork.org*>.

   See Charlie Cook's Weekly Political Report, "Off to the Races," which contains polling and specific race updates at <*http://nationaljournal.com*>.

(Continued on page 98)

Recommended resources for preparing to communicate with executive branch officials:

Conduct a press search to determine agency controversies. Search for press on the agency head's confirmation hearing if applicable. If the agency head was confirmed by the Senate, review committee transcripts at <*www.gallerywatch.com*>.

Links to all web resources are available on the Resources page for this book: <*www.LobbyingAndAdvocacy.com*>.

§3.10
The Seven Ps

5. Promoters

Questions to consider before communicating with policymakers:

Remember the old saying, "You dance with the one who brought you." Legislators tend to listen to and "dance with those who brought them." Think about who "brought them" and what they may have promised them before the dance.
1. Which groups or individuals actively helped the policymaker get elected? Who has supported the policymaker financially and otherwise?
2. Who are current supporters or legislative allies?

Recommended resources for preparing to communicate with legislators:

Campaign contributor databases:
1. View the FEC's disclosure database to look up political contributions by individuals and candidates at <*www.fec.gov*>.
2. Search campaign finance reports and view actual disclosure reports filed at <*www.fec.gov*>.
3. Search the *CQ MoneyLine* by Congressional Quarterly at <*www.cqmoneyline.com*>.
4. Search the *Center for Responsive Politics* contribution database and obtain customized election data, if needed, at <*www.opensecrets.org*>.
5. The National Institute on Money in State Politics provides a free searchable database of all state level political campaign contributions at <*www.followthemoney.org*>.

You can conduct research via the Internet and press tracking services referenced above to ascertain some of the candidate's endorsing organizations. For example, conduct a search for the candidate's name and the word "endorses" or "endorsed."

Recommended resources for preparing to communicate with executive branch officials:

1. Who are the trusted allies of key players in the administration?
2. Who does the agency head turn to for advice? Check for advisory board membership appointed by the agency head on the agency's web page.
3. Who are the legislative allies, such as committee chairs or highest-ranking members of the minority party who have been supportive of the agency head?

Project Vote Smart (<*www.vote-smart.org*>) provides interest-group ratings with background information on the pertinent interest group.

Links to all web resources are available on the Resources page for this book: <*www.LobbyingAndAdvocacy.com*>.

§3.11
The Seven Ps

6. Priorities

Questions to consider before communicating with policymakers:

Before visiting a member or staff member, remember that decision-making is not done in a vacuum. Members and staff are running at 100 miles an hour, juggling priorities and issues. The more you are informed on what these priorities and issues are, the better.

1. When is the policymaker up for re-election?
2. Is he or she in a competitive race? What criticisms have been raised or are anticipated?
3. What criticisms have been made of the policymaker by his or her opponents to which he or she may be sensitive?
4. What are the members' future ambitions or interests; for example, vying for a chairmanship, running for a party leadership position, or for a state-wide position such as senator or governor?
5. What are the legislator's big-picture priorities, issues, or concerns that could have a bearing on how this issue is perceived by the member or how much attention the legislator can give the issue?
6. How does the legislator spend his or her time?

Recommended resources for preparing to communicate with legislators:

TheCapitol.Net's *Congressional Directory* is available at <*www.CongressDirectory.com*> and indicates committee

(Continued on page 100)

and subcommittee positions for each member of Congress as well as each senator's election date. (All House seats are up for re-election in even-numbered years.)

Determine whether a senator is up for re-election this "election cycle" (two-year period) or if the House member (up for re-election every two years) is in a competitive race. Incumbents will be seeking to counter criticisms from their challengers.

Charlie Cook, nationally recognized political campaign handicapper, provides excellent reports on House and Senate competitive races as well as past election statistics at *<www.cookpolitical.com>*.

Check the member of Congress' seniority on various committees to find out if the member is in line to chair a committee or move up through the ranks of leadership.

Much information on the future plans and aspirations of members of Congress can be learned from daily reading of congressional publications such as *Roll Call* (*<www.rollcall.com>*), *Congressional Quarterly* (*<www.cq.com>*), *National Journal* (*www.nationaljournal.com*), and *The Washington Post* (*<www.washpost.com>*). If you don't know about the policymaker, you can rest assured that someone in Washington, DC, has studied that member of Congress thoroughly. You may have colleagues or coalition members who have contacts and are personally familiar with the particular member of Congress and could provide you with insights on his future aspirations.

Recommended resources for preparing to communicate with executive branch officials:

Has the official been confirmed by Congress or scheduled for confirmation hearings? If so, review any confirmation hearing press or transcripts to determine controversial issues confronting the official or her agency. How might any controversies that the official is confronting affect the consideration of your issue or the congressional reaction to it?

Search the Library of Unified Information Sources (LOUIS) at *<www.louisdb.org>* to search numerous federal documents, including congressional hearings for reference to a specific executive branch official's name or agency.

Search Open Hearings at *<www.openhearings.org>* to view schedules of current and future Senate committee hearings that may involve an executive branch official.

For an electronic copy of testimony prepared by executive branch officials appearing before Congress, check the relevant congressional committee's homepage at <*www.house.gov*> or <*www.senate.gov*>.

Commercial services, such as Gallery Watch (<*www.gallery watch.com*>), Lexis-Nexis, and Congressional Quarterly (<*www.cq.com*>) provide congressional hearing transcripts.

Some hearing testimony is available via the Internet on the Thomas web site at the Library of Congress (<*www.thomas.gov*>). In addition, published hearing testimony is generally available through the federal depository library system. There are approximately 1,350 federal depository libraries throughout the United States and its territories, at least one in almost every congressional district. See <*www.gpoaccess. gov/libraries.html*> to locate the federal depository library in your area. The libraries provide free public access to a wide variety of federal government information in both print and electronic formats, and have expert staff available to assist users.

Links to all web resources are available on the Resources page for this book: <*www.LobbyingAndAdvocacy.com*>.

§3.12
The Seven Ps

7. Personal
   Experience

Questions to consider before communicating with policymakers:

Has the policymaker had a personal experience on the issue that may shape his or her perspective on the issue? Personal experiences are extremely powerful and factor significantly into decision making. The underlying significance of the personal experience may not be apparent, even after speaking with a legislator in person, but opinions formed in the crucible of personal experience and reinforced over a period of years can be extremely powerful in driving a legislator's policy positions.

Recommended resources for preparing to communicate with legislators:

Occasionally, members of Congress will discuss personal situations in public that have driven their convictions or positions on specific legislation. This information may be available through searching the policymaker's remarks on the topic in the *Congressional Record* (via <*www.thomas.gov*> or other print media sources referenced in §§ 3.6–3.12).

Conversations with people who know the policymaker personally, including staff and former staff, can also reveal this type of inside information.

(Continued on page 102)

The Open Secrets Personal Financial Disclosure Database: <*www.opensecrets.org*> provides financial information on every member of Congress since 2005 (such as net worth, stock holdings, assets, and outside income).

Recommended resources for preparing to communicate with executive branch officials:

Personal information regarding agency officials is sometimes communicated during a confirmation hearing or in news releases announcing the official's appointment.

Conversations with people who know the policymaker, including supporters, staff, and former staff, can reveal personal experience information regarding an official.

The Open Secrets Personal Financial Disclosure Database (<*www.opensecrets.org*>) provides financial information on every executive branch official since 2005 (such as net worth, stock holdings, assets, and outside income).

§3.13 Understanding and Monitoring the Broader Political Landscape and Environment

While a positive legislative environment and macro-political issues can provide a hook, negative conditions can also provide disadvantages that could hinder the prospects or timing of your issue. The emergence of a new hot legislative priority could send your once timely issue to the back burner or make it politically unattractive. For example, the day after the Enron scandal broke would not have been the best time to approach a legislator to cosponsor legislation that would have been characterized as favorable to big business. Conducting political environmental scans can enable lobbyists to:

- Determine the conditions or timing most favorable for legislative or grassroots activities.
- Respond quickly and appropriately when circumstances change.
- Conduct advance planning to determine various scenarios and establish back-up plans.
- Strike while the iron is hot and take action.

Each issue is unique and the importance and effect of the political environment varies by issue. See Chapter Five for a discussion of taking the public's pulse through polls and surveys. The outcome of policy issues depends on political circumstances, and political circumstances change regularly. It's no wonder that effective lobbyists spend a significant amount of time tracking political circumstances and dynamics that could shape their issues.

§3.14 How to Conduct Legislative Forecasting

Forecasting the legislative environment is similar to forecasting the weather: you meticulously monitor certain indicators, constantly contemplate various scenarios, but remain mindful that everything can change without warning with one political gale force.

The winds of political change blow swiftly. A number of factors can influence your issue in terms of substance, timing, and support. A new legislative priority can eclipse your issue or offer a new legislative vehicle for its speedy advancement. The emergence of a hot new issue could result in a stepped-up desire for policymakers to champion it or a compelling reason to oppose it. Recommended resources for tracking political indicators and legislation, as well as strategies for overcoming obstacles are provided in Chapter Five.

§3.15 Worksheet: Evaluating the Political Environment

Determine how your issue fits within the context of the political environment and how the environment will affect your issue. You can use the following worksheet on evaluating political barometers to assist with your political issue forecasting:

KEY: 1 = Conditions are currently ideal for the issue's success.

2 = Conditions tend to be favorable for the issue's success.

3 = Condition is unknown.

4 = Conditions tend to be unfavorable for the issue's success.

5 = Conditions are definitely unfavorable for the issue's success.

Condition	Ranking (1-5) (Circle One)	Notes: Resources Monitored and Scheduled for Monitoring
Public Opinion: Congress reflects and reacts to public sentiment. What is the condition of public opinion or perceived public opinion on the issue or related issues? How might it shift? What surveys or public opinion polls have been released on the topic? Chapter Ten discusses strategies for influencing or shaping prevailing opinions within certain segments of the population.	1 2 3 4 5	

There are a number of well-known general polling firms:

• Gallup: <*www.gallup.com*>
• Rasmussen:
  <*www.rasmussenreports.com*>

(Continued on page 104)

Condition	Ranking (1-5) (Circle One)	Notes: Resources Monitored and Scheduled for Monitoring
• Zogby International: <*www.zogby.com*>		
• Mason-Dixon Polling and Research: <*www.mason-dixon.com*>		
• The Polling Company, Inc.: <*www.pollingcompany.com*>		
• Quinnipiac University Polling Institute: <*www.quinnipiac.edu*>		
• Survey USA: <*www.surveyusa.com*>		
• American Research Group: <*www.americanresearch group.com*>		
Interest groups frequently conduct their own surveys and polls or purchase questions on more broadly based surveys like Gallup or the National Journal's Hotline.		
The Hotline's "Blogometer" report, which takes the temperature of the political blogosphere, is posted every weekday at noon at <*http://blogometer. nationaljournal.com*>		
Issue Priority: What is the level of commitment among supporters and allies? Have competing issues arisen? Are compromises between key players possible? Have new concerns emerged that could change the level of focus or attention given the issue by key players?	1 2 3 4 5	

Condition	Ranking (1-5) (Circle One)	Notes: Resources Monitored and Scheduled for Monitoring
Issue Engagement: What players and what groups are engaged in the issue? Are relevant committee and party leaders engaged? Is the public interested or concerned (especially in the districts or states of key legislators)? What is the level of interest in and involvement by the press, the administration, key interest groups, celebrities, and experts?	1 2 3 4 5	
Issue Leadership: Do the key policymaker champions have the positional, relational, and personal ability to advance the issue? What if your champion announced retirement? Do you have a back-up plan? How might changes in congressional composition, leadership, party strength, or priorities affect the leadership of your issue?	1 2 3 4 5	
Economic and Other Environmental Conditions: How might economic conditions, such as the unemployment rate and consumer price index, affect the consideration or outcome of the issue? Data on trends are published by a myriad of sources, depending on the topic. Subject-matter experts are often good sources for identifying trends in a specific issue area. In addition, think tanks and associations have staff committed to identifying and tracking trends.	1 2 3 4 5	

(Continued on page 106)

Condition	Ranking (1-5) (Circle One)	Notes: Resources Monitored and Scheduled for Monitoring
Distractors: What makes, or could make, the issue unattractive to the public, policymakers, the press, or the administration? What developments could come to light that could trigger negative press and public perceptions? See Chapter Six for resources on conducting opposition research.	1 2 3 4 5	
Situational Opportunity: What are the logistical considerations? You may have a great issue, but no parliamentary or time opportunity, given impending congressional adjournment. Is a legislative vehicle available or a funding offset required to pay for your measure? Is a workable parliamentary situation feasible under the political circumstances? Does an upcoming election make consideration of your position more or less attractive? Do political circumstances discourage bipartisanship on the issue at play?	1 2 3 4 5	
Political Strength: Do you have the votes in committee or on the floor or could more support be garnered under various scenarios? What might happen before the vote that could reduce your political strength? Chapter Eight provides tips for developing a vote count through target lists. Your congressional champions can also work closely with allies and party leadership to determine how members are expected to vote.	1 2 3 4 5	

Condition	Ranking (1-5) (Circle One)	Notes: Resources Monitored and Scheduled for Monitoring
Gallup's periodic generic congressional ballot and job approval surveys can provide insight into a political party or particular member's political strength. You can search Gallup polls at Gallup Brain: <http://brain.gallup.com>.		
President's Approval Rating: There is a strong correlation between the political support of members of Congress and the president's approval. Changes in presidential approval may increase or decrease congressional support for a specific issue.	1 2 3 4 5	

§3.16 The Significance of Congressional and Party Leadership

The congressional party numbers determine which party is in the majority and gets to select committee chairs, set agendas and schedule the consideration of legislation. The political party division of the current Congress is available at <*www.CongressNumbers. com*>. The political agenda of congressional leaders is determined through discussions in various party and leadership meetings and communicated by the leaders through press communications.

The established priorities of congressional leadership, as well as the priorities of the individuals serving in various leadership positions, play a large role in shaping the congressional agenda. Accordingly, congressional leaders tend to receive significant media coverage of their actions and communications. Party leaders refine and promote their messages at key times such as:

- Leadership retreats prior to a congressional session,
- Before and after significant votes,
- Prior to returning home to communicate with constituents for a congressional recess,
- Before and after presidential messages, such as the State of the Union, the Weekly Radio Address, the release of the budget, and other announcements.

§3.17 Lobby Tips

How to Determine and Track
Congressional Leadership Priorities

- A good indication of the majority party's overall legislative wish list for a congressional (two-year) session can be seen by reviewing the "top ten": the first ten bills introduced in the U.S. Senate and House of Representatives. For the Senate, go to *<www.thomas.gov>* and search for the bill texts and Congressional Record statements for Senate bills S. 1 through S. 10. The House leadership's legislative priorities for the session are reflected in the leadership sanctioned-bills introduced as H.R. 1 through H.R. 10. The minority party broadcasts its legislative priorities through House and Senate bills numbered 11-20, which may also be found at *<www.thomas.gov>*.

- To track the current political party division of members of Congress, go to *<www.CongressNumbers.com>*.

- Pay careful attention to the statements by the party leaders on the Senate or House floor. Leaders frequently make statements at the beginning of the day or at key moments, such as prior to or following consideration of a high-priority issue. See Chapter Four for tips on monitoring floor action.

- Regularly check congressional leadership web sites for video footage, schedule updates, and releases (links are available at *<www.CongressLeaders.com>*). Some leaders allow the general public to sign up to receive email updates from their office on a regular basis.

- Review the House Majority whip notices, The Daily WhipLine, at *<www.majoritywhip.gov>*.

- Obtain House Floor Hourly Recaps at *<http://clerk.house.gov>*.

- See the Senate Daily Floor Schedule at *<www.senate.gov>*.

- Of course, the most effective method is to establish reliable information sources with people on the inside, but you still need to know what is said publicly. You will want to perform press searches and obtain transcripts regarding congressional leaders of particular interest to your issue, such as congressional party majority or minority leaders, committee chairs, subcommittee chairs, and caucus leaders. See Chapter Five for resources for conducting press research.

- Monitor C-SPAN TV or radio schedules at *<www.cspan.org>* for upcoming press conferences by congressional leaders. These press events are often scheduled on short notice as issues emerge and votes occur.

- Subscribe to congressional daily publications with email alert services such as *Roll Call* at *<www.rollcall.com>*, Congressional Quarterly's *Daily* at *<www.cq.com>* and the National Journal's *Congress Daily* at *<http://nationaljournal.com>*. These alerts help lobbyists to stay abreast of leadership announcements, political dynamics, and changing priorities.

§3.17 Lobby Tips (Continued)

- Watch daily and weekly news talk shows. Monitor program websites for upcoming guest schedules and online viewing information. See Chapter Ten for a chart of scheduling, guest, and online viewing information for weekly television news talk shows.

- Develop credibility with key leadership staff. Remember that many scheduling decisions are made behind closed doors long before they become public. Congressional leadership staff frequently email regular schedule information such as whip notices of upcoming floor action and a summary of the outcome to their allies and members of the press. Receiving regular or informal scheduling information from leadership staff can be extremely useful.

The following quotation from former congressional leader Martin Frost explains the intense dynamics of congressional leadership politics that occur behind the scenes:

"Campaigning for a leadership position in your own party conference or caucus (they are the same entity but with different names), is highly personal. The only people who can vote are your Congressional colleagues.

"Your colleagues have several reasons for deciding whom to support. First and foremost is that the person elected will be thrust into the national spotlight as a spokesman for his or her party. As a member of the Republican Conference or the Democratic Caucus, each Congressman must decide who is the right voice and right face for his party. They must decide who will make their own re-elections back home easier and who will help them retain or gain majority status.

"And then there are personal considerations. Which candidate will help further the voter's personal ambitions for key committee appointments or for projects for his particular district? Also, each Congressman voting in the election must decide whether or not a particular candidate for a leadership position would be a plus should they come into that Congressman's district to help with his or her re-election campaign.

"Additionally, one of the candidates for the leadership position may have already earned a particular Congressman's vote by things done for him or her in the past—money raised for re-election or past support for a particular legislative project."

Congressman Martin Frost (D-TX, 1979–2005), January 16, 2006,
"Behind the Scenes: How Congress Elects Leaders," FoxNews

§3.18 Beyond Party Numbers and Partisan Discipline

"Even in the best of times, control of Congress is an optical illusion. In a political crisis, it vanishes altogether."

Bruce Reed, *Slate Magazine*, October 2006, "Mark of Distinction, What the Democratic Field Can Learn from Mark Warner"

While much truth is reflected in the old saying that "He who has gavel, wins," partisan strength and political leadership do not solely determine outcome. The ability of congressional leadership to advance its priorities and exert party discipline depends on a number of factors including:

- How fragile is their majority (numeric margin and party strength) and how powerful is the minority?
- How is the issue playing back home for the members of Congress?
- How is the leadership's standing with their party members?

While the majority party has the gavel and can set the agenda, the minority party also has certain rights and power. For example, in the Senate, 60 votes are needed to break a filibuster. Political party affiliation alone is not an adequate predictor of voting or a complete indicator of political philosophy. Certain Democrats are more conservative on some issues than certain Republicans. Nevertheless, political party has significance in terms of the way that the agenda is established and how the power is divided in Congress.

§3.19 Consider Committees

As a lobbyist, you will need to keep your eye on committee and subcommittee chairmanships, agendas, and dynamics. You must monitor *all* of the committees that could become involved in your issues, such as the House Rules committee as well as oversight, appropriations, and budget committees. A death or scandal could quickly change committee leadership or composition and subsequently, the consideration of an issue. Study the seniority and maintain communications with future as well as current leaders. Majority control can change quickly, especially in the Senate, which would result in a change in committee chairmanships.

§3.20 Recommended Resources

Tracking Committees

- Congressional committee materials available online from the Government Printing Office: *<www.gpoaccess.gov>*.
- Links to House Committee web sites: *<www.house.gov>*.
- Links to Senate Committee web sites: *<www.senate.gov>*.
- Search congressional committee records through LOUIS, The Library of Unified Information Sources at: *<www.louisdb.org>*.
- For Senate hearing schedules and live audio, go to *<www.openhearings.org >*. The page provides schedules of Senate committee hearings and links to live audio. Users can subscribe to receive hearing updates via RSS feed or iCalendar. The site also allows users to import the "Live Hearing" view into a personalized Google home page.
- For campaign contribution information broken down by congressional committee members, see *<www.opensecrets.org>*.

§3.21 Consider Caucuses and Specialized Groups (Congressional Member Organizations)

In addition to committees, Members of Congress join their own party committees, caucuses, and informal interest groups. These groups are based on many factors ranging from common issue interests (for example, the Congressional Coalition on Adoption) to political alignment such as conservative Democrats who comprise the Blue Dogs Coalition and moderate Republicans comprising the Main Street Republicans' Coalition. For more information, see §§ 7.60–7.61 in the *Congressional Deskbook*.

 §3.22 Recommended Resources

Tracking Congressional Organizations

- Information on congressional organizations can be found via LexisNexis *<www.lexisnexis.com>* and Wikipedia *<http://wikipedia.org>* (search for "Caucuses of the United States Congress").
- Information on House organizations can be found via the House Committee on Administration: *<http://cha.house.gov>*.

§3.23 Lobby Tips

Utilize the Trade Press in
Environmental Assessment and Trend Tracking

A federal or state lobbyist who is serious about a particular substantive issue area should subscribe to relevant trade publications in their area of engagement such as the CCH and Bureau of National Affairs (BNA) daily publications. For example, a tax lobbyist would subscribe to the *Daily Tax Reporter via BNA*, which provides daily reports on federal and state legislative, regulatory, judicial, and policy developments with the text of important and timely government documents frequently included. Most trade associations and NGOs also have their own publications, and many have government affairs sections on their web sites.

§3.24 Lobby Facts

Volumes of State Legislation

According to the July 2002 edition of *The American Prospect* magazine, approximately 150,000 bills are considered annually by the fifty state legislatures and about 25 percent of them become law. Compared to Congress, state legislatures generally have fewer staff resources and less partisan staff. Accessing a state legislator is also much different than trying to get an appointment with a member of Congress through a scheduling secretary. State legislators may not have staff to schedule their appointments for them, so you may need to catch them in the hall.

> *"The range of public laws enacted as a percentage of the total bills introduced in Congress varies significantly from year to year and tends to fall into a range between approximately 2 percent and 9 percent. Given the nearly 200,000 bills introduced in the states every two years, this amounts to the enactment of some 40,000 or 50,000 new laws every two years."*
>
> Paul W. Hallman, President, MultiState Associations, Inc.

§3.26 Assessing the Executive Branch
Political Policy-making Environment

See §§ 3.5–3.12 for resources to use in determining White House priorities and controversial agency issues that could affect an agency's consideration of a public policy issue. The timing of elections, the degree and nature of congressional oversight, pending confirmations for agency officials, and the timing of appropriations hearings and legislation are all factors that can potentially influence executive branch policymaking.

§3.25 Recommended Resources

Tracking State Legislative Environments

- **National Conference of State Legislatures** (NCSL) provides links to state legislatures, issues, party composition and calendars: <*www.ncsl.org*>.
- **Guide to State Legislative Lobbying**, by Robert L.Guyer, copyright 1999, Published March 2000 by Engineering THE LAW, Inc.
- **Various interest groups and associations** track state legislation and provide predictions on the movement of state bills to their members. Most national trade associations have state legislative staff dedicated to monitoring state legislation.
- **Stateside** <*www.stateside.com*> provides state legislative monitoring and regulatory forecasting.

§3.27 Nature or Nurture?

Keep in mind that a system designed to respond to citizen interests is not solely directed by the nature of the political environment. Lobbyists tend to spend much of their time tracking politics and often enjoy discussing political developments with their colleagues. While lobbyists should study and respect the macro political environment and political "determinants" for the purpose of tailoring and adjusting strategies, lobbyists should not become so consumed with merely watching and discussing the political situation that they forgo opportunities for shaping or changing the outcome. As former Senate Republican Steering Committee Staff Director Jade West observed:

> *"Sometimes conventional wisdom about what is achievable needs to be proven wrong."*
>
> Source: The Hill, April 23, 2007, Tuesday profile: "Wholesaler-Distributors lobbyist helped stop overhaul of healthcare," by Ian Swanson

The remainder of this book discusses strategies and actions for taking effective actions.

> *"Knowledge might be power, but only when you take action."*
>
> Richard Keeves

§3.99 Chapter Summary

- Understanding the current political environment and the determinants that drive positions is an essential part of any effective strategy. (§ 3.1)
- Effective lobbying involves learning about the personal and professional background, constituency, and interests of specific elected officials before attempting to communicate with them. (§ 3.2)

- Studying the determinants that drive a policymaker's decision-making process provides many benefits (§3.3). Researching the official and the constituency in advance helps to maximize the communications opportunity, build stronger and deeper relationships with officials and staff, and avoid making irrelevant or offensive comments.
- § 3.5 provides recommended resources for researching key determinants before communicating with legislative and executive branch policymakers. These sections are provided as a tool to assist in researching the following "Seven Position Drivers" (also known as "The Seven Ps") that drive a policymaker's policymaking process:
  1. Profile (constituency represented) (§ 3.6)
  2. Previous experience (§ 3.7)
  3. Positions (§ 3.8)
  4. Press/public opinion (§ 3.9)
  5. Promoters (§ 3.10)
  6. Priorities (§ 3.11)
  7. Personal experience (§ 3.12)

  Sample questions to examine before communicating with policymakers are included. Recommended resources to assist with answering questions related to each determinant before communicating with legislative and executive branch officials are provided, as well as recommended resources for preparing to communicate with legislators and executive branch officials. These sections can also be used as a guide for group discussions during governmental affairs department staff meetings or strategic planning sessions.
- The macro-political environment changes regularly. Forecasting the political environment and making necessary adjustments are essential elements of effective lobbying. (§ 3.13)
- Consider your issue in the context of the macro-political environment, and time your activities accordingly. (§§ 3.13–3.14)
- Tips for conducting legislative forecasting and a worksheet for evaluating the political environment are provided. (§§ 3.14–3.15).
- Although congressional leadership priorities and the political party division of the current Congress should be reviewed, political party affiliation alone is not an adequate predictor of voting nor does it universally reflect political philosophy. (§ 3.18)
- While the majority party may set the agenda, the minority party also retains certain rights and powers as well. (§ 3.18)
- The role and strength of congressional and political party leadership (§ 3.16) as well as congressional caucuses and specialized groups should be considered in the evaluation of the political landscape (§ 3.21).
- Tips for determining and tracking congressional leadership priorities. (§ 3.17)
- The trade press can be a valuable resource for assessing the political environment. (§ 3.23)
- Resources are provided for assessing executive branch (§3.26) and state legislative (§ 3.25) environments.

CHAPTER 4

Understanding Governmental Institutions and Processes

"Once begin the dance of legislation, and you must struggle through its mazes as best you can to the breathless end—if any end there be."

Woodrow Wilson

§4.1 Introduction

This chapter briefly describes the major aspects of the public policy process with the best resources for digging in deeper and communicating with others who are new to legislative or regulatory advocacy. It is not designed to serve as an exhaustive source of information on the intricate legislative and regulatory processes and institutional structure of Congress (for that, see the *Congressional Deskbook* by Michael Koempel and Judy Schnieder). Rather, it is meant to assist by providing recommended resources for your communications with your association members, staff, associates, or clients on the public policy process and governmental institutions.

This chapter can serve as a resource for new employee orientations and a training tool for junior-level staff. For not-so-junior staff, the references can serve as a go-to guide for rekindling or replenishing current process knowledge. The recommended resources will provide much greater depth for those subjects of interest.

While the legislative and regulatory processes described here represent the way that they are intended to function, remember that in political environments rules are at times waived or ignored. As German Chancellor Otto von Bismarck famously said, "To retain respect for sausages and laws, one must not watch them in the making." (The quotation is also attributed as "*People who love the law or good sausage should never watch either being made.*")

§4.2 Importance of Gaining and Maintaining a Working Knowledge of the Governmental Institutions and Processes

Lobbyists will be at an advantage to know and appreciate how the institutions that they are lobbying originated, how they function, and how they are organized. The following hypothetical scenarios illustrate why an effective lobbyist's knowledge base and familiarity cannot be limited to a particular substantive issue area:

1. Imagine that you are watching the full House of Representatives consider a bill that is a top priority for those whom you represent. You watch on C-SPAN as the House goes into the "Committee of the Whole" and passes a "motion to recommit" with specific instructions that are read quickly by the House Reading Clerk. The measure passes. It happens so quickly that you're not sure what transpired. You are under a deadline to quickly communicate the outcome of the vote to your membership or client. How do you explain the action? (*Note:* The answer can be found in Appendix 4, Select Glossary of Lobbying Terms, Abbreviations, and Acronyms.)

2. Picture yourself guiding a group of your own members or clients through the halls of Congress or your statehouse. You pass a prominent exhibit and the conversation turns to the history of the institution. You wish you had a relevant observation to provide, but you don't, so you change the subject.

3. You receive a phone call from a reporter asking you to provide a comment on a new "NPR" in your area of engagement. You're not sure what he's talking about.

You don't realize that "NPR" refers to a federal executive branch agency's "Notice of Proposed Rulemaking." (See the Glossary of Lobbying Terms in Appendix 4 for a definition.) After trying to figure it out, you ask the reporter to explain, diminishing your credibility.

Most lobbyists and government affairs professionals have a degree of familiarity with the legislative and regulatory processes. Indeed, most lobbyists have worked in Congress or in state legislatures and many have taken several classes on parliamentary procedure. Some lobbyists even pursue advanced degrees in public policy. However, with the relentless press of legislative activity, lobbyists do not always take the time to periodically renew their familiarity with the process and update their resources for communicating the process to others. Additionally, most federal lobbyists lobby the executive branch, but relatively few have had experience working directly in the executive branch. As a result, lobbyists can be caught off-guard or perplexed by the federal agency policymaking process.

Lobbyists who focus exclusively on their particular issue areas, without gaining and maintaining a full understanding of governmental processes and structures, typically fail to be fully effective. Effective lobbyists are not required to be experts on the details of every parliamentary maneuver or regulatory function, but they must be able to:

- Follow and explain the process and parliamentary procedures and discern the implications of those procedures on their issue of concern,
- Navigate the regulatory process and be able to communicate it to others,
- Know basic differences between federal and state legislative processes, and
- Know where to find answers quickly to technical questions regarding public policy processes and governmental institutions.

This chapter highlights governmental institutions and the public policy processes, with recommended resources that can be noted on your planner, bookmarked on your computer, and incorporated into your grassroots, organization, or client communications.

§4.3 Recommended Resources

Capitol History

See book's Resources web page for links: <www.LobbyingAndAdvocacy.com>.
- Library of Congress: <www.thomas.gov>
- Senate: <www.senate.gov>
- U.S. House of Representatives: <www.house.gov>
- Architect of the Capitol: <www.aoc.gov>
- US Capitol Historical Society: <www.uschs.org>
- C-SPAN Capitol History Videos and Podcasts: <www.c-span.org/capitolhistory>

§4.4 A Brief Timeline: Hallmarks of Our Congress and Capital City's History

Historic Highlights: Congress, The Institution

1774: The First Continental Congress met, representing twelve of the thirteen colonies.

1776: On July 4, 1776, the Second Continental Congress adopted the Declaration of Independence. Under the Articles of Confederation, the "Congress of the Confederation" was designed as a unicameral body. Each state was equally represented and had veto power over most decisions.

1785: New York was selected as the first capital. Congress met in City Hall (Federal Hall) from 1785 to 1790.

1787: Weaknesses of the Articles of Confederation resulted in the Convention of 1787, where our Constitution was drafted. A compromise was reached to provide representation proportional to population for the House of Representatives and equal representation for each state in the Senate. Senators were originally elected by state legislatures.

1789–1791: The First Federal Congress created the government as defined by the U.S. Constitution, passed amendments to the Constitution (Bill of Rights), established a revenue system for the new nation and a national bank, and chose Washington, DC, as the location for the nation's capital.

1913: The Constitution was amended to allow for direct election of senators by the people of the state instead of the individual state legislatures.

Historic Highlights: The Capital City

1790–1800: The capital was moved from New York to Philadelphia. During that time, Congress met in the Philadelphia County Building (Congress Hall).

1791: President Washington selected the District of Columbia as our new capital, in accordance with the "Residence Act" passed by Congress in 1790, from land ceded by Maryland. In the meantime, plans were drawn to move the capital, and the Capitol, to what is now Washington, DC.

1793: George Washington laid the cornerstone of the Capitol building, located near the Old Supreme Court.

1800: The Senate wing was completed.

1811: The House wing was completed.

November 17, 1800: First Session of Congress held in the new Capitol building.

August 24, 1814: The British army burned the White House and the Capitol during the War of 1812. Senators were forced to meet in emergency headquarters in Blodgett's Hotel in northwest Washington until a temporary facility could be built.

1819: Reconstruction completed, adding the center Rotunda area and the first dome.

1850s: Capitol was expanded dramatically. Thomas U. Walter was responsible for the wing extensions and the cast-iron dome.

1904: The East Front of the Capitol building was rebuilt.

1909: The Senate's first permanent office building opened, later named for Senator Richard Russell of Georgia. Other office buildings, named after prominent members of Congress, followed in later years.

1958-1962: A marble duplicate of the sandstone East Front was built.

June 20, 2000: Ground was broken for the Capitol Visitor Center, a massive underground structure that was chronically delayed, scheduled to open by the 2009 Presidential Inauguration. It provides a grand entrance hall, a visitors theater, room for exhibits, and dining and restroom facilities, in addition to space for building infrastructures such as an underground service tunnel. For a map of the Capitol complex, see Appendix 3.

§4.5 **Congress's Design of Balance and Deliberate Delay**

*"All legislative Powers herein granted shall be vested in a Congress of the
United States, which shall consist of a Senate and House of Representatives."*
Article 1 of the U.S. Constitution: Section 1

The framers designed Congress to guard against impetuous action by instituting a bicameral structure with different representational systems, terms of office, and powers. They created a balanced and complex process to allow for responsive representation:

*"Congress is functioning the way the Founding Fathers intended-not very
well. They understood that if you move too quickly, our democracy will be
less responsible to the majority."*
Barber B. Conable

The House of Representatives has 435 voting members serving two-year terms. Each member represents a congressional district, with seats apportioned among the states based on population. Alaska, Delaware, Wyoming, South Dakota, Vermont, North Dakota, and Montana are currently the states with only one "at large" House member due to their relatively small populations. American Samoa, the District of Columbia, Guam, and the United States Virgin Islands send non-voting delegates to the House; Puerto Rico sends a non-voting Resident Commissioner who serves a four-year term; and the Northern Mariana Islands are not represented. Periodically, legislation is introduced in Congress to provide voting rights for the District of Columbia's representative.

The Senate has 100 voting members (not including the vice president of the United States, who only votes in the event of a tie vote and who officially serves as the Senate's president even though the Senate majority leader leads the Senate on a day to day basis). Senators serve staggered six-year terms. Each state has two senators, regardless of the state's population. Every two years, approximately one-third of the Senate is elected. George Washington reportedly likened the Senate's role of cooling House legislation to that of a saucer that is used to cool hot tea. The founders envisioned the Senate as a "necessary fence" against public "fickleness and passion" that tend to influence House members. The Senate is sometimes referred to as the "world's greatest deliberative body," because of its design and rules that encourage discussion, allow for extended debate, and require 60 votes to stop a filibuster.

§4.6 Recommended Resources

Basics on Members of Congress and the Legislative Process

- To help constituents determine their **Members of Congress**:
  1. Use Capitol Advantage's member locator by entering the constituent's zip code at *<www.congress.org>*,
  2. Search by zip code and access zoomable congressional district maps at *<www.govtrack.us>*, or
  3. Call the U.S. Capitol Switchboard at 202-225-3121 and ask for contact information for their House member or two senators by providing their state and zip code.

- **List of House Members:** *<www.house.gov>*

- **List of Senators:** *<www.senate.gov>*

- **Congressional Directory:** online *<www.congress.org>*; print *<www.CongressDirectory.com>*

- **Congressional Leadership** (provides photos and web site links as well as a 2-page PDF): *<www.CongressLeaders.com>*

- **Senate Leadership:**
  - List and Overview of Senate Leaders: *<www.senate.gov>*

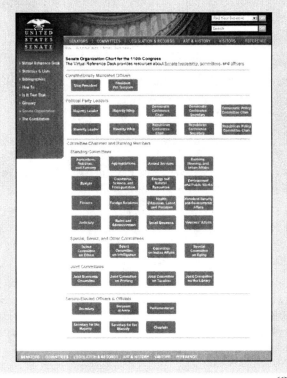

(Continued on page 122)

§4.6 Recommended Resources (Continued)

- **Senate Leadership (continued):**
  - Overview of role of the Vice President, President Pro Tempore, Party Secretaries, Conference Chairpersons, Policy Committee Chairpersons, and Conference Chairpersons: <*www.senate.gov*>
  - Democratic Leadership: <*http://democrats.senate.gov/leadership*>.
  - Republican Leadership: <*http://republican.senate.gov*>.
  - Democratic Steering and Coordination Committee: <*http://democrats.senate.gov*>
  - Republican Conference Chair: <*http://src.senate.gov*>
  - Senate Republican Conference: <*http://src.senate.gov*>
  - Republican Policy Committee: <*http://rpc.senate.gov*>
  - Democratic Policy Committee: <*http://democrats.senate.gov/dpc*>
  - Democratic Senatorial Campaign Committee: <*http://dscc.org*>
  - National Republican Senatorial Committee: <*www.nrsc.org*>

- **House Leadership:**
  - Overview of House Leaders: <*www.house.gov*>
  - Office of the Speaker: <*http://speaker.house.gov*>
  - Office of the Democratic Leader: <*http://democraticleader.house.gov*>
  - Office of the Republican Leader: <*http://republicanleader.house.gov*>
  - Democratic Whip: <*http://democraticwhip.house.gov*>
  - Republican Whip: <*http://republicanwhip.house.gov*>
  - Democratic Caucus: <*http://dems.gov*>
  - House Democrats: <*http://housedemocrats.gov*>
  - House Republican Conference: <*http://gop.gov*>
  - House Republican Policy Committee: <*http://policy.house.gov*>
  - House Republican Conference Secretary: <*http://gopsecretary.gov*>

- "How Our Laws Are Made" from the Library of Congress is an excellent resource for participants in the process of all levels to have on hand.

- Every lobbyist should have the *Congressional Deskbook* by Michael L. Koempel and Judy Schneider on her bookshelf. It should be kept close at hand to answer questions that arise regarding essentially every aspect of the Congress and the legislative process <*www.CongressionalDeskbook.com*>.

- Customizable Booklet: "Congress and the Legislative Process in a Nutshell" may be customized with your organization's logo and contact information for trade show giveaways, gifts for new members or contributors, handouts for events and mailers to a specific target group (all booklets fit in a standard # 10 business envelope). For additional information: <*www.TCNBooklets.com*>

§4.6 Recommended Resources (Continued)

- Lobbyists should participate in at least one comprehensive training class on the entire congressional process and make an effort to stay current on the legislative process and parliamentary procedure.

- Several types of training on the congressional and executive branch processes are available through TheCapitol.Net at <www.HowCongressWorks.com>. Advanced classes are also available. Professional associations such as the American League of Lobbyists (<www.alldc.org>) also periodically offer congressional process classes.

- Appendix 4: Select Glossary of Lobbying Terms, Abbreviations, and Acronyms.

- The Federal Government's Financial Health: A Citizen's Guide to the 2007 Financial Report of the United States Government (U.S. Government Accountability Office at <www.gao.gov/financial/fy2007financialreport.html>).

- You can call the House Legislative Resource Center at 202-226-5200 to learn the status of House or Senate legislation. Several commercial companies, such as Congressional Quarterly <www.cq.com> and Gallery Watch <www.gallerywatch.org> provide legislative tracking services.

- In the course of their work and life, lobbyists have numerous opportunities to explain or clarify governmental processes to children. The following resources can assist lobbyists in those efforts:

  ○ Ben's Guide to the U.S. Government for Kids at <http://bensguide.gpo.gov> provides material according to grade level, activities, links to government resources, and an image map with quick facts about each state.

  ○ The Dirksen Congressional Center's Congress Link home page at <www.congresslink.org> provides resources that help children understand various aspects of the government:

  ○ Learn About the Constitution, the three branches of government, the U.S. election process and other historical information at <http://congressforkids.net>.

  ○ The classic ABC Schoolhouse Rock (America Rock) depiction of singing "Bill's" travels through the halls of Congress is a fun, yet educational way to introduce the legislative process to children. The Schoolhouse series was broadcast on television in the seventies and is still available from <www.amazon.com>.

§4.7 Legislative Process Flowchart

Legislation may begin in either chamber. Similar proposals are often introduced in both chambers.

Measure introduced in the House *§ 8.20*	Measure introduced in the Senate *§ 8.20*
Measure referred to committee, which holds hearings and reports measure to the House *§§ 8.30, 8.40, 8.50, 8.60*	Measure referred to committee, which holds hearings and reports measure to the Senate *§§ 8.30, 8.40, 8.50, 8.60*

OR

For important measures, special rule reported by the Rules Committee and adopted by the House *§§ 8.90, 8.100*

Leadership schedules measure for floor consideration *§ 8.70*	Leadership schedules measure for floor consideration *§§ 8.160, 8.170*
House debates and can amend measure *§§ 8.110, 8.120*	Senate debates and can amend measure *§§ 8.180, 8.190, 8.200, 8.210, 8.220, 8.230*
House passes measure *§§ 8.130, 8.140*	Senate passes measure *§§ 8.240, 8.250*

Measures must pass both the House and the Senate in identical form before being presented to the President.

One chamber agrees to the other chamber's version *§ 8.260*	OR	Each chamber appoints Members to a conference committee, which reconciles differences and agrees to a conference report *§ 8.280*	OR	House and Senate exchange amendments to bill and reach agreement *§ 8.270*

House approves conference report

Senate approves conference report

Legislation presented to the President.

President signs measure	If President does not sign measure into law within 10 days *§ 8.290*		President vetoes measure
Measure becomes law	If Congress is in session, measure becomes law	If Congress is not in session, measure does not become law ("pocket veto")	Measure does not become law, unless both chambers override veto by 2/3 majority

§4.8 **Basic House and Senate Differences**

"Each House may determine the Rules of its Proceedings."
Constitution, Section 5 [2]

Lobbyists need to understand and stay refreshed on the institutional and procedural differences between the House and the Senate. Lobbyists with experience working in either the House or the Senate need to round out their knowledge of the procedures in the other body. § 4.9 lists basic House and Senate differences and § 4.24 provides a comparison of the basic differences between a House Special Rule and a Senate Time Agreement. However, advanced legislative process classes, such as those provided by The-Capitol.Net, are recommended for updating a lobbyist's knowledge of the technical aspects of House and Senate procedures. (See § 4.6.)

§4.10 **The Annual Budget and Appropriations Processes**

"A billion dollars here, a billion dollars there
and pretty soon you're into real money."
Senator Everett M. Dirksen (R-IL, 1950–1969)

Congress passes "authorization" bills that provide program authority and "appropriations" bills that fund various programs. On the first Monday in February, the president submits a budget to Congress ("the President's Budget"). For the next six weeks, Budget Committee members and staff prepare reports on their views and estimates for the Budget Committee. Executive branch officials testify before the relevant subcommittees prior to passage of the funding bills. Appropriations hearings provide an opportunity for members of Congress to publicly raise concerns regarding agency programs or policies. Beginning in June and continuing through October, the House and Senate spend a significant amount of floor time addressing the thirteen appropriations measures that fund the federal government.

In order to keep the government funded, congressional appropriations bills must be passed by the beginning of the fiscal year on October first. If they are not, Congress may pass temporary stop-gap legislation to keep the government from closing down until the appropriations bills are finalized. These measures are referred to as Continuing Resolutions, or CRs.

The appropriations process drives much of the congressional agenda and lobbyists need to track and respect the demands of the process on congressional schedules, even if they are not directly involved in lobbying appropriations legislation. Additionally, significant policy issues related to a lobbyist's area of interest may be considered and resolved quickly as amendments to appropriations bills. Separate or "free standing" legislation of interest to lobbyists can also be added into "omnibus" measures that combine two or more of the thirteen appropriations bills as Congress completes appropriations action in the fall. Congressional members and staff are especially challenged during the

§4.9 Differences between the House and the Senate at a Glance

House	Senate
Larger—435 members	Smaller—100 members
Shorter term—2 years	Longer term—6 years
Four calendars (Union, House, Private, and Discharge)	Two calendars (Legislative and Executive)
Less procedural flexibility/more restraints	More procedural flexibility/fewer restraints
Stronger Leadership—power less evenly distributed	Weaker Leadership—power more evenly distributed
Role of Rules Committee and special rules to govern floor consideration	Unanimous consent and complex unanimous consent time agreements to govern floor consideration
Scheduling by Speaker and majority-party leadership, with limited consultation among members	Scheduling by majority-party leadership, with broad consultation among all members
Germaneness of amendments generally required	Germaneness of amendments rarely required
Presiding officer has considerable discretion in recognition; rulings rarely challenged	Presiding officer has little discretion in recognition; rulings frequently challenged
Debate always restricted	Debate rarely restricted
Debate-ending motions by majority vote (218 representatives)	Cloture invoked by three-fifths vote (60 senators)
Quorum calls permitted in connection with record votes	Quorum calls permitted almost any time and used for constructive delay
Narrower constituency—House District	Larger constituency—entire state
Elections generally less competitive	Elections generally more competitive
Specialists	Generalists
Less reliant on staff	More reliant on staff
Less media coverage	More media coverage
More partisan	Less partisan
Adjourns at end of day	Recesses at end of most days

Source: *Congressional Deskbook*, §§ 8.150-8.151. This chart and more is online at <*www.CongressNumbers.com*>. Congressional pay and perquisites are available at <*www.CongressPay.com*>.

final days of the process, which generally involve a heightened workload and many late-night sessions. Consequently, provisions may be included with little or no warning or public scrutiny as the appropriations process draws to a close. Lobbyists should establish rapport and proactively educate appropriations committee members and staff regarding their subject of concern prior to the commencement of the appropriations season if at all possible.

The "Congressional Budget Process Flowchart" is available in the *Congressional Deskbook*, by Michael Koempel and Judy Schneider, at § 9.53.

§4.11 Congress's Constitutional "Power of the Purse"

Revenues and Borrowing

The Congress shall have the Power

1 To lay and collect Taxes, Duties, Imposts, and Excises . . .

2 To borrow Money on the credit of the United States . . .

(U.S. Constitution, Art. I, sec. 8.)

Spending

No money shall be drawn from the Treasury,

but in Consequence of Appropriations

made by Law . . .

(U.S. Constitution, Art. I, sec. 9, cl. 7.)

§4.12 The Magnitude of the Federal Budget: An Historical Perspective

"The federal budget for 2007 is $2.8 trillion, the highest in history; one in six Americans relies on government assistance; we spend $586.5 billion on Social Security, $372.3 billion on Medicare, $268.5 billion on health care, and $93 billion on education, training, employment and social services. If you laid the dollar bills composing the federal budget end to end, the chain of cash would circle the equator approximately 11,000 times— or reach from Earth to the sun three times over. To put our budget in historical perspective, the federal government spends approximately $9,300 per person in the United States; a century ago, the federal government spent just over $7 per person."

"Is The Era Of Small Government Over?"
by Ben Shapiro, Townhall.com, March 21, 2007

§4.13 Outstanding Government Promises vs. Assets and Historic Revenues

The following graphic illustrates projected government deficits and key dates.

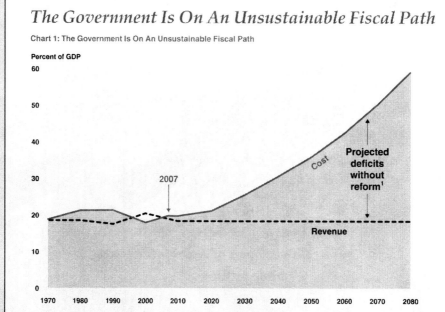

The Government Is On An Unsustainable Fiscal Path

Chart 1: The Government Is On An Unsustainable Fiscal Path

Key dates

2007 — Medicare Part A benefit payments began to exceed the program's tax revenue.

2017 — Social Security benefit payments will begin to exceed the program's tax revenue.

2019 — Medicare Part A Trust Fund assets will not be enough to pay full benefits. Under current law, benefits would be reduced to 79 percent of scheduled benefits in 2019, declining to 29 percent by 2081.

2040 — Federal debt held by the public will exceed the historical high of 109 percent of GDP.

2041 — Social Security Trust Funds' assets will not be enough to pay full benefits. Under current law, benefits for all retirees would be reduced to 75 percent of scheduled benefits in 2041, declining to 70 percent by 2081.

2080 — Total government cost will be more than three times revenue.

Notes:

1. Projected deficits represent projected cost in excess of revenue, where revenue as a percent of gross domestic product (GDP) is set equal to its historical average and projected cost is based on scheduled Social Security and Medicare benefits and current cost trends. While the precise amounts of the government's financial responsibilities are far from certain—they are based on many complex calculations and assumptions, including life expectancies and health care cost—their magnitude and the need to control them are evident.

2. The dates and events presented above are taken from the 2007 Annual Reports of the Social Security and Medicare Boards of Trustees and the *2007 Financial Report of the United States Government*.

Source: The Federal Government's Financial Health: A Citizen's Guide to the 2007 Financial Report of the United States Government, U.S. Government Accountability Office, page 2.

§4.14 Recommended Resources

The Budget and Appropriations

- Information on the President's Budget, which is transmitted annually to Congress by the first Monday in February, reflects administration policies and is available at: <*www.budget.gov*> or <*www.gpoaccess.gov/usbudget*>.

- Prepared federal agency testimony on appropriations bills are available on federal agency and congressional Appropriations Committee web sites. Transcripts reflecting questions and concerns by Appropriations Committee members are eventually available from the congressional Appropriations Committees, but more quickly available from the Library of Unified Information Sources (LOUIS, named after Supreme Court Justice Louis Brandeis) at <*www.louisdb.org*> or commercial subscription services such as Congressional Quarterly's Budget Tracker and Gallery Watch.

- Congressional Budget Office, <*www.cbo.gov*>

- U.S. House of Representatives Budget Committee, <*http://budget.house.gov*>

- U.S. Senate Budget Committee, <*http://budget.senate.gov*>

- U.S. House of Representatives Appropriations Committee, <*http://appropriations.house.gov*>

- U.S. Senate Appropriations Committee, <*http://appropriations.senate.gov*>

- Appropriations bills scheduling information:

  - Check the Appropriations Committees' web sites or call the relevant Appropriations Committee or subcommittee to determine if a meeting has been scheduled.

  - The Government Accountability Office's (GAO's) Brochure on Fiscal Stewardship, Publication GAO-07-362SP, January 31, 2007.

  - An audio course on "Authorizations and Appropriations in a Nutshell" is available at <*www.CapitolLearning.com*>. The course provides a basic overview of authorizations and appropriations.

  - Seminars are provided by TheCapitol.Net on "Understanding Congressional Budgeting and Appropriations" at <*www.FederalBudgeting.com*>. Other professional organizations such as the American League of Lobbyists (<*www.alldc.org*>) offer seminars and topical speakers during the appropriations season.

§4.15 Know the Legislative Language

"I should apologize, perhaps, for the style of this bill. I dislike the verbose and intricate style of the modern English statutes .... You 'however' can easily correct this bill to the taste of my brother lawyers, by making every other word a "said" or "aforesaid," and saying everything over two or three times, so that nobody but we of the craft can untwist the diction, and find out what it means . . ."

Thomas Jefferson, 1817

§4.16 Congressional Approval Terminology

Term	Used For
Adopted	Conference Reports
Agreed To	Amendments Simple Resolutions Concurrent Resolutions
Concur	Amendment of Other Chamber
Ordered	Engrossment Previous Question Third Reading Yeas and Nays
Passed	Bills Joint Resolutions
Sustained	Points of Order Rulings of Chair

Only members of Congress can offer bills and amendments. Bills and amendments introduced by members of Congress may be initially suggested or drafted by staff or an outside entity, but the House or Senate offices of Legislative Counsel help congressional representatives format the language. If you are trying to get a bill or amendment offered, a congressional member or staff representative will need to work with the House or Senate Legislative Counsel's office to finalize the language into the appropriate format.

Source: *Congressional Deskbook*

 ## §4.17 Recommended Resources

Legislative Language

- Appendix 4: Select Glossary of Lobbying Terms, Abbreviations, and Acronyms.
- *Legislative Drafter's Deskbook, A Practical Guide*, by Tobias A. Dorsey, <*www.LegislativeDraftersDeskbook.com*>
- See TheCapitol.Net's Legislative Glossary online at <*CongressGlossary.com*>.
- Training on the processes and related terms is highly recommended. (See § 4.6 for potential providers.)
- U.S. House of Representatives Committee on Rules: <*http://rules.house.gov*>
- Standing Rules of the Senate: <*http://rules.senate.gov/senaterules*>

Capitol Hill has its own vocabulary. Lobbyists generally learn this language through their own Hill experience and in classes (as referenced in § 4.6). A glossary of lobbying terms is provided in Appendix 4. Terminology used to describe the approval of various measures is provided in § 4.16.

§4.18 Bill Introduction

Approximately 10,000 bills are introduced in Congress every year, but only a fraction of those bills make it through the entire legislative process to become law (see *<www. CongressNumbers.com>*). Bills can begin in either the House or the Senate and different or similar versions of the same bill can move through the respective chambers concurrently. However, revenue bills must originate in the House (U.S. Constitution, Art. I, sec 7).

Bill introduction highlights follow:

- Policy ideas can originate anywhere, but bills can only be introduced by members of Congress.
- New bills are numbered and sent to the appropriate committees.
- Senate bills start with S. and House bills start with H.R. House and Senate bills that are very similar are called companion bills. The member introducing the bill is referred to as the primary sponsor, and an unlimited number of members may co-sponsor a bill. Significant co-sponsorship, that is, a large number of bipartisan co-sponsors, and support from key congressional leaders can help the bill progress.
- Members of Congress circulate "Dear Colleague" letters to urge their colleagues to co-sponsor their legislation (see §§ 8.20–8.22 in the *Congressional Deskbook*).

§4.19 The Critical Role of Committees

" . . . Congress in session is Congress on public exhibition, whilst Congress in committee rooms is Congress at work."

President Woodrow Wilson in "Congressional Government: A Study in American Politics" (1885)

The substantive work to consider and revise legislation performed in congressional committees is frequently under-observed and not fully recognized. However, committees have a huge role in shaping legislation, even though the public and the press tend to give more attention to final floor action.

A count based on congressional committee web sites reveals that in 2005 alone, approximately 7,553 witnesses testified before Congress in 1,546 congressional hearings.

There are three types of committees (see § 7.50 in the *Congressional Deskbook*):

1. Standing Committees have their legislative authority determined by chamber rules. Committees also have oversight authority for the federal programs and issues within their jurisdiction, and some committees are focused on oversight activities.

2. Temporary Select or Special Committees can be created for a specified purpose and time period.
3. Joint Committees have members from both the House and Senate and are usually permanent with administrative or study authority.

Each committee is led by a chair that is appointed by House or Senate leadership. A small fraction of the bills referred to a committee actually receive action from the committee. The committee chair establishes the agenda that identifies the bills that will move through the committee. The staff director and other majority party employees report to the committee chair. Subcommittee chairs also tend to have staff support. The highest-ranking members of the minority party, known as the "Ranking Members," lead the minority party's efforts on the committees and subcommittees and employ minority committee staff.

Committee work is generally delegated to subcommittees, which consider and pass the legislation prior to full committee consideration. Subcommittee chairs are generally seen as the "go to" people by the leadership on the issues within their jurisdiction. High priority issues may be addressed at the full committee level.

A bill comes under its most intense scrutiny while in committee, and many bills die in committee. Examples of committee activities follow:

- Bills may be referred to more than one committee or subcommittee and joint hearings may be held.
- Public or closed hearings are held to receive testimony by invited experts or affected parties and in some cases subpoenaed witnesses. Parties who were not invited to testify may submit statements to be published in the hearing record, consistent with the specific committee's rules. A committee may also submit a bill to the Government Accountability Office for recommendations.
- See Chapter Ten for "Tips for Testifying before Congress" and "Your Rights and Expectations as a Congressional Witness." See also § 8.41 "Tips on Keeping Up with House and Senate Committee Hearings" in the *Congressional Deskbook*.
- After one or more subcommittee hearings, the subcommittee holds a "mark up" of the bill, which involves voting on amendments or even entire substitutes to the proposal while progressing line-by-line through the bill. After the subcommittee reports the bill, the full committee considers the measure and can "report out" a bill with a recommendation to the full House or Senate. The committee staff writes a "committee report" which describes the purpose of the bill. Committee reports are a significant part of a bill's "legislative history" as federal agencies, the courts, policy experts, and the public access the document to determine (or debate) a law's purpose.

See also § 8.52 "Tips on Keeping Up with House and Senate Markups" in the *Congressional Deskbook*.

§4.20 Recommended Resources

Committees

- List of House and Senate committees linked from web sites: <*www.house.gov*> and <*www.senate.gov*>

Live Coverage of Committee Meetings:

- Check the relevant congressional committee's web site at <*www.house.gov*> or <*www.senate.gov*> to determine if they are broadcasting the event live via their committee homepage.

- C-SPAN broadcasts certain congressional hearings on C-SPAN 1, C-SPAN 2, and C-SPAN 3 television and on C-SPAN Radio. If hearings are held during C-SPAN's gavel-to-gavel coverage of full House or Senate floor action, C-SPAN may broadcast them at a later time that week (including nights and weekends). C-SPAN also provides links to congressional broadcasts of hearings. Check <*www.cspan.org*> for committee broadcast schedules and archives, which can be viewed via the Internet. C-SPAN archives are typically available online for a couple of weeks but may be purchased from C-SPAN.

- Go to <*www.openhearings.org*> to view a mini-site of schedules of current and future Senate committee hearings and links to live audio and video of hearings in progress. Users can subscribe to receive updates for all committees and hearings via RSS feed or iCalendar. The site also provides the ability to import the "Live Hearing" view into a personalized Google web site.

To obtain written U.S. House or U.S. Senate hearing testimony or Committee Reports:

- For an electronic copy of testimony prepared by committee witnesses, check the relevant congressional committee's web site <*www.house.gov*> or <*www.senate.gov*>.

- Search for hearing records at the Library of Unified Information Sources (LOUIS), at <*www.louisdb.org*>.

- Search Open Hearings at <*www.openhearings.org/live*> for hearing links.

- Some hearing testimony is available via the Internet on the Thomas web site at the Library of Congress (<*www.thomas.gov*>).

- Published hearing testimony is generally available through the federal depository library system. There are approximately 1,350 federal depository libraries throughout the United States and its territories, at least one in almost every congressional district. See <*www.gpoaccess.gov*> to locate the federal depository library in your area. The libraries provide free public access to a wide variety of federal government information in both print and electronic formats, and have expert staff available to assist users.

- Subscription services such as Gallerywatch (<*www.gallerywatch.com*>), Congressional Quarterly (<*www.cq.com*>), and National Journal (<*www.nationaljournal.com*>).

§4.21 **Floor Action**

After clearing the relevant committees, priority bills can move to the entire House or Senate for a "floor" vote, a reference to the place where the debate and votes take place. House and Senate leadership schedule floor votes in accordance with their chamber's rules for bringing up a measure. See § 4.9 for a general comparison of selected House and Senate procedures.

§4.22 **The House Rules Committee and House Floor Votes**

The full House will vote on approving a special "rule" issued by the powerful Rules Committee prior to voting on the actual bill. The Rules Committee plays a role similar to a traffic cop by directing consideration of legislation moving to the full House. The committee plays an extremely important role by deciding the rules of debate, including which amendments will be in order, for each bill. The Rules Committee issues a "rule" for the bill, which includes the types of amendments that can be offered, time limitations, and how the allowed time will be divided. Closed rules prohibit any amendments, but allow the incorporation of amendments that were passed in congressional committee. Open rules allow any member to offer an amendment, and modified-open rules allow specified amendments. Additional types of rules are described in § 4.24. Members wishing to offer amendments on the House floor must submit their amendments to the committee in advance of the committee's meeting and may be permitted to testify to make the case for allowing the House to consider their amendment. See § 8.91, "Special Rules Glossary," in the *Congressional Deskbook*.

The full House will vote on approving the rule issued by the Rules Committee prior to conducting a general debate and proceeding to vote on the bill and related amendments. The floor debate time is generally evenly divided between the two parties with a "floor manager," appointed by each party's leadership, managing their side's speakers. The floor manager is typically the chair of the committee that has had jurisdiction for the legislation.

To speed debate on some bills, the House meets as the "Committee of the Whole," which can amend a bill, but cannot pass it. See § 4.27 and Appendix 4, Glossary, for an explanation of the Committee of the Whole procedure. Immediately after a bill is passed, a "motion to recommit" (see Appendix 4, Glossary, for definition) may be offered with or without instructions to change the bill in a specific way. It may be done virtually immediately (within seconds) and brought back for consideration by the full House (as modified by the motion to recommit).

§4.23 **Senate Floor Votes**

Under most circumstances, senators may speak at any length on any topic, Senate amendments are not required to be germane, and amendments can be offered at any time during the consideration of legislation. Any senator (or group of senators) can stop the advancement toward a vote by attempting to talk a bill to death with a "filibuster." Debate can be ended by a "unanimous consent" motion (with no senator objecting), or by invoking a motion to cut off debate called "cloture." (See Appendix 4, Glossary, for definition of cloture.) The stages to invoking cloture under Senate Rule XXII are:

1. At least sixteen senators sign a cloture motion, commonly called a "cloture petition."
2. The motion is initially presented on the Senate floor, where it is read by the clerk.
3. The motion needs to "mature" or "ripen" before it can be considered. This does not happen until the second calendar day on which the Senate is in session.
4. When the vote occurs, it requires a roll call vote. It generally requires three-fifths of the currently serving senators (sixty votes if there are no vacancies) unless it is a motion to amend actual Senate rules (which requires a two-thirds vote of the Senators present, typically sixty-seven senators).
5. Amendments must be submitted in writing before the vote on the cloture motion and must be germane to the subject at hand.
6. First-degree amendments must be filed by 1:00 p.m. on the day the cloture motion is filed, and second-degree amendments must be filed at least one hour before a cloture vote begins.
7. If cloture is invoked, effectively ending the filibuster, a "time cap" of thirty hours is provided for the Senate to finish debating the measure.

For more information, see § 8.230, "Cloture in Senate Floor Proceedings," in the *Congressional Deskbook.*

§4.24 Comparing a House Special Rule and a Senate Time Agreement

House Special Rule	Senate Time Agreement
Called up as a simple resolution	Called up by unanimous consent
Requires majority vote for passage	Agreed to by unanimous consent
Specifies time for general debate	Specifies time for debating amendments
Permits or prohibits amendments	Generally restricts only the offering of nongermane amendments
Does not specify date for vote on passage of measure	Generally sets date for vote on final passage
Effect is often to waive House rules	Effect is often to waive Senate rules

Source: *Congressional Deskbook,* § 8.202

§4.25 Recommended Resources

Floor Votes

1. **C-SPAN** provides live gavel-to-gavel coverage of the U.S. House on C-SPAN 1 and the U.S. Senate on C-SPAN 2. C-SPAN radio also frequently broadcasts floor coverage. Check <*www.cspan.org*> for scheduling information as well as live and archived webcasts.

2. **Congressional Quarterly's CQ Floor Video Service** (<*www.cq.com*>) helps you monitor and analyze House and Senate floor debate by allowing you to pinpoint, watch, and email video of the statements that impact your interests. You can review video from statements made on the House or Senate floor moments after the words are spoken and up to a full day before the *Congressional Record* is available. The service enables you to email video clips to your members, clients, or colleagues, search for floor debate dating back to 2003 and receive email alerts when action occurs on your issues.

3. **Metavid** (short for meta and video) at <*http://metavid.ucsc.edu*> captures, streams, archives, and facilitates real-time collective remediation of federal legislative proceedings, including House and Senate floor proceedings from 2006 to present. Footage can be searched by the name of a specific member of Congress. Close-captioned transcripts are also available.

4. **Congressional Record** is the official record of House and Senate floor proceedings, which has been published by the Government Printing Office (GPO) since 1873. Information such as letters and statements are also inserted by members of Congress and published in the record. GPO publishes new issues of the record daily and transmits each new issue to the Library of Congress overnight. Typically, the following morning a new issue becomes available from the Library of Congress on THOMAS. Posting takes longer after late-night sessions. Issues are available online from 1989 (the 101st Congress) to the present. Search the *Congressional Record* online at <*www.thomas.gov*>.

   In addition, the *Congressional Record* may be browsed through the federal depository library system. There are approximately 1,350 federal depository libraries throughout the United States and its territories, at least one in almost every congressional district. See <*www.gpoaccess.gov*> to locate the federal depository library in your area. The libraries provide free public access to a wide variety of federal government information in both print and electronic formats, and have expert staff available to assist users.

   The *Congressional Record* is also available for browsing at <*www.gpoaccess.gov/crecord*>.

§4.26 **Amendments and Parliamentary Procedures**

"You have to learn the rules of the game.
And then you have to play better than anyone else."
Albert Einstein

Understanding the amendment process and parliamentary procedure is important since amendments can significantly modify, expand, or gut a bill. The majority of legislation passes as an attachment to other legislation. Lobbyists are often asked to explain or clarify the amendment process to their members, colleagues, or clients who are confused by it. Familiarity with the House amendment tree and amendment process terms is useful for explaining or clarifying the process. See § 8.122, "Basic House Amendment Tree," in the *Congressional Deskbook*.

§4.27 **Talking Points for Explaining the Amendment Process**

Simplified talking points that may be helpful as you explain the amendment process to others:

- Amendments can change important aspects of legislation such as the bill's scope, coverage, and penalties for non-compliance.
- An amendment "in the nature of a substitute" can replace the entire text of legislation with alternative language that completely changes the nature of the bill.
- First-degree amendments change the text of the actual legislation under debate. Second-degree amendments change first-degree amendments. First-degree amendments are offered first, but second-degree amendments are voted on first. Perfecting (second-degree) amendments are voted on before substitute amendments are voted on.
- A group of amendments can be offered after obtaining unanimous consent. This is called "en bloc" (as a block).

House Highlights:

More than one-third of all measures considered by the House are brought to the House floor under a procedure called "suspension of the rules." This procedure is designed for considering relatively non-controversial items. Suspension measures can be brought to the floor on Monday and Tuesday of each week, and during the last six days of a session. Suspension votes can be considered on other days as well by unanimous consent or a special rule.

Most amending on the House floor is done in the Committee of the Whole House which is not a typical committee, but a meeting under parliamentary rules that includes all members of the House of Representatives and allows expedited consideration of legislation through:

- A smaller quorum requirement (only 100 instead of the 218 required in the full House);
- The prohibition of certain motions; and
- A five-minute rule for debate on amendments.

The Committee of the Whole cannot pass the measure. The legislation is reported back to the full House for final consideration. The full House then votes on the amendments that were passed in the Committee of the Whole before final passage of the legislation. See § 8.112, "House versus Committee," in the *Congressional Deskbook*.

A motion to recommit a bill, traditionally offered by a minority party member, can be offered immediately before the final vote on the measure. The motion is typically one last chance for a minority member to attempt to change or kill a bill in the House. The motion can contain specific "instructions" to change the bill. If a motion to recommit the bill with instructions passes, the bill is sent back to the reporting committee (in a matter of moments) and the bill, as amended by the motion to recommit is then sent back and considered by the full House. See § 8.140, "Motion to Recommit and Final Passage," in the *Congressional Deskbook*.

Senate Highlights:

Since rules allow senators to speak for any amount of time on the Senate floor, time agreements are used to expedite consideration of legislation and set scheduling. Typically, Senate amendments do not need to be germane to the subject at hand, and unrelated amendments are referred to as riders. Measures that become loaded with numerous non-germane amendments are often referred to as "Christmas-tree" bills.

The Senate Majority Leader has three options for bringing up legislation:

1. A "unanimous consent agreement" for non-controversial items, which can be stopped by a single objecting senator,

2. A negotiated "time agreement" (a complex unanimous consent agreement), and

3. A "motion to proceed to consideration" (a motion to proceed), which needs only a majority vote.

Germaneness is required in some Senate circumstances:
- When cloture has been invoked,
- During consideration of concurrent budget resolutions,
- During consideration of appropriations bills, and
- Under consent time agreements.

For a complete discussion of Senate legislative procedure, see §§ 8.160 et seq in the *Congressional Deskbook*.

§4.28 Recommended Resources

Amendments and Parliamentary Procedures

- See Appendix 4 for a Select Glossary of Lobbying Terms.
- Abridged Dictionary of Parliamentary Terms via the House Rules Committee: <www.rules.house.gov>
- Pocket Dictionary of Legislative Terms: <www.TCNBooklet.com>
- Glossary of Federal Budget Terms via the House Rules Committee: <www.rules.house.gov>
- House Floor Procedures Manual from the Congressional Institute: <www.conginst.org>
- Explanation of the House "Committee on the Whole" Procedure via the Library of Congress: <www.thomas.gov>
- *Riddick's Senate Procedure*, named after former Senate Parliamentarian Emeritus Floyd M. Riddick, contains the Senate's practices and precedents and is updated by the current Senate parliamentarian, at <www.senate.gov>.
- Links to all web resources are available on the Resources page for this book: <www.LobbyingAndAdvocacy.com>

§4.29 What is an Earmark?

Rules for public disclosure of the sponsors of congressional earmarks (also called "directed congressional appropriations" and "pork" or "pet projects") that members of Congress insert into spending bills and the congressional procedures for objecting to their approval were a contentious issue during the 2006 and 2007 lobbying reform debates. (See Appendix 4, Glossary, for a definition of earmarks.) A House Rule adopted on January 4, 2007 requires the disclosure of earmarks in legislation and bans all earmarks in spending bills that would financially benefit members, their families, or special interest groups. In accordance with the Honest Leadership and Open Government Act (HLOGA) (Pub. L. 110-81) (available in *Lobbying and Advocacy Sourcebook*), all ear-

§4.30 Recommended Resources

Earmarks

- Office of Management and Budget's Earmark Database: <www.earmarks.omb.gov>
- Citizens Against Government Waste (CAGW) Earmark Database: <www.cagw.org>
- Earmark and budget training is available from TheCapitol.Net, both live courses and audio courses.

marks in tax, tariff, and spending bills or conference reports, and their sponsors, must be disclosed on the Internet at least forty-eight hours before Senate votes. Earmarks must be certified as meeting rule requirements by the Senate committee chairmen and the Senate majority leader instead of the Senate parliamentarian. Several members of Congress opposed the final earmark reform provision as insufficient and have pledged to push Congress to reconsider the issue in the future.

§4.31 Moving through the Second Chamber

Legislation moves separately (and sometimes concurrently) through the House and Senate. Once one chamber (either the House or Senate) has voted to pass a bill, the other chamber may:

- Pass it with the language intact;
- Refer it to a committee for scrutiny or alteration (the committee may or may not act on it);
- Reject the entire bill, informing the other chamber of its actions; or
- Ignore the bill, while continuing to work on its own version of the legislation. If the second chamber does not pass the legislation, it dies at the end of the second year of the "Congress."

§4.32 Moving to Conference

After the two chambers pass differing versions of legislation, the bill goes to conference. Conferees are chosen by party leaders and typically include members from the House and Senate committees who worked on the bill. Conferees are not allowed to write new legislation; they must work within the boundaries of the differences in the House and Senate bills. When the conferees have reached agreement, they submit a report of their recommendations to each chamber for approval. The text of conference reports can be found via the Clerk of the House *<clerk.house.gov>* or the Thomas web site *<www.thomas.gov>*.

"Fast track" procedures prohibit amendments but require a two-thirds majority for approval. Per recently enacted lobbying reform legislation, provisions added in conference at the last minute—so-called "dead of night" provisions—would have to receive sixty votes in order for the conference report to survive challenges on budget points of order.

For more information, see § 8.280, "Conference Committees," in the *Congressional Deskbook*.

§4.33 **Presidential Consideration**

- **Enactment:** The Speaker of the House and the President of the Senate both sign the approved bill and send it to the president. If the president signs it, it becomes law. The date that he signs it is the date of "enactment." The bill is assigned a public law number such as Pub. L.. 111-1, which would indicate that it was the first public law enacted in the 111th Congress. New laws are posted on the National Archives and Records Administration (NARA) web site at <*www.archives.gov*>; 202-741-6043. Specific provisions in the new law become effective according to the "effective date" specified in the text of the legislation.
- **Veto and Congressional Override Votes:** The president may "veto" the entire bill. The bill goes back to Congress for a second vote, in which it must get a two-thirds majority of votes in each chamber in order to become law.
- **Pocket Veto:** If Congress adjourns within ten days of giving the bill to the president, and he does not sign it, the bill dies.
- **Enactment without Presidential Signature:** If Congress is in session, and the president does not sign the bill within ten days (Sundays excepted), the bill becomes law without his signature.

Congress passed the *Line Item Veto Act of 1996*, which temporarily granted the president the power to veto single budget items ("line items") and send the bill back to Congress with a two-thirds majority of votes in each chamber required for the measure to become law. The line-item veto authority was provided until June 1998, when the U.S. Supreme Court struck down the law as violating the Presentment Clause of the U.S. Constitution (*Clinton v. City of New York in 1998*, 524 U.S. 417 (1998)). Presidential and congressional interest remains in restoring the line-item veto in a manner that would avoid constitutional concerns.

For more information, see § 8.290, "Presidential Action on Enacted Measures," in the *Congressional Deskbook*.

§4.34 **Respect Congressional Timing and Schedules**

> *"There is a tide in the affairs of men*
> *Which taken at the flood, leads on to fortune."*
> Brutus in Julius Ceasar, Act IV, Scene 3, William Shakespeare

Never did the phrase that "timing is everything" ring truer than in its frequent use to describe congressional work. A lobbyist needs to respect congressional schedules and organize activities and initiate communications at the best time of the day and week. Members of Congress and staff tend to be the most difficult to reach during the middle of the week, when the House and Senate are in session and committee meetings occur. Staff is usually more accessible and conversational when their boss is out of town, on Fridays or Monday mornings or during congressional recesses.

§4.35 **Congressional Sessions and Recesses**

Each two-year "Congress" is comprised of two "sessions":

110th Congress, Session I	2007
110th Congress, Session II	2008
111th Congress, Session I	2009
111th Congress, Session II	2010
112th Congress, Session I	2011
112th Congress, Session II	2012

In non-election years (Session I), Congress frequently is in session close to Christmas. In election years (Session II), Congress usually recesses in October and November, so that the members can go home and campaign, frequently returning after the election to complete action on funding the government. The most significant items tend to pass the last few days of a session or before Congress recesses for a break. The upcoming deadline of a recess inserts a timed end on negotiations, which are often needed to get agreement to finalize priority legislation.

Congressional recesses present excellent opportunities to meet congressional staffers in Washington, DC, or members back in their home districts or states. See "The Lobbyists Annual Calendar: Key Dates and Activities Template with Annual Schedule Highlights" in Appendix 5 for suggestions on specific activities timed to coincide with the legislative cycles.

The least busy times for Congress are during congressional recesses. January and February are typically slow before the budget is received on Capitol Hill. The full House and Senate floors are not as busy during this time while committees are holding hearings and marking up legislation before it is ready to come to the floor.

At the beginning of each year, the House and Senate leadership publish calendars of scheduled recesses on their homepages at <*www.house.gov*> and <*www.senate.gov*>.

Federal holidays are observed and congressional recesses typically occur around:

- President's Day,
- Memorial Day,
- Easter/Spring Break,
- Independence Day (Fourth of July),
- The entire month of August, returning after Labor Day, and
- Christmas/New Year's.

§4.36 The Principle of Early Intervention: Life Cycle of Lobbying

As soon as a bill is introduced, interest groups tracking the issue through a variety of databases and tracking systems (described in § 5.5) begin lobbying the legislation. Many reporters monitor congressional committee consideration closely and ask members of Congress questions about their position on the legislation. As the measure receives increased public awareness through interest groups and the media, constituents learn about the legislation and ask their members of Congress to reveal their positions on the proposal. By the time a bill moves to the floor, most members of Congress have already determined their position, even if it has not yet become publicly known. Therefore, communications should be made early in the process, before a member has formulated a position on the bill.

You will have much more influence in shaping legislation and member votes if you concentrate your efforts early in the legislative life cycle. However, even if you achieve early victories, do not stop working and communicating with Capitol Hill. The lobbying intensity, press, and pressures that mount immediately before a vote can cause changes in positions and the degree of support.

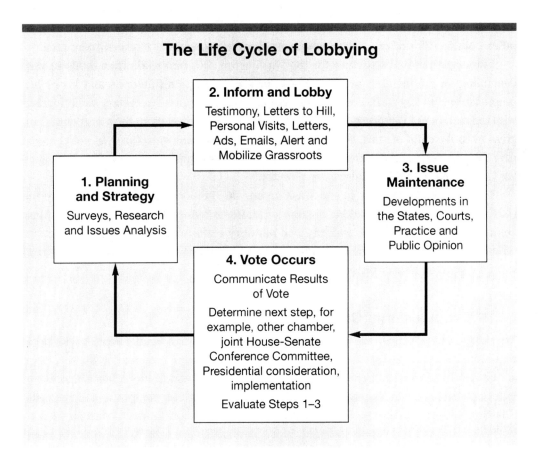

The Life Cycle of Lobbying

2. Inform and Lobby
Testimony, Letters to Hill, Personal Visits, Letters, Ads, Emails, Alert and Mobilize Grassroots

1. Planning and Strategy
Surveys, Research and Issues Analysis

3. Issue Maintenance
Developments in the States, Courts, Practice and Public Opinion

4. Vote Occurs
Communicate Results of Vote

Determine next step, for example, other chamber, joint House-Senate Conference Committee, Presidential consideration, implementation

Evaluate Steps 1–3

§4.37 **Congressional Offices Overview**

Congressional offices provide logistical, political, and substantive support for the members of Congress. § 4.40 discusses the functions of a legislative office and §§ 4.38 and 4.39 examine the structure and environment of congressional offices.

Every member of Congress has an individual office, referred to as a "personal office" which is in one of the congressional office buildings in Washington, DC, as well as offices in their home district or state. Members who hold key leadership or committee leadership positions have additional offices and staff in the congressional complex. The House office buildings (Rayburn, Longworth, and Cannon) are on the south side of the Capitol and the Senate office buildings (Russell, Dirksen, and Hart) are on the north side of the Capitol building. See § 4.48 for an explanation of the office building numbering system.

§4.38 **Congressional Office Staffing**

Because of the dramatic increase in citizen communications to members of Congress (further discussed in Chapter Seven), congressional offices are spending more of their limited staff resources addressing constituent correspondence. According to the Congressional Management Foundation, the average House office contains nine staffers and they spend 50 percent of staff time answering constituent mail. The average Senate office contains 22 staffers, five of whom are devoted exclusively to constituent mail.

The organizational structure for the Washington, DC, personal office tends to vary depending on the member of Congress' emphasis on certain functions and his or her relationship with key staff. For example, depending on the press secretary's relationship with the member of Congress, he or she may either report directly to the member of Congress or to the chief of staff. While in many ways, the staffing structure has not changed over the last thirty years, a few of the titles have. For example, Senate "office manager" has been replaced by "administrative director."

The most senior staffer in the Washington, DC, personal office is most likely the chief of staff. The highest-ranking committee staffer is referred to as staff director. Most committees are divided into majority and minority staffs with separate staff directors, offices and staff. The most senior staff in the state or district office is typically referred to as the state or district office director.

§4.39 **Congressional Office Structures**

The congressional offices are like 535 small companies all individually dealing with organizational structure and staffing issues. While there are some common attributes, there are unique features within each office that do not correspond to any other office. Some offices even share Washington, DC, staff for positions such as computer professionals. Educational levels and experience vary widely with the more junior positions such as staff assistant and legislative assistant. More similarities are seen in the education and

§4.40 Different Roles and Responsibilities of Various Types of Congressional Offices

	Personal Office Senate	Personal Office House	Committee Office (if Committee Chairman or High Ranking Minority)	District Office (House) State Office (Senate)	Campaign Office
Typical Title for Highest Ranking Staff	Chief of Staff	Chief of Staff has replaced the previous title of Administrative Assistant	Staff Director	District Director or State Director	Campaign Director
Purpose	Legislative correspondence; legislative support to Senator; bill and issue tracking; assist constituents visiting DC from their state (Capitol and White House tours). Analyze and develop positions, prepare press communications.	Legislative correspondence; legislative support to House member; bill and issue tracking; assist constituents visiting DC from their congressional district (Capitol and White House tours). Analyze and develop positions, prepare press communications.	Majority office directs and implements agenda of committee chair. Minority office directs and implements minority committee activities.	Determine constituents' opinion; case work (helping constituents solve problems such as missing social security checks); local offices for the member of Congress.	Elect/re-elect candidate
Type of Work	More issue-oriented than the state office. Addresses a very wide range of issues and handles inquiries from across the state. Tends to be more politically focused and more loosely connected to the senator than any committee office he or she may run.	More issue-oriented than the district office. Addresses a very wide range of issues and handles inquiries from his/her particular congressional district. Tends to be more politically focused and more loosely connected to the member than any committee office he or she may run.	Substance-oriented. Focus is on particular issues and staffers generally have subject matter expertise.	More constituent (and casework) oriented than the DC office. Focuses on district or state meetings and activities.	Extremely political. Activities include fundraising, preparing for appearances and debates, updating strategies, and opposition research.

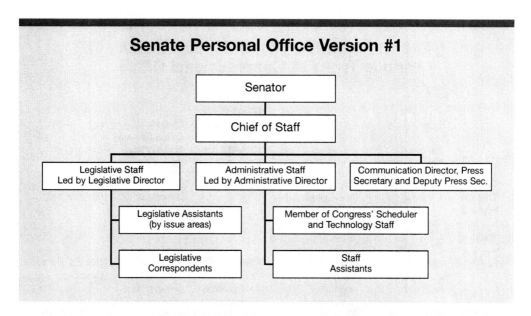

Senate Personal Office Version #1

- Senator
- Chief of Staff
  - Legislative Staff Led by Legislative Director
    - Legislative Assistants (by issue areas)
    - Legislative Correspondents
  - Administrative Staff Led by Administrative Director
    - Member of Congress' Scheduler and Technology Staff
    - Staff Assistants
  - Communication Director, Press Secretary and Deputy Press Sec.

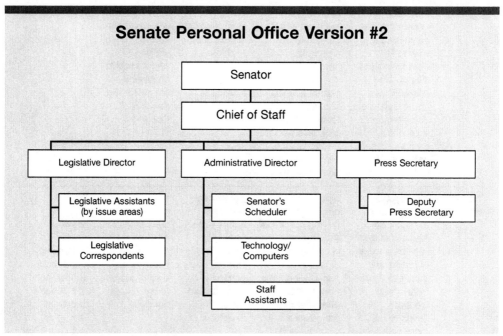

Senate Personal Office Version #2

- Senator
- Chief of Staff
  - Legislative Director
    - Legislative Assistants (by issue areas)
    - Legislative Correspondents
  - Administrative Director
    - Senator's Scheduler
    - Technology/ Computers
    - Staff Assistants
  - Press Secretary
    - Deputy Press Secretary

experience profiles of top staff, where advanced degrees and management experience are more common. Overall, the majority of staff for any given office are recruited from that member's home state, but this is less often the case for the more senior positions, where more varied experience, such as previous work in another member's office, is more often the case.

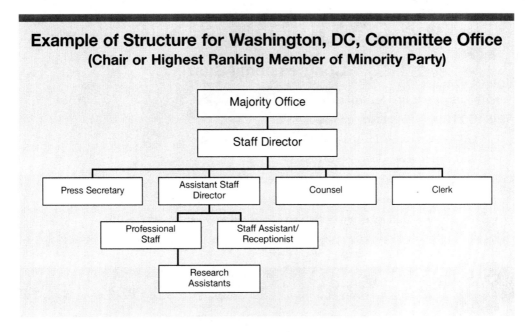

Example of Structure for Washington, DC, Committee Office
(Chair or Highest Ranking Member of Minority Party)

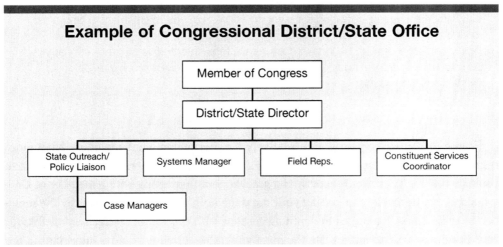

Example of Congressional District/State Office

§4.41 Essential Role of Congressional Staff

While understanding office structure is critical to success in lobbying, it's important to be courteous to everyone on the Hill, regardless of their title or position.

Many constituents are disappointed when they are not able to meet directly with the House member or senator, especially once they notice the age of the young congressional staffer that is attending the meeting on behalf of the member. (According to the Congressional Management Foundation, the average congressional staffer is 28 years old, with a bachelor's degree and 1.8 years of experience on the job.) However, it is important not to ever dismiss or underestimate the role of congressional staff.

§4.42 Recommended Resources

Congressional Staff

- Congressional staff listings are available from:
  - CQ Press: <*http://csd.cqpress.com*>
  - LexisNexis: <*www.lexisnexis.com*>
  - Knowlegis: <*www.knowlegis.net*>
  - Congressional Yellow Book: <*leadershipdirectories.com*>
  - Almanac of the unelected: <*www.bernan.com*>
- Congressional staff roles are described at <*www.congress.org*>

§4.43 Lobby Tips

Respect the Role of Staff

Many staffers exercise considerable authority, more than you might imagine, and most staffers start in an entry-level position and move up quickly. Today's receptionist is tomorrow's chief of staff. Be kind and courteous to everyone; one day they may answer the phones, and the next day, they answer your senator's question on a piece of legislation that's important to you.

While they may be young and relatively inexperienced, staff members have more responsibility within the office and more influence with the member of Congress than you may realize. They are frequently the gatekeepers to meeting with a member of Congress and can be the key to getting your message considered or even used by the member. In some cases, having an in-depth discussion with the senior staffer responsible for your issue who will actually write the members' talking points is more important in the long run than having a brief courtesy meeting directly with a member who may not remember the exchange.

Members of Congress rely on staff so extensively because they are responsible for making important decisions on a host of complicated issues, and they are supposed to be several places at once throughout the day. With limited time and resources, members of Congress entrust their staff with significant authority to handle issues on a day-to-day basis. Since staff can focus more specifically on issues and often become subject-matter experts, legislators often rely on their recommendations when it is time to make a decision on legislation. While this may seem shocking or even irresponsible at first, keep in mind that members attempt to recruit staffers with a consistent political philosophy to theirs and expect them to stay informed and updated on their policy preferences in specific areas so that staff can faithfully exercise a good deal of judgment within those areas. Accordingly, the staffer operates within a framework of understanding the member's positions and philosophies. For example, if the member of Congress's campaign platform included opposition to all new employer mandates, the staffer can evaluate new legislative proposals in light of the member's political philosophy and draft letters to constituents explaining the position.

It is important to note that while members of Congress rely heavily on their staffers, staffers are not always completely in sync with their members' viewpoint and they may not be aware of all of the conversations that the member is having concerning an issue. It is therefore critical to communicate with the member of Congress directly at some point in order to confirm the members' official position on a matter. While congressional staffers are extremely important as advisors to members of Congress, ultimately, the member is the only one who votes.

The level of expertise among staff varies considerably. For that reason, it is important to neither assume too much knowledge nor talk down to the staffer. Instead, start by asking questions as to how familiar the staffer is with the issue. Some staffers are entry level and performing relatively minor tasks while others may be serving on a committee as a policy expert, but virtually all are among the best and brightest individuals in the nation.

§4.44 The Pace and Stress of the Legislative Office Environment

The high pressure, long hours, unpredictable schedule, and highly visible environment on Capitol Hill create unique opportunities and stresses. Accordingly, the turnover rate of congressional staff tends to be significantly higher than many private sector jobs. In the wake of 9/11, security concerns and associated warnings or evacuations contribute to the environmental stress.

§4.45 Example of a Senior Staffer's Daily Workload

- 5,000 steps a day AT WORK
- 300–400 emails per day, and about 150–175 requiring responses
- Rarely less than 12 hours per day
- Rarely time for a lunch break or any break at all
- Long meetings last 30 minutes; most meetings much shorter

In general, a frenetic pace that requires constant prioritizing among the urgent, the less urgent, and the truly important things.

Source: Bill Wichterman, Former Chief of Staff to two members of Congress and Former Policy Advisor for the Senate Majority Leader

§4.47 Recommended Resources

Congressional Staff Salaries

- Legistorm <*www.legistorm.com*>: Browse congressional staff salaries by state, House or Senate office, last name, committee, leadership office, or administrative office. Salaries are approximate since they represent only a portion of a year and bonuses are not included. Additionally, some staff are paid from more than one office (for example, a House personal office and a committee office).

- A CRS Report, "Legislative Executive and Judicial Officials: Process for Adjusting Pay and Current Salaries," RL33245, lists the salaries of certain government officials and describes the process for updating government officials' salaries (see <*www.LobbyingAndAdvocacy.com*>).

For information on congressional pay and perks, see <*www.CongressPay.com*>.

§4.46 Congressional Staff Pay

Congressional staff salaries, typically ranging from the 20's for entry-level positions to $115,000 for senior leadership staff, is well below the national average as living expenses in the Washington, DC, area are extremely high. I recall hearing one staffer joke about the inconsistent relationship between pay and power on Capitol Hill by claiming that "I could make more by knowing me than by being me." Nonetheless, the staffers wield a lot of power, and securing positions at all levels, many of which are stepping stones, is competitive.

Vacancies are usually filled by word of mouth, with constant movement between offices on Capitol Hill, especially with the more senior positions. A new labor pool is created every two years after many members are defeated or retire. Their staff often seek new employment from the newly elected legislators who seek experienced staff as they arrive on Capitol Hill.

For more information, see the *Congressional Deskbook*, Chapter Four, "Supporting Congress: Allowances and Staff."

§4.48 Location and Facilities of Congress

This section provides general information on the congressional facilities. Information useful for bringing members or clients into Washington, DC, is provided in a "Practical Guide to Working the Hill" (Appendix 3).

The United States Capitol Complex is comprised of the Capitol, the House and Senate Office Buildings, the U.S. Botanic Garden, the Capitol Grounds, the Library of Congress buildings, the Supreme Court Building, the Capitol Power Plant, and various support facilities. In addition, the new Capitol Visitor Center, an underground facility located beneath the Capitol's east front plaza, opens in December 2008.

§4.49 Recommended Resources

Capitol Facilities

- The Architect of the Capitol has a wealth of information for further research: *<www.aoc.gov>*
- Appendix 3: A Practical Guide to Working the Hill
- Maps and directions from TheCapitol.Net: *<www.CapitolHillMap.net>*

"The Capitol is one of the most widely recognized buildings in the world. It is a symbol of the American people and their government, the meeting place of the nation's legislature, an art and history museum, and a tourist attraction visited by millions every year." Reference: *<www.aoc.gov/cc/index.cfm>*.

The United States Capitol in Washington, DC, is among the most architecturally impressive and symbolically important buildings in the world. It has housed the meeting chambers of the Senate and the House of Representatives for almost two centuries. Begun in 1793, the Capitol has been built, burnt, rebuilt, extended, and restored; today, it stands as a monument not only to its builders but also to the American people and their government.

Underground tunnels (and even a private underground railway) connect the main Capitol building with each of the congressional office buildings. All rooms in the Capitol are designated as either S (for Senate) or H (for House), depending on whether they are north (Senate-side) or south (House-side) of the Rotunda. Similarly, rooms in the congressional office buildings are designated as HOB (for House Office Building) or SOB (for Senate Office Building). The abbreviations for buildings use the first letter of the building name followed by HOB, so, CHOB means the Cannon House Office Building. Rooms in the Cannon building have three digits—100 CHOB—rooms in the Longworth building have four digits with one as the prefix—1100 LHOB—and rooms in the Rayburn building have four digits with two as the prefix—2100 RHOB. Senate buildings have similar abbreviations (SR for the Senate Russell building, SD for the Senate Dirksen building, and SR for the Senate Hart building).

Additionally, most addresses in Washington, DC, are designated NE, NW, SE, or SW, in relationship to the Rotunda. (Since the Capitol Rotunda is not located in the center of the District—it is slightly farther east—the four DC quadrants are not the same shape and size.)

For more information, see Appendix 3 and the *Congressional Deskbook*, Chapter Six, "Supporting Congress: The Capitol Complex."

§4.50 **Congressional Support Organizations**

Architect of the Capitol

The Architect of the Capitol is responsible to the United States Congress for the maintenance, operation, development, and preservation of the United States Capitol Complex. The architect acts on the Senate side subject to the approval of the Senate Committee on Rules and Administration, and actions on the House side are subject to the approval of the Speaker and the Committee on House Administration. Reference: <*www.aoc.gov*>.

Congressional Budget Office (CBO)

CBO's mandate is to provide the Congress with:

- Objective, nonpartisan, and timely analyses to aid in economic and budgetary decisions on the wide array of programs covered by the federal budget and
- The information and estimates required for the Congressional budget process.

Reference: <*www.cbo.gov*>.

Government Accountability Office (GAO)

GAO, commonly called the investigative arm of Congress or the congressional watchdog, is independent and nonpartisan. It studies how the federal government spends taxpayer dollars. GAO advises Congress and the heads of executive agencies . . . about ways to make government more effective and responsive. GAO evaluates federal programs, audits federal expenditures, and issues legal opinions. When GAO reports its findings to Congress, it recommends actions. Its work leads to laws and acts that improve government operations, and save billions of dollars. Reference: <*www.gao.gov*>.

Government Printing Office (GPO)

GPO is the federal government's primary centralized resource for gathering, cataloging, producing, providing, authenticating, and preserving published information in all its forms. GPO is responsible for the production and distribution of information products and services for all three branches of the federal government. Reference: <*www.access. gpo.gov*>.

Library of Congress/Congressional Research Service (CRS)

The Congressional Research Service is the public policy research arm of the United States Congress. As a legislative branch agency within the Library of Congress, CRS works exclusively and directly for members of Congress, their committees, and staff on a confidential, nonpartisan basis. Reference: <*www.loc.gov*>.

Chief Administrative Officer (CAO)
for the U.S. House of Representatives

The Office of the Chief Administrative Officer (CAO) provides operations support services and business solutions to the community of 10,000 House members, officers, and

§4.51 Lobby Tips

GAO Reports

Stay abreast of GAO publications and reports addressing your issues. Search for GAO reports at *<www.gao.gov>* and at LOUIS, the Library of Unified Information Sources, at *<www.louisdb.org>*.

staff. The CAO organization is comprised of more than 600 technical and administrative staff working in a variety of areas, including information technology, finance, budget management, human resources, payroll, child care, food and vending, procurement, logistics, and administrative counsel. Source and reference: *<http://cao.house.gov>*.

Clerk of the House

Performs a variety of duties, including:
- Prepare the roll of members-elect.
- Call the members-elect to order at the commencement of each Congress; call the roll of members-elect, and, pending the election of the Speaker, preserve order and decorum; and decide all questions of order.
- Prepare and distribute at the beginning of every session a list of reports required to be made to Congress.
- Note all questions of order, and decisions thereon, and to print these as an appendix to the Journal of each session of the House.
- Prepare and print the House Journal after each session of Congress, and distribute the Journal to Members and to the executive and the legislature of each state.
- Attest and affix the seal of the House to all writs, warrants, and subpoenas and formal documents issued by the House.
- Certify the passage by the House of all bills and joint resolutions.
- Receive messages from the president and the Senate when the House is not in session.
- Prepare and deliver messages to the Senate and otherwise as requested by the House.
- Retain, in the official library, a permanent set of the books and documents generated by the House. Administer lobbyist reporting.
- Manage the office and supervise the staff of any deceased, resigned, or expelled member until a successor is elected.

Reference: *<http://clerk.house.gov>*.

§4.52 Lobby Tips

CRS Reports

Many topical issue papers written for members of Congress by the Congressional Research Service are available to the public at *<www.opencrs.org>*. An index of CRS reports that can be purchased through a subscription service is available at *<www.pennyhill.org>*. CRS reports can also be obtained, for free, from your member of Congress.

Secretary of the Senate

The Secretary of the Senate has Senate responsibilities similar to the Clerk of the House:
- Expedites the day-to-day operations of the United States Senate.
- Administers the lobbying registration and disclosure requirements under the Lobbying Disclosure Act (under its Office of Public Records).

Reference: *<www.senate.gov/reference/office/secretary_of_senate.htm>*.

§4.53 General Overview of the Regulatory Process

The Office of Management and Budget (OMB), created in 1970, is the president's arm in the rulemaking process. Formally located within the Executive Office of the President, OMB's role is to apply government-wide discipline to rulemaking while implementing the president's priorities and assuring consistency among federal agencies. Where disagreements arise between OMB and agency heads, the president and the White House staff must resolve them. Independent agencies are exempted from OMB review and approval of their proposed regulations. OMB implements its regulatory responsibilities through its Office of Information and Regulatory Affairs (OIRA).

The Office of Information and Regulatory Affairs (OIRA) is a federal office that Congress established in the 1980 Paperwork Reduction Act. OIRA reviews draft regulations under Executive Order 12866 and develops and oversees the implementation of government-wide policies in the areas of information technology, information policy, privacy, and statistical policy. OIRA also oversees agency implementation of the Information Quality Law, including the peer review practices of agencies.

Reference: *<www.whitehouse.gov/omb>*.

OIRA Reports to Congress are available at: *<www.whitehouse.gov/omb/inforeg/reg pol-reports_congress.html>*.

The administration's Semiannual Regulatory Agenda (Unified Agenda) is published in the Federal Register, usually in April and October. The agenda summarizes the rules and proposed rules that each federal agency expects to issue during the next six months. The agenda is published by the Office of the Federal Register National Archives and Records Administration (NARA). Current and previous issues may be searched at <*www.gpoaccess.gov/ua*>.

While the Unified Agenda contains an official list of anticipated regulatory actions, some regulatory actions remain on the agenda for several years. Effectively influencing the regulatory process involves establishing relationships with agency officials on the inside who have insight and can provide updates as to whether or not specific proposals listed in the Unified Agenda will actually move forward. There are links to current and past regulations under review (updated daily), as well as links to letters from the Office of Management and Budget to federal agencies with comments on specific regulations (for example, return letters responding to a draft rule, prompt letters, suggesting an issue worthy of agency priority and post review letters sent after an OMB review), at <*www.whitehouse.gov/omb*>.

The annual State of the Union is provided, by law, to a joint session of Congress in January. The president's speech presents administration priorities, and may include references to forthcoming regulations.

See §§ 3.6–3.12 for recommended resources on executive branch positions and priorities.

§4.54 **Selected Regulatory Agency Laws and Rules**

- Administrative Procedures Act, 1946 (5 U.S.C. § 500 et seq.): Establishes the basic rules for federal agency procedures, covering rulemaking, fact finding, adjudications, and other issues.
- Congressional Review Act, 1996 (5 USC § 801 et seq.): Creates the process allowing the House and Senate to review and block "major" new final rules by adopting a joint resolution with presidential concurrence.
- Freedom of Information Act, 1996 (5 U.S.C. § 552): Guarantees public access to government-held information (with specified exceptions) and creates processes to obtain it.
- Government in the Sunshine Act, 1976 (5 U.S.C. § 552b): Requires multi-headed agencies to conduct meetings in public (with specified exceptions).
- Federal Privacy Act, 1974 (5. U.S.C. § 552a): Creates rights against agency disclosure of information on individuals.
- National Environmental Protection Act, 1969 (42 U.S.C. § 4331 et seq.): Requires agencies to draft and publish environmental impact statements on environmentally sensitive rules.
- Paperwork Reduction Act, 1980 (44 U.S.C. § 3501 et seq.): Creates standards for agency imposition of information-collection burdens on the public.
- Regulatory Flexibility Act, 1980 (5 U.S.C. § 601 et seq.): Creates procedures for agencies to consider the impact or burden of new rules on small businesses.

§4.55 Recommended Resources

Tracking Executive Branch Actions

Lobby Fact: The *Federal Register* contained approximately 75,000 pages in 2006.

Federal Register

Published by the Office of the Federal Register, National Archives and Records Administration (NARA), the *Federal Register* is the official daily publication for rules, proposed rules, and notices of federal agencies and organizations, as well as executive orders and other presidential documents. Searchable *Federal Register*: *<www.gpoaccess.gov/fr>*, *<www.archives.gov>*

Public Laws Electronic Notification Service

Available at *<www.archives.gov>*.

Code of Federal Regulations

The Code of Federal Regulations (CFR) is the codification of the general and permanent rules published in the *Federal Register* by the executive departments and agencies of the federal government. It is divided into fifty titles that represent broad areas subject to federal regulation. Each volume of the CFR is updated once each calendar year and is issued on a quarterly basis. Searchable CFR: *<www.gpoaccess.gov/CFR>*, *<www.archives.gov>*

Executive Orders

Available at *<www.archives.gov/federal-register/executive-orders>*.

- C-SPAN provides archives of previous State of the Union addresses at: *<www.c-span.org/executive/stateoftheunion.asp>*.
- The State of the Union is also published in the *Congressional Record*, which is searchable at *<www.gpoaccess.gov/crecord>*.

Administration Positions on Legislation

The administration develops a Statement of Administration Policy (SAP) and at that time congressional liaison offices in the federal agencies may become engaged on the Hill. Executive branch agency staff review legislation and weigh in with the opinion of the administration. See § 2.3 for Anti-Lobbying Act restrictions.

Agency representatives may be asked about the administration's position on legislation in congressional hearings, through letters from members of Congress and through press inquiries to agency officials and at the daily White House Press briefings.

Links to Statements of Administration Policy, executive branch reports to Congress, and OMB officials' testimony before Congress can be accessed from OMB at *<www.whitehouse.gov/omb>*.

Additional Resources

- See §§ 3.6–3.12 for resources for determining the seven "Position Drivers" of executive branch officials.

§4.55 Recommended Resources (Continued)

- Submit comments online at Regulations.gov: *<www.regulations.gov>*.
- See GSA's regulatory guide at *<www.reginfo.gov>*. Regulations active under the Regulatory Planning and Review process (E.O 12866 review and its predecessor, E.O. 12291) are linked to as well as regulatory reviews completed in the last thirty days and OIRA's letters to agencies.
- OMB's Office of Information and Regulatory Affairs: *<www.whitehouse.gov/omb/inforeg>*
- TheCapitol.Net regulatory links: *<www.AdminResearch.com>*
- *Federal Regulatory Process Poster* by Kenneth Ackerman: *<www.AgencyPoster.com>*.
- RegScan (subscriber service): *<www.regscan.com>*

Links to all web resources are available on the Resources page for this book: *<www.LobbyingAndAdvocacy.com>*

EXECUTIVE ORDERS:

- E.O. 12688: Regulatory Planning and Review: Details the role of OMB in the federal rulemaking process and requires non-independent agencies to analyze the costs and benefits of significant rules.
- E.O. 12988: Civil Justice Review: Requires agencies to review new rules and legislation to improve legal clarity and enhance the civil justice system.
- E.O. 13132: Federalism: Requires agencies to consult with state and local governments on rules that affect them. E.O. 13175 requires consultation with Indian Tribal governments.
- E.O. 13211: Energy: Requires agencies to analyze significant new rules involving energy supply, distribution, or use and prepare a Statement of Energy Effects.
- OMB Circular A-4: Updated guidelines for agencies conducting Regulatory Impact Analysis on proposed significant rules.

Source: *Federal Regulatory Process Poster*, by Kenneth Ackerman *<www.AgencyPoster.com>*.

§4.56 Understand the Major Differences between Federal and State Legislative Processes

"Lobbying is lobbying, whether at the federal, state, or local level, because lobbying is communications. The major difference is that the vast majority of state legislators are in session part time, even though it's full-time work."

The Hon. Peggy Kerns, Director of the Center for Ethics in Government at the National Conference of State Legislators and former legislator (former Colorado House Minority Leader)

§4.57 Recommended Resources

State vs. Federal Legislative Processes

Resources for assessing lobbying and ethics laws applicable to state and local lobbying engagements are provided in § 2.3 and resources for identifying and tracking state legislative issues are provided in § 3.25. Specific resources useful for federal lobbyists who wish to learn more about the differences between federal and specific state legislative processes are below:

- *Guide to State Legislative Lobbying*, by Robert L. Guyer
- National Conference of State Legislatures (NCSL): <*www.ncsl.org*>.
- American Legislative Exchange Council (ALEC): <*www.alec.org*>.
- The State Government Affairs Council (SGAC): <*www.sgac.org*>.
- Council of State Governments (CSG): <*www.csg.org*>.
- Many states have an office located at the Hall of States in Washington, DC (444 North Capitol Street NW, near Union Station on the Senate side of the Capitol). The state office staffs monitor federal legislation from their state's perspective and have access to numerous resources including a State Services Organization (SSO) library (<*www.sso.org*>).

Links to all web resources are available on the Resources page for this book: <*www.LobbyingAndAdvocacy.com*>.

§4.99 Chapter Summary

- Lobbyists need to understand and stay updated on the governmental institutions and processes to effectively navigate and influence the legislative and regulatory processes. Resources on communicating parliamentary procedure and various legislative and executive branch processes are provided throughout the chapter.
- Lobbyists are frequently called upon to explain and clarify features of the legislative and regulatory processes to association members, staff, associates, or clients. While most lobbyists have worked in Congress, they need to round and maintain their knowledge base and maintain resources for explaining and clarifying the processes with others. (§ 4.2)
- A brief timeline (§ 4.4) and recommended resources (§ 4.3) are provided to assist lobbyists in explaining historical information on the Capitol (institution) and the capital (city).
- Lobbyists need to understand and appreciate the differences between the House and Senate (§ 4.8) and know how to communicate them.
- Annual budget information is given, including authorization and appropriations timetables (§ 4.10), the historical context of the federal budget (§ 4.12), and helpful resources to further research the subject (§ 4.14).

- Capitol Hill has its own language (§ 4.15). The vocabulary is best learned by immersion into the culture. Classes can also be taken to round one's knowledge of legislative and regulatory terms. The chapter defines congressional approval terminology (§ 4.16) and provides recommended resources on legislative language (§ 4.17).
- § 4.19 discusses the crucial role of congressional committees in developing legislation. Types of committees, leadership, and committee work are outlined in this section.
- Rules for debate are proposed by the Rules Committee and approved by the full House (§ 4.22). Terms and procedures for debate in the Senate are discussed and defined (§ 4.23).
- § 4.25 shows lobbyists how to access live gavel coverage, review video, and locate official records of House and Senate proceedings.
- The impact of congressional scheduling on the work of the lobbyist is presented in § 4.34. Timing your efforts and activities while keeping in mind the timing of sessions, recesses, and the introduction of a bill are imperative (§§ 4.34–4.36).
- A lobbying life cycle depicts various lobbying activities to coincide with the phases of the legislative process. (§ 4.36)
- Congressional offices provide members of Congress the support needed to represent and respond to constituents, as well as provide information and services to the member. (§§ 4.37–4.41)
- Although the structure of congressional offices can be similar, each office varies depending on the preferences of the member of Congress (§§ 4.39 and 4.40). It is imperative to extend professionalism to all staff members, regardless of rank or seniority.
  - The high pressure and fast pace of the legislative office environment results in frequent turnover and requires constant prioritization of issues and tasks (§ 4.41, 4.44).
  - § 4.46 contains information about congressional staff salaries, and §§ 4.48 and 4.49 give information about the location and features of the Capitol building itself.
  - Roles of support organizations such as the Congressional Budget Office (CBO) and Government Printing Office (GPO) are outlined in § 4.50. § 4.50 also provides information about accessing reports written for Congress by the Congressional Research Service (CRS) and lists the duties of the Chief Administrative Officer (CAO) of the House and the Clerk of the House.
  - § 4.53 describes the regulatory process, including the role of the Office of Management and Budget in the rulemaking process. Selected executive branch laws and rules are provided in §4.54, and §4.55 gives the lobbyist resources for tracking the status of key legislation.
  - Specific resources are provided to assist federal lobbyists who wish to learn more about the differences between federal and state legislative processes. (§ 4.57)

CHAPTER 5

Know
Your Issue
(Well Enough for the
Toughest Questions)

*"I've learned that you can get
by on charm for about fifteen
minutes. After that, you'd
better know something."*

Ronald K. Pendleton, Ph.D., Professor of Education
California State University, San Bernardino

Chapter 5: Know Your Issue
(Well Enough for the Toughest Questions)

§5.1 **Introduction**

Your issue needs to be analyzed and messaged before you can promote and defend it effectively. As Vidal Sassoon said, "The only place where success comes before work is in the dictionary." (Also attributed to Donald Kendall.) Chapter Five provides effective methods for researching a public policy issue and discusses special considerations so that your issue can withstand the scrutiny of opposing viewpoints in the public policy environment. The chapter contains a worksheet to assist with taking stock of your issue and specific resources to enable quick, effective, and thorough research.

Since information is power and can bring legislative advantage on a hotly contested issue, information presented in the legislative environment is often reviewed and criticized intensely from a variety of perspectives. Lobbyists and those with whom they work are frequently called upon to speak to the media and debate issue opponents. A lobbyist must know his or her issue well enough to respond to the toughest questions.

§5.2 **Prepare before the Session**

"The will to win is important, but the will to prepare is vital."
Coach Joe Paterno

Since quality research takes time, developing and honing expertise in an issue area is best done before a congressional session starts. Therefore, issue research and updates should be scheduled into a lobbyist's legislative action plan and calendar. (See Chapter Six.) Since time to research new issues is not a luxury available for most lobbyists, they must possess and refine the ability to quickly analyze, assess, and present information, so that they can respond quickly and credibly to legislative situations. However, the problem is that lobbyists, like most professionals, have not been adequately trained to conduct Internet research. According to a Convera® December 19, 2006, release entitled, *Consumer Search Engines Leave Professionals at a Loss, says Convera® Survey:*

- A commanding 95 percent of professionals find Internet search engines an aid for conducting work, yet only 40 percent are very satisfied with the results.
- Less than 25 percent are very confident that when using popular Internet search engines they've looked everywhere to find answers.
- Businesses pay employees to hunt for information that can't be found and make decisions without all the facts.
- More than 60 percent do not ask for help when they need it, while 80 percent have never been trained to use the advanced search feature.

As "knowledge power" has increased in value on Capitol Hill, and expanding resources have contributed to "legislative information overload," effective lobbyists must develop their research skills to make the most efficient use of their research time. Lobbyists in the middle of a legislative floor vote cannot waste time chasing down Internet rabbit trails. Presenting relevant and credible information, especially as it relates to

§5.3 Recommended Resources

Conducting Legislative Research

- Highly recommended: *Real World Research Skills* by Peggy Garvin, (formerly with the Congressional Research Service) available at *<www.RealWorldResearchSkills.com>*
- The following classes on conducting research are provided by TheCapitol.Net (with CEU credits available from George Mason University *<www.DCResearchSkills.com>*:
  - ◦ "Research Skills for the Real World: Going Beyond Google"
  - ◦ "Tracking and Monitoring Legislation"
  - ◦ "Searching for Legislative Intent: How to Research and Compile Legislative Histories"
- Capitol Learning Audio Courses, including "Researching Legislative Histories: Finding Legislative Intent in Bills and Committee and Conference Reports" *<www.CapitolLearning.com>*.

specific legislative constituencies, has become the new currency on Capitol Hill, and the stakes for performing excellent research, often under strict time constraints, are higher than ever. To respond quickly to developing legislative situations with research and analysis that policymakers will trust and rely upon, lobbyists must learn to think like researchers.

§5.4 Special Considerations for Legislative Research

Lobbyists must exercise caution while preparing research that will be used in the rough-and-tumble world of politics. The American League of Lobbyists' "Lobbyists' Code of Ethics" underscores the importance of providing policymakers with current and accurate information. According to the Code, when a lobbyist discovers that he or she has provided inaccurate information, the lobbyist needs to go back and notify the public official:

- *A lobbyist should be truthful in communicating with public officials and with other interested persons and should seek to provide factually correct, current and accurate information. (1.1)*
- *If a lobbyist determines that the lobbyist has provided a public official or other interested person with factually inaccurate information of a significant, relevant, and material nature, the lobbyist should promptly provide the factually accurate information to the interested person. (1.2)*
- *If a material change in factual information that the lobbyist provided previously to a public official causes the information to become inaccurate and the lobbyist knows the public official may still be relying upon the information, the lobbyist should provide accurate and updated information to the public official. (1.3)*

The full Code is in Appendix 6 and on the ALL website *<www.alldc.org>*.

§5.5 General Research Tools for Lobbyists

Tool	Description
General web search engines	Generally easy to use, free of charge, and effective for finding information that is readily available on the Internet. Examples include:
	<www.google.com>
	Highbeam offers searches of articles and includes some government documents at *<www.highbeam.com>* (titles can be retrieved without purchasing the text of the articles).
	See § 1.01, list of search engines, in *Real World Research Skills.*
	The Wayback Machine at *<www.archives.org>* for Internet archives.
Web sites for finding resources	See § 1.11 starting points on the Web, in *Real World Research Skills.*
Email alert services	See § 1.51, *Real World Research Skills.*
Blogs	See § 1.53 and § 1.54, *Real World Research Skills.*
TheCapitol.Net research links and reference tools	*<www.TheCapitol.Net/Research>* *<www.LobbyingAndAdvocacy.com>*
Transcripts and newswires	LexisNexis offers searches of print media, *<www.lexisnexis.com>*
Federal News Service (includes electronic media coverage and transcripts)	*<www.fnsg.com>*
Commercial Online Services	See § 1.53 and § 1.56, *Real World Research Skills.*
Macroreference Index	*<www.cam-info.net/enc/index.html>*
Freedom of Information Act (FOIA)	See §§ 4.50–4.51, *Real World Research Skills.*
Factiva, owned by Dow Jones Reuters Business Interactive, offers searches from Dow Jones Interactive Publications Library. Registration is free, but viewing articles is fee-based.	*<www.factiva.com>*
Opposition Research by Investigative Research Specialists, Inc.	*<www.researchops.com>*
Yearly summaries of Congressional policy decisions are available from Congressional Quarterly.	CQ Almanac Plus: *<www.cqalmanac.com>*

Links to all web resources are available on the Resources page for this book: <www.LobbyingAndAdvocacy.com>.

(Continued on page 166)

Books on Research

- *Real World Research Skills* by Peggy Garvin, a highly recommended, essential tool for today's lobbyists. *<www.RealWorldResearchSkills.com>*

- *United States Government Internet Manual*, by Peggy Garvin (Bernan Press). A solid, thorough, accessibly organized reference book of World Wide Web sites corresponding to countless institutions of the American Government, as well as state and local government information, and a special section of government information for numerous nations.

- *Internet Tools of the Profession: A Guide for Information Professionals*, 2nd edition, Hope N. Tillman (editor), paperback (Special Libraries Association, 1997). Go to *<www.sla.org>* to see links to resources provided.

- *Public Records Online: The Master Guide to Private and Government Online Sources of Public Records*, edited by Michael Sankey (Facts on Demand Press, 2006).

- *Super Searchers Go to the Source: The Interviewing and Hands-On Information Strategies of Top Primary Researchers–Online, on the Phone, and in Person*, by Risa Sacks and Reva Basch, paperback (Cyberage Books 2001). Almost 400 pages of examples, case studies, strategies, and stories. Each interview ends with a list of Super Searcher Tips, and the appendix includes helpful references to websites, databases, books and articles.

- *Super Searchers on Competitive Intelligence: The Online and Offline Secrets of Top CI Researchers*, by Margaret Metcalf and Reva Basch, paperback (Information Today 2003). This book presents 15 leading CI researchers and their hard-earned secrets. These CI researchers are from such Fortune 100 firms as Compaq Computer, Dell Computer, Lockheed Martin, Merck, and United Technologies. The tips, techniques, and models provided can be successfully applied to any business intelligence project.

Members of Congress

(See §§ 3.6–3.12 for additional resources for researching members of Congress and their constituencies.)

The Almanac of American Politics by Michael Barone and Richard E. Cohen, of National Journal Group, provides descriptions of congressional districts, states, and bios.	*<http://nationaljournal.com>*
Politics in America by CQ Press provides detailed state and district profile information.	*<http://www.cqpress.com>*
Access a printable congressional district map	*<www.nationalatlas.gov>*
Access congressional profile information and bill information with RSS feeds on all federal legislators and legislation	*<www.opencongress.org>*

Links to all web resources are available on the Resources page for this book: <www.LobbyingAndAdvocacy.com>.

Legislation

Alert services for tracking and monitoring legislation	*<www.cq.com>* *<www.gallerywatch.com>* See § 2.50, *Real World Research Skills.*
C-Span Television and Radio	*<www.cspan.org>*
Senate committee hearings and links to live audio and video of hearings in progress	*<www.openhearings.org>*
Some hearing testimony is available on Thomas.	*<www.thomas.gov>*
Published hearing testimony is generally available through the federal depository library system.	*<www.gpoaccess.gov/libraries.html>*
Congressional Quarterly's Floor Video Service	*<www.cq.com>*
Metavid—House and Senate floor proceedings	*<http://metavid.ucsc.edu>*
Congressional Record	*<www.thomas.gov>*
OMB's Earmark Database	*<www.earmarks.omb.gov>*
Congressional committee activity	*<www.thomas.gov>* *<www.gallerywatch.com>* *<www.cq.com>*
Search bills from Thomas	*<www.thomas.gov>*
New laws are posted by National Archives and Records Administration (NARA).	*<www.archives.gov>*
Public Laws Electronic Notification Service	*<www.archives.gov>*
United States Code (USC)	See §§ 2.60–2.70, *Real World Research Skills.*

States

Links to state homepages and state legislature homepages.	*<www.statelocalgov.net>*
Governor re-election schedule	*<www.nga.org>*
Political party composition of state legislatures broken down by chamber	*<www.ncsl.org>*

Links to all web resources are available on the Resources page for this book: <www.LobbyingAndAdvocacy.com>.

(Continued on page 168)

States (continued)	
Nexus of federal and state regulatory issues	Each federal agency has an intergovernmental affairs department, which monitors state legislative and regulatory activities. See §§ 3.6–3.12 for federal agency directory information or check the agency's web site for intergovernmental affairs department contact information. Many states have offices at the Hall of States on Capitol Hill.
General state issues	Search the USNewswire (also known as PRNewswire) for state information by using the following steps: 1. Go to <*www.prnewswire.com*>. 2. In the left-hand column, select "Policy and Public Interest" or "Federal and State Legislation." 3. Search all releases using a particular state name: go to the search box in the bottom left corner and put in a state name. For the full text of every governor's annual state of the state speech, go to <*www.stateline.org*>. For comprehensive state legislative monitoring and profiling (including information about existing state laws and regulations, and issues developing across states and localities), go to <*www.stateside.com/intelligence/state.shtml*>. *Governing* magazine provides a guide to city, county or state official web pages at <*www.governing.com*>. The Council of State Governments (CSG) provides the *Book of the States*, state directories, and a state news magazine at <*www.csg.org*>.
Comprehensive state legislative monitoring and profiling	<*www.stateside.com*>
Links to state legislatures	<*www.ncsl.org*>
Model state legislation	<*www.ncsl.org*>, <*www.alec.org*>, <*www.csg.org*>, <*www.stateside.com*>. National associations frequently develop issue-specific model legislation. National Conference of Commissioners on Uniform State Laws: <*www.nccusl.org*>.

Links to all web resources are available on the Resources page for this book: <www.LobbyingAndAdvocacy.com>.

Executive Branch

The Plum Book (officially titled, the *United States Government Policy and Supporting Positions*) lists the names and titles of all federal political appointees.	*<www.gpoaccess.gov/plumbook>*
U.S. Government Manual online for free. It contains very basic federal agency contact information and descriptions of federal programs.	*<www.gpoaccess.gov/gmanual/browse>*
Executive Orders	*<http://archives.gov>*
Statements of Administration Policy	*<www.whitehouse.gov>*
Executive Branch Reports to Congress	*<www.whitehouse.gov>*
OMB Officials' Testimony before Congress	*<www.whitehouse.gov/omb>*
Lobbyist databases to determine which lobbyists are contacting specific federal agencies (also searchable by state)	*<www.lobbyists.info>* or *<www.senate.gov/lobby>*
Database of federal government contracting and spending	*<www.USASpending.gov>*
USAGov—links to federal, state, and local government web sites	*<www.USA.gov>*
Executive branch staff contact information	*<www.leadershipdirectories.com>*
Search multiple government databases	*<www.gpoaccess.gov/multidb.html>*

Tracking and Monitoring Regulations

Office of Information and Regulatory Affairs (OIRA)	*<www.whitehouse.gov/omb/inforeg>*
OIRA Reports to Congress	*<www.whitehouse.gov/omb/inforeg>*
Semiannual Regulatory Agenda (Unified Agenda)	*<www.gpoaccess.gov/ua>*
Current and past regulations under review, along with comments	*<www.whitehouse.gov/omb>*
The Federal Register	*<www.gpoaccess.gov/fr>* *<www.archives.gov/federal-register>*
Proposed regulations	*<www.regulations.gov>*
Compilation of web links on federal regulations	*<http://reginfo.gov>*
Code of Federal Regulations (CFR)	*<www.gpoaccess.gov/CFR>* *<www.archives.gov/federal-register/cfr>*
RegScan (subscriber service)	*<www.regscan.com>*

Links to all web resources are available on the Resources page for this book: <www.LobbyingAndAdvocacy.com>.

(Continued on page 170)

Budget and Appropriations

President's Budget	*<www.gpoaccess.gov/usbudget>* *<www.budget.gov>* *<www.whitehouse.gov/omb>*
Federal agency testimony on appropriations bills	Library of Unified Information Sources (LOUIS, named after Supreme Court Justice Louis Brandeis) at *<www.louisdb.org>* Commercial subscription services such as *<www.gallerywatch.com>* and *<www.cq.com>* The web pages for individual congressional committees from *<www.house.gov>* or *<www.senate.gov>*
Congressional Budget Office	*<www.cbo.gov>*
U.S. House of Representatives Budget Committee	*<http://budget.house.gov>*
U.S. Senate Budget Committee	*<http://budget.senate.gov>*
U.S. House of Representatives Appropriations Committee	*<http://appropriations.house.gov>*
U.S. Senate Appropriations Committee	*<http://appropriations.senate.gov>*

Trade Publications

- The Bureau of National Affairs (BNA) offers a full range of daily public policy publications.
- Also see subject-matter trade association web sites and periodicals.

Associations

National Trade and Professional Associations and State and Regional Associations	*<www.associationexecs.com>* (A free 5-day trial is available online.)
The Gale Group provides the *Gale Encyclopedia of Associations:* *National Organizations of the U.S.,* as well as a state encyclopedia of associations.	*<www.galegroup.com>* (Register for a free trial.)
Google list	*<www.goodle.com/Top/* *Business/Associations>*

Links to all web resources are available on the Resources page for this book: <www.LobbyingAndAdvocacy.com>.

Nonprofits

Financial and organization profile information on nonprofits are available through several search engines.	If you don't see a nonprofit's Internal Revenue Service Report 990 posted voluntarily on the organization's homepage, you can search for the 990 Form and additional profile information with the following databases:
	The Guidestar database at *<www.Guidestar.org>* allows the user to locate Internal Revenue Service Report 990s in a PDF format. Additional financial information also is available for descriptions of an organization's staffing, board of directors, and goals.
	The Economic Research Institute's search engine may be accessed at *<www.eri-nonprofit-salaries.com>*.

Issue Analysis and Publications

Government Accountability Office (GAO) reports and publications	*<www.gao.gov>*
GPO Publications	*<www.access.gpo.gov>*
Library of Congress (LOC)/ Congressional Research Service (CRS) reports: An index of CRS reports, and organizations that provide CRS reports.	*<www.loc.gov/index.html>* *<www.opencrs.org>*, *<www.pennyhill.org>* CRS reports also may be obtained from your member of Congress.

Lobbyists

Information on registered lobbyists at the federal and state levels is available on several databases.	A database of federal registered lobbyists (legislative and executive branch): *<www.lobbyists.info>* by Columbia Books.
	View a lobbyist database with PDF files of actual reports filed by lobbyists on the Congressional lobbyist database at *<www.senate.gov/lobby>* and *<http://lobbyingdisclosure.house.gov>*.
	Some states provide a database of registered lobbyists online. Run a Google search (without using quotation marks): *state registered lobbyists online*.

Links to all web resources are available on the Resources page for this book: <www.LobbyingAndAdvocacy.com>.

(Continued on page 172)

Businesses	
Information on companies	*<www.goliath.com>* and *<www.sec.gov>*

International	
CIA *The World Factbook*	*<www.cia.gov>*

Media	
See § 13.51 in the *Congressional Deskbook*.	

Links to all web resources are available on the Resources page for this book: <www.LobbyingAndAdvocacy.com>.

§5.6 Ten Considerations for Lobbyists Conducting Research— 1. Double-Check and Verify Everything

Ronald Reagan's signature phrase, *"Trust but verify,"* is germane throughout the research process. As you connect with experts or organizations, be careful to make sure that you are reaching the intended source or organization. Names of individuals, organizations, Internet web pages, or legislation can be similar and easily mistaken or misspelled. Always check web page addresses after typing them to make sure that they are accurate and operational. One way of determining an organization's credibility is to check with a trusted expert in the field. It is a good idea to second-check the information's veracity with an authoritative source before forwarding the information to a policymaker or legislative staffer who may rely on the information without verifying it. Check to make sure that your intended recipient did in fact receive the information and was able to access it. See §§ 1.40–1.44, *Real World Research Skills.*

§5.7 Ten Considerations for Lobbyists Conducting Research— 2. Consider Confidentiality

Relevant information can be quickly and widely forwarded in an electronically oriented legislative environment. People you provide information to can lose a laptop or Blackberry or mistype email addresses. Information can also be forwarded to opposing interests and can be leaked to the general media. A good rule of thumb is to never put in writing anything that you wouldn't want to see on the front page of a national newspaper.

Use appropriate discretion when contacting independent-sounding think tank associations or "experts." Consider who is in charge, where they came from, that is, background of staff leaders and members of the board of directors, and campaign donations of the individuals involved. Brief junior staff about the importance of safeguarding the confidentiality of politically sensitive research projects.

§5.8 Ten Considerations for Lobbyists Conducting Research— 3. Source Everything and Give Credit Where Credit Is Due

As you verify your information, keep a thorough record of your references, since your information may be scrutinized (fairly or unfairly) in a public forum. Consider the source. One person's fact is another person's fabrication. Not everything you read on the Internet is trustworthy. Consider the political leanings of the organization. Many organizations publicly posing as "nonpartisan" have a political agenda. Research into an organization's board of directors, funding sources, and leadership can provide insight into potential biases.

Do not forward a document prepared by someone else without proper attribution. It is not only a matter of providing credit where credit is due, but there also may be problems with the document.

§5.9 Ten Considerations for Lobbyists Conducting Research— 4. Anticipate Scrutiny and Criticism

Legislative research is released into a forum where the stakes can be high and much can be gained or lost on the basis of good information that is effectively presented. Because the information can be subject to intense scrutiny and criticism, lobbyists must consider the conflicting views and what might be said about the information by opposing interests or the media.

To prepare for the scrutiny, lobbyists must critique their own work by answering the following questions:
- What are the weak points or incomplete aspects of your perspective?
- Does the information contain biases?
- Are survey results statistically significant?
- Are the questions leading?
- Is the information dated?
- Is other information more representational, current, or credible?

§5.10 Ten Considerations for Lobbyists Conducting Research— 5. Consider Where Your Information May End Up

While the information you prepare may be directed to a specific staff person or member of Congress, keep in mind that the information may be quickly forwarded to others by the person for whom you prepared it. For example, an informal or candid email may be forwarded by a legislative assistant to the chief of staff or even directly to a member of Congress. Information that you may intend for a specific person may end up being quoted on the House or Senate floor by a member of Congress months later. Make sure that the information is written in a way that would allow those unfamiliar with the issue to understand it: cite all sources, including bill numbers and names, and spell out acronyms and abbreviations. Always source your information and specify the scope and any caveats (for example, whether it's dated or limited in scope).

Congressional staffers may not acknowledge receipt of your information, but that does not mean that he or she is not utilizing it, or may not use it in the future, or that it will not be used publicly by a Senator or House member.

§5.11 Ten Considerations for Lobbyists Conducting Research—
6. Be Concise and Relevant: Tailor Your Information to the Policymaker's Interests

Use information from a senator's or House member's own state whenever possible. See §§ 3.5–3.11 for specific research resources regarding the "Seven Position Drivers" that influence a policymaker. Neither elected officials nor their staffs have time to sift through voluminous information to figure out how it might affect their constituency. If you must provide unfiltered information or information that relates to numerous states, if possible, reference specific sections up front and flag the information that is pertinent to their constituency.

§5.12 Ten Considerations for Lobbyists Conducting Research—
7. Clarify Expectations and Deadlines in Advance

What is the purpose of your information? How do you expect the information to be used and by whom? How much time will you be given to provide the information? You want to avoid developing an extensive policy paper on an issue only to be told later by the staffer that he or she needed only a few talking points, or that the senator is really just interested in a specific aspect of the issue. What format is most useful to your audience? Clarify exactly when the information is needed and provide updates on your progress. If you encounter problems that could affect your ability to meet a deadline, notify the person for whom the information will be provided as soon as possible.

§5.13 Ten Considerations for Lobbyists Conducting Research—
8. Utilize Training before the Session to Enable Efficient and Effective Research

While lobbyists should utilize environmental scanning to identify issues for research (discussed in Chapter Three), lobbyists often find themselves having to analyze an issue area very quickly, yet thoroughly and credibly. For this reason, professional development is needed to refine and update research skills before the legislative session begins. (See § 5.3 for information.)

§5.14 Ten Considerations for Lobbyists Conducting Research— 9. Consider Your Contacts: The Act of Conducting Research Itself Can Be News

Legislative research often involves confidential issues or proposals and may involve work to assist a high-profile government official. Lobbyists may also be involved in research related to hotly contested election campaigns. Simply phoning an expert on a specific sensitive issue can tip off certain groups that a proposal is being developed or a specific argument is being advanced.

For example, the *Dallas Morning News* reported that *New York Times* reporters were phoning various adoption attorneys with questions regarding unsealing John Roberts' children's adoption records at the time of his Senate confirmation consideration. The research efforts conducted by *The New York Times* reporters then became news itself when the National Council for Adoption issued the following statement denouncing *The New York Times'* decision to investigate the adoption records of Judge Roberts' two young children:

> *"The adoption community is outraged that, for obviously political reasons, the* Times *has targeted the very private circumstances, motivations, and processes by which the Roberts became parents."* The *Times* responded with a response, initially posted on Michelle Malkin's web site, stating that *"[o]ur reporters made initial inquiries about the adoptions"* and *"[t]hey did so with great care, understanding the sensitivity of the issue."*

§5.15 Ten Considerations for Lobbyists Conducting Research— 10. Opposition Research: Know Thy Enemy (and Especially Thy Enemy's Arguments)

"Every man is entitled to his own opinions,
but he is not entitled to his own facts."
Former Senator Daniel Patrick Moynihan (D-NY 1977–2001)

Arguments of interest groups allied with members of Congress often become the public arguments of members of Congress. You will need to track or check your opposition's arguments regularly through resources such as:

- Web pages and print publications.
- Publication distribution lists and widely attended events, if possible.
- Daily press updates.
- Quarterly lobbying reports at *<www.senate.gov/lobby>* or *<www.lobbyists.info>*).
- Nonprofit IRS 990 forms and additional organizational information at Guidestar *<www.guidestar.com>* or the Economic Research Institute *<www.eri-nonprofit-salaries.com>*.
- Obtain additional resources at: *<www.researchops.com>*.

§5.16 **Five Basic Steps of Public Policy Research**

1. Survey and collect pertinent existing public information (§ 5.17)
2. Identify and collect existing information from credible experts (§ 5.18)
3. Study and evaluate existing sources of information (§§ 5.19 and 5.20)
4. Develop and formulate your information (§ 5.21)
5. Update your facts, data, and arguments (§ 5.22)

§5.17 **Public Policy Research— Step 1: Survey and Collect Existing Information**

From the number of general research tools available, knowing which resources to use can make all of the difference. See § 5.5 for a list of recommended general research tools for identifying and collecting existing information. Many of the tools and resources in § 5.5 are gleaned from *Real World Research Skills* by Peggy Garvin. Garvin's book is highly recommended as an essential tool for today's lobbyists.

§5.18 **Public Policy Research— Step 2: Identify and Collect Existing Information from Experts**

Experts and insiders can be invaluable resources for unpublished information, opinions, evaluations, referrals, and an overall perspective on your issue. Consider whether email, a phone conversation, or an in-person meeting would be the best format for gathering information. When contacting a source, be sure to introduce yourself, explain why you are making the contact, ask your questions, and listen carefully to the answers. When concluding, verify follow-up information and make sure to thank the person, even if they cannot provide you with what you need.

See §§ 6.00–6.02 in *Real World Research Skills*.

§5.19 **Public Policy Research— Step 3: Study and Evaluate Existing Sources of Information**

"Knowledge is power."
Sir Francis Bacon

The following template will assist you in taking stock of your issue:

§5.20 Issue Evaluation Template

Aspect of Issue	Existing Information and Resources	Additional Information Needed
History (including legislative, regulatory, and legal)		
Current practice/trends		
Practical, short-term and long-term ramifications		
Surveys		
Public opinion polls		
Direct consequences:		
Universe of affected parties		
Who or what benefits and how?		
Who or what is negatively affected?		
Indirect consequences:		
Are there others indirectly affected? What are potential unintended consequences?		
Costs/benefits analysis:		
Has GAO conducted a report?		
Have think tanks examined the issue?		
Who are your opponents?		
What are your opponents' arguments and how are you rebutting them?		
Who are your allies? What are your allies saying and doing? Is the message consistent or complementary? How are they different? Could information released by current allies undercut your message or information?		
What are the most politically attractive arguments in light of the current political environment? (See § 3.15 for a Worksheet for Evaluating the Political Environment.) How can your message be shaped to maximize its impact based on the current environment, trends, and news cycles?		

§5.20 Issue Evaluation Template (continued)

Aspect of Issue	Existing Information and Resources	Additional Information Needed
What information have you prepared for your grassroots? What else is needed to maximize the effort? What is the schedule for providing additional grassroots resources?		
What is the current message in the media? What are the other messages out there that need to be countered, modified, or reinforced?		
What media strategies are being employed by the opposition?		
What are the leading studies and reports associated with the issue and what is the message gleaned from them?		
What are the implications of state laws, regulations, or practices?		
What are the overall political risks for policymakers who support your cause? How can the risks be diminished?		
Identify experts:		
What resources are opponents putting into it? What resources are you able to put into it?		
Anecdotes (including outside the beltway spokespersons and examples)		
Inspiring quotations		
Political considerations:		
How will the issue provide visibility or strengthen constituent relationships for the policymaker?	(See §§ 3.6–3.12 for additional resources for researching members of Congress and their constituencies.)	

§5.21 Public Policy Research— Step 4: Develop and Formulate Your Information

Select the most effective approaches and communication delivery methods for your message based on current practices, your legislative strategy, and your resources. See Chapter Ten for a discussion of effective methods for communicating your issue in the public arena.

What do you have, and what do you need? Who is the audience? Consider the following formats:

- **One-pager (Fact Sheet):** Lobbyists need to be able to boil their issue down to a "one-pager" for Hill visits. (See § 8.30.)
- **Position Papers/Principles:** Especially useful within your own organization to communicate your official position, for example, policies approved by your board of directors on broad issues. Organizations frequently establish principles that are designed to enable them to respond to specific legislative or regulatory proposals over the long-term.
- **Frequently Asked Questions (FAQs) and Answers:** Useful for policymakers, grassroots, and the media.
- **Myths vs. Realities:** Particularly useful when confronted with a need to counter several opposing arguments.
- **Surveys and Public Opinion Polls:** Surveys and public opinion polls can be extremely useful, but lengthy surveys must be summarized in a press release or cover letter given policymakers' time constraints. What is the bottom line? Why does the member of Congress need to know the information? Highlighting a survey's findings from the policymaker's constituency can be especially effective.
- **Photographs, Charts, and Graphs:** Pictures are worth a thousand words. Members of Congress frequently use charts and oversized photographs of individuals and locations during committee meetings and on the House or Senate floor. Advocates frequently use graphics in congressional testimony, press briefings, and correspondence. After obtaining congressional staff approval and meeting specific measurement requirements, congressional witnesses often bring oversized charts with them to display on an easel during their testimony.
- **Timelines:** Timelines can be an effective method of graphically conveying the sequence of several key events in order to emphasize a particular point.
- **Briefing Books:** Briefing books should be used sparingly. Most policymakers don't have time to read one or the space to store one. However, briefing books are very useful for preparing congressional witnesses. See Chapter Ten for information on preparing a congressional briefing book including sample briefing book contents.
- **Elevator Speech:** Every lobbyist needs to rehearse an elevator speech on each of his or her issues. Lobbyists are frequently asked to discuss their priorities and explain their issues in a few minutes or even a few seconds.

How to effectively present your message to policymakers is addressed in Chapter Eight.

§5.22 Public Policy Research—
Step 5: Update Your Facts, Data, and Arguments

Those people who develop the ability to continuously acquire new and better forms of knowledge that they can apply to their work and to their lives will be the movers and shakers in our society for the indefinite future.
Brian Tracy

Presenting obsolete information is a good way to lose credibility. Build issue-analysis updates into your legislative action plan, and schedule periodic reviews to ensure currency. (See Chapter Six.) Establish a free flow of information with experts who will periodically furnish you with updates on your issues of concern.

§5.23 Frequent Mistakes Lobbyists Make in
Providing Information to Policymakers

The following list addresses some of the frequent mistakes lobbyists make when providing information to policymakers.

- Providing too much information: Lobbyists need to understand the constraints on congressional staff and members' time and only provide information that they can use. (Lobbyists need to get to the bottom line quickly and then present the backup.)
- Lobbyist's contact information is not clearly available at top of document or on front cover.
- Providing old information.
- Information is not verified.
- Information is not sourced.
- Failure to check the legitimacy of source.
- Failure to check the currency of information.
- Presenting rumor as fact.
- Failure to consider the information's ownership, confidentiality, attribution, legal limits, copyright, privacy, or national security implications.
- Information that makes your friends, allies, and supporters look bad.

"Knowledge will forever govern ignorance. And a people who mean to be their own governors must arm themselves with the power that knowledge gives."
James Madison

§5.99 Chapter Summary

- Plan to include time for researching your issue, but also be prepared to quickly analyze and present information when needed (§ 5.2). Use the recommended resources in § 5.3 for tips on conducting research.

- Knowing which resources to use can make all of the difference. Included in § 5.5 are extensive resources for research, including identifying members of Congress, tracking and monitoring regulations, issue analysis, and publications. Also included are a list of books on research.

- Lobbyists must carefully check sources and information for accuracy. If inaccurate information is disseminated, it should be corrected according to the policies set forth in the Lobbyists' Code of Ethics. (§ 5.6)

- Always consider confidentiality, and remember that you never know where the information may be sent once it leaves your hands. Ensure that information is cited properly, giving credit to other individuals when necessary. (§§ 5.7, 5.8)

- Remember to only provide information that the policymaker needs. Clarify in advance the format for the information as well as deadlines. (§§ 5.11, 5.12)

- Be sure to research and anticipate the arguments of the opposition and critique your own work in advance of scrutiny by your opponents or the media. Know that the act of research itself may give advance notice to others that your issue is being developed. (§§ 5.9, 5.14)

- Use the Issue Evaluation Template in § 5.20 to study each aspect of your issue. Determine what information you have and what you need on the history of your issue, current practices and trends, and short and long-term ramifications. Assess the effect your issue has on other parties, and whether a cost/benefit analysis has been conducted. Review your opponents and allies, as well as their messages, resources, and strategies. (§ 5.20)

- Select a format to communicate your message. A one-page fact sheet is essential, and a position paper expresses the position of your organization. Anticipating a list of frequently asked questions and their answers can be helpful, and preparing a list of myths vs. realities enables you to counter opposing arguments. Determine whether it is productive to include surveys and opinion polls, as well as photos, charts, graphs, or timelines. (§ 5.21)

- Avoid common mistakes, such as providing too much information, not presenting your information clearly, and giving old, outdated, or unverified information. Always check the legitimacy of your source and the currency of your information, and never present rumor as fact, or disseminate anything that would be unintentionally damaging to your allies and supporters. (§§ 5.22, 5.23)

CHAPTER 6

Build the Right Plan

"The road to success is always under construction."

John W. Patten, President, *Business Week*

Chapter 6: Build the Right Plan

§6.1 **Introduction**

"The afternoon knows what the morning never suspected."
Swedish Proverb

A high-pressure legislative environment presents challenges to getting out of the weeds and thinking strategically. However, organizations that take the time to invest significantly in strategic government affairs, goal updates, and staff training and development have reaped many rewards in both the short- and long-terms. These rewards include sustained legislative successes, effective representation of member or client interests as situations change, improved relationships (externally and internally), and crisis and failure avoidance.

Chapter Six outlines the necessary steps for creating and maintaining an effective government affairs planning process. This chapter also concentrates on determining the needs of your members or clients, evaluating and planning issues, and determining long-term goals, as well as updating and revising your plan as necessary.

§6.2 **Basic Government Affairs Planning Strategies**

Several basic strategies must be considered to assist with effective government affairs planning:

1. Plan your planning. If practical and feasible, schedule strategic planning sessions during congressional recesses or other times when lobbying work may be slow. Planning requires intensive concentration and freedom from distractions.

2. Remove distractions and obtain expertise. As with all strategic planning, an external facilitator and a change of venue can help your legislative team develop fresh perspectives and new synergies as you revamp and refine your plans. To minimize interruptions, establish some ground rules for using electronic devices such as cell phones and Blackberries.

3. Expect the unexpected. Build flexibility into your plans and resources to allow for unexpected developments and new issues.

4. Set priorities. Effective lobbyists must balance advocacy, communication with those they represent, and internal organizational responsibilities. They are constantly setting priorities in their work to maintain the proper balance between monitoring legislation and actually influencing it. Lobbyists are especially challenged to balance:

- Advocacy work (direct lobbying),
- Interacting with those they represent,
- Departmental and inter-departmental organizational activities, and
- Activities to meet long-term goals that may require sustained effort over time.

5. Work with the end in mind. Reactive activities in the heat of a session can sometimes inadvertently reflect a "ready, fire, aim" rather than a "ready, aim, fire" approach. Legislative and executive branch action plans are essential in preparing for an upcoming legislative session. As Stephen Covey said in *The 7 Habits of Highly Effective People*, "Start by keeping the end in mind." Picture yourself giving a presentation at the end of the year to your stakeholders (members, leaders, employees, or clients). What would you be the most proud to announce? What would they most like to hear? Then develop a plan and go out and make it happen.

An important input to the planning process is incorporating key legislative dates, cycles, and lobbying activities. See Appendix 5 for a "Lobbyists' Annual Calendar: Key Dates and Activities Template" with important congressional schedule, regulatory announcements, and compliance dates that you can incorporate into your planning and goals.

§6.3 Turning Planning into Execution

Most of us recognize this all-too-common experience: Your organization or client conducts an intensive strategic planning session, often off-site and facilitated by planning experts. During the session the enthusiasm is evident and contagious, and the participants seem to "catch the vision." Then the session ends, and everyone returns to their regular jobs and routine; after a few days the strategic plan occupies a comfortable space on desks or shelves, or remains in a folder on your organization's network drive, somewhat forgotten. No doubt, managers and staff will refer to it on occasion, and it might be brought up in monthly and quarterly meetings, but once the enthusiasm wanes, the vision fades and somehow, the plan simply does not live up to its billing once the rubber hits the road. To avoid this disappointment, planning must be integrated into your overall efforts, and must be used as a guiding compass for daily activities. The following diagram illustrates the role planning and strategy play in the context of integrated business functions associated with lobbying, public policy, and legislative actions.

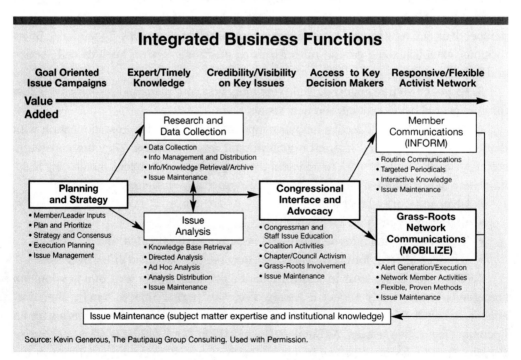

Source: Kevin Generous, The Pautipaug Group Consulting. Used with Permission.

§6.4 Ten Steps of Legislative Action Planning

The major steps to building and maintaining a legislative action plan are as follows:

- **Step 1:** Obtain Member or Client Input (§ 6.5)
- **Step 2:** Evaluate the Political, Legislative, Regulatory, and Judicial Environments (§ 6.6)
- **Step 3:** Consider Your Organization's History and Capabilities (§ 6.7)
- **Step 4:** Prepare for Planning (§ 6.8)
- **Step 5:** Identify and Prioritize Your Issues (§ 6.9)
- **Step 6:** Develop Legislative and Regulatory Action Plans with Goals for Each Issue (§ 6.10)
- **Step 7:** Emphasize Long-Term Goals (§ 6.11)
- **Step 8:** Establish Short-Term Priorities with Metrics to Measure Achievement (§ 6.12)
- **Step 9:** Regularly Update the Plan (§ 6.13)
- **Step 10:** Communicate Your Successes (§ 6.14)

§6.5 Legislative Action Planning— Step 1: Obtain Member or Client Input

"Every well-built house started with a definite plan in the form of blueprints."
Napoleon Hill

Determining the concerns, priorities, and preferences of your members or clients is the foundation for effective planning. Given the nature of the legislative environment, it is important to identify issues, receive direction from those you represent, and develop broad-based principles and policy statements reflecting their concerns.

Methods to utilize:

- Surveys
- Committees of member experts
- Focus groups
- Member meetings and discussions (local chapters, etc.)
- Specific comments provided by individuals (relationships with member experts, large number of complaints)

Strategies to Maximize Effectiveness:

Think Long-Term

Design survey questions and other feedback tools to receive input on both general and specific parts of an issue as well as short- and long-term issues.

Have a Rapid Response Mechanism and Expert Contacts in the Wings

Have a process in place for quick input by members so that you can address and respond to urgent issues that surface quickly, while maintaining your responsibility to represent your members. A legislative committee or board, a quick mini-survey of your grassroots network, or a sampling of your membership can not only provide guidance and justification for taking a position, it also can provide timely and useful information when communicating with policymakers.

Know When Not to Take a Position

When survey results are mixed or a position is unknown, it may be in your members' or clients' best interest to refrain from taking a position. In that circumstance, you can notify the membership of the impending legislative action and let them weigh in with policymakers individually when time does not permit official position development. It is better to remain silent on an issue than to compromise your position development process and risk misrepresenting your members or clients and their interests. For example, in 1989, the national representatives of the American Association of Retired Persons (AARP) took a position to Capitol Hill supporting a catastrophic health-care bill without checking with their dues-paying grassroots members. The measure was swiftly enacted. When AARP's grassroots members learned about the new law and the controversial position taken by their national organization, they chased down members of Congress in the street and lobbied on Capitol Hill opposing their national organization's position. Within a year, the provision was repealed. AARP's reputation suffered for several years and the lobbying efforts of their national representatives were greatly impeded because members of Congress questioned whether the organization's lobbyists really reflected the view of their constituency.

Results to Aim For

- Compile a list of issues, concerns, positions, and opinions of various potential member, client, or organization spokespersons.
- Set priorities for issues in order of importance and intensity of opinions by members.
- Capture perceived risks, impacts, and benefits to members on each issue.
- Solicit and obtain additional information, documentation, expertise, and "real world" knowledge of how the issue truly impacts people and organizations.
- Integrate your information-gathering efforts into supporting efforts to build a network of members that is active, informed, and comfortable with providing you with regular and candid feedback, including a cadre of true experts with in-depth knowledge. (See Chapter Seven addressing grassroots for more information.)
- Educate members on potential pitfalls, unintended consequences of legislation, little-known facts, and so forth.

§6.6 Legislative Action Planning— Step 2: Evaluate the Political, Legislative, Regulatory, and Judicial Environments

Information and data, once gathered, should be analyzed as part of the planning process. Consider the political and legislative environment as part of your planning:

- Macro-environmental factors, such as, economic upturns and downturns, natural disasters, wars, and international politics. (See § 3.15 for a worksheet to use for evaluating environmental factors.)
- Changes associated with your issues (take stock of your issue periodically using the worksheet in § 3.15):
  - Events impacting the issue
  - Publicity regarding the issue
  - Shifts in public opinion
  - New studies or reports issued or published
- Changes in the legislative and regulatory environments (see §§ 3.15, 3.20, and 3.23 for recommended resources for monitoring changes in the legislative environment):
  - Makeup of Congress, leadership, or committee chairs
  - Congressional agenda and priorities
  - New bills and legislation introduced, moving through committee, passed, or enacted
  - Changes in the executive branch agenda as well as changes in executive branch staff
  - Changes to lobbying laws and rules (see § 2.3)
- Potential judicial decisions that could trigger or shape legislative action
- Changes to other stakeholders and coalitions (see Chapter Nine):
  - New and existing supporters and opponents on the issue
  - New initiatives and strategies adopted by supporters and opponent organizations
  - Changes to the makeup of coalitions, coalition strategies and priorities, a new competing coalition, etc. (See Chapter Nine for tips on maintaining your priorities within your coalitions.)
- Changes to your organization or client:
  - Internal changes within the organization or client organization that could impact legislative representation and government affairs; for example, a new CEO with different priorities, new spokespersons who need to be trained, a new board of directors that wants to emphasize a certain issue, or a new event, program, or publication that needs to be coordinated with government affairs activities

Through this analysis, identify the opportunities and threats posed by your environment, and changes to the environment. List the opportunities and threats for consideration of how they may impact your planning goals, priorities, and schedules.

§6.7 Legislative Action Planning—
Step 3: Consider Your Organization's History and Capabilities

History

British statesman Edmund Burke once said, "Those who don't know history are destined to repeat it." Similarly, those who don't know the legislative and public policy history of their own organization are destined to reinvent the wheel or encounter embarrassment. Some politicians never forget. Imagine your CEO caught off-guard by a congressional committee chairman's criticism of your organization's past legislative position, activity, or faux pas. You will be better able to respond if you are well-versed in your organization's history. A friend shared this story with me: he was doing damage control with an important congressional committee chairman. A department staff person had made a key promise to a member of Congress, but in the shuffle of a staff transition, the promise to the member of Congress was forgotten. The broken promise infuriated the committee chairman, who happened to be critical to their interests.

Considering Capabilities

- Consider your organization's or client's leadership support for lobbying and government affairs. In what ways can this support be strengthened or improved?
- Evaluate how each of the following functions in your organization support and integrate with the government affairs function. How can government affairs better support the other organizational functions, which can be challenging given unpredictable legislative schedules?
  - Media and public affairs
  - Technology (how it can be leveraged to assist in your research and communications)
  - Printing, graphics, and publications support
  - Membership (how new members can be recruited for the organization and for the grassroots efforts, etc.)
- Assess the knowledge and skills possessed by your team, including consultants (both in terms of the legislative and regulatory process), research, contacts, and issues. (An evaluation and planning by issue exercise follows in § 6.10, and managing performance is addressed in Chapter Eleven.)
- What level of resources and funding is available for governmental affairs? How are government affairs resources being spent?
- Describe your organization's reputation on Capitol Hill, in the executive branch agencies, state legislators, etc. What are your "reputational goals"? What are specific areas that need to be strengthened or improved? Do policymakers approach your organization for input and expertise?

It is important to know the history of specific legislative issues, your organization's or client's positions taken, advocacy successes and failures, as well as any government officials who were offended or critical of your organization or client in the process. If your organization or client took a controversial position in the past, how will you address it if it is referenced in the future? How did your organization or client justify the position at the time, or how can the position be explained in the context of current issues? Were there specific criticisms from key policymakers or the press?

Maintain a useful legislative archive system (with backup) that includes information on congressional contacts from all of your staff members. See Chapter Eleven for recommendations on establishing and maintaining useful government affairs databases and archive systems.

§6.8 Legislative Action Planning— Step 4: Prepare for Planning

"The journey of a thousand miles begins with a vision."
Anonymous

Set the stage for your planning efforts:
- Review your organization's mission statement and how it relates to your governmental affairs efforts.
- Review the government affairs aspects of your organization's strategic plan.
- Solicit and evaluate the priorities and concerns of your organization's leadership (or those of your clients).
- Assess your specific government affairs goals. Do you have clearly defined, time-specific, and measurable goals in place for your government affairs program? If not, how can they be established or clarified?

§6.9 Legislative Action Planning— Step 5: Identify and Prioritize Your Issues

Identifying and prioritizing your current and future issues is a challenging, yet central, aspect to government affairs successes. Synthesize the information gathered from your members or clients, the environment, and your organization, and use the results to develop or update your list of issues that concern you and your members, clients, or organization.

While you may be expected to at least monitor every issue that could impact your members or clients, remember that there is great power in focus. Not everything can be priority Number One. What are your "must win issues"? What are the lower priority issues? Making a deliberate decision to de-emphasize certain issues, eliminate certain low-priority goals or activities, or reduce your activity in certain coalitions can help you focus your efforts, resources, and activities on those that matter most. Remember to stay in close communication with those you represent to ensure that your priorities match their interests.

§6.10 Legislative Action Planning— Step 6: Develop Legislative and Regulatory Action Plans with Specific Goals for Each Issue

"Although we strive for excellence, we set sensible goals because one of the most frustrating things in the world is to set our goals so high that we have no chance of reaching them."
Bart Starr

You will need to evaluate and develop a legislative action plan with specific goals for each issue. As you evaluate and develop goals for each issue, consider the following:

- Incorporate priority ranking into your legislative action plan. Remember that you have limited staffing and resources. Avoid the temptation to develop excessively ambitious goals, particularly for issues that may be of secondary importance. Your clients, members, or staff easily can be demoralized by unrealistic expectations.
- As you plan, identify how your issues relate to one another, and how you can create synergy between multiple issues and contacts.
- Assign specific responsibility for action steps, along with measurable outcomes and deadlines.

The following planning framework example can be adopted or modified to meet your organizational needs.

Legislative or Regulatory Issue Planning Worksheet

Issue Title/Description:

Identify a specific individual with lead responsibility on the issue as well as others who share responsibility (consistent with LDA filings):

- Name of individual with primary responsibility
- Names of individuals with secondary or back-up responsibility (especially useful in staff transitions or during staff absences or unavailability)

Importance: (score or ranking)

Organization's or client's official statement of position:

Details of organization's or client's position (specific member/client concerns and requests on the issue):

Long-term objective (3-5 years):

Short-term objective (this legislative session):

Opportunities/threats posed by the current/anticipated environment:

Political obstacles:

Opponents' likely strategy:

Risks, key upcoming dates or deadlines to note, and possible future events/trends to monitor:

Planning Area	Describe As-Is	Target/Objective	Action Steps
Lobbyists' issue research (see Chapter Five)			
Monitoring and tracking of legislation and regulations			
Educating grassroots on issue			
Coordinating with coalitions/partners			
Select/prioritize target members/legislators/staff /agencies/officials. For anticipated new bills, plan to secure a sponsor and co-sponsors.			
Develop messaging			
Work media to get message out			
Contact/visit members/ legislators/staff/agencies/ officials			
Alert grassroots to personally contact members/legislators/ staff/agencies/officials			
Develop and present comments to Congress, state legislatures, and/or executive agencies			
Pass or advance friendly legislation			
Stop or slow hostile legislation			
Internal staffing dedicated or available for the issue			
Budget dedicated or available for the issue in specific areas			

§6.11 Legislative Action Planning— Step 7: Emphasize Long-Term Goals

"If you don't know where you're going, you will probably end up there."
Yogi Berra

While much of your day-to-day focus will be necessarily on issue-specific lobbying activities, much of your long-term success will hinge on the overall capabilities, prioritization of resources, and infrastructure that you plan and develop over time. (Providing professional development for government affairs staff is addressed in Chapter Eleven.) Consider incorporating the following long-term goals in your government affairs planning.

Staffing and Consultant Development

See Chapter Eleven for details addressing the following topics that should be included in your planning:

- Recruiting (from Capitol Hill or the executive branch)
- Skills and knowledge enhancement (research, ethics compliance)
- Evaluating performance (goal-setting and self-appraisals)
- Motivation, incentives, and compensation
- Selecting, acquiring, and managing consultants

Grassroots Recruiting and Development

See Chapter Seven for details addressing the following topics that should be included in your Grassroots Action Plan goals:

- Identifying and reaching individuals and groups that may join or support your organization or client effort;
- Recruiting and organizing new activists;
- Educating, training, and equipping grassroots members;
- Identifying and organizing leaders and special experts among your grassroots;
- Obtaining sufficient input from your members and supporters;
- Training constituents on how to effectively interact with legislators in their home districts, for example, how to host a visit from a member of Congress (addressed in Chapter Seven) and participation in town hall meetings hosted by members of Congress;
- Coordinating and managing a Capitol Hill Day/Legislative Conference;
- Ensuring recognition of grassroots accomplishments;
- Ensuring that grassroots members or clients are satisfied with your positions, priorities, strategies, and accomplishments;
- Increasing the quality and number of contacts by grassroots members to members of Congress.

Research Capability

See Chapter Five for details addressing the following topics that should be included in your planning:

1. Surveying and collecting pertinent existing public information
2. Identifying and collecting existing information from credible experts
3. Studying and evaluating existing sources of information
4. Developing and formulating your information
5. Updating your facts, data, and arguments

Media Relations

See Chapter Ten for details addressing media relations including:

- Positive visibility (if desired) in the public, press, and on the Hill
- Number of hits, effectiveness of the coverage, in what media, number of readers/viewers, nature of coverage, and feedback received

Coalition Development

See Chapter Nine for details regarding coalition development including:

- Leadership role within a coalition in order to advance your members'/clients' interests
- Building stronger coalition relationships—role in coalitions and meetings on behalf of those whom you represent, not just the visibility gained, but also the extent of actual or meaningful contributions toward success on behalf of those whom you represent. Another important coalition goal is to avoid being associated with positions that do not represent your organization or client.

Congressional, State Legislative, and Executive Branch Relationships

Planning should concentrate on:

- Relationship building and goodwill efforts with key members, committees, legislators, executive agencies, and public officials. This is difficult to quantify since credibility is so important, but consider evaluating your relationships with members and staff, at least informally.
- Quality and number of meetings and visits.
- Key staffers seeking assistance and utilizing the organization's information and input.
- Assisting congressional staffers and members with information, strategy, advice, coordination, etc. To what extent do they use or rely on that information?
- If you value visibility, perhaps you would like to set a goal on the number of times that you testify before Congress or submit written testimony. Of course, the quality of the appearance or submission is extremely important, but each appearance or submission on the record provides visibility for your organization with policymakers and throughout the policymaking community.

Integration of Efforts with Other Components of Your Organization or Client Organization

See Chapter Eleven for details addressing the following topics that should be included in your planning:
- Establishing win-win relationships with other functions within your organization such as membership relations and services, issues management, information technology, legal compliance, accounting, media, graphics, printing, and publications, to include such elements as:
  - Sharing information
  - Integrating scheduling in advance of events and requirements
  - Communicating effectively
  - Coordinating priorities and activities
  - Sharing resources, tools and systems

Budgeting and Resource Allocation

See Chapter Eleven for details addressing the following topics that should be included in your planning:
- Reviewing prior years' budgets and actual spending
- Consider major new requirements or initiatives that will require resources
- Identify areas of savings and improved efficiencies
- Develop budget
- Pitch budget and priorities to your organization or client
- Establish systems and procedures to track actual spending, and revenue, if applicable, against your budget (consistent with disclosure filings)

Develop Regulatory Action Plan

Most of the elements of issue planning addressed in the previous section should apply. In addition, consider the following in your planning efforts:
- Build in a review of the administration's Semiannual Regulatory Agenda (Unified Agenda). (See the Lobbyist's Annual Calendar: Key Dates and Activities Template in Appendix 5.)
- Build in any anticipated regulatory comment periods and associated deadlines (or estimated deadlines, if unknown).
- Develop objectives related to submitting comments under various scenarios, such as, seeking input from membership or clients, experts, and consultants.
- Set targets for quantity and quality of comments submitted and included in the public record on key regulatory priorities. Perhaps they were referenced by policymakers in the final rule, quoted by the media or cited by members of Congress in a letter to the agency or during a public hearing. Did the comments make a difference?
- Consider ways to increase your organization's credibility and influence in the long-term with key policymakers in the executive branch, such as inviting officials to speak or participate in events. (See § 2.3 for ethics restrictions.)

Coordinating State/Local and Federal Efforts

The skilled federal lobbyist is also aware of (and likely involved in) state or local public policy activity on his or her issues. This is because federal lobbyists have long recognized that state legislative activities can drive federal legislation and affect the political disposition of federal policymakers toward an issue. Members of Congress frequently publicly point to the experience of their states in making the case for or against federal legislation or regulations. Do laws on your issue already exist in certain states? If so, how might they influence policy at the federal level? Consider objectives such as:

- Promoting or opposing state legislation (for example, developing talking points or model legislation)
- Finding opportunities for state legislators or governors to testify before Congress
- Using a state law as a model for federal legislation or a number of state laws to make the case for a certain federal law.

The following table lists the strategic planning goal areas discussed in this chapter and may be customized for your organization.

Planning Area	Describe As-Is	Target/Objective	Action Steps
Staffing and consultant development			
Grassroots recruiting and development			
Research capability			
Media relations			
Coalition development			
Congressional/state legislature/executive branch relationships			
Integration of efforts with other components of your organization or client organization			
Budgeting and resource allocation			
Development of Regulatory Action Plan			
Coordination between federal, state, and local issues			

§6.12 Legislative Action Planning—
Step 8: Establish Short-Term Priorities
with Metrics to Measure Achievement

You will need to establish and maintain a system that will regularly measure and evaluate progress, accomplishments, and performance and then recognize successes in tangible ways. While much government affairs work is difficult to quantify, some performance-based outputs can be effectively quantified with a little thought and effort. See Chapter Eleven for suggestions for linking staff performance to goal achievement. Remember, you will get more of whatever is measured, tracked and rewarded, regardless of whether or not you are conscious of your informal rewards system. In the absence of an effective goal-tracking system, specific unspoken goals can become paramount, such as, getting press for the organization or impressing board members, at the expense of other important, but less visible goals. Examples of areas that might be quantified and tied to employee performance are included in Chapter Eleven.

§6.13 Legislative Action Planning—
Step 9: Regularly Update the Plan

"For time and the world do not stand still. Change is the law of life. And those who look only to the past or the present are certain to miss the future."
John F. Kennedy

Legislative plans tend to have a short shelf life. Political winds shift quickly. New issues emerge suddenly in response to national and international events and associated national news cycles. An unexpected development can instantly kill the prospects of a once-promising priority. Continually update your approach as situations evolve, but establish specific reporting deadlines, for example, quarterly, for goal achievements. Set aside time during each congressional recess to update your plans.

A new contingency plan may need to be incorporated. An election or a new development such as the resignation of a key administration contact or congressional ally may necessitate reevaluating the bottom line of what your organization is willing to accept. Update fallback positions (or "doomsday" plans) as situations warrant. What are the new options under the worst-case scenario, and what would your organization accept under various scenarios? How will you coordinate with your allies on potential compromises? Don't compromise too early or too late. Maintaining relevant plans for various scenarios will produce sound decisions when the heat is on.

"There is no point at which you can say,
'Well, I'm successful. I might as well take a nap.'"
Carrie Fisher

Continually identify new interests and clarify priorities as circumstances change. Check with your members or clients periodically to ensure effective representation and resource allocation.

§6.14 Legislative Action Planning— Step 10: Communicate Your Successes

Communicating successes will help you generate more buy-in and involvement at all levels within your organization:

- How have your government activities and successes contributed to advancing your organization's goals?
- Have you stopped or delayed legislation that would have cost your members or clients millions of dollars to implement?
- Have you been instrumental in achieving passage of legislation that has had significant benefits?
- Have you changed legislation to make it work more effectively for those whom you represent?
- Have you contributed to member, employee, or client retention or expansion?
- Have you provided press or other types of visibility that have increased the credibility of your organization?
- Will the visibility you received help your organization compete to recruit new members and to retain existing members?
- Did you avoid potential criticisms from members, employees, or clients for not taking an active role on an issue important to them?
- How has your government affairs work contributed toward the bottom line?

Be sure to communicate success to your members, and give credit to your members or clients whenever possible.

§6.15 Tips for Executing Your Plan

Your message must be communicated proactively to maximize your ability to shape positions. Your strategies must also be customized and adapted as situations change. Officials or staff that you were counting on may resign, be replaced, or forget your issue. Unexpected deals may be cut, legislators may change their minds at the last moment, and conflicts within coalitions may cause immediate problems that must be addressed. New players can enter the scene with undeveloped but politically attractive alternative proposals. One press article or vivid story presented by a member of Congress can change the entire legislative climate on an issue.

Flexibility is often required in refining your approach and finding the right vehicle for a proposal. Your House strategy may be very different from your Senate strategy and your methods may vary from committee to committee and member to member. You must

---

§6.16 Quotes for Overcoming Obstacles

"Obstacles are those frightful things you see when you take your eyes off your goal."
—Henry Ford

"Being defeated is often a temporary condition. Giving up is what makes it permanent."
—Marilyn vos Savant

"Failure is a part of success. There is no such thing as a bed of roses all your life. But failure will never stand in the way of success if you learn from it."
—Hank Aaron

"Problems cannot be solved by the same level of thinking that created them."
—Albert Einstein

---

be flexible to deal with a range of obstacles including partisan conflicts, coalition divisions, and tender egos.

Effective lobbyists plan for various scenarios, but respond swiftly and competently when confronted with unexpected developments, obstacles, failures, or disappointments.

§6.99 Chapter Summary

- During strategic-planning discussions, brainstorm areas such as: issue development, the relative prioritization of issues, fall-back strategies, coalition involvement, and risk evaluation to assess priorities and determine long-term goals. Organize each of your strategic goals with specific action items. (§§ 6.2, 6.3)
- Surveying your members to determine their opinions and priorities will enable you to represent your constituency effectively. Build a network of active, informed members who can provide you with regular and candid feedback. (§ 6.5)
- The Ten Steps of the Government Affairs Planning Process are discussed:
  - Step 1: Obtain Member or Client Input (§ 6.5)
  - Step 2: Evaluate the Political, Legislative, Regulatory, and Judicial Environments (§ 6.6)
  - Step 3: Consider Your Organization's History and Capabilities (§ 6.7)
  - Step 4: Prepare for Planning (§ 6.8)
  - Step 5: Identify and Prioritize Your Issues (§ 6.9)
  - Step 6: Develop Legislative and Regulatory Action Plans with Goals for Each Issue (§ 6.10)
  - Step 7: Emphasize Long-Term Goals (§ 6.11)

- Step 8: Establish Short-Term Priorities with Metrics to Measure Achievement (§ 6.12)
- Step 9: Regularly Update the Plan (§ 6.13)
- Step 10: Communicate your Successes (§ 6.14)

- Familiarize yourself with your organization's legislative history, including advocacy successes and failures. Maintain a legislative archive system, including contact information and your organization's relationship history with specific members of Congress. (§ 6.7)

- Create specific goals that reflect your members' priorities and your strategic plan. Recognize the need to develop a system to accommodate changing priorities. (§§ 6.10, 6.13)

- Develop legislative and regulatory action plans, and establish and enforce deadlines to keep your plan updated. Think through obstacles and opponents' strategies, prioritize goals, and track and communicate your successes. Give ownership and responsibility to specific individuals by connecting the achievement for each goal to individual performance evaluations and salary reviews. (§§ 6.11, 6.13, 6.14)

Develop, Never Devalue, Grassroots

"We in America do not have government by the majority. We have government by the majority who participate."

Thomas Jefferson

Chapter 7: Develop, Never Devalue, Grassroots

§7.1 **Introduction**

As discussed in Chapter Six, constituent contacts are the most effective type of congressional communication. They are more effective because all members of Congress are motivated by the same thing: getting re-elected. However, in the press of legislative activity, it is easy for professional lobbyists to forget that the strongest force in the political process is the individual constituent. Too frequently, lobbyists become consumed by "inside the (Washington, DC) beltway" politics at the expense of informing, equipping, and alerting the affected citizens who are best positioned to determine the outcome. In essence, "the law of lost perspective" is an axiom that is too often illustrated by those who tend to lose perspective after serving in positions of power for several years.

Lobbyists recognize the importance of activating grassroots when they need them for an important vote, but often overlook adequate training "out of season" that makes effective activation possible. Some concerned citizens are reluctant to participate because they don't think they can make a difference, or they think that they lack adequate political experience to get involved. An underrated and underappreciated, but critical aspect of effective lobbying involves equipping and motivating affected citizens to become involved in the American political process.

Chapter Seven highlights the critical need of citizen involvement. Grassroots development tips are provided to assist the lobbyist in organizing and maintaining an effective citizen network. Sample material is provided as a model to overcome "involvement inhibitors" by motivating citizens to become more involved.

> *"Each of the great social achievements of recent decades has come about not because of government proclamations but because people organized, made demands and made it good politics to respond. It is the political will of the people that makes and sustains the political will of governments."*
> James P. Grant, Former Executive Director, UNICEF

§7.2 **Remember Who You Work For**

> *Remember who you work for. Just as an elected representative's power is derived by the consent of the governed, a lobbyist's power is derived from those whom they represent and their consent is needed on an ongoing basis. You are in your position to represent, not to expand your power base as a free agent.*
> The Tenth Law of Lobbying, § 8.4

Many lobbyists are quick to recite former Speaker of the House Tip O'Neill's timeless truth, "all politics is local," and certainly grassroots efforts are a central component of many government affairs strategy and coalition discussions. However, as lobbyists strive to balance the two major components of their work, advocacy, and communicating with their represented interests, the daily, and sometimes mundane, work that it takes to successfully maintain effective communications with their interests is overlooked or inadvertently deemphasized. Lobbyists can become more focused on pleasing coalition colleagues or congressional players than on accurately reflecting their principal's positions and priorities. Lobbyists consumed by a frenetic pace of high-profile Washington, DC, activities may feel "interrupted" by routine grassroots events and inquiries. Similarly, more mundane grassroots or client meetings and conferences can often conflict with important legislative opportunities or significant congressional events. While there are practical ways to minimize these conflicts, such as assigning specific staff to communicate with the grassroots or clients on a daily basis and scheduling conferences during congressional recesses, maintaining an outlook that the citizen is central to the representational process will help you to keep things in perspective.

I have attended coalition meetings where lobbyists have boasted how they will get their grassroots to assist them with their legislative projects. Citizen advocates who are identified with a specific lobbying organization are sometimes referred to as a lobbyist's "grassroots assets," as if they are owned or possessed. Like everyone else involved in the public policy process, lobbyists must work to keep perspective, accurately represent the interests who sent them, and remember that they are accountable to their principals: their members, constituents, or clients.

> *"We all have the ability to be great because we all have the ability to serve."*
> Martin Luther King

§7.3 Checklist for Organizing and Maintaining an Effective Grassroots Network

"You get the government you deserve."
"Those who are engaged win the day."
Meredith McGehee, C-SPAN's Washington Journal

Tips for organizing a grassroots network:

- Make network building a priority: Given the press of legislative events, the long-term developmental work to establish and maintain a network of equipped and involved citizens is often overlooked or inadvertently deemphasized.
- Consider the source: Where do your current, or potential, grassroots individuals come from?
- Establish communications goals: Set specific goals to maintain interactive communication and constant honing of priorities based on member or client feedback.
- Prioritize: Don't go to the well too often, but check with the grassroots frequently to make sure that you are accurately representing their interests.
- Keep members, clients, or employees involved year-round: Recruit, train, and equip before and between votes; don't wait until the ball game starts to start your training.

- Keep the channels of communication open: Make sure to share the outcome and successes after engagement efforts. Use surveys and various mechanisms to receive regular feedback and invite constructive suggestions from participants.
- Keep it interesting: Use hooks such as legislation anniversary dates, themes, or contests. Share motivating examples of success stories.

Typically you are facing one of the following scenarios:

1. Organized formal membership

Your current and potential grassroots activists are formal members of the organization, and they are organized in groups such as local or state chapters. Mature associations and labor unions fall into this group. An active commitment at the highest levels is essential for effectively developing, equipping, and energizing these local groups to facilitate additional political involvement.

This scenario is optimal since you already have information on a large pool of potential activists. Primarily, your job will be to develop existing members into a strong grassroots network of informed activists. Much of the foundational work has been done, but the key will be in finding new ways to motivate and involve individuals and effective ways to help them build their talent. Common challenges that can arise in this situation are a lack of consistency between local and national groups on legislative positions, as well as confusion over the usage of copyrighted information from the national organization.

2. Unorganized formal membership

Under this scenario, the organization has formal members, but the members are not organized into local chapters or groups. Typically they consist of individuals or businesses on mailing lists, perhaps dues-paying members who rarely or never meet together.

This scenario presents more of a challenge to develop members into a strong grassroots network of informed activists. You will need to work to develop some strategies for organizing and engaging them, and you may want to give them an opportunity to join a more organized effort such as a network or coalition.

3. No formal membership

Under this scenario, the organization does not have formal members. If you are fortunate, a segment of the population, including organizations, will support your interest. You can reach out to organizations that are potential allies and to citizens likely to support your cause to build a grassroots effort.

If you fall under scenarios 2 or 3, you can build a stronger organization over time, and you can develop a separate function or resource (for example, web-based) for legislative engagement efforts. Some of the best lobbying is done internally while working within your own organization to promote a stronger organizational commitment to the government affairs function.

§7.4 Seven Components for Building and Maintaining an Effective Grassroots Network

1. Identify and Recruit (§ 7.5)
2. Motivate (§ 7.7)
3. Organize (§ 7.9)
4. Educate (§ 7.10)
5. Energize (§ 7.11)
6. Recognize (§ 7.13)
7. Evaluate (§ 7.14)

§7.5 Components for Building and Maintaining an Effective Grassroots Network—1: Identify and Recruit

One overlooked contribution that lobbyists make to the public policy process is how they motivate and equip citizens to become involved and engaged in the governmental process. Identifying citizens who may be concerned about your issue is a fundamental step toward building an effective grassroots network. Who are your potential grassroots activists? What is their typical profile? The worksheet at § 7.6 may be useful for developing your recruitment strategy.

---

§7.6 Worksheet for Identifying Grassroots Recruiting Resources

Potential characteristics that may assist with grassroots identification and recruitment	Check (√) if applicable to your recruitment campaign	List potential recruiting resources: upcoming meetings that you could attend to recruit, membership lists you could purchase
Geographic area		
Field of work or expertise		
Demographics		
Interests and passions		
Membership in state, local, or national organizations		
Events or meetings attended		
Education level and area		
Web sites and blogs accessed		

Some of your best recruiters may be current grassroots activists. Train them and include them in your outreach efforts. Make sure that your materials are easily transferable from one activist to another. Consider key congressional districts and states as you conduct your outreach. Examples of grassroots technology venders that can assist you with your outreach efforts are found in § 7.19.

---

§7.7 Components for Building and Maintaining an Effective Grassroots Network—2: Motivate

"If you want to build a ship, don't herd people together to collect wood and don't assign them tasks and work, but rather teach them to long for the endless immensity of the sea."
Antoine de Saint-Exupery

"Ordinary people accomplish extraordinary things every day."
Marilyn King

Motivating members to become involved as effective advocates is an essential element in recruiting them. Some of your members or clients will already be motivated and

---

§7.8 Encouraging Citizen Engagement: Motivational Notes and Quotes

We hire and fire a member of Congress with our vote, but it's more than that. An employer wouldn't hire someone and then wait months later until the performance appraisal to first determine how the employee is doing on the job and provide necessary feedback. A successful employer is engaged and provides ongoing input to the employee to maximize his or her effectiveness. So it should be with citizen involvement. Our responsibility of good citizenship does not end with our vote. Our engagement is an ongoing process.

"The political world is stimulating. It's the most interesting thing you can do. It beats following the dollar."
—John F. Kennedy

"I have come to the conclusion that politics are too serious a matter to be left to the politicians."
—Charles DeGaulle

"A person may cause evil to others not only by his actions but also by his inaction, and in either case, he is justly accountable to them for the injury."
—John Stuart Mill

"The human race is divided into two classes: those who go ahead and do something, and those who sit still and inquire, 'why wasn't it done the other way?'"
—Oliver Wendell Holmes, Jr.

"All tyranny needs to gain a foothold is for people of good conscience to remain silent."
—Thomas Jefferson

"Turn on to politics, or politics will turn on you."
—Ralph Nader

Examples of the power of one:
- Texas was brought into the union by one vote.
- English became our official language instead of German by only one vote.
- Hitler gained control of the Nazi party by one vote.

equipped and are already enjoying being engaged. Others will need to be encouraged and assisted. Make sure that your training includes a balance of informational and motivational materials. Providing specific examples of how government or the specific issue at stake touches their lives directly and the difference that one person can make reminds citizens of the political power that they possess and motivates them to participate.

§7.9 Components for Building and Maintaining an Effective Grassroots Network—3: Organize

Are the interested citizens, members, or clients already organized by chapter, state, region, or issue interest? Have they participated in surveys that indicate their concerns and interests?

There are several ways to organize your information about your activists to facilitate rapid and targeted communications, including:

- **Geography** (crucial for determining legislative representatives): State and zip code/congressional district (see § 7.19 for grassroots technology information).
- **Expertise**: Issue-area specialists, previous involvement such as prior testimony before Congress or at the state level on behalf of your organization or others.
- **Expressed Interests/Past Involvement**: Determine specific areas of concern from surveys as well as previous actions. The best indicator of future involvement can be past involvement. Database services such as Capitol Advantage (see § 7.19) can permit identification and list creation of grassroots members who have contacted their members of Congress. These lists can be especially useful in identifying activists for specific legislative opportunities such as testifying before Congress or a legislative fly-in to meet with specific members of Congress.

Are there issues or aspects of issues that certain grassroots members want to specialize in? Providing an array of issues and involvement opportunities can help in recruiting, effectively involving, and assisting a broad representation of citizen activists. Build in mechanisms to ensure currency of contact information, such as regular inquiries to obtain change of address/email/phone information.

§7.10 Components for Building and Maintaining an Effective Grassroots Network—4: Educate

"[W]henever the people are well-informed, they can be trusted with their own government; that, whenever things get so far wrong as to attract their notice, they may be relied on to set them right."
Thomas Jefferson

Just as an "informed citizenry is the bulwark of a democracy," an enlightened constituency is central to any effective grassroots program.

It is important to educate those whom you represent not only on the issues, but also on the importance of respectful and effective congressional communications and courtesies. Do not encourage unpredictable or hot-tempered individuals to take leadership roles or to speak with members of Congress on behalf of your organization. Similarly, in the interest of your organization's long-term reputation, you have to know when to fire clients if they refuse to appreciate basic congressional courtesies.

Just one disastrous exchange between your grassroots member or client and a key member of Congress can cause damage that can take months to repair. This damage can affect more than just the success of your immediate legislative effort; it can taint your organization's reputation for years. With the implementation of new ethics laws in 2007 (see Chapter Two), unapprised grassroots activists who inadvertently break ethics laws can be subject to substantial penalties.

Options for providing grassroots training include:

- Sessions during existing conferences.
- Web-based, CD, telephone or video training sessions.
- Resources such as legislative tool kits (hard copy or online).
- Orientation sessions: Arranging meetings and the distribution of material upon joining as a member or election to office.
- Training in conjunction with other groups at the state and local levels.

The following training features should be incorporated into your planning process and your personalized "Lobbyist's Calendar Template" (see Appendix 5):

1. Motivation (see "How to Encourage Citizen Engagement: Sample Motivational Notes and Quotes" in § 7.8).
2. How to communicate effectively with policymakers (Chapters Eight and Ten) (for example, writing, meeting, emailing, and testifying).
3. Policy for distribution of materials, such as sensitive legislative information and newsletters policy.
4. Policies for developing or communicating organizational public policy positions.
5. Ethical compliance with all applicable lobbying and ethics laws, including gift restrictions, awards, campaign dos and don'ts, sponsorship of trips or events, and non-profit activity restrictions (see Chapter Two).
6. Testimony checklist (see Chapter Ten, § 10.61).
7. Policy briefings with associated materials, such as sample letters, model state legislation, or testimony on a specific issue.
8. Town hall participation opportunities.
9. How to invite legislators to participate in an event and how to conduct a site visit (see § 7.15).
10. Assist grassroots leaders, sometimes referred to as grass tops, in their efforts to identify, mobilize, and educate their own local contacts.

§7.11 **Components for Building and Maintaining an Effective Grassroots Network—5: Energize**

"Knowledge might be power, but only when you take action."
Richard Keeves

Once your network is organized, you will be able to alert members of involvement opportunities with periodic "alerts" or "calls to action." Without going to the well too often, it's important to keep members regularly informed about engagement opportunities.

Communicating the level of the priority is helpful. For example, note when a specific call to action reflects the organization's top priority or the most important legislative involvement opportunity of the year.

Make sure that efforts are recognized. Grassroots technologies (see § 7.19) can generate automatic thank-you notes from your organization to grassroots communicators. Keep things interesting. People like to hear updates regarding the effort. And they like to win prizes, so, for example, announce tally updates on congressional communications or regulatory comments by state or congressional district. Call attention to outstanding examples of communication to recognize and motivate others.

§7.12 **Case Study: The Power of Personal Involvement**

In 1980, Carole Young stopped by a Dallas mall in the middle of the day to purchase a gift for a friend. She returned to the parking lot and unlocked her car only to be grabbed from behind by a man with a knife. He shoved her into her car, cut her, took her keys and threatened her life. They struggled as he drove. She tried to unlock her door, and he automatically relocked it. She tried to cause him to go off of the road, to no avail. Carole then took a deep breath and decided to try to a different approach: She would try to talk him out of hurting her. She told him that he really seemed like a nice person and that she couldn't believe that he would do something like this. She told him that it was not too late and that she wouldn't turn him in if he'd just let her out. However, to her surprise, it was he who eventually exited the car, saying that he had heard enough and that he had to get away from her! Her life was spared.

Understandably, Carole was extremely upset by the experience and concerned about the lack of security in mall parking lots throughout Dallas. The next week, she ran into Steve Bartlett, then a city council member, at church. As it turned out, he served on the council's safety committee, so Carole thought that he would be the best person to take on the issue. She told him her story, then she said, "Dallas has a problem in its mall parking lots that I believe the council should address." Steve agreed and explained the work that he was personally doing with the council, but then he challenged her by asking, "What are *you* going to do about it?" Carole was furious because she had expected her governmental representative to take the problem and solve it. She went home and recapped the conversation with her husband who replied, "Well, maybe Steve has a point. Maybe you should consider doing something about it."

After much reflection, Carole again approached her city council member and explained that she wanted to help, but she didn't know what to do. He invited her to help, but she said that she just didn't feel qualified. He then arranged for her to attend a safety meeting at the local Chamber of Commerce. He even drove her to the meeting and encouraged her to launch a mall safety initiative. She ended up chairing a significant mall security effort and initiated a number of crime prevention projects. Carole's committee hosted luncheons that brought area law enforcement and mall security together to coordinate their efforts for the first time. As a direct result of the meetings, parking lot security was improved measurably and the crime rate in parking lots throughout the city dropped dramatically. This happened because one person took the initiative to get involved and tell her personal story. It also happened because a motivating leader was available to assist and encourage her in her efforts.

Carole was subsequently asked to serve on a number of committees and task forces at both the city and state levels. She was eventually appointed to a state-wide board overseeing the Texas prison system. As part of her work on this board, she initiated a program that allowed incarcerated offenders to build homes for Habitat for Humanity. The charity was helped, but so were the prisoners, who developed carpentry skills and earned certifications as they worked on cabinets and roofs. A ceremony was held for the single mother and her kids who were receiving the home. The prisoners were allowed to participate in the dedication ceremonies for the homes that they had built. They were quite obviously proud of their work, and Carole could sense that they had learned more than carpentry skills. At one such event, she noticed a man wearing street clothes standing among the prisoners. Carole discovered that it was a prisoner who had been released two weeks earlier. He had worked on the project and was so proud of the effort that he wanted to stand with the prisoners even though he had been released.

All of this happened because of Carole's difficult experience. I interviewed Carole to see what advice she would give to those who are concerned about a political issue, but reluctant to get involved.

The following is an excerpt from that interview:

Q. What were the keys to your success in getting changes made?
A. "My passion carried me a long way. When something like this happens, a certain amount of negative energy is created. You become frustrated and want to do something, but may not know where to turn. That negative energy has the potential to make you a fearful and bitter person, but if turned in a positive direction, it can give you the momentum to effect significant change. If you channel it in a positive direction, you can do a lot."

Q. Is there any specific advice that you would offer someone just starting out on a political issue that they are concerned about?
A. "Find others to join you on your team and research your issue. I initially worked through the Chamber of Commerce. And when overseeing the health care of the offenders in Texas prisons, I sat in on some classes at the medical school to better understand

the health care issues of an incarcerated population. You will discover that you can do a lot of things that you didn't think you could. I never dreamed I could have accomplished what I've accomplished."

Q. What is a good first step to mounting a campaign?
A. "The best way to go about most everything I've ever done is to start small. Figure out how you can make a difference in one area. If you can make one small difference—kind of like a pilot—then you have leverage, and you can expand your success. You have to find vehicles to work with and surround yourself with people who can help you gather support."

§7.13 Components for Building and Maintaining an Effective Grassroots Network—6: Recognize

You always get more of whatever is recognized and rewarded. Examples of recognition include:

- Annual awards for outstanding citizen efforts (presented at a major event and covered in publications, as appropriate).
- Receptions at legislative conferences that allow an informal sharing session with a microphone for citizens to share success stories from their Hill visits in front of their peers.
- Profiling activists and their success stories in publications.
- Publicly recognizing successful advocates in front of their peers during speeches or meetings.
- Video/slide shows of advocates testifying before Congress or state legislatures.
- Be creative! Provide an appropriate gift for specific contributions to the public policy process, such as a t-shirt with the message, "I survived testimony before the U.S. Congress," for your testifying members. The U.S. Capitol Historical Society (<*www.uschs.org*>) offers a range of excellent gifts suitable for presentation including items made from the original Capitol building.
- If a constituent's letter or information is used in a congressional publication or event (for example, a letter is inserted into the *Congressional Record* by a member of Congress, or a constituent's example is referenced during a hearing), provide a tape or copy of the publication to the constituent, with an extra copy for his or her boss, if appropriate.
- Recognizing grassroots and grasstops members for effective recruiting of their peers.
- Providing access to premium information and opportunities such as invitations to important meetings, conference calls, or inclusion in an organization's advisory council.

§7.14 Components for Building and Maintaining an Effective Grassroots Network—7: Evaluate

Evaluate your programs regularly. You will need to incorporate periodic program evaluation such as satisfaction surveys into your planning, your grassroots action plan and your "Lobbyists' Calendar." (See Appendix 5 for a Lobbyist's Annual Calendar: Key Dates and Activities Template.)

Identify "involvement inhibitors" such as feelings of inadequacy, lack of time, and cynicism through grassroots participation surveys and personal conversations. Consult the chart below for examples of actions to address your identified "involvement inhibitors" that you can include in your grassroots action plan.

It is important to organize an effective feedback network by designing a process for regular input from those you represent. For example:

- Track the quality as well as the quantity of participation. Use the methods and worksheets in Chapter Six to build metrics, establish a grassroots action plan, and conduct regular evaluations of your program's effectiveness. Review the accomplishment of your grassroots action plan goals and address the results of grassroots satisfaction surveys.

- If you are a contract or consultant lobbyist, ask for honest feedback upon client termination so that you can constantly hone the quality of your services.

- Schedule brainstorming sessions. Perhaps you have a board of directors, chapters, or committee members engaged in public policy. Work to strengthen these relationships. Some of your organization's best and most creative legislative

Examples of Actions to Address Identified "Involvement Inhibitors"

Examples of Identified "Involvement Inhibitors"	Examples of Specific Actions to Include in Grassroots Action Plan
Feelings of inadequacy	Include success stories/testimonials from previously intimidated citizens in publications
Feeling unqualified	Explain that no previous political experience is needed and stress how inexperienced congressional staff (average age of 30 years old) benefit from hearing constituent concerns
Too busy/multiple priorities	Explain how it will only take a few minutes to make a phone call or send an email to a member of Congress
Feeling cynical (they won't listen anyway)	Provide examples in your communications and conversations of how just one person has made a difference. (See also § 7.8 for sample talking points for encouraging citizen engagement.)

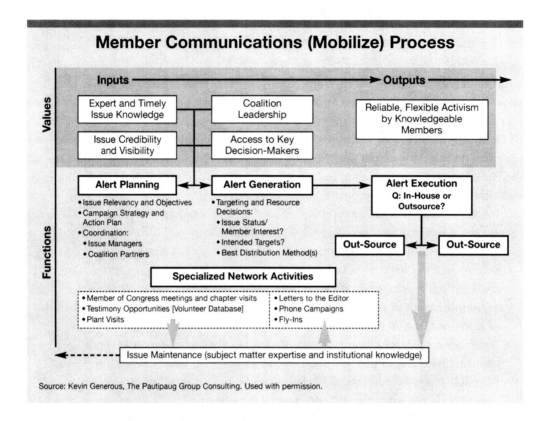

Member Communications (Mobilize) Process

Values

Inputs ──────────────────────────────────► **Outputs** ──────►

| Expert and Timely Issue Knowledge | Coalition Leadership |
| Issue Credibility and Visibility | Access to Key Decision-Makers |

Reliable, Flexible Activism by Knowledgeable Members

Functions

Alert Planning ◄────► **Alert Generation** ─────► **Alert Execution**
Q: In-House or Outsource?

Alert Planning:
• Issue Relevancy and Objectives
• Campaign Strategy and Action Plan
• Coordination:
  • Issue Managers
  • Coalition Partners

Alert Generation:
• Targeting and Resource Decisions:
  • Issue Status/ Member Interest?
  • Intended Targets?
  • Best Distribution Method(s)

Out-Source ◄────► Out-Source

Specialized Network Activities

• Member of Congress meetings and chapter visits
• Testimony Opportunities [Volunteer Database]
• Plant Visits

• Letters to the Editor
• Phone Campaigns
• Fly-Ins

◄─────── Issue Maintenance (subject matter expertise and institutional knowledge)

Source: Kevin Generous, The Pautipaug Group Consulting. Used with permission.

ideas might come from them. These individuals also can provide invaluable candid feedback on your grassroots efforts.

• Regularly invite input and respond to constructive criticisms from your grassroots whom you serve.

"The government relations (GR) professional who wants to stay ahead of the curve has to constantly re-examine and, as necessary, re-tool, their government relations operations to remain a cutting edge GR provider.

"In particular they should use strategic planning to account for trends shaping the GR industry. Three trends in particular have over the last decade changed the way GR organizations operate today: 1) changes in the public policymaking environment; 2) the average American's more direct communications with her legislator because of ready, low-cost access to policy information; and 3) the continued expansion of trade and professional association member services. The future promises even greater change at an accelerated pace. Experienced GR professionals can turn these changes to their advantage by giving their GR organization a 'performance checkup' via benchmarking, monitoring key performance indicators, incorporating performance metrics, and focusing on business process change and improvement."
Kevin Generous, President and Principal, The Pautipaug Group Consulting (a strategic planning firm)

§7.15 Checklist for Planning and Executing a Site Visit

"The key to the whole visit is to know why you want them to come and visit you and everything should be structured around that."
Andrew M. Mekelburg, Vice President, Federal Government Relations, Verizon

Determine the Purpose

- Make sure you know the point you want to make and have the tour make that point.

Design the Tour

- Don't just take them into a conference room. People like to see the company and the employees working.
- Respect legislative ethics requirements, such as meals, travel, or gift restrictions. (See Chapter Two for specific restrictions.)

Coordinate Details with Congressional Office

- Prepare written agenda in advance and provide to congressional office.
- Communicate logistics and the nature of the tour with key congressional staff.
- Include key staff if possible.
- If the government official is expected to speak, work with the office in advance to help with comments.

Prepare and Brief Employees

- Brief all employees in advance and get their buy-in and participation.
- Make sure employees are aware and will recognize the member and know how to address him or her.
- Brief any employees who will have a speaking part so that they are comfortable with anticipated questions that could arise.
- Also have spokespersons who are ready to step in to keep things moving or address an unexpected or awkward situation.
- Orchestrate logistics, paying attention to every detail from beginning to end: Who will be waiting at the door? Who will be waiting at stops along the tour? Who will provide introductions of the member if remarks will be made? Taking a senator up the wrong elevator or accidentally ending up in the kitchen won't make a good impression. If you are looking for a photo opportunity, plan it through and get multiple photos so that you can choose from several options.
- Prepare principals and spokespersons. Make sure that they will recognize the policymaker and know how to greet the policymaker. (See §§ 3.2–3.12 for policymaker background research information.)
- Prepare for down time. Small talk can go a long way. It's always a good idea to think in advance about one point that you would like to make if you have a chance for a personal conversation.
- Prepare handouts and any formal presentations.

§7.16 A Practical Example of a Legislative Conference Grassroots Success

A new, but unworkable Medicare-Medicaid data bank law was repealed in 1996 as a direct result of a meeting between several Society for Human Resource Management (SHRM) members and their member of Congress as part of the organization's annual legislative conference in Washington, DC. The human resource professionals met with their representative, Rep. Tillie Fowler (FL), and explained how the newly enacted law simply did not work. Although the citizens were not especially politically connected and the organization did not have a Political Action Committee (PAC), they made a compelling case and effectively presented the issue to Rep. Fowler, drawing from their own experiences as practitioners and using information provided by their national association. The Congresswoman was persuaded and soon introduced legislation to repeal the data bank law. Her legislation was enacted and the ill-conceived data bank requirement was permanently repealed.

 ## §7.17 Recommended Resources

How to Get Around on Capitol Hill

- The *Congressional Directory* with a fold-out map by TheCapitol.Net: <www.CongressionalDirectory.com>
- A Practical Guide to Working the Hill (Appendix 3)
- Capitol Learning Audio course from TheCapitol.Net: What your Member of Congress Can Do For You

Conduct the Tour

- Provide transportation (arranged in advance if you can in light of legislative ethics restrictions) and have appropriate staff accompany the legislators to talk on the way over. (*Note:* Congressional ethics rules prohibit registered federal lobbyist attendance on trips. See Chapter Two for additional details.)
- The tour guide should not become distracted or leave the member of Congress.
- The role of the host is to arrange for the participants to talk to the policymaker and introduce them to the experts in the field.

Debrief with the Official (on the Ride Back or During a Planned Conversation)

- Thank the participants again for spending the time to take the tour.
- Offer to follow-up and answer any additional questions.

Potential Questions for Congressional Representatives

- What was your impression?
- Do you have any other questions?
- What was the highlight for you?
- Reemphasize the point that you wanted them to focus on, that is, why your product is good for them, the district and the country.

Debrief with Your Staff

Use the following sample points and questions to discuss with your staff:

- Clarify follow-up responsibilities.
- Make sure that anything that was promised before, during, or after the trip was provided.
- Did you meet your objective?
- Should you use photos in company newsletter, on web site, etc? If so, notify the member of Congress.
- Send a thank you letter to the member of Congress and any involved staffers.
- What can be improved for the next site visit?
- Should you offer additional tours for other government officials?

§7.18 Grassroots Databases

Many grassroots databases are available to communicate with your grassroots members and facilitate their communications with Congress. These databases can be useful, convenient tools for grassroots members to contact their member of Congress while providing you with the benefit of their communications information.

Common database features include the following mechanisms:

- Write or email a member of Congress. (*Note:* Given the dramatic increase in communications to Capitol Hill, some congressional offices have established barriers to these systems such as logic games that require constituents to answer a question online before an email will be accepted.)
- Track who is hitting your web site. And use your web site as a tool to recruit.

However, such services must be weighed against confidentiality of data. An associate once advised me never to give an outside provider my grassroots or membership lists. Most venders have confidentiality provisions within their contracts, but recognize that the communications information on political activists can be extremely valuable, especially for those involved in political campaigns. Electronic information can be accessed in a number of ways by unauthorized people, including disgruntled employees or through security breaches. If you do decide to make your membership or grassroots contact information available to outside vendors, always seed the list by placing a false

§ 7.19 Grassroots Communications Vendors

Vender	Service	Contact Information/ Homepage
Capitol Advantage/ Knowlegis	A convenient mechanism allows your grassroots to email or write their members of Congress and contact the media. The Capitol Advantage system also facilitates citizen comments to agency officials on regulatory proposals. You are provided with a copy of their communications which are well organized in a database hosted by Capitol Advantage. Features include: • Updated congressional staff information; • Search capabilities by legislator, committee, congressional staff name, state, and zip code; and • Up-to-date news features, press releases and town hall meetings lists.	*<www.knowlegis.net>* Or phone 703–289–9816
SoftEdge	The Soft Edge provides software and internet applications for government relations and grassroots advocacy.	*<www.thesoftedge.com>* Or phone 703–442–8353
Congress Plus	Congress Plus Mobile provides Congressional contact information via internet application, access from PDA (Personal Digital Assistant), laptop, or desktop. Features include: • Grassroots contacts matched by congressional district • All members of Congress, state legislators and committees updated daily • Hill office issue-specific staff, with email, title, and phone • Track meetings, bills, and votes • Share your notes with colleagues • Congressional staff locator • Zip code-to-district locator	*<www.congressplus.com>*

Vender	Service	Contact Information/ Homepage
Advocacy Inc.	Advocacy Inc. sells email and phone list services. Lists are available by several demographic categories including: geographic location, precinct, congressional district, state legislative/school district, age, county, city/town, zip code, voting history, and voting frequency.	*<www.advocacyinc.com>*
Democracy Data & Communications (DDC)	DDC offers technology products and professional services for a variety of government affairs functions including grassroots.	*<www.democracydata.com>*
Aristotle	Various technology products including grassroots.	*<www.aristotle.com>*

Links to all web resources are available on the Resources page for this book: *<www.LobbyingAndAdvocacy.com>*.

 # §7.20 Recommended Resources

TheCapitol.Net Training

Information on TheCapitol.Net training and audio learning is available at: *<www.TheCapitol.Net>*.

name and address in the database, one that is sent to your home address or a specified email address, so that you know with certainty if your membership data has been misused.

Examples of grassroots communications venders are included in § 7.19. However, given the rapid pace of development of technology, lobbyists should monitor the development and availability of new technologies through groups such as the American League of Lobbyists, *<www.alldc.org>*.

§7.99 **Chapter Summary**

- In the press of legislative activities, professional lobbyists often overlook or inadvertently deemphasize the importance of developing and maintaining a network of involved citizens. Lobbyists must remember that constituent contacts are the most effective type of congressional communication. Despite multiple priorities and full schedules, lobbyists must also remember for whom they work (the interests they represent) and take care not to devalue them. (§§ 7.1, 7.2)
- A checklist for organizing and maintaining an effective network is provided in § 7.3 and includes the following tips:
  - Keep members, clients, or employees involved all year. Recruit and train before and between votes. (Don't wait until the ball game starts to start your training.)
  - Make network building a priority: Given the press of legislative events, the long-term developmental work to establish and maintain a network of equipped and involved citizens is often overlooked or inadvertently deemphasized.
  - Consider the source: What are the sources of your current, or potential, grassroots participants?
  - Establish communications goals: Set specific goals to maintain interactive communication and constant honing of priorities based on member or client feedback.
  - Prioritize: Don't go to the well too often, but check with the grassroots frequently to make sure that you are accurately representing their interests.
  - Keep the channels of communication open. Make sure to share the outcome after engagement efforts. Use surveys and various mechanisms to receive regular feedback and invite constructive suggestions from participants.
  - Keep it interesting. Use hooks such as legislation anniversary dates, themes, or contests. Share motivating examples of success stories.
- The following seven components of an effective grassroots capability are discussed:
  - #1: Identify and Recruit (§ 7.5)
  - #2: Motivate (§ 7.7)
  - #3: Organize (§ 7.9)
  - #4: Educate (§ 7.10)
  - #5: Energize (§ 7.11)
  - #6: Recognize (§ 7.13)
  - #7: Evaluate (§ 7.14)
- Various considerations are discussed for recruiting grassroots. (§ 7.5)
- An example of a motivating case study that can be used to overcome involvement barriers is included in § 7.12. The study profiles an ordinary citizen with no political experience who became passionate on an issue with a highly successful outcome.
- A chart is provided in § 7.14 listing potential actions to address your identified grassroots "involvement inhibitors," such as feelings of inadequacy or time constraints.

- One effective grassroots activity is to invite legislators to a facility. A practical checklist for planning and executing a site visit is provided in § 7.15.
- Organizers of association government affairs programs and others involved in major legislative efforts frequently design legislative conferences or "Hill Days," which facilitate constituent meetings in Washington, DC, and brief citizens on key issues. Legislative conferences are an excellent opportunity to make a difference on key issues. A practical example of a successful legislative conference grassroots meeting is provided in § 7.16. Recommended resources for legislative conferences are included in § 7.17.
- Technology is an extremely useful tool for facilitating grassroots involvement and tracking participation, but technology must be used judiciously and the security of membership or grassroots information must be safeguarded. (§ 7.18)
- A chart is provided in § 7.19 listing contact information for grassroots communications venders, but lobbyists are encouraged to track emerging technologies given rapid developments in the field.
- Additional information on communications with legislators is included in Chapter Eight.

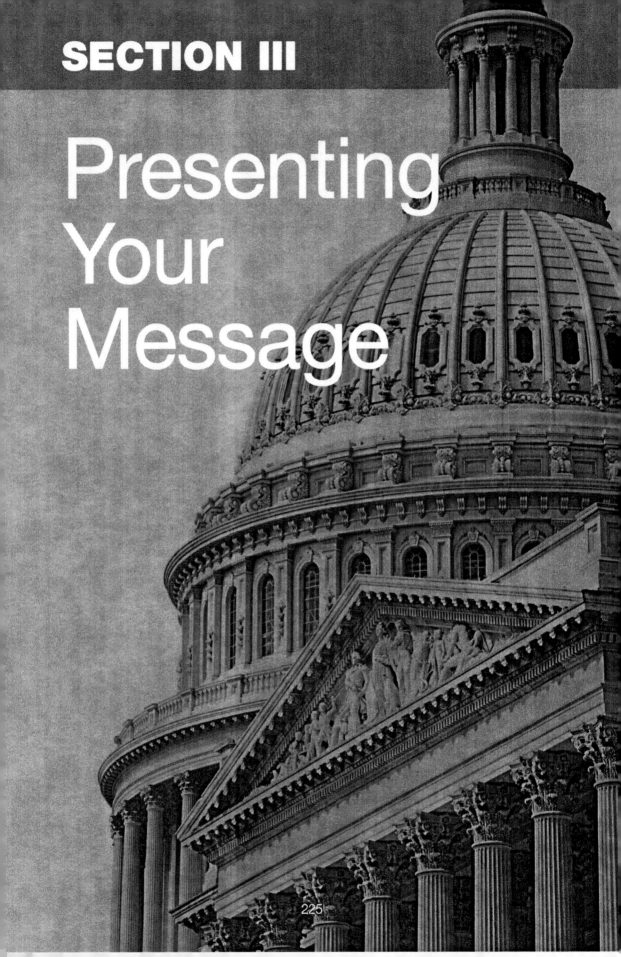

Presenting Your Message

Communicate Effectively with Policymakers:

Personal Meetings, Letters, Phone Calls, and Electronic Communications

Chapter 8: Communicate Effectively with Policymakers:
Personal Meetings, Letters, Phone Calls, and Electronic Communications

§8.1 Introduction

Every day that Congress is in session, thousands of citizens enter congressional buildings in an attempt to influence legislative actions in meetings and hearings; millions of emails, phone calls, and letters flood Capitol Hill; advocates hold briefings and press conferences; and organizations issue media releases designed to influence the legislative process. Simultaneously, communications flood the offices of executive branch officials and state and local policymakers.

Which emails and letters are ignored, and which meetings and events are quickly forgotten? Which modes and methods of communication connect and actually influence policy? How can your message be presented so that it is heard above the din?

Whether communicating as a company representative or as an association spokesperson, representing a client's interest or solely your own, specific methods have been proven to be effective for communicating with policymakers. Chapter Eight gives you the tools that you need to target and integrate your legislative communications. It's not just what you say, but how you say it. It is not just your information or your position, but how you present it. Chapter Eight provides practical tips, sample formats, and research-based methods for communicating most effectively with policymakers in every venue, including telephone conversations, email, congressional meetings, and letters. Congressional testimony is one of the most effective ways to weigh in on the legislative process. Chapter Ten provides an overview of what is expected from a congressional witness. It also includes a useful checklist to guide you as you assist in the preparation of a congressional witness or with your own testimony before Congress as well as tips for covering congressional hearings.

The goal of Chapter Eight is to enable you to provide constituent-oriented and results-centered communications that will help you develop and increase your long-term credibility and influence.

§8.2 Basic Dos and Don'ts That Apply to All Modes of Lobbying Communications

<u>Dos</u>

1. Respect the Importance of Personal Constituent Contact and Ties to the Constituency

> *All politics is local. Where they stand depends on where they sit. Every member of Congress is motivated by the same thing: getting re-elected. Nothing trumps the power of the constituency. Local issues and perspectives can drive public policy and strongly influence viewpoints.*
> The 30 Laws of Lobbying: 2 (§ 8.4)

Given the unequivocal power of their constituency to influence legislators, constituent contacts and ties to the constituency should be the focus of all lobbying communications. When the word "constituent" is mentioned in any congressional office, it is as though bells and whistles have sounded. As discussed in Chapter Seven, we must get beyond the platitudes and focus our daily lobbying activities on the political truism that "All politics is local."

Members of Congress are naturally most interested in the implications of legislation on their particular constituency. Effective advocacy groups recognize this and tailor their messages accordingly. For example, during periodic congressional debates over minimum wage increase proposals, the Economic Policy Institute, which strongly supports minimum wage increases, presents information to lawmakers on how many workers in their state would benefit by a minimum wage increase. Simultaneously, the Employment Policies Institute, which opposes minimum wage increases, lobbies Congress armed with information on how many jobs will be lost in each specific state or district.

For example, an Economic Policy Institute media release on Connecticut legislation stated that:

> "*New analysis of Census Bureau data by Dave Macpherson of Florida State University shows that the bill would cost the state over $25 million and an estimated 500 jobs. Worse, those who will benefit from the wage hike aren't in low-income families. The data shows the average family income of those benefiting from the hike is nearly $75,000 per year. Unfortunately, the 500 lost jobs will be concentrated on those Connecticut workers with the fewest skills. According to the economist David Neumark of the University of California at Irvine, for every 10 percent increase in the minimum wage, employment for high school dropouts and young black adults and teenagers falls by 8.5 percent.*"

Source: PRNewsire Release, EPI Calls on Connecticut Legislature to Uphold Minimum Wage Veto; Research Shows the Legislation Hurts Those it Claims to Help, June 23, 2007

2. Recognize that Personalization is Power

> ***All politics is personal.*** *Never underestimate the power of personal persuasion and the value of personal relationships. Technology will never replace the benefits of face-to-face conversations. Technology will never vote, people always will.*
>
> The 30 Laws of Lobbying: 3 (§ 8.4)

Because of the truism that all politics is local, many services and technologies have arisen to help organizations expedite grassroots communications to policymakers and to make grassroots communications more convenient for citizens. These services include:

- Systems such as Capitol Advantage (<*www.capwiz.com*>) and Convio (<*www.convio.com*>) that allow organizations to launch massive email and letter writing campaigns by providing alerts to constituents with several sets of pre-written talking points conveniently arranged in an email or letter writing system.

- Tools and strategies for conducting an inventory of your organization's potential activists and micro-targeting of your stakeholders to determine their interests, contacts, and ability to be effective advocates ("advocability"). For example, The Felkel group offers an online survey tool for purchase that provides an internal audit and inventory of an organization's positive actionable relationships with over 28,000 elected officials.
- Services that provide toll-free phone numbers for constituents to phone for assistance in connecting with Congress or the White House. Citizens calling the toll-free number may receive quick coaching on the legislation before the consultant patches their phone call through to the appropriate policymaker.
- Telemarketers who call targeted constituents of certain demographic groups and legislative districts to attempt to motivate them to weigh in on a legislative issue before offering to transfer the motivated constituent through to their lawmaker's office.

Technology and information can motivate and facilitate grassroots communications, but they should never replace them. There is no short cut for sincere grassroots expressions and no substitute for informed constituents weighing in with their own views. We can take former House Speaker Tip O'Neill's "All politics is local" insight a step further: Lasting political persuasion is personal.

Technology-based services or grassroots firms should never be used to mislead constituents into weighing in on something that they don't really understand or believe. Congressional offices can often recognize manufactured efforts, often referred to as "astroturf," instead of grassroots. As illustrated in the following quote, manufactured grassroots campaign are often detected by the congressional staff receiving constituent phone calls:

> *"Gary Lindgren, press secretary for Rep. Steve Chabot (R-Ohio), a target of the campaign, says Chabot's office received quite a bit of mail and phone calls, but that they clearly originated from an astroturf effort. It's often easy to tell when a lobbying campaign is not generated in the district, Lindgren notes, because "a lot of times, people are reading off a prepared script." He says many who called Chabot's office seemed poorly informed about the legislation."*
>
> Source: "Hello. I'm calling this evening to mislead you."
> By Ken Silverstein, *Mother Jones* magazine, November/December 1997 Issue

While isolated, a few efforts to actually fabricate grassroots have been revealed in the press. Such efforts devalue authentic citizen contacts and can raise doubts about authentic citizen mobilizations and expressions. Also, as referenced in Chapter Seven, organizations should take measures to safeguard member, client, or constituent contact information accessible to third-party providers.

3. Study and Listen First

*"No one would talk much in society if they knew
how often they misunderstood others."*
Goethe

Most lobbyists make their pitch before they have fully determined the position and current thinking of the policymaker with whom they are communicating. Chapter Three provides tools for evaluating the environment and the factors that are driving a policymaker's position, and Chapter Five provides tips for conducting research on the representative prior to your meeting.

Start your meetings and telephone conversations by first getting a gauge of how familiar the representative is with the issue and his current thinking on the legislation. Asking questions to determine specific opinions, opinion drivers, and concerns that may exist is extremely useful. Then you can tailor your pitch to her level of familiarity and concerns. Ask if the policymaker has already decided or where he is in the decisionmaking process. Ask when they expect to make a decision on the issue and when you should check back. Ask what considerations are likely to shape their decision.

4. Consider the Messenger

It's not just what you say and how you say it. It is also who is saying it. Think strategically about your message and the ideal messengers to connect with specific legislators. Messengers can be effective for a variety of reasons, for example, their expertise, credibility on the issue, reputation, profile, or personal relationship with the elected official. See § 3.10 for information on the representative's "promoters."

5. Provide Practical Examples and Experiences

Practical examples and relevant real-life experiences have tremendous power on Capitol Hill because they help members of Congress to understand the realities of proposals. Any effective legislative strategy should include an array of examples illustrating the practical ramifications of the proposal. These examples can be obtained from individuals who would be directly affected by the legislation and from subject matter experts with experience on the topic.

6. Mindset Matters

*"Coca Cola does not view Pepsi drinkers as the enemy.
Coca Cola views Pepsi drinkers as potential Coke drinkers."*
The Power of Personal Persuasion, Deanna R. Gelak

Mindset matters during lobbying conversations. People perceive how you view them in your consciousness. Seek to make a difference in every encounter, even when you meet resistance. Effective lobbying can overcome negative stereotypes and make some small difference in every situation.

7. Choose One Issue, Be Concise, and Avoid Tangents

All modes of legislative communication should be modeled with the following reality in mind: the person on the receiving end, whether an entry-level legislative correspondent managing the reply to your letter or a U.S. senator answering your question during a town hall meeting, is processing multiple priorities and will respond best if you keep your argument succinct and focused on one issue. You must know your issue (as discussed in Chapter Five). Concisely make your case, stick to the subject, and avoid tangents.

Regardless of the mode of communication, it is important to know exactly which piece or pieces of legislation you are talking about. Knowing your piece of legislation involves not only understanding its substance, but also whether there is competing legislation, whether there is companion legislation in the other chamber (House or Senate), and how the legislation might move, such as whether it is moving as a freestanding bill or whether it is likely to be considered as an amendment (or rider) to other legislation, which is frequently the case. Even though more legislation has been introduced in recent years, fewer free standing bills have been enacted into law. This fact underscores the need for lobbyists to discern which legislation is likely to move and how it might be attached to other proposals (commonly referred to as vehicles). See Chapter Four for more information on the legislative process, including the Life Cycle of Lobbying, and for examples of the need to be concise in all congressional communications.

8. Be a Reliable Resource

> *"The immature mind hops from one thing to another;*
> *the mature mind seeks to follow through."*
> Harry A. Overstreet, Social Psychologist and Educator

A Senate staff member shared a vivid example with me of his experience with a lobbyist's inadequate follow-through. The staff member attended a meeting where a lobbyist had promised the senator that he would prepare some critical information for the senator to be used in an upcoming floor debate. The lobbyist did deliver on his promise, but the material did not arrive until several hours after the Senate debate had ended. The lobbyist failed to notify the staff or senator of the delay. The senator, who had been counting on the information, was extremely unhappy, and the staff member decided not to work with that particular lobbyist again.

Legislative decision-making depends on responsible relationships and reliable information. Policymakers turn to experts and sources they trust when they need information and input. Be a reliable resource, and keep your promises. Ultimately, the goal is to develop and maintain a relationship of trust with information exchanged in both directions.

9. Be Persistent but Not Overbearing

Check back periodically to see if a decision has been made, but know when to stop. Frequently providing useful information without becoming annoying is a skill developed and refined over time. If you don't know whether your contacts are too frequent, you can always ask the staffer, making it clear that you want to be helpful, but also you want to be respectful of his or her time. Seek clarification on the legislator's information, format, and communication preferences.

- Try to exceed expectations on the usefulness of the material and provide information earlier than expected.
- Set clear expectations on when and how promised information will be delivered to the legislative representative.
- Confirm receipt of promised information by phone or email.
- When you encounter problems or delays, let the person know about the problem or delay as soon as possible.
- Ask the recipient if anything else is needed.
- Don't put all your eggs in the basket of one specific staff person. A decision tree exists in every office, and only the legislator votes.

Don'ts

1. Don't Violate Lobbying Laws or Standards

The first great truth from the Hippocratic Oath developed for physicians serves as a rule to guide all types of legislative communications: "First do no harm."

> *"No 'quid pro quos.' Bribing a public official is a felony. Be familiar with the ethics rules that apply to public officials and never do anything to encourage or cause a policymaker to violate ethics standards or laws."*
> The 30 Laws of Lobbying: 6 (§ 8.4)

> *"Stay above reproach. Guard your reputation by avoiding not only the substance but the appearance of wrongdoing. Be strict in complying with the letter and spirit of lobbying and ethics laws, and remember that laws and professional standards are a floor, not a ceiling."*
> The 30 Laws of Lobbying: 13 (§ 8.4)

Before conducting lobbying of any type, it is essential to recognize the "ethics imperative" as discussed in detail in Chapter Two. Lobbyists must take great care to avoid violating any ethics laws or rules including those pertaining to gifts, events, quid-pro-quos (bribes), and lies to Congress.

§ 8.3 Making Your Message Stand Out from the Din:
Postal and Email Communications to Capitol Hill 1995–2004

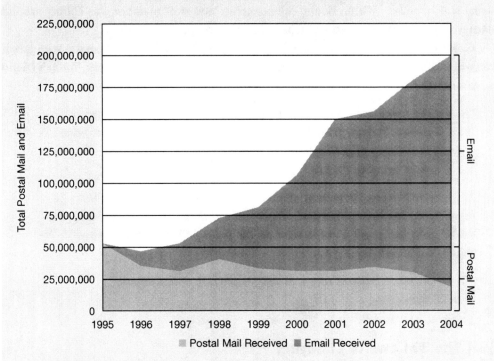

Postal Mail Received ■ *Email Received*

(House email and postal mail data provided by the Office of the Chief Administrative Officer of the House of Representatives. Senate email data provided by the Senate Sergeant at Arms. Senate postal mail data provided by the Office of the Senate Postmaster. These volumes do not include faxes or phone calls, which cannot be measured in aggregate. Email data prior to 1998 in the House and 1999 in the Senate was not available and is only an estimate.)

Since the Internet was introduced to Capitol Hill in 1995, total communications received by Congress have increased significantly. As this chart shows, total postal mail and email to Capitol Hill have increased from approximately 50 million in 1995 to 200 million in 2004, nearly a 300 percent increase. These data represent all incoming email and postal communications to the House and Senate, not only communications from constituents to their elected representatives. However, most offices have experienced comparable growth in constituent communications.

Source: Congressional Management Foundation

2. Don't Threaten

"Never threaten. This goes for subtle or veiled threats as well. Threats only make people increase their resolve against your views or agenda."
The 30 Laws of Lobbying: 4 (§ 8.4)

3. Don't Gossip or Violate Confidences

Choose your words carefully and take care to safeguard confidences. I attended a coalition meeting where several attendees complained extensively about a certain congressional staff member. Within hours, the congressional staff member was calling around town wanting to know exactly who had said what about him.

Gossip undermines your trust in the person you gossip to, as that person wonders if you will talk about her the same way. Also, be aware of changing alliances. Today's friend is tomorrow's foe, and today's coalition confidant could be tomorrow's opponent.

> *"Resist the temptation to gossip. Washington is a much smaller town than it seems. Today's friend may be tomorrow's opponent. Words have a mysterious way of getting back to people."*
> The 30 Laws of Lobbying: 7 (§ 8.4)

> *"Safeguard the confidences of others as carefully as you would your own. Apply the newspaper test: Never put anything in writing, including email, that you don't want to read on the front page of the newspaper."*
> The 30 Laws of Lobbying: 8 (§ 8.4)

> *"Great people talk about ideas. Small people talk about others."*
> Unknown Author

§8.4 The 30 Laws of Lobbying

1. **Trust is everything.** What kills trust is a lack of truthfulness, exaggerations, excessive spin beyond simply framing things positively, and omitting key facts or factors. Always be completely honest, even when it's hard. Your word is your bond. Trust is the lifeblood of politics. It's okay to say you don't know if you don't know. Professionally, all you have in the long-term is your reputation and your integrity.

2. **All politics is local.** Where they stand depends on where they sit. Every member of Congress is motivated by the same thing: getting re-elected. Nothing trumps the power of the constituency. Local issues and perspectives can drive public policy and strongly influence viewpoints.

3. **All politics is personal.** Never underestimate the power of personal persuasion and the value of personal relationships. Technology will never replace the benefits of face-to-face conversations. Technology will never vote, people always will.

4. **Never threaten.** This goes for subtle or veiled threats as well. Threats only make people increase their resolve against your views or agenda.

5. **Never assume.** Always verify each position directly with the policymaker and never take anything or anyone for granted. Positions can change based on time, circumstance, and the specific nature of the issue or situation.

6. **No "quid pro quos."** Bribing a public official is a felony. Be familiar with the ethics rules that apply to public officials and never do anything to encourage or cause a policymaker to violate ethics standards or laws.

7. **Resist the temptation to gossip.** Washington is a much smaller town than it seems. Today's friend may be tomorrow's opponent. Words have a mysterious way of getting back to people.

8. **Safeguard the confidences of others as carefully as you would your own.** Apply the newspaper test: Never put anything in writing, including email, that you don't want to read on the front cover of the newspaper.

9. **What goes around comes around . . . even though it may take some time.** Do not be disheartened when people seem to get away with unethical behavior.

10. **Keep a check on the way you view those you represent.** Just as an elected representative's power is derived by the consent of the governed, a lobbyist's power is derived from those whom they represent and their consent is needed on an ongoing basis. You are in your position to represent, not to expand your power base as a free agent.

11. **Be kind to everyone.** The Golden Rule works on the Hill. It's not always apparent who actually wields the most influence and who might in the future. Today's receptionist is tomorrow's chief of staff. Today, a congressional staff member answers the phones. Tomorrow, that staffer may answer the Senator's question on an issue important to you.

12. **When in doubt, check it out.** Address your ambiguities, because policymakers, those whom you represent, the media, or your competition might! Don't disseminate information that you haven't verified. More people have been burned by not verifying information than would care to admit it.

13. **Stay above reproach.** Guard your reputation by avoiding not only the substance but the appearance of wrongdoing. Be strict in complying with the letter and spirit of lobbying and ethics laws, and remember that laws and professional standards are a floor, not a ceiling.

14. **Avoid personal attacks.** Never ascribe motives or call names. Don't assume to know someone's motivation. Name-calling will diminish your credibility, especially with those who have not yet decided on your issue. The goal is to win on the issue, not to make enemies or make people look bad.

15. **Always have a backup.** Anticipate the unexpected. Be prepared to go to Plan-B for your lobbying strategy, your meeting plans, and your technology.

16. **Make planning a priority.** No one ever plans to fail, but many fail to plan. Use down time to update your goals and action plans. Know your issue well enough for the most difficult questions and know your opposition. Knowledge is power. Become a student of the person you are trying to persuade.

§8.5 Five Principles for Effective Legislative Communications:
The "CHATS℠ Method" for Communicating with Congressional Members and Staff

C-onnect to Find Something in Common

"When I'm getting ready to reason with a man, I spend one-third of my time thinking about myself and what I am going to say—and two-thirds thinking about him and what he is going to say." —Abraham Lincoln

Learn what is important to the policymaker. Where they stand depends on where they sit. Make your connection to the member's constituency. What is your interest's relationship to the district or state? What are the factors that will drive the member's decisionmaking process? Does the member have a leadership role on any committees, caucuses or informal groups? How will your position help him or her in effectively representing the constituency? Be a student of the policymaker and his or her past statements or positions on the issue (including press received and statements made during political campaigns). What press has the member received? What is the member's professional background and how might it influence his or her thinking on the issue? What press releases are posted on the member's web site? (They are a reflection of the member's priorities.) See Chapter Three for tips and resources to assist you with determining a legislator's "Position Drivers" and Chapter Five for tips on conducting research on the policymaker and the constituency.

H-ear

"Don't ever talk until you know what you're talking about." —Sam Rayburn

One of the greatest secrets of effective lobbying is to listen first. Sincere listening cannot be faked. Our mindset matters. What is the member's real priority or concern? Does he or she have any remaining questions on the issue?

"We forget that listening is a powerful action in itself. Active listening means challenging ourselves to stay engaged with the speaker and remember not just what is said but why it is being said." —The Power of Personal Persuasion, Deanna R. Gelak

A-void Arguing

"I never saw an instance of one or two disputants convincing the other by argument." —Thomas Jefferson

"Arguments only confirm people in their own opinions." —Booth Tarkington

"Interestingly, a person's commitment to a particular point of view actually increases when he or she speaks up and defends it. Like a muscle, it builds strength by applying resistance. . . We want to avoid this 'boomerang' effect. . . . When we find that our conversation is turning into an intellectual competition, it is time to take a deep breath, step back, and try a different approach." —The Power of Personal Persuasion, Deanna R. Gelak

T-ake the Temperature

Questions are powerful. Ask questions to take the temperature and determine where they stand on the issue and try to determine if they have made a decision before making your pitch. Silence does not indicate consent. Watch body language and ask how they are doing on time. Ask questions to understand the thinking behind their position or concerns and to ensure a dialogue instead of alternating monologues. Know when to be silent and know when to stop.

"Occasionally allow yourself the luxury of an unexpressed thought." —Sen. Everett Dirksen

S-ow Seeds for Consideration

"We are usually convinced more easily by reasons we have found ourselves than by those which have occurred to others." —Blaise Pascal

Securing a commitment or change to an established position usually takes some time. We should not expect a dramatic or instant change in the course of just one lobbying meeting. People often need numerous additional credible and influential contacts to change their position. People need time to process a new position and "own" it. Leave them with a "point to ponder" that they can consider. Follow-up and be persistent without becoming annoying.

17. **Allow for Murphy's Law.** If something can go wrong it will and usually it will at the worst possible moment.

18. **Everything is always more complicated than it seems.** Simple tasks can take longer and require more resources than originally intended. We lobby in an age of "the increasing complexity of everything" (a phrase dubbed by *Wall Street Journal* columnist Peggy Noonan).

19. **Be proactive.** Don't wait until problems pop up to take proper care of priorities. This includes legislative plans, compliance with disclosure reporting and ethics laws, technology, and relationships!

20. **Inform policymakers of the opposition's position as you communicate your own.** They'll hear it anyway, so you might as well frame it for them before you shoot it down.

21. **Be respectful.** Arrive at meetings on time or early. Briefings should be brief. Poor time management communicates lack of value and respect. Know when to stop. Always say thank you.

22. **Use the power of momentum.** Success can breed success and one success can lead to another.

23. **Develop and motivate those you represent.** It's not just about the numbers. It's about passion, commitment, and multiplying converts.

24. **Train, develop relationships, and recruit year-round.** Both in season and out of season, what players do on and off the field will reap dividends on the field when the big vote is announced.

25. **Timing is everything.** Evaluate not just what to do, but when. What is the best time to push the issue or communicate with an individual considering various legislative cycles, work schedules, and circumstances?

26. **Break the barrier.** When contacting a legislative office, never give a screener (such as, a receptionist or an appointment secretary) a chance to say no. Find out which staff person currently has responsibility for your issue area and get to know him or her.

27. **Sound policy is sound politics.** Even the best strategy can't compensate for poor policy. Would it work in the real world?

28. **Admit your mistakes right away.** Accept responsibility and offer to make amends. No one is perfect. In matters large and small, the cover-up can be worse than the crime. Practice humility.

29. **Guard against cynicism.** Enthusiasm is contagious, but so is cynicism. There is no shortage of cynics. Resolve to be part of the solution.

30. **Keep it all in perspective.** Never lose your sense of humor. Don't forget about the people who will still be in your life ten years from now. The people who didn't return your calls before you came to Washington probably won't after you leave.

"Do the right thing. It will gratify some people and astonish the rest."
Mark Twain

§8.6 Determining the Best Mode of Communication

With a dramatic increase in legislation pending in Congress and an exponential increase in congressional communications, advocates face increased challenges to connect with policymakers to get their message heard above the din.

As illustrated in the chart at § 8.3, the volume of constituent communications to Capitol Hill has increased dramatically over the past decade as web site and Internet use has facilitated more communication.

While the conventional order of congressional communications is listed in § 8.10, successful advocates use several types of communication simultaneously, integrating effective grassroots contacts and national lobbyist contacts throughout the legislative process.

Letters are still important for certain reasons, for example, to express gratitude for a meeting or to communicate an organization's official position; however, they only work if time permits, since congressional security and screening measures delay mail delivery. While email facilitates congressional communications, it is important to recognize the limits of technology. As discussed in § 8.39, some massive email-only campaigns have

§8.8 Lobby Tips

Getting Connected Quickly
and Breaking the Barrier

Typically, the best order for contacting a member of Congress is to write first, to phone second, and then to meet personally: write, call, meet. Of course, sometimes you don't have the time to move through all three steps, so you need to be able to get past the office's screening system to speak to the staffer with responsibility for your issue or with enough authority to set up a meeting.

When you do not know the name of the staffer handling your issue area, phone the office and ask the receptionist the name of the legislative assistant handling your issue, and then phone the office again later and ask to speak to the specific person by name. Make sure that you mention your connection to the interests that you represent in the state or district. Most legislative staff members schedule their own meetings, but meetings directly with members of Congress are arranged through the policymaker's scheduler and may be expedited by another legislative staff member in the office, such as, the chief of staff or legislative director.

Making and keeping the right connections also applies to your stakeholders. Knowing your advocates, their interests, their compelling stories, and their personal relationships with elected officials is a critical success factor. Develop and refine effective methods of mining your organization data to identify effective advocates and potential spokespersons in key congressional districts.

raised suspicions with policymakers, who sometimes question the authenticity of some of the contacts.

When citizens are truly concerned about an issue, they express their concerns in several ways: by calling, writing, emailing, speaking at town hall meetings, personal contact directly with the policymaker, and writing the local newspaper. Authentically engaged citizens are also likely to contact congressional district or state offices as well as the Washington, DC, office. Effective lobbying involves integrating various approaches, modes, venues, and styles of communications.

§8.7 Respect Individual Communication Preferences

People have different communications types and preferences. Some rely mostly on email and prefer it to a phone call. Others are very slow to check emails and virtually never acknowledge them. Some congressional staffers tend to ignore many emails because of the volume they receive, but can be very responsive in person when they see you in a congressional hallway or meeting.

§8.9 Recommended Resources

Making and Keeping the Right Connections

Contact information for congressional staffs is found in numerous commercial directories including: The Congressional Yellow Book (<*www.leadershipdirectories.com*>), Capitol Advantage's online services (<*www.capitoladvantage.com*>), Convio, formerly GetActive (<*www.convio.com*>), The Soft Edge (<*www.thesoftedge.com*>), and TheCapitol.Net (pocket directory) <*www.CongressionalDirectory.com*>.

Links to all web resources are available on the Resources page for this book: <*www.LobbyingAndAdvocacy.com*>.

§8.10 The Typical Order of Congressional Communications

1. Write: A letter written on the organization's or individual's letterhead is sent to the policymaker expressing the organization's official position and requesting a certain action, for example, that the legislator cosponsor and actively support specific legislation.
2. Call: A phone call is made to the congressional office requesting a personal visit with the policymaker to discuss the letter and the policymaker's position.
3. Visit: A personal visit occurs with the policymaker or a staff representative.
4. Follow-up phone calls and emails are made, as appropriate, and numerous targeted communications are coordinated with grassroots activities, with the goal of influencing the position and establishing ongoing relationships and communication.

§8.11 An Example of Simultaneous and Integrated Washington Lobbyist and Grassroots Activities

- The national organization sends a letter and phones the appropriate staff person in the DC office referencing the letter and requesting a meeting with the DC staff. Numerous congressional briefings are held, featuring constituent presentations and coalition meetings.
- Meanwhile, a host of grassroots activists are phoning and emailing the Washington, DC, staff responsible for the issue, writing, emailing, and visiting the legislator's district office, writing letters to the editor of the local newspapers, and raising the issue directly with the legislator at congressional district/state public events.

§8.13 Continually Cultivate Contacts

I recall a situation when I had been preparing for months for a key floor vote and developed several relevant research papers and charts that were used by legislators. I was honored to be asked by the congressional leadership to be available in a Capitol office

§8.12 Lobby Tips

Early Identification and
Contact of the Key Influentials

"He who frames the issue tends to determine the outcome of the vote. That's a basic rule of political consultants that applies to elections and to the legislative process, as well."

—Michael Barone, September 3, 2007, Surge Politics, Townhall.com

You want to start with the key decision makers on the issue and the leaders that other members will look to in developing their own position. Neglecting top leaders and other influential members on the issue is a mistake since they will quickly influence other members and could even become solidified against your position if opposing interests reach them first. One of the first steps is to identify and connect with, or cultivate, champions for your cause.

- Identify key committee and personal staff early and focus on key leaders and decision makers on the issue.
- Work both the House and Senate. It's easy to neglect one chamber when action is occurring in the other chamber, but both should be worked and monitored to at least some degree.
- Approach relevant executive branch officials early in the process.
- Don't wait until the bill is out of committee to start working on influential members, including leadership. Even though it may be very challenging to get their attention on an issue before it's out of committee, at least starting grassroots activity early will help to make sure they are sensitized and sympathetic to your perspective, especially if your issue could move to the floor quickly.
- See §§ 3.5 and 5.5 for resources for researching members of Congress and their constituencies.

in case questions arose during the floor vote. Staff relied heavily on the information that I provided and asked me to be available during the legislative debate and to even help myself to refreshments from their refrigerator. I felt a sense of importance camped out in their office as the debate unfolded and questions and issues were raised and answered.

However, when I returned to the same office the next day to retrieve some charts that had been used by members of Congress on the House floor, I noticed that a different receptionist was working in the leadership office. I introduced myself and she returned the greeting politely, but I realized that I was, to her, a stranger. Another group of people involved in another floor vote were now in the lobby working closely with staff. The focus of the office had moved on to the next issue without hesitation.

Appreciation has a short shelf-life on Capitol Hill. You need to continue to work hard to maintain your usefulness as a credible resource. To provide valuable information and stay in contact without becoming annoying is a skill developed and refined over time.

Contacts are an important advocacy success factor. Keep the channels of communication open with your Hill contacts, and look for new opportunities to provide useful information and strengthen your relationships.

§8.14 **Identify Legislative Leaders and Potential Champions**

Your ideal champion will have the credibility and clout, as well as the time and attention, to focus on advancing the issue. You can use the Target List Template for ranking legislators' positions in § 8.18 to identify several potential champions. The following distinctions contribute to issue leadership:

- Committee chairs for the House or Senate committees or subcommittees of jurisdiction or the highest-ranking member of the opposite party.
- Key committee members (consider seniority and other committee responsibilities).
- House or Senate party leaders (although it may be difficult to get their attention).
- Leaders of relevant congressional caucuses or informal congressional groups (such as the House Blue Dogs).
- Member who has a compelling experience with or personal interest in the issue.
- Members who have been quoted in the press on the issue.
- Public effectiveness.
- Ability to recruit support, for example, from key targets and both political parties.
- Available to work the issue, that is, willing to send Dear Colleague letters or to speak to members of Congress personally.
- Past champions on the issue or similar issues (see Chapter Five for tips and links for researching members of Congress).
- Try to avoid negatives, such as strained relationships with other influentials or targets, those under investigation, or with lame duck status.

§8.16 **Develop a Target List**

Lobbyists should focus both time and resources contacting members of Congress who they have determined are undecided on how they will vote on their issue. Lobbyists, typically in coalitions, work to determine where members of Congress stand on their issue early in the legislative process so that they can focus their efforts on those members. Generally, lobbyists refer to these members as "targets."

The Target List Template in § 8.18 may assist you with ranking members of Congress on your issue and sharing your intelligence with your colleagues. In filling out your ranking form, it is important to note the exact source of the intelligence. Was the intelligence obtained directly from the member of Congress or a staff person? Staff titles and dates of communication can be extremely helpful as several lobbyists compare their notes.

Your strong supporters should not be ignored; you may be able to encourage them

§8.15 Lobby Tips

Cultivating Legislative Champions

- Have regular meetings or conference calls with congressional staff/members to work together on identifying potential allies and addressing targets.

- Sometimes members who can't be out front for political reasons can help in other ways behind the scenes, by lobbying their party leadership to block or schedule the proposal or by supporting specific amendments.

- Consider administration spokespersons and agency legislative liaisons. Is the administration supportive? If so, perhaps administration key officials can help contact select members of Congress who would tend to be influenced by the administration. Identify the key decision makers within the administration on the issue, for example, the assistant secretary for congressional affairs at the relevant cabinet agency, and request meetings with them on your issue. Ask them where they are in the decisionmaking process, for instance, what has been discussed regarding a letter of intent (communicating the president's intention to veto or sign the legislation) or a Statement of Administration Policy (SAP), which are prepared by the Office of Management and Budget on major legislation prior to House or Senate floor consideration.

- A public statement or phone call from another elected official from the state may be helpful depending on the circumstances.

- See Chapter Five for tips on researching members of Congress, other public officials, and staff members.

- Use the worksheet in §§ 3.6–3.12 as a guide to research the background of members of Congress on your issues of concern.

to take a more active or visible role. They may even be willing to help you to approach other members of Congress. You will most likely want to avoid personal meetings or phone calls with those who are actively working against your position, yet grassroots contacts are important so that they cannot say publicly that they have not heard anything from your side of the issue. Besides, effective constituent contacts can actually mute or, under the right circumstances, even change an established position.

While it is possible to make some difference in every encounter if the right approach is used, it makes the most sense to focus your limited time and attention on those who have not yet decided how they will vote.

§8.17 Identify Key Committee and Personal Office Staff

The most important assets and resources that a lobbyist has is Hill contacts. Make a list of contacts that you need to establish that are strength-based on committee jurisdiction and target considerations. While developing strong relationships with key individuals is critical, remember not to place all of your eggs in one basket. Staff turnover on Capitol Hill is extremely high and staff members can be unavailable. It is a good idea to have multiple contacts in key offices and committees.

You need to connect your issues with the committees that have jurisdiction over them. Committee chairs, subcommittee chairs, and their ranking minority counterparts will be contacted about the issue by their own party leaders, outside groups, and the press. You need to make sure that you have addressed all of the subcommittees of jurisdiction and others that will become involved, for example, the House Committee on Rules that will issue a rule regarding the amendment process for House consideration of your issue.

§8.18 Making a Target List for Ranking Legislators' Positions

As you make contacts and gather intelligence on legislators' positions, you will need to develop a systematic method of recording and updating the intelligence that you receive. The Target List Template below allows lobbyists to narrow down their target list, to focus their resources on those who have not yet decided, and, as appropriate, to share information within their organization or with coalition colleagues efficiently.

The headings below are used to rank each member of Congress according to his or her level of support or opposition. Separate forms should be developed for House and Senate members. In ranking positions, always note the direct source of the information. Did the reading come from staff or from the member of Congress directly? Inserting direct quotations from the legislator or staff, with the staff title can be helpful in sharing information and assessing the level of commitment or opposition.

Target List Template

1. **Supports Your Position:** A #1 ranking indicates that the policymaker enthusiastically supports your position, and that position is not expected to change. Your strong supporters should not be neglected as you may be able to encourage them to take a more active or visible role and to help to approach other members of Congress.

2. **Leaning for Your Position:** These are the key members that should be solidified as soon as possible. Determine the reasons for any reservations and work to address them.

3. **Undecided or Position Is Not Known:** While it is possible to make some difference in every encounter, it makes the most sense to focus your limited time and attention on those who have not yet decided how they will vote.

4. **Leaning Against Your Position:** Approach with caution, recognizing that they are not predisposed to favor your arguments. Be especially careful in tailoring your message as well as the messenger (for example, an influential constituent with good ties to the policymaker).

MEMBER NAME (Include political party and state/district)	1. Strongly supports our position	2. Leaning toward supporting our position	3. Undecided or position is not known	4. Leaning against our position	5. Strongly opposed to our position
List all House members or senators (or state legislators) here The roster can list members either alphabetically or by state.	Do they need information or talking points? What actions are they willing to take, for example, cosponsor the bill, hold hearings, send a Dear Colleague letter of support, speak, or work behind the scenes to convince other members?	The egg hasn't hatched. How can the commitment be solidified and confirmed at the member level? Would the member be interested in making a public statement of support? If so, how can that be encouraged and appreciated if it does happen? What is the member hearing from the other side? Is the opposition targeting this member?	Is the member really undecided or just appearing to be so? Who else could check? What are the factors that are likely to carry the most weight with this member? (See Chapter Three for the 7 Position Drivers.)	How did the member develop the position? What are the driving forces?	Could something be done to make the member less enthusiastic about vocalizing the position? Contact by the member's allies on other issues/friends/financial supporters? Press?

5. **Opposes Your Position:** While effective lobbying can make a difference in any situation, you need to exercise caution in contacting those who are actively working against your position. Effective citizen activist contacts still can be useful in muting their position, or occasionally even helping to change it under the right circumstances, such as when an unexpected amendment or alternative is considered.

§8.19 Tips for Personalized Letters

Ideally, you will first write a letter to a congressional office so that you are officially on record and then phone later to confirm receipt and request a meeting. Recognize that because of security issues, congressional mail may take several weeks to be irradiated and arrive at the Capitol Hill destination and overnight service or courier deliveries may not be accepted. However, depending on the security situation, a special procedure may be available for expediting the delivery of congressional mail. These procedures are included in § 8.23. Unfortunately, faxes are generally considered junk mail and thrown away without being read.

§8.20 Personalized Letters vs. Form Letters

The Congressional Management Foundation surveyed congressional staff to determine the influence of personalized postal letters: *"This chart compares the impact of identical form postal mail with that of individualized postal mail. The differences between the two are significant. In cases where the member/senator has not reached a firm decision on an issue, 44 percent of staff surveyed said that individualized postal communications have 'a lot' of influence, compared to only 3 percent for identical form communications. This preference for individualized communications over form communications was a theme that staff repeatedly emphasized throughout our research, some quite passionately."*

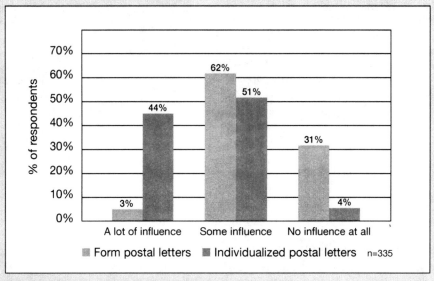

"Communicating with Congress," Congressional Management Foundation, 2005

The correct format for addressing a letter to a member of Congress is included in § 8.22. As illustrated in § 8.20, personalizing the letter is critical. Additional communication tips—making a clear connection to the constituency, including practical examples, and keeping your points concise—are discussed in § 8.2. Whether the letter is handwritten or typed, it needs to be easily readable by a busy person. Only address one issue and try to limit the letter to one page if possible. Letters to House members should reference the House version of the legislation (including a description and bill number) and letters to senators should reference Senate legislation.

Given the volume of mail received by congressional offices daily, junior staff members known as legislative correspondents log a record of the letter into their computer system and prepare an appropriate, frequently canned, response which generally ends

§8.21 Lobby Tips

Assisting Constituents Writing Letters

Advise the citizens with whom you work to send their letters only to their own elected representatives. Constituents frequently desire to write to several legislators who may have a role on their issue of concern but who do not represent them. However, due to congressional courtesies, members of Congress receiving non-constituent letters simply forward the letter to the writing constituent's representative, based on his zip code.

To determine their representative, constituents can:

- Enter zip code at <*www.house.gov/writerep*> or
- Call the U.S. Capitol switchboard at 202–225–3121 and ask the operator to advise them of their House member and two Senators (based on their zip code).

§8.22 Congressional Letter Formatting

House:

The Hon. [INSERT FULL NAME]
U.S. House of Representatives
Washington, DC 20515

Dear [Congressman/Congresswoman] [INSERT LAST NAME]:

Senate:

The Hon. [INSERT FULL NAME]
U.S. Senate
Washington, DC 20510

Dear Senator [INSERT LAST NAME]:

If appropriate, use Chairman/Chairwoman/Chair as the title (depending on the preference of the recipient), instead of Congressman/Congresswoman or Senator. Senators should be referred to as Senator or Chairman, but not as Representative or Congressman.

with a non-committal sentence such as, "I assure you that I will keep your view in mind as I consider this critical issue." Given the numbers of letters received on Capitol Hill daily, members of Congress don't read the letters themselves, but rely on staff to keep them apprised of how their mail is running and to pull letters that demand their personal review. In addition to sending the official letter to the congressional office, send a copy of the letter to the appropriate senior congressional staff handling your issue area, and bring a copy of the letter with you to meetings with staff in Washington, DC, or the district or state.

§8.23 Lobby Tips

Expedited Delivery of Letters to Congress

Security procedures permitting, same day delivery of correspondence to the full House of Representatives or Senate can be achieved by sending unsealed mail through the House or Senate distribution facilities. You can place a specific note at the top of the page, for example, "Time Sensitive Material," or "Attention: Education Legislative Assistants," or "Please Post this Invitation." The House location does not accept expedited mail for the Senate, and the Senate location does not accept expedited mail for the House. Instructions for Senate and House expedited delivery procedures follow, but should be verified prior to sending mailings.

Senate Expedited Delivery Information:

Delivery time
Items are sorted in the early afternoon for delivery the following day. Orders with ten or fewer letters are delivered within 24–36 hours. Orders with eleven or more letters are delivered within 36–48 hours.

Restrictions
Unsealed letters or packages (non perishable) no larger than 4"D X 14"W X 18"H are accepted. Identical letters distributed to all offices do not need to be addressed. For alternate delivery information on items that do not meet the standard criteria, contact the Congressional Acceptance Site at 202-224-5600 or at <congressional_acceptance_site@ssa.senate.gov>.

Payment
Stamps, postage meter, or a money order, made payable to the U.S. Postmaster, must be included. Checks are not accepted. Call for current rates.

Location
Time-sensitive letters and packages can be sent by courier to the Senate Congressional Acceptance Site at 160 D Street NE for expedited delivery to Senate offices. The site is located across from the Capitol Police headquarters.

Advance notification required
Notify the Congressional Acceptance Site prior to sending mail or packages at 202-224-5600 or at <congressional_acceptance_site@ssa.senate.gov>.

House Expedited Delivery Information:

Delivery time
Mailings will be delivered within 24 hours of receipt, provided all requirements are met.

Restrictions
Mailings should NOT be in envelopes, press kits or conference pocket folders, plastic covers or any other containers. Sheets of paper are accepted that can be either be folded or stapled to many other sheets of paper. Booklets in an opened box are accepted. No sealed items will be accepted.

§8.23 Lobby Tips (Continued)

Distribution options
Unaddressed letters must be sorted in one of the following groups:
- All mail stops (700 boxes),
- All Members and Delegates (440 boxes),
- All Members and Committees (490 boxes),
- All Members, Committees, and Subcommittees (625 boxes),
- All Democrats (219 boxes) (this includes 5 Delegates and 2 Independents), or
- All Republicans (221 boxes).

Mailings to any other group of members must be individually addressed.

Payment
Mail directed to members of the U.S. House of Representatives, House offices or House staff sent without postage affixed to the separate pieces is subject to a delivery fee. You can phone the House Postal Operations Call Center at 301–336-8820 (from 8:30 a.m. to 5:30 p.m. Eastern time) for current delivery fees.

Payment for House mailings must be in the form of a check (company, personal, cashiers, etc.) or money order, payable to the United States Treasury.

Cover letter requirements
All mailings must be accompanied by a cover letter on your letterhead that includes:
- Distribution requirements,
- Individual weight of the pieces,
- Number of pieces,
- Rate per piece,
- Total money sent,
- Check or money order number,
- Name and phone number of a contact person, and
- An address where the receipt can be mailed.
  (Note in the cover letter if the mailing is being sent for a different entity.)

Location
Mailings should be delivered between 8 a.m. and 7 p.m. Monday–Friday to: House Postal Operations, 9140 East Hampton Drive, Capitol Heights, MD 20743.

Contact information for House mailings:
House Postal Operations Call Center
8:30 a.m. to 5:30 p.m.
301-336-8820
<pbms.callcenter@mail.house.gov>
Fax 1: 301–336–7081
Fax 2: 301–336–6860

§8.24 **Effective Phone Calls**

> *"**Break the barrier.** When contacting a legislative office, never give a*
> *screener (a receptionist or an appointment secretary) a chance to say no.*
> *Find out which staff person currently has responsibility for your issue*
> *area and get to know him or her."*
> The 30 Laws of Lobbying: 26 (§ 8.4)

While numerous hard-copy and online congressional directory and biographical information services are available for purchase (see § 3.7), constituents may call the Capitol
switchboard and ask the operator to connect them to their House member or one of their
two senators based on their zip code and state. The phone number to the Capitol Switchboard is 202–224-3121 or 202–225-3121. Calls may also be placed to the policymaker's
local office. Contact information for state and district offices is available on the representative's web page, in the local phone directory, and in commercial directories.

The Four Cs of Congressional Calls follow:

1. Connect
- Connect to the right person
- Make your connection to the member's constituency clear

2. Be Clear
- Make a specific request (What legislation you are talking about and what your
  request is; for example, I want to set up a meeting to discuss cosponsorship.)

3. Be Concise
- Recognize the time constraints and conflicting priorities

4. Be Careful
- Be careful what you leave on voice mail
- Use technology wisely (for example, patch through calls)

Commercial services expedite constituent phone calls to their representatives by providing toll-free numbers that connect constituents directly with their legislators (referred to
as "patch through" calls). Phone banks can also provide services such as grassroots alert
calls, rally or event notifications, or get out the vote calls.

    While these services can be effective for rapidly motivating massive numbers of con-
stituents, facilitated efforts can annoy lawmakers and backfire if they are viewed as manufactured. As with all grassroots communications, constituents phoning congressional
offices should authentically believe in what they are doing as opposed to having words
put into their mouths. They don't have to be experts on the issue at hand, but they do
need to have a full awareness of the issue that they are calling about.

§8.25 Lobby Tips

Call-in Days

Organizations frequently establish a specific date for a legislative Call-in Day on a specific issue to encourage grassroots to call Capitol Hill at a strategic point in the legislative process. Ten to fifteen calls into an office on the same issue and on the same day are likely to get the attention of Congressional staff.

Use Voice Mail Cautiously

Get right to the point when leaving voice mails. Legislative staff don't have time to listen to long, drawn-out messages and may delete your message before listening to the entire recording if you are too long-winded. Always speak your name and phone number slowly and clearly, and repeat your phone number. Never assume that your frequent contacts have your phone number. Save them a step and always leave it for their convenience.

Controversial voice mails can be saved by the recipient and played for the media. I recall reading in the media when a senior congressional staff person called a press conference to play a voice mail from a lobbyist threatening the senator with negative advertisements if the senator did not support his organization's position on a bill. Similarly, the press released a voice mail message left by Senator Larry Craig concerning his controversial potential resignation from the Senate. The senator had inadvertently dialed the wrong number and left the message on the wrong telephone voicemail.

§8.26 The Importance of Effective Congressional Meetings

Given the frenetic pace on Capitol Hill, you may face obstacles in connecting with the right person and getting in the door. Some of your best lobbying may be determining how to get in the door. As you attempt to schedule your meeting, reference any presence you have in the state/district.

The most effective meetings are personal meetings from constituents. Research conducted on the effectiveness of various contacts to members of Congress has revealed that contacts by constituents—who have the power of the vote—carry more weight than contacts by Washington, DC, lobbyists. The chart at § 8.27 demonstrates the powerful role of constituent contacts in congressional decision making.

§8.27 Constituent Meetings Compared to Other Congressional Communications

The following "Influences on Member Decision-Making" chart illustrates the power of personal constituent meetings.

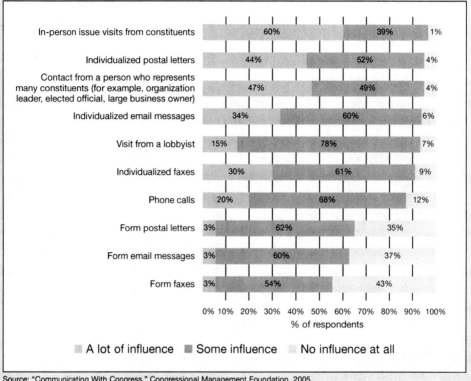

Source: "Communicating With Congress," Congressional Management Foundation, 2005.

"Staff report that personal interactions between members and their constituents— whether through in-person visits or personalized postal or e-mail messages—have far more impact on members' decision-making processes than do identical form communications or visits from lobbyists."

"If your member/senator has not already arrived at a firm decision on an issue, how much influence might the following advocacy strategies directed to the Washington office have on his/her decision?"

As discussed in § 8.2, members of Congress are most interested in the viewpoints of their constituents and in the implications of legislation on their constituency. Consider various venues for meetings including district or state offices, site tours (see Appendix Two for how to host a site visit) or briefings at unique locations that will provide practical insight as well as a visual experience.

§8.28 Ten Tips for Effective Meetings

- Be honest
- Be prepared
- Be prompt
- Listen
- Be a resource
- Ask thoughtful questions
- Respect protocol and the decision tree
- Respect staff, but remember that only the legislator votes
- Say thanks
- Follow-up and maintain communication

§8.29 Reminders for Hill Visit Participants
Respect the Role of Staff

Don't be disappointed when you meet with the staff instead of a member of Congress. While the average age of staff is approximately 30 years old, lawmakers rely heavily on them for legislative recommendations and information. Most staff members do not have the benefit of non-governmental job experience, so they benefit greatly from receiving input from informed constituents.

Use Practical Examples

Practical examples can get a lot of attention on Capitol Hill because they help members of Congress to understand the real-life realities of proposals. Any effective legislative strategy should include several examples of the practical consequences of the proposal.

Respect the Decision Tree

Ask if a decision has been made or when one could be expected. Explain that you will be checking back to determine the legislator's position. Keep current and keep educating the legislator as well as the staff members as the vote approaches. Work to establish several contacts within the office and seek opportunities to interact directly with the member of Congress before the vote occurs.

Don't Cancel

Cancel or re-schedule meetings only as a last resort; try very hard to stick with the original schedule. Any rescheduling will result in a withdrawal of your goodwill account with congressional officials. Try to emphasize the relational costs of cancelling with your visiting grassroots constituents, those within your organization, and with your client as well.

- Phone the congressional office if an unavoidable emergency causes you to run late or cancel the visit. Canceling is bad enough, but not showing up without phoning will hurt the organization's reputation on Capitol Hill.
- Do not be disappointed if you meet with congressional staff. They have more power than you realize. Although typically young, these staffers have been given responsibility by the policymakers to be their eyes and ears on specific issues and to make specific recommendations. Members of Congress have so many commitments and responsibilities that they may not remember you or think to contact you for advice in the future, but the staff representative specifically charged with responsibility for your issue might, and probably represents a more realistic opportunity to establish an ongoing relationship that will eventually lead to meaningful legislative input.

Dress Appropriately

- Wear appropriate business attire (don't dress like a tourist), but wear comfortable shoes since you will do a lot of walking.
- Consult a map and chart your walk in advance. Become familiar with the map of Capitol Hill and the House and Senate office buildings. (See Appendix 3 for a Practical Guide to Working Capitol Hill and a map).

Be Prompt and Respect Their Time

> *"**Be respectful.** Arrive at meetings on time or early. Briefings should be brief. Poor time management communicates lack of value and respect. Know when to stop. Always say thank you."*
> The 30 Laws of Lobbying: 21 (§ 8.4)

Be on time, but don't be impatient if congressional staffers or members keep you waiting, which is frequently the case. Don't enter the office too early, because the rooms are cramped; usually, there is not a good place to wait. Coordinate cell phone numbers of all participants in advance so that you can make plans in case of emergency or delay. If you have to cancel, do it as soon as possible.

Never Underestimate the Role of Congressional Staff

> *"**Be kind to everyone.** The Golden Rule works on the Hill. It's not always apparent who actually wields the most influence and who might in the future. Today's receptionist may be tomorrow's chief of staff. Today, a congressional staff member answers the phones. Tomorrow, that staffer may answer the senator's question on an issue important to you."*
> The 30 Laws of Lobbying: 11 (§ 8.4)

Citizens may be surprised when they discover that they are scheduled to meet with congressional staff instead of the legislator. However, as discussed in Chapter Four, it is important to never underestimate the role of congressional staff members. It may be better to have a twenty-minute substantive meeting with a legislative aide handling your issue than a three-minute meeting with the legislator, who won't remember you the next day.

Use your down time while waiting for congressional appointments to build relationships with additional staff through networking. Even entry-level staff and interns can be very helpful and frequently rise quickly within congressional ranks.

Be Prepared

- Know what you expect from the meeting. What is your want—your "ask"? You won't get it if you don't ask for it.
- If you are asking the policymaker to change his or her established position provide justification, such as, a description of conditions changed or new information on the issue is available that justifies rethinking the issue.
- Coordinate with other attendees in advance
- Select one issue and stick to the point
- Be a resource (ask how you can help)
- Listen and ask thoughtful questions
- Do not forget to say thank you
- Follow up
- Never assume
- Do not threaten
- Stick to the subject and avoid tangents
- Make sure that you coordinate your message with others in your group before the meeting. What are you asking for? Who will give an example or anecdote from the state or district? What materials will be provided and by whom?
- If you are planning a legislative conference, it is important to allow an opportunity for those attending the same Hill meetings to get together and coordinate their plans before their meeting.

Imagine that you are a congressional staff member. The legislator comes in and tells you that he or she needs a brief summary of a key legislative issue within the next hour. You have not dealt much with the issue directly, but you have met with a few people who are interested in the legislation. You reach for your file and see several items. You see a concise one-pager (§ 8.30) that effectively summarizes the issue and provides relevant talking points, information on the bill's status, and contact information from the expert lobbyist who provided the information on the issue. Also in your file is a huge packet of paper provided by a lobbyist, but it has too much information for you to sort through to determine what is relevant and what isn't. You can't recall who gave you the packet and the contact information is not apparent. You will undoubtedly rely on the concisely presented information, and may well call the lobbyist that provided it for some quick assistance.

§8.30 Sample One-Pager

Sample One-Pager

[Name of Issue]

Your Organization's LOGO

[Contact Information: name, title, e-mail, organization and web site]

ISSUE:

Members of Congress and staff have limited time to review material received concerning important legislative issues. A One-Pager is an effective tool for congressional visits and provides a method for leaving a tangible resource that succinctly summarizes your most compelling points. One-Pagers may also be used as enclosures to congressional correspondence and handouts for briefings or press conferences.

BACKGROUND:

Congressional communications have increased exponentially. According to the Congressional Management Foundation, communications to Capitol Hill have increased 300 percent over a decade (see § 8.3). Therefore, communications must be concise and relevant (see §§ 8.2 and 8.5).

CONSIDER VARIOUS FORMATS:

- **Problem and Solution**
- **Talking Points**
- **Myths vs. Reality**
- **Frequently Asked Questions (FAQs)**

See § 5.21 for ideas on formulating your information.

Consider opposing arguments (see § 5.15), congressional messages (see § 3.8), and press themes (see §§ 10.6–10.7) on conducting a media audit on an issue or organization.

STATUS:

Indicate committee status, e.g., specific committee(s) where the legislation is pending, date passed by committee or the other chamber, and the date(s) that hearings, mark-ups, or floor activity are scheduled.

ESSENTIAL INGREDIENTS:

- Your organization contact information and relevant web site
- Background
- Problem to/impact on constituency
- Status
- Solution (What are you asking?)
- Relevant web site links
- Most compelling statistics, surveys, and examples, with relevant local statistics if possible
- Long-term and practical ramifications
- Relevant bill numbers
- Support (e.g., bipartisan congressional support, names/number of key endorsing organizations
- Consider referencing Frequently Asked Questions, talking points, analysis, and status information on your web site to draw them to it.

See § 5.20 for an Issue Evaluation Template.

SUMMARY:

A One-Pager is a calling card and a tool to facilitate further engagement. It is not an end unto itself. Integrate it with your meeting; use it to refer congressional representatives to your web page and to other relevant resources, e.g., studies and statistics.

What to Bring

- Bring a concise summary of your points (a one-pager or list of FAQs with useful web page URLs referenced). See § 8.30 for a sample one-pager format.
- Statistics or examples from the district or state
- A copy of a letter sent by your organization to the legislator on the topic (Most likely, staff will ask you during your meeting whether you have sent an official letter, so be sure to bring a copy with you to your lobbying meetings.)
- A web site printout if it contains useful information, such as data specific to the issue under discussion
- Your business card

What Not to Bring:

- Leave sharp objects, such as knives and scissors, at home. Carrying mace and firearms is prohibited in the congressional buildings and the District of Columbia. Make sure that all meeting attendees understand that they should be prepared to go through metal detectors to enter congressional buildings.
- Don't make bad jokes regarding security. Capitol Police don't laugh at good-natured jokes intended to pass as small talk when they mention bombs or anthrax. While this may seem obvious, it's good to remind those whom you may be escorting to the Hill to avoid any potentially embarrassing situations.

"The Hill is all about relationships. When a lobbyist wants to meet with a member but instead gets an appointment with a staffer, this is not a bad thing. It is the staffer who will make the recommendation on the request. Therefore be prepared to give the staffer background on the issue, connect the issue to the member's district, base, or committee assignment and raise the action items that you want the member to take. Hand the staffer a one-pager and be sure to note what you will do to help the member find support. You need to let the staffer know that you are willing to work to get this done. Don't leave the staffer with the impression that you are making a request and expecting the staffer and the member to get 'er done."

Cassie Statuto Bevan, Senior Professional Staff Member, International Relations Committee, U.S. House of Representatives (Congressional staff member for twenty years)

§8.31 Legislative Conference/ Hill Day Checklist for Event Organizers

- Provide enough time for constituents to travel between their House and Senate meetings and map out in advance the most convenient way for them to do so in light of changing security procedures and construction.
- Before the conference, verify visitor entrances and the availability of Capitol building transit passes with the House Sergeant at Arms office at 202–225–2456 and the

Senate office at 202–224–2341. Depending on security procedures, constituents with appointments on both the House and Senate sides of the Capitol may be able to avoid walking around the entire Capitol block. This may be done by obtaining a transit pass from the appointment desks on the first floor of the north or south side of the Capitol. The Capitol appointment desk staff will need to see the constituent's driver's license and may call the office to confirm the pending appointment.

- Bring contact information regarding logistical information important in addressing problems or emergencies that may arise, for example:
  - Your organization's Hill meeting coordinator (Contact information should be provided to attendees in case constituents arrive and the congressional office appears to be unaware of the appointment.)
  - Bus drivers
  - Hotel reception coordinator
  - Scheduling secretaries or administrative assistants of all speakers
  - Cell phone numbers for staff from your organization and other individuals who are essential to the program (providing speaker introductions, receiving awards)
  - Information to answer constituent questions, such as, Metro stops, cab phone numbers, restaurants, etc. (See A Practical Guide to Working the Hill and Guiding Congressional Witnesses/Hill Visitors in Appendix 3.)
  - Confirm the time/place that you will meet after the visits (bus pickup or hotel) and emergency evacuation and inclement weather contingency plans (See the Top 100-Plus Best Home Pages for Lobbyists on this book's web site at <*www.LobbyingAndAdvocacy.com*>.)
  - Use the talking points in § 8.29 to remind Hill visit participants of essential considerations before and during your conference

§8.32 Coaching Grassroots: Practice for Personal Meetings

Since the average congressional meeting lasts approximately ten minutes, you will want to make the most of every second. Practice makes perfect and increases confidence. Conduct role-play exercises with other members of your group. One person can play the member of Congress and the other person can be the lobbyist. This can be done on stage in front of an audience at a legislative conference using the components and script provided in §§ 8.34–8.36. You can also ask your members in the audience to pair up and take turns playing a member of Congress and constituent. Emphasize the best points to stress on your issues.

§8.33 How to Construct a Role Play Exercise: Preparing to Meet with a Member of Congress

A mock meeting with a member of Congress can be effectively utilized at Hill Days or legislative conferences to prepare constituents for their personal meetings. The following script provides guidelines that you can use to construct your own role play exercise tailored for your issues. The role play exercise described in §§ 8.34–8.36 involves two exercises with the same actors: 1. "How not to" followed by 2. "How to." You need a volunteer from the audience and an experienced government affairs staff member. The volunteer acts as the member of Congress and the government affairs staff member plays the role of constituent.

Additional actors can be added. You may choose to vary the parts and add actors. The components and script are simply guides to use in tailoring your own exercise for your constituents, issues, and meetings.

§8.34 Components: How *Not* to Meet with a Member of Congress Exercise

A narrator announces that the first exercise will demonstrate how not to meet with a member of Congress.

MEMBER of Congress: *Thank you for stopping by.*

Constituent:

- Asks a question that puts the member on the spot, for example, "Do you remember me?" (Of course, the member does not.);
- Gives opinion right away on a number of issues;
- Doesn't mention specific legislation or make a specific request;
- Goes on tangents (mentions that he has been wanting to request a tour of the Capitol and rambles about how his business is doing);
- Didn't take the time to research the member's position on the issue. Doesn't know where the member stands on an issue even though the member has been public on it;
- The constituent mentions too many issues, talks too much and doesn't listen;
- The constituent doesn't know when to stop and wrap things up, and misses cues by the congressional official that it's time to end the meeting.

MEMBER of Congress: *Abruptly ends the meeting.*

§8.35 Components: How *to* Meet with a Member of Congress Exercise

Member of Congress: *Thanks the constituent for stopping by.*

Constituent:

- Makes tie to district right away (for example, the number of employees represented, importance of the company's services to the district);
- Asks if the member has any questions about the issue or bill and listens closely to the response, taking careful notes;

- Has an "ask," that is, Do you think that you would be able to support the bill? Have you decided how you would vote? (without placing the member on the spot or pressuring for an answer);
- Asks the member whether he or she needs any information that would help with the decision;
- Provides concise information (one-pager) customized to the district or state; and
- Politely requests the staff member's email address and asks when to check back for a decision.

MEMBER of Congress: *Thanks the constituent for the helpful input and the staffer promises to follow up shortly.*

§8.36 Example Script: Role Play Exercise

The narrator announces that the next exercise will demonstrate some Hill visit tips through a sample role play exercise with a member of Congress.

How *Not* to:

MEMBER: *Thanks for stopping by.*

Constituent: Hello Congressman. I met you once a couple of years ago at the festival back at the district. Do you remember me?

MEMBER: *[politely searches for a response], "Maybe so . . ." [but doesn't];*

Constituent: I'd like to talk to you about the farm bill. Are you familiar with it?

MEMBER: *Yes. I actually serve on the Agriculture Committee.*

Constituent: Really? You're on the Agricultural Committee? I didn't realize that.

MEMBER: *ACTUALLY, I chair a subcommittee. In fact, I issued a press release last week regarding my position on the farm bill. It has been on my web page.*

Constituent: Well I have other issues I'd like to talk to you about. . . .

[**MEMBER:** *Looks at the time and announces, "Unfortunately I have another meeting."*]

Constituent: I'd like to send you some information on the farm bill, so can I have your email address?

[**MEMBER** *directs constituent to the receptionist and makes a quick exit.*]

How to:

MEMBER: *Thanks the constituent for stopping by.*

Constituent: [Gives a firm handshake while saying,] Nice to meet you, Mr. Chairman. I run Fresh Farm on Serenity Road in your district, which employs 100 of your constituents. We have been recognized by the Chamber of Commerce for our exemplary business practices and we are extremely involved in supporting the community, including several local charities. I would like to talk to you regarding bipartisan legislation that will ensure that common animal agriculture operations are not considered toxic waste sites. Senators Chambliss, Lincoln, and Domenici are sponsoring S. 807, Ag Toxic Waste Designation legislation. I wonder if you have had an opportunity to take a look at the legislation or if you have any questions about the issue?

MEMBER: *I am beginning a comprehensive review of all Ag legislation as we set our agenda for the upcoming Congress, and I will be taking a look at that bill, but I haven't looked at it in detail at this point.*

Constituent: Congressman, as you may know, the bill would clarify that manure is not a hazardous substance, pollutant, or contaminant—under the Comprehensive Environmental Response, Compensation and Liability Act—and the Environmental Planning and Community Right to Know Act.

[Hands congressman a paper with his business card attached.]
I would like to give you our one-pager that documents the need for the legislation. For example, manure is not a toxic waste—and Congress never intended for toxic waste laws to apply to its routine production and use. It's disturbing that some states and environmental groups are trying to apply federal toxic waste laws to normal, routine, agricultural operations. The law was never intended to be used to address the normal application of animal manure as fertilizer. The web site listed at the top of the page will provide updated statistics on the issue as the legislation progresses.

My own experience on the farm in your district documents the need for the legislation. We have an outstanding safety process and are already under a number of regulations. We are trying our best to hold down the prices of pork, but unnecessary regulations will add to the costs, which will have a heightened impact on your low income constituents.

MEMBER: *Do the labor unions have a position on this?*

Constituent: The opposition is mainly pushed by some environmental groups and there has been some action at the state level, but not in ours. But actually there is broad support for the measure. Several farm groups from our state as well as the American Meat Institute have stepped up in support. Will you be able to cosponsor and actively support S. 807?

MEMBER: *I'll have to take a closer look at the legislation.*

Constituent: Do you need any information to help in your decision?

MEMBER: *Is there any information on the costs to the federal government on enforcing this as a toxic substance? I wonder if the case could be made that it would drain valuable resources away from enforcement of real toxic substances.*

Constituent: That is an excellent point. I serve on a national committee of the National Pork Producer's Council. I'm sure they've considered that point and I'll check and get back to you on the issue. You may be hearing from Kate in their office.

I'd also like to invite you and your staff to tour our farm so that you can see our processing procedures first-hand, and your kids would have a great time on the farm!

MEMBER: *Sounds great. I'd actually be interested in that.*

Constituent: Great! What would be the best way for me to go about setting that up?

MEMBER: *Mary is my scheduler.*

Constituent: Great. I'll check with Mary right away to get her contact information and follow-up. Also, who is the best person to check with in your office regarding your decision on cosponsorship?

MEMBER: *Bill Smith handles my agriculture committee issues, so he'd be your contact.*

Constituent: Great! I want to respect your time. *[Stands.]* Congressman, thank you for taking time out of your busy schedule to meet with me. *[Shakes hand.]* I will follow up with Mary and Bill right away, and we look forward to seeing you and your family out on the farm soon.

MEMBER: *Thank you for your helpful input. I enjoyed our conversation. I will take a close look at the issue and will see you back in the district.*

§8.37 Tips for Sending Email

The following tips are provided to help you send effective email that will be read and considered by legislative staff:

- Because congressional staffs are bombarded with emails, send them only what they need to know and tell them why they need to know it right up front.
- If you need to paste or include lengthy material, consider the format that will make their review of the information as efficient as possible (paste the text of the full article at the bottom of the email instead of just a link). As discussed in Chapter Five, consider transferability and where your information could end up.
- Communicate your punch line or primary point in the first one or two sentences, stick to the point, and keep the communication brief.
- Do not include congressional staff or agency officials on bulk emails that won't interest them. Blind copy (bcc:) staff on group emails if necessary to avoid broadcasting their email addresses to external parties.

§8.38 Sample Email to Congressional Staff

SUBJECT: Rep. Jones' Constituent Request on H.R. 1234

Dear John,

While we have not yet had the opportunity to meet personally, I thought that you would find the analysis below from one of your constituents valuable as the Congressman determines his position on H.R. 1234. Our organization represents 500 members from your district who have similar concerns with the legislation. Additionally, our letter that we sent to Congressman Jones on April 3 on the proposal is pasted below.

I understand that the Committee on Rules will soon consider the legislation. I will call you shortly to determine your availability for a brief meeting to discuss the ramifications of this legislation on your constituents.

Sincerely,

[Insert name, title, organization, and phone number]

- Use email appropriately; don't overuse it.
- Don't rely solely on email in direct lobbying or grassroots. (See § 8.39 for a discussion on the limitations of email-only campaigns.)

> *"All politics is personal. Never underestimate the power of personal persuasion and the value of personal relationships. Technology will never replace the benefits of face-to-face conversations. Technology will never vote, people always will."*
>
> The 30 Laws of Lobbying, 3 (§ 8.4)

- Watch what you write. Mistyping an email address by just one character or accidentally typing .org instead of .com on the end of an email address will send your candid and confidential comments to a complete stranger or opponent. Such mistakes are occasionally highlighted in the press to the great embarrassment of the sender. For example, an August 21, 2007 article in *The Hill* newspaper, "Senate earmark battle turns very personal," contained the text of extremely candid comments sent by a congressional communications director calling a senator a derogatory name. The email was intended solely for three colleagues in his own office, but the sender was just one letter off on one of his colleague's name, which landed his confidential email in the inbox of a staffer in a different Senate office.

> *". . . Apply the newspaper test: Never put anything in writing, including email, that you don't want to read on the front cover of the newspaper."*
>
> The 30 Laws of Lobbying, 8 (§ 8.4)

§8.39 The Limitations of Email-Only Grassroots Campaigns

Just as personalized letters carry more weight than form letters, personalized emails sent directly to the appropriate congressional staff person carry more weight than form emails sent to the congressional representative's general email address.

A few cases have surfaced that revealed that form emails had been fabricated by zealous grassroots firms who falsified citizen communications. To thwart such misuse of technology, congressional offices have set up systems such as logic games, which require emailing constituents to type in an answer to a logic question before their email will be processed by the congressional office. While even form-email campaigns may represent citizens' authentic expression of their First Amendment rights, they are often not personalized and can be disregarded by congressional staff. From a grassroots perspective, the success of email-only campaigns is limited. An integrated approach with a number of approaches such as personal visits, letters, and town hall meetings, as well as personalized emails, will carry more weight with policymakers.

§8.40 Follow-up and Continue to Build a Relationship

"The only way to have a friend is to be one."
Ralph Waldo Emerson

Make sure that you respond to any requests for information made during a meeting. Send periodic notes and useful information. Stay in touch and be persistent, but not overbearing. Aim to stengthen the relationship. Information and updates received directly from knowledgeable congressional members and staff can be invaluable.

Follow-up from home state or district contacts is critical.

Meeting opportunities with legislators while they are in Washington, DC, have become less frequent over the years since legislative business frequently occurs between Tuesday and Thursday, resulting in members spending more time in their district or state offices. Additionally, fewer members have chosen to move their families to the DC area due to the increased cost of living and the expectation of shorter tenures. These developments highlight the need for contacts to be made and meetings to be held in the members' home state or district. Another advantage of home state contacts is that policymakers usually have more time and ability to focus when at home since they are distracted by votes and committee meetings when they are in Washington, DC.

§8.41 Special Considerations for State and Multi-State Lobbying

While the basic lobbying communication strategies presented in this chapter apply to state lobbying communications, some significant differences exist, especially in access and timing. For example, most state legislators are in session part time and have fewer staff resources. Therefore, gaining access to a state legislator is much different from trying to arrange an appointment with a member of Congress through a scheduler. State legislators may not have staff to schedule their appointments for them, so you may need to catch them in the hall. They may also answer their own email.

State legislative action can also be more focused. According to the July 2002 edition of *The American Prospect* magazine, approximately 150,000 bills are considered annually by the fifty state legislatures and about 25 percent of them become law. According to Paul W. Hallman, President of MultiState Associates, Inc., "The range of public laws enacted as a percentage of the total bills introduced in Congress varies significantly from year to year and tends to fall into a range between approximately 2 percent and 9 percent. Given the nearly 200,000 bills introduced per biennium in the states, this amounts to the enactment of some 40 or 50,000 new laws every two years." Because of restrictions on how many days the legislature is in session, some states restrict the number of bills introduced per legislator:

> *"Several states restrict the ability of legislators to introduce bills, mostly to manage the workload of legislatures that have tight restrictions on how many days they can be in session, said Brenda Erickson of the National Conference of State Legislatures. For instance, the Colorado Legislature limits each member to five introduced bills in each session, she said."*
> More Bills, More Lawyers for Leg. Office, March 28, 2007, By Paul Singer, *Roll Call* Staff

While legislation introduced the first year (first session) of a two-year Congress carries over to the second year (second session), states have different laws regarding whether legislation can "carry over" to the next year. States also have introduction deadlines and deadlines for crossing over from the chamber of origin to the other legislative chamber.

Coordinating your efforts with other groups engaged in multi-state efforts can be very effective. For example, various national interest groups and associations involved in tracking and lobbying state bills and multi-state corporations frequently coordinate their lobbying efforts. These groups often develop issue-specific model legislation. Public opinion, constituent-focus, and effective coalitions are as important at the state level as they are at the federal level. Chapter Nine addresses effective coalition building at the state level and Chapter Ten addresses public opinion, surveys, and media communications.

Most governors have a state office located at the Hall of States in Washington, DC (444 North Capitol Street near Union Station, on the Senate side of the Capitol). The state office staffs are monitoring federal legislation from their state's perspective and have access to numerous resources including a State Services Organization (SSO) library.

Each federal agency has an intergovernmental affairs department that monitors state legislative and regulatory activities. See §§ 3.6–3.12 for federal agency directory information or check the agency's web site for intergovernmental affairs department contact information.

§8.42 **The 25 Fundamentals for Successful State Lobbying**

By Robert L. Guyer, Esq.

1. Your threshold question of each lawmaker is, "Why would that lawmaker give me his or her vote?" Until you can answer that question, you are not likely to get the vote.
2. Lawmakers are your "customers." Customers buy to meet their needs, not yours.
3. Winning a lawmaker's vote is 10 percent access and 90 percent heat. Access is easy. "Political heat" is a few active trustworthy constituents, both those in- and out-of-district.
4. Get past "nice" to get lawmakers' votes. A lawmaker's being "nice" isn't a vote.
5. "Lobbying is a dance of seduction." Find and use each lawmaker's susceptibilities.
6. "Facts don't vote." A lawmaker votes his or her own peculiar political calculus. Seldom are material facts alone sufficient to get votes; political facts may be.
7. 70 percent of winning a lawmaker's vote occurs before talking to the lawmaker.
8. Lawmakers are almost wholly motivated by special interests. Lobby the special interests that put and keep a lawmaker in power before you lobby that lawmaker.
9. 80–90 percent of lawmakers are irrelevant to your winning or losing your bill. The relevant ones are on key committees and the few, if any, who actually care.
10. Lobby first to get those few relevant lawmakers to "partner" with you. You must show each why partnering with you is good for him or her, politically.
11. Most lawmakers' votes are won or lost at fish fries, not in committee meetings.
12. Most committee meetings are theater since the votes were committed at the fish fry.
13. There is no unimportant staff. You may not need a staff person's support, but you can't afford his or her opposition. Build warm relationships with staff!
14. "The lower you shoot, the higher you hit." Lobby staff, then members of the committee of first reference, its chair, then gatekeeper committees. Lobby leadership last, if at all.
15. The more work you do for lawmakers and especially staff, the more likely your ideas will become law. Materials that don't help them do their jobs end up in the trash!
16. Legislatures operate on three types of rules: 1) written; 2) unwritten; 3) unwritten and unspoken. Violate any of the three and your influence with lawmakers will suffer!
17. Unwritten rule one—you have to talk to groups you don't like, and who don't like you.
18. Unwritten and unspoken rule one—"Thou shalt make campaign contributions" to be a long-term capitol player. Money is good; constituent support is better.
19. Coalitions are indispensable. They exist for advantage—not for love, loyalty, or debt. Don't pre-qualify or disqualify a potential partner. "Politics makes strange bedfellows."

§8.43 Recommended Resources

Effective State and Local Lobbying

- Position statements on state candidates: <*www.ontheissues.org*>
- State and local campaign contributions: <*www.followthemoney.org*>
- Links to state legislatures, state legislature issues, party composition, and calendars: <*www.ncsl.org*>
- *Guide to State Legislative Lobbying*, by Robert L.Guyer. Robert Guyer also provides seminars on state lobbying. See <*www.lobbyschool.com*>.
- See §§ 3.6–3.12 for a worksheet that can be used to assess the factors (the Seven P's or "position drivers") that drive state policymakers' positions.
- Resources for identifying and tracking state legislative issues are provided in § 3.25.

State policy and lobbying organizations:

- ○ National Conference of State Legislatures (NCSL): <*www.ncsl.org*>
- ○ American Legislative Exchange Council (ALEC): <*www.alec.org*>
- ○ The State Government Affairs Council (SGAC): <*www.sgac.org*>
- ○ Council on State Governments (CSG): <*www.csg.org*>
- ○ *Governing* magazine: <*www.governing.com*>
- State Capital Global Law Firm Group offers a variety of legal and compliance information resources, including publications and conferences, for multi-state lobbyists:
  - ○ "Lobbying, PACs and Campaign Finance: 50 State Handbook" by ThompsonWest
- See § 4.64 for resources on state and federal legislative process differences.
- Resources for assessing lobbying and ethics laws applicable to state and local lobbying engagements are provided in § 2.3.
- Trade publications can be a valuable tool to assist with state legislative monitoring. Issue-specific newsletters such as those provided by the Bureau of National Affairs <*www.bna.com*> are extremely helpful to federal lobbyists who want to generally monitor state developments in a specific issue area. BNA reporters occasionally develop charts highlighting state laws in key areas.

20. Most contract lobbyists have little personal political power. Don't confuse a lobbyist's ability to say "hi" to the lawmaker with the ability to get that lawmaker's vote.

21. Your contract lobbyist should be a better lobbyist for the legislature overall. Your members should be better lobbyists for their districts' lawmakers.

22. The best time to lobby is when you don't need anything.

23. What the legislature *giveth* an executive agency can *taketh* away. And what the legislature wouldn't give you, an executive agency might.

24. Facts, law, a desire to carry out its mission, and its own politics motivate an agency. Show the agency how doing what you want achieves what it wants.
25. Nobody cares about your issue as much as you do. Neither money nor the best contractors can win your battles for you. If you don't make it happen, it won't.

§8.44 Special Considerations for Executive Branch Lobbying

The same basic communications principles that apply to lobbying Congress also apply to lobbying the executive branch. Personal contacts, long-term credibility, effective analysis, and practical examples are all very powerful. There is also strength in a large number of quality comments on proposed regulatory actions since agencies typically report on the number of comments received. Also, the comments filed are part of the public record, which can be reviewed by the media and legislators.

The main difference between lobbying agency officials and lobbying Congress relates to the decision-making process. An individual member of Congress can decide on a legislative position and take action very quickly. However, administration positions are developed in light of the president's agenda and are generally developed through an extensive process that involves multiple agencies and officials and includes sign off by the Office of Management and Budget. The clearance process for a cabinet secretary's letter to Capitol Hill can involve clearance by numerous divisions within an agency and dozens of administration officials. Similarly, the development of regulations involves numerous officials and requires sign off by the Office of Management and Budget.

§8.45 Executive Branch Lobbying—Do Your Homework: Understand Existing Administration Policies

Whether lobbying the administration on a regulatory proposal, a judicial nomination, or seeking to shape the administration's position on legislation, understanding any existing administration activities in the area and contacting administration officials early in the process is essential. Agency representatives may be asked about the administration's position on legislation in congressional hearings through letters from various policymakers, through meetings with organization leaders, and through press inquiries to federal agency officials and White House spokespersons. Lobbyists need to determine if their issue has already been discussed within the administration and where it stands in the decision-making process.

It is important to know of existing administration policies, statements, or activities on your issue before lobbying an agency official. See the worksheet in §§ 3.6–3.12 for recommended resources on executive branch positions and priorities. § 4.55 provides recommended resources for tracking executive branch actions. See Chapter Nine (coalitions) for suggestions on working with allies to expand your executive branch lobbying efforts. See the Lobbyist's Annual Calendar Template in Appendix 5 for key dates relating to lobbying the executive branch.

§8.46 Executive Branch Lobbying—Respect Executive Branch Ethics and Disclosure Requirements

Effective lobbying of executive branch officials involves understanding and respecting the special restrictions, ethics laws, and disclosures that apply to lobbying federal employees. Organizations lobbying executive branch officials must register as a federal lobbyist with the House and Senate under the Lobbying Disclosure Act of 1995 (LDA). A discussion of registration procedures as well as legal and ethics requirements applicable to federal employees are provided in Chapter Two.

§8.47 Executive Branch Lobbying— Understand the Environment and Position Determinants

See the worksheet at §§ 3.6–3.12 for resources to use in determining White House priorities and controversial agency issues that could affect an agency's consideration of a public policy issue. The timing of elections, the degree and nature of congressional oversight, pending confirmations for agency officials, other priorities, and the timing of appropriations hearings and legislation are all factors that can potentially influence executive branch policymaking.

§8.48 Executive Branch Lobbying— Know the Process and Work it

The *Federal Register* contained approximately 75,000 pages in 2006 alone. Federal policy affecting your interests can be changed with the stroke of a pen. Effective lobbying involves having a working knowledge of the executive branch policymaking process. Many of the processes and deadlines are dictated by statutory requirements unfamiliar to many federal lobbyists. While most federal lobbyists' responsibilities include executive branch advocacy, most federal lobbyists do not have previous job experience working in a job in the federal government. It is therefore essential that federal lobbyists increase their familiarity with the regulatory and executive branch public policy position process by consulting a general overview of the regulatory process at § 4.53 and taking at least one seminar (in person or by audio course available through groups such as TheCapitol.Net at <*www.TheCapitol.Net*> or the American League of Lobbyists at <*www.alldc.org*>).

§8.49 Executive Branch Lobbying—Respect Agency Staff

> *"We the people of the people, decided to hire these people. Where do*
> *we get this term bureaucrat? Don't ever call someone a bureaucrat."*
> Paul Orfalea, Founder of Kinko's, C-SPAN, April 4, 2007

Agency officials at all levels can be extremely knowledgeable and helpful. Every federal agency has a congressional affairs office dedicated to handling the agency's legislative

§8.51 How to Contact the White House and Agency Officials

The process for sorting correspondence for the president and cabinet officials is similar to the congressional mail processing system. Given the vast amount of mail received, the staff review and tally the mail for appropriate responses, which typically contain canned text, acknowledging the receipt of the correspondence and conveying the official's position as appropriate. Significant delays in mail delivery are experienced due to an extensive security screening process. Due to the large volume of email received, the White House cannot respond to every message; however, responses are tabulated similar to congressional email.

While large numbers of citizen letters, emails, and phone calls to the White House Comment Line are likely to be noticed by administration officials, effective White House and agency lobbying involves establishing relationships. While organizations often need to send a letter to the president to officially weigh in on an issue, this action alone is not likely to accomplish much, if anything. In the executive branch, as with Congress, all politics is personal. Establishing credible relationships and communications with agency and White House officials responsible for your issue area is much more effective than simply sending correspondence that will receive a canned reply. Bring copies of your letter to the president or agency heads with you to your meetings as a tool for communicating your perspective on the issue.

Mailing Address: The White House
1600 Pennsylvania Avenue NW
Washington, DC 20500

White House Switchboard: 202-456-1414 (to be connected with specific White House offices or staff)

White House Comment Line: 202-456-1111 (to register your opinion)

Visitors Office: 202-456-2121

Email: <comments@whitehouse.gov>, <vice_president@whitehouse.gov>

Invitations: Check the White House web page at <www.whitehouse.gov> for guidelines on extending an invitation to the president or vice president or their spouses.

Communications With Other Federal Government Agencies: If you have a question about a particular government benefit, program, or service, visit <www.USA.gov>. USA.gov is the official gateway to all government information and is a catalyst for a growing electronic government. Verify an official's title before corresponding in any mode, for example, cabinet secretaries are referred to as Mr. Secretary or Madame Secretary and the "The Honorable" precedes their name when their first and last names are used:

The Honorable Elaine L. Chao
Secretary of Labor
U.S. Department of Labor
Frances Perkins Building
200 Constitution Ave. NW
Washington, DC 20210

Dear Secretary Chao:

See § 8.53 for agency contact resources.

activities. These are typically extensive operations with knowledgeable staff that can be an excellent resource as you lobby your issue. See § 8.51 for staff contact resources.

§8.50 Tips for Providing Official Comments on Proposed Federal Regulations

Anticipate action in advance and incorporate comment deadlines into your Executive Branch Action Plan as soon as they are known. Determine areas of upcoming regulatory action through research, personal contacts with agency officials, trade publications, and a daily review of the *Federal Register*. Review the Semiannual Regulatory Agenda (Unified Agenda), which is published in the *Federal Register* (usually in April and October). It summarizes the rules and proposed rules that each federal agency expects to issue during the following six months. The agenda is published by the Office of the Federal Register National Archives and Records Administration (NARA). Current and previous issues may be searched at *<www.reginfo.gov>*.

Confirm all submission requirements, including contact information for the designated federal official receiving the comments. Specific instructions are included in the *Federal Register* notice of the action and comments may be submitted online at *<www.regulations.gov>*.

Regularly review active regulations under the Regulatory Planning and Review process (E.O 12866 and its predecessor, E.O. 12291): *<www.reginfo.gov>*. (Regulatory reviews completed in the last thirty days and OMB's Office of Information and Regulatory Affairs' (OIRA) letters to agencies are also listed.).

§8.52 Preparing for Executive Branch Meetings

See § 8.29 for tips on what to bring and what to leave at home. The general preparation and communication tips for Hill visits apply to agency meetings. In addition, you need to make sure that you bring a valid photo ID and the phone number of your agency official contact so that you can successfully negotiate the agency building entrance and security clearance process. Recognize that there may be a public record of your meeting with a high level official that can be accessed through Freedom of Information Act requests or otherwise.

§8.55 Advocacy and the Judicial Process

While the legislative and judicial branches are separate, there is much interplay between these functions as public policy is developed and refined as part of our foundational system of checks and balances. Citizen interests weigh in with the judicial process by submitting or signing on to amicus curiae (friend of the court) briefs. These briefs provide justices with information that can help them reach and express their decisions. Such information can also reinforce the arguments of parties to the litigation.

§8.53 Recommended Resources

Effective Executive Branch Lobbying

- Prior to meeting with agency officials, utilize the worksheet at § 3.5 to determine the factors that are driving their positions.

- **Statements of Administration Policy** (statements issued by the Office of Management and Budget on major legislation issued before House or Senate floor votes): *<www.whitehouse.gov/omb>*.

- Numerous criminal and civil statutes as well as disclosure requirements apply to federal lobbyists lobbying the executive branch as well as federal employees involved in congressional liaison, such as, anti-bribery statutes, revolving door requirements, and the Anti-Lobbying Act of 1919. See Chapter Two for a discussion of these laws as well as resources for staying up to date on them as they change.

- *Congressional Quarterly's* Federal Staff Directory (print or online) *<www.cqpress.com>*.

- **Project Vote Smart** (*<www.vote-smart.org>*) provides information including biographical information and public statements on executive branch agency heads.

- For current and past regulations under review (updated daily) as well as links to letters from the Office of Management and Budget (OMB) to federal agencies with comments on specific regulations (return letters responding to a draft rule, prompt letters, suggesting an issue worthy of agency priority and post review letters sent after an OMB review), go to *<www.regulations.gov>*.

- TheCapitol.Net regulatory links: *<www.AdminResearch.com>*.

- GSA's regulatory guide, "RegInfo": *<www.reginfo.gov>*.

- Federal Regulatory Process Poster by Kenneth Ackerman: *<www.AgencyPoster.com>*.

- Louis Database: *<www.louisdb.org>*.

- **The Plum Book** (officially titled, the United States Government Policy and Supporting Positions) lists the names and titles of all federal political appointees. The book may be obtained from the House Committee on Oversight and Government Reform (*<http://oversight.house.gov>*) or the Government Printing Office bookstore (*<http://bookstore.gpo.gov>*).

- **U.S. Government Manual** is free and available online at *<www.gpoaccess.gov>* and contains basic federal agency contact information and descriptions of federal programs. However, subscription services, such as the Federal Yellow Book (*<www.leadership directories.com>*) provide more current contact information. Some information is available on agency web sites, but direct phone numbers and email addresses of high-ranking officials generally are difficult to find.

- RegScan (subscriber service): *<www.regscan.com>*.

- **Executive Branch Lobbyists:** Check lobbyist databases to determine which lobbyists are contacting specific federal agencies (also searchable by state): *<www.lobbyists.info>* or *<www.senate.gov/lobby>*.

- A list of federal agency acronyms is available at *<www.whitehouse.gov/appointments/ list.html>*. Contact information for more than 44,000 federal agency staff within the Washington, DC, metropolitan area is available at: *<www.leadershipdirectories.com>* (subscription). Search across multiple government databases, including presidential documents and the free online Government Manual at *<www.gpoaccess.gov/multidb.html>*.

§8.54 Number and Turnover Rate of Political Appointees in Cabinet-Level Agencies

According to the Office of Personnel Management, approximately 3,100 of the 1.8 million federal government employees are political appointees who serve at the pleasure of the President. The following chart shows the percentage of non-career executives (excluding Schedule C's) for the Cabinet level agencies.

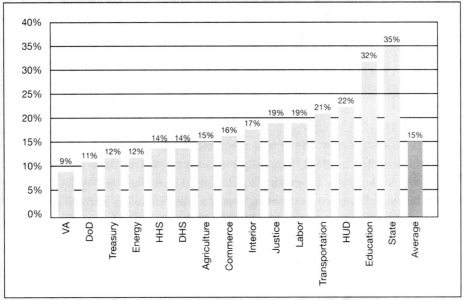

Source: "Addressing the 2009 Presidential Transition at the Department of Homeland Security," June 2008. Research conducted by the National Academy of Public Administration. Data from Fedscope as of September 30, 2007, adjusted for Transportation Security Agency executives who are not identified in Fedscope. Fedscope information is for filled positions. Accurate information from OPM on authorized executive positions is not available.

A 1994 GAO study documented the average political lifespan of political appointees (including political appointees requiring Senate confirmation) to be 1.8 years of service. *Source: Political Appointees: Turnover Rates in Executive Schedule Positions Requiring Senate Confirmation, General Accounting Office (now named the Government Accountability Office), April 1994.*

Since the executive branch revolving door turns steadily, lobbyists must establish and maintain political appointee contacts on an ongoing basis to achieve executive branch advocacy objectives.

§8.56 Lobby Tips

U.S. Supreme Court

- Transcripts of oral arguments are posted on the Supreme Court Web site on the same day an argument is heard by the Court at: *<www.supremecourtus.gov>*. Archives are available for cases argued starting in October 2000. Bound copies of individual transcripts may be purchased by contacting Alderson Reporting at 202-289-2260 or *<www.aldersonreporting.com>*. Supreme Court opinions are available at *<www.supremecourtus.gov>*.
- The ABA publishes a useful newsletter and accompanying web site, "Preview of United States Supreme Court Cases," *<www.supremecourtpreview.com>*.
- See *<www.LobbyingAndAdvocacy.com>* for a primer on the judicial process.

Through judicial review, the courts overturn unconstitutional laws and executive actions. Additionally, Congress frequently responds to controversial judicial decisions with legislation or hearings. Interests also file lawsuits challenging legislation and regulations as unconstitutional or as violating specific laws, including statutes governing the legislative or regulatory processes. Accordingly, litigation strategies are frequently coordinated with legislative and agency lobbying strategies.

§8.99 Chapter Summary

- Remember that since all politics is local, communications that come directly from constituents and address the implications of legislation on the policymaker's constituency will be the most effective. (§ 8.2)
- Know your issue, listen to the policymaker's concerns, provide reliable information, and always follow through when you have agreed to provide additional information to the policymaker. During your communications, determine the policymaker's familiarity with your issue, and use this information to tailor your approach, using practical examples and experiences. (§ 8.2)
- Avoid any type of conduct that could be considered a violation of current laws or ethical standards for lobbyists. Never threaten, gossip, or violate confidences (§ 8.2). Familiarize yourself with the 30 Laws of Lobbying, and use the scientifically based CHATS℠ method to ensure effective communication with congressional members and staff (§§ 8.4, 8.5).
- Consider timing and respect the communication preferences of your recipient when determining the best methods of personal communications. Remember that effective lobbying requires integrating various approaches of communicating. (§§ 8.6, 8.7)

- Identify key leaders and decision makers in both the House and the Senate early, and continue to cultivate potential champions for your issue. (§§ 8.12–8.15)
- Determine where members of Congress stand on your issue early in the legislative process. Make a list of contacts in key offices and on committees. As you make contacts and gather information, use a tool such as the template in § 8.18 to rank each member of Congress according to his or her level of support or opposition for your issue. Ranking sheets can be an effective method for coordinating intelligence with colleagues and coalition members. (§§ 8.16–8.18)
- Utilize the format in § 8.22 when preparing correspondence for individual policymakers. Remember that a personalized letter is always more effective than a form letter, as illustrated in the chart in § 8.20. While security procedures typically result in significant delays in the delivery of mail to Congress, an expedited procedure is usually available that may allow you to have your mail delivered to House or Senate offices within 24 to 48 hours (§ 8.23).
- Tips are provided to ensure successful phone communication (the Four C's of Congressional Calls listed in § 8.24). Consider the use of call-in days to maximize constituent efforts, but remember that congressional staff can be skeptical of efforts that appear to be manufactured. (§§ 8.24, 8.25)
- Recognize that the most effective communications are personal meetings with constituents (§§ 8.26, 8.27). Use the Top Ten Tips for Effective Meetings and the reminders listed in § 8.28 to prepare for a successful meeting. Know what to bring with you as well as what *not* to bring to your meeting (§ 8.29).
- Several tools are provided for governmental affairs professionals who arrange legislative conferences and Hill days with congressional meetings for constituents. These tools include a checklist for Hill event organizers (§ 8.31) and a list of reminders for Hill visit participants (§ 8.29). §§ 8.32–8.36 provide specific instructions for coaching citizens prior to their meetings, including scripts for role play exercises on "How to" and "How Not to" meet with a member of Congress.
- Use the email tips provided in § 8.37 and the sample email to congressional staff (§ 8.38) to help you send emails that will be read and considered by legislative staff. Remember that congressional staff are often skeptical of the authenticity of email-only grassroots campaigns and easily recognize form emails with canned language as coordinated efforts. (§ 8.39)
- Avoid pressuring citizens to communicate on issues that they don't really believe in or understand and encourage them to personalize their communications. Using an integrated approach with various communication formats will provide the most impact. (§ 8.39)
- Know that policymakers are usually busy and distracted by competing activities and votes while in Washington, DC, and that communications with the legislator in his or her state or district are often more effective. (§ 8.40)

- While most strategies listed in Chapter Eight apply to state legislators as well as members of Congress, lobbyists should recognize that differences exist as well (§ 8.41). Use the resources listed in § 8.43 to ensure effective state and local lobbying.
- Essential guidelines to follow when lobbying the executive branch. (§ 8.44)
- Tips for giving official comment on proposed federal regulations are provided (§ 8.50). Lobbyists can use the provided format for contacting White House and agency officials (§ 8.51) or for helping citizens to do so.
- Tips are provided for effective executive branch meetings (§ 8.52) and resources are recommended for accessing federal and regulatory information (§8.53).
- A number of opportunities exist for advocates to shape public policy issues through involvement in the judicial process. For example, advocates can weigh into the judicial process with amicus curiae (friend of the court) briefs. There is significant interplay between Congress and the judiciary with Congress responding to controversial judicial decisions and interests filing lawsuits to challenging enacted legislation or regulations. (§ 8.55)

Multiply Your Influence:
Coalitions and Partners

"The way a team plays as a whole determines its success. You may have the greatest bunch of individual stars in the world, but if they don't play together, the club won't be worth a dime."

Babe Ruth

Chapter 9: Multiply Your Influence: Coalitions and Partners

§9.1 Introduction

"None of us is as smart as all of us."
Japanese proverb

On April 17, 2007, House Ways and Means Committee Chairman Charlie Rangel recounted a story involving the power of coalition organization. When asked why he voted for gun control when 85 percent of his constituents were against it and 15 percent were for it, he replied, "because the 15 percent are organized!"

Coordinated legislative efforts are a feature of most legislative campaigns. Nearly all lobbyists work through legislative coalitions. This is because they recognize not only that there is great strength in numbers, but also that there is great impact in coordinating strategies and pooling resources. Chapter Nine helps you identify existing efforts in your issue areas and coordinate with various groups and individuals in order to get your message across.

§9.2 Benefits of a Coalition Effort

"The whole is greater than the sum of its parts."
John Wooden

Lobbyists devote much of their work time to coalitions because they understand that there is great strength in numbers. Coalitions allow lobbyists with common interests to pool resources, contacts, expertise, and intelligence, and to coordinate their message. A well-coordinated coalition of interests can reach legislators more quickly and effectively than any single group working alone. Presenting a unified front, especially when non-traditional allies are included, can be impressive to the policymakers, the media, and the public.

§9.3 A Profile of Coalition Utilization

An informal 2007 Coalition Building Survey of Federal Lobbyists by Columbia Books (see § 9.4) found that most lobbyists are involved in several coalitions and put a considerable amount of time into their efforts. Sixty-five percent of responding lobbyists had been a member of two to five coalitions during the past twelve months, and more than 18 percent had been a member of more than five coalitions in that time period. The survey showed that 35.9 percent devoted on average more than one day a week to coalition building; 27.2 percent spent approximately one day a week; and 37 percent spent less than one day a week.

In 2007, the database of registered lobbyists at *<www.lobbyists.info>* contained 424 formal federal legislative coalitions; however, the true number of federal coalitions is much higher since coalitions can be extremely informal and can organize and disband over the course of just a few weeks. Coalitions range from the spontaneous "paper only"

§9.4 Coalition Involvement Survey

Coalition Building Survey

1. On average how much of your time is devoted to coalition building? (Select one)

	Response Percent	Response Count
Approximately one day per week	27.2%	25
Less than one day per week	37.0%	34
More than one day per week	35.9%	33
answered question		92
skipped question		1

2. How many coalitions have you participated in during the past 12 months.

	Response Percent	Response Count
0	3.3%	3
1	13.0%	12
2-5	65.2%	60
more than 5	18.5%	17
answered question		92
skipped question		1

3. How useful do you find the following factors in deciding whether to join a coalition being formed by another group?

	Very Useful	Somewhat Useful	Rarely Useful	Never Useful	Rating Average	Response Count
Shared interest in a specific issue	86.0% (80)	12.9% (12)	1.1% (1)	0.0% (0)	1.15	93
Shared interest in a specific policy or piece of legislation	92.5% (86)	7.5% (7)	0.0% (0)	0.0% (0)	1.08	93
Common industry	30.4% (28)	62.0% (57)	7.6% (7)	0.0% (0)	1.77	92
Compatibility of organization types (labor union, business group, corporation, etc.)	17.4% (16)	67.4% (62)	15.2% (14)	0.0% (0)	1.98	92
answered question						93
skipped question						0

efforts, with several groups sending a group letter to Capitol Hill, to the more formal coalitions that have membership dues, paid staffs, and dedicated offices.

§9.5 Disclosure of Lobbying Activities

As discussed at length throughout this book, lobbyists must continually be aware of lobbying laws and ethics requirements in all facets of their work. This includes coalition

§9.4 Coalition Involvement Survey (continued)

4. Which of the following resources do you use in your coalition-building efforts? (Select all that apply)

	Response Percent	Response Count
Personal/industry networking	98.9%	92
Print news items, periodicals and white papers	75.3%	70
Electronic news items, periodicals and white papers	66.7%	62
Electronic databases like Lobbyists.info, SOPR, or OpenSecrets	20.4%	19
Contact management software	4.3%	4
Other (please specify)	5.4%	5
answered question		93
skipped question		0

5. How do you use existing technology to assist you in building coalitions? (Select all that apply)

	Response Percent	Response Count
For identifying potential allies or adversaries	55.4%	51
For establishing contact with other coalition members or potential members	83.7%	77
For disseminating relevant information or core issue messages to constituents, members, or elected officials	**84.8%**	78
For tracking the latest developments on a specific issue, policy or piece of legislation	83.7%	77
Other (please specify)	1.1%	1
answered question		92
skipped question		1

Source: 2007 Coalition Involvement Survey, Columbia Books, Inc.

work and contributions. In addition to the lobbying ethics, gift, and activity restrictions discussed in Chapter Two, coalition leaders and members should confirm that their coalitions are properly registered and that contributions are disclosed in keeping with federal, state, and local requirements.

Cleta Mitchell, a partner at Foley & Lardner LLP, succinctly describes the federal coalition reporting requirements under the Lobbying Disclosure Act of 1995 (as amended by the Honest Leadership and Open Government Act of 2007):

"Lobbyists must register the name, address, and principal place of business of any organizations other than the client, that contribute more than $5,000 to the registrant or client during the quarter to fund lobbying activities of the registrant and actively participates in the planning, supervision, or control of lobbying. No disclosure is required if the organization to be identified lists the client on its web site as being a member of, or contributor to, the client unless the organization in whole or major part plans, supervises, or controls lobbying activities. Additionally, the organization must disclose the coalition's internet address on its registration."

Cleta Mitchell, partner, Foley & Lardner LLP, September 17, 2007

§9.6 Challenges Confronting Legislative Coalitions

While lobbyists find much utility in working through coalitions, the dynamics of individual groups with their own institutional interests attempting to work together can present challenges. Competitive interests within and among coalitions can distract from legislative goals and convey division to policymakers.

NON SEQUITUR ©1998 Wiley Miller. Dist. By UNIVERSAL PRESS SYNDICATE.
Used with permission. All rights reserved.

§9.7 Frequent Coalition Challenges and Solutions

Problem:
Negative Competition between Participants and Inflated Egos

- Vying or even undercutting each other for press.
- Unhealthy competition for visibility with public officials, such as negative characterizations or gossip regarding other coalition members in an attempt to magnify one's status.

(*Note:* Such undercutting tends to prevail when organizations compete with each other for members or clients.)

Effect:

- Detracts from achievement of results-oriented legislative goals.
- Can undermine effectiveness to external parties, for example, Hill allies, and result in deal-making by a single member or without the knowledge or support of the entire group.

Solution: Share the Credit

- Provide numerous visibility opportunities such as meetings with influential legislative officials and media contacts (but only provide as much visibility as an organization desires).
- These opportunities and regular reminders will help participants become confident that coalition activities will strengthen and not threaten their relationships with their own members.
- The goal is to share the credit as well as the work and to help each participating organization achieve victory for their membership, clients, or company.
- When coalition members understand the benefit that a well-coordinated joint effort will bring to each organization, they will be more likely to share the work and the credit.
- Find specific and tailored ways to recognize all member contributions and provide visibility to members who seek it: praise specific efforts in front of influential policymakers or staff, create co-chairs of major efforts and subcommittee leaders, feature various organizations on the coalition web page, hold joint press conferences and produce joint correspondence as appropriate.
- You can establish subcommittees, such as grassroots, press, policy/legislative analysis, legal, finance, outreach, and lobbying (to coordinate House and Senate meetings and other communications, not only to facilitate activities, but also to provide visibility opportunities and recognition for active leaders within the group).

(Continued on page 286)

§9.7 Frequent Coalition Challenges and Solutions
(continued)

Problem: **Free-riders**	**Effect:** • Can dishearten coalition members who make meaningful contributions, and serve as a disincentive for those considering contributions. • Raises questions concerning the free-rider's organization's commitment to the issue.

Solution:

- Define expectations from the very start, including financial contributions, commitments, member responsibilities, and benefits.
- Fashion several levels of involvement to reflect differing levels of commitment.
- Clearly express expectations. (Levels of commitment can vary, but can be anticipated; the role and commitment of each participant should be delineated early in the process.)
- Gently remind participants that members are expected to contribute to the effort. Coalitions are not established merely to exchange information (as substitute newsletters, or to expand contacts for people who are not committed to the cause).
- Ignoring problems with members who do not contribute and are uncommitted can undermine the value of the contributions of those members who are actively contributing and are effectively engaged to advance the coalition's mission.

Problem:
Lack of Structure

Effect:

- While some coalitions operate better when they are loose-knit or short-term, the absence of structure and clear expectations can lead to internal competition, communication problems, and a lack of organizational commitment.

Solution:

- Develop the appropriate structure in light of the nature of the effort.
- For all but extremely short-term efforts, develop a formalized work plan and budget with short- and long-term goals, priorities, and clear coalition structure options.

§9.7 Frequent Coalition Challenges and Solutions
(continued)

- Discuss options for various levels of organization and structure as the coalition is conceived, and obtain buy-in from all key players. A candid discussion during a coalition meeting may help to constructively identify and satisfy participants' own organizational needs.

Problem: Moles	
Problem: Moles	**Effect:**

**Problem:
Moles**

Effect:

- Disclosing your coalition's strategies to the opposition can cause extreme damage and even result in defeat.

Solution:

- Determine the level of commitment of every person on your distribution lists.
- Require participants to sign in at meetings, and follow up with new members or interested parties to determine the nature of their interest and level of commitment.
- Don't send sensitive information to individuals or large groups you don't know.
- Require all conference call participants to identify themselves and obtain a list of participants from the provider of participants.

**Problem:
Lack of
Resources**

Effect:

- Limited effectiveness; you can't change the world if you can't pay the rent.

Solution:

"Many hands make light work."—John Heywood
- Motivate coalition members to help you expand the effort.
- Place coalition expansion on each meeting agenda.
- Consider allowing potential members who lack the financial resources for membership to contribute "in-kind" by covering certain coalition expenses, such as support staff for an effort, printing, or food (if allowable under gift rules).
- Use effective research strategies, databases, and legislative contacts to identify potential members and contributors. (See § 9.8.)

§9.8 **Expanding Your Efforts**

"Every man owes a part of his time and money to the business or industry in which he is engaged. No man has a moral right to withhold his support from an organization that is striving to improve conditions within his sphere."

President Theodore Roosevelt

1. Use your Networks and Connections

Networking within your existing associations, organizations, coalitions, and associates is an excellent way to determine which groups and individuals are already involved or who might be interested in your specific issue. This can range from making an announcement at the end of a coalition meeting to sending an email to your existing contacts who have an interest in your issue area.

2. Ask Established Legislative Leaders and Experts in the Area

Ask legislative staff and administration allies for advice. A strong supporter on the Hill may be able to refer groups that have contacted him. Conduct a media search and identify experienced lobbyists and state advocates who may have battled for your issue or are in a position to help you identify potential players.

3. Search Public Records and Lobbying Disclosure Databases

One method of identifying existing lobbying efforts and potential federal or state allies is to search federal and state lobbying registration forms by a variety of categories. Federal lobbying registrations identify the House and Senate bills lobbied, as well as the executive agencies lobbied by specific organizations and lobbyists along with their office's contact information. The 2007 "Lobbyists Coalition Involvement Survey," by Columbia Books, Inc., revealed that lobbyists tend to underutilize technological tools available to them to identify potential allies. Federal lobbyist registration forms can be searched by using a variety of criteria including subject matters lobbied, states represented, and specific governmental agencies lobbied (see Chapter One for a list of the various subjects). For example, you can search for all federal lobbyists registered in 2007 who represented California interests on homeland security issues or those who have recently registered to lobby the Department of Homeland Security. Also, state lobbyist registrations may be used to identify potential state and federal coalition members. The following lobbyist databases can be searched to identify lobbyists and clients by issue area, geographical region, and federal or state agency lobbied:

- Federal lobbyists: *<www.lobbyists.info>*, *<www.disclosure.senate.gov>*, and *<www.house.gov>*
- State lobbyists: *<www.publicintegrity.org>*
- Also see this book's web site for more resources: *<www.LobbyingAndAdvocacy.com>*

Also, you can select registrations by year and subject if you are looking for lobbyists who may have been engaged in previous legislative battles.

Use the following criteria to search and view federal lobbyist registrations via the Secretary of the Senate's Office of Public Records by accessing <*www.disclosure.senate.gov*>.

Query the Lobbying Disclosure Act Database

Search Filings

Step 1 of 3: choose up to five search options

you have not selected any fields.

Registrants	Clients	Lobbyists
☐ registrant name	☐ client name	☐ lobbyist name
☐ registrant country	☐ client state	☐ lobbyist status (active or terminated)
☐ registrant ppb country	☐ client country	☐ lobbyist covered position description (for electronic filings only)
	☐ client ppb country	☐ lobbyist covered government position indicator (yes or no)

Filings	Affiliated Organization	Foreign Entities
☐ report type	☐ affiliated organization name	☐ foreign entity name
☐ amount reported	☐ affiliated organization country	☐ foreign entity country
☐ date, filing received		☐ foreign entity ppb country
☐ filing period		☐ ownership percentage
☐ filing year		
☐ government entity contacted		
☐ issue area (lobbying activity)		
☐ specific lobbying issue (for electronic filings only)(text)		

submit

(Please note that your search results will be limited to the first 1000 records returned.)

Disclosure Home

---

4. Online and Hard-Copy National and State Association Directories

Go to <*www.associationexecs.com*> for online and print editions of *National Trade and Professional Associations and State and Regional Associations*, from Columbia Books. A free five-day trial is available, and information can be downloaded into Excel or Outlook functions.

5. Media Searches and the Public Record

To search congressional hearing records to identify groups that have weighed in on the issue or similar issues in the past, use the Library of Unified Information Sources (LOUIS) at <*www.louisdb.org*> or use commercial services such as Gallery Watch (<*www.gallerywatch.com*>) or CQ <*www.cq.com*>.

6. Campaign Contributors

Another way to determine potential allies is to examine the records of those who are politically active through their campaign contributions, as well as interested parties that have contributed to specific policymakers. Political campaign contributions to federal and state elected officials can be searched in a variety of ways. Consider using the following state and federal databases:

- View the FEC's disclosure database to look up political contributions by individuals and candidates, search campaign finance reports, and view actual disclosure reports filed at *<www.fec.gov>*.
- Search CQ MoneyLine by Congressional Quarterly at *<www.fecinfo.com>*.
- Search the Center for Responsive Politics contribution database at *<www.opensecrets.org>*.
- Obtain customized election data, if needed, at *<www.opensecrets.org>*.
- The National Institute on Money in State Politics provides a free searchable database of all state level political campaign contributions at *<www.followthemoney.org>*.

7. Consider State-Related Groups as Resources

The following groups are known as the Big Seven:
- National Governors Association: *<www.nga.gov>*
- National Conference of State Legislatures: *<www.ncsl.org>*
- Council of State Governments: *<www.csg.org>*
- National Association of Counties: *<www.naco.org>*
- U.S. Conference of Mayors: *<www.usmayors.org>*
- National League of Cities: *<www.nlc.org>*
- International City/County Management Association: *<www.icma.org>*

For these resources and more, see this book's web site: *<www.LobbyingAndAdvocacy.com>*.

8. Consider Non-traditional Alliances

> *"There are no permanent allies ... only permanent interests."*
> 19th century British Foreign Secretary Lord Palmerston

Consider potential allies based on the nature of your issue. Presenting a united front, especially when non-traditional allies are included, can be impressive to the policymakers, the press, and the public. Consider thinking outside the box to engage governmental leaders whom you may not work with traditionally.

§9.9 **Effectively Addressing Conflict**

Conflict will inevitably develop between individuals and groups both within and among coalitions. Groups with the same membership base may vie for visibility in the press and on the Hill by attempting to undercut or discredit their coalition partners. While some competition can be healthy, competition that undercuts the efforts and injures relationships can cause long-term rifts between organizations that could work together. Knowing how to finesse these types of challenges will aid you in achieving legislative victories through effective coalitions. Maintaining civility when your organization or effort is criticized by opposing interests is important to achieving success. Sometimes it's not my way or your way, but a third way that works for both interests.

§9.10 Example of a Typical Coalition Meeting Agenda

I. Legislative Developments
- Update from committee staff members
- Update on new legislation

II. Grassroots
- State captain reports (via speaker phone): Reports on town hall meeting participation, state team expansion efforts, and letters to the editor.

III. Targets
- Update House and Senate rankings

IV. Potential Senate Hearing
- Update on timing and potential witnesses

V. Administration Position
- Upcoming meetings with key officials

VI. Press
- Discussion of media plans for targeted states
- Status of editorial board visits

VII. Upcoming Congressional Staff Briefing
- Timing and participants

VIII. Expanding the Coalition
- Brainstorming on new allies and members

IX. Status of New Survey/Polls
- Association survey efforts and upcoming Gallup Poll

X. New Business

§9.12 Coalition Organization: Examples of Varying Degrees of Structure

Informal	Formal
No paid staff Coalition letter to Capitol Hill	Paid staff
Short-term coordination of Hill visits, Grassroots	More long-term coordination/ formalization
Short-term basis	Dedicated office/staff
No membership dues	Established dues structure Standing committees
No office	Hired consultants

§9.11 Motivating Quotes for Coalition Teamwork

"Individual commitment to a group effort . . . that is what makes a team work, a company work, a society work, a civilization work."
Vince Lombardi

"Teamwork is the fuel that allows common people to produce uncommon results."
Unknown

"Michael, if you can't pass, you can't play."
Coach Dean Smith to Michael Jordan in his freshman year at UNC

"The ratio of We's to I's is the best indicator of the development of a team."
Lewis B. Ergen

"It is amazing how much can be accomplished if no one cares who gets the credit."
John Wooden

"In cooperative situations, others are depending on you to succeed. In competitive situations, others hope to see you fail."
Unknown

"A team should never practice on a field that is not lined. Your players have to become aware of the field's boundaries."
Former NFL Coach John Madden

"Never doubt that a small group of thoughtful, committed people can change the world. Indeed, it is the only thing that ever does."
Margaret Mead

§9.13 A Tool to Empower Allies to Maintain Effective Coalitions

Many associations make grassroots and legislative information available on their web site, such as this page on the American Veterinary Medicine Association (AVMA) web site: *<www.avma.org/advocacy/state/coalitions.asp>*.

AVMA

Home | News | Issues | My AVMA | Jobs | Animal Health | Public Health

Search AVMA

Search Tips | Advanced Search

Search State Legislative Resources

Search within State Legislative Resources only. Go

About us

State legislative updates

Contact us

Issues

Animal welfare

Business issues

Dog bite prevention

Euthanasia

Non-economic damages

Ownership vs. guardianship

Pharmacy and vaccination

Scope of practice issues

Trends

Resources

Resources by state

Advocacy tools

= AVMA/SAVMA Members Only

Get Acrobat Reader

Some files on this page require Adobe Acrobat Reader software. Click on the image above to download it for free from the Adobe site.

State Legislative Resources

Advocacy > State legislative resources > Advocacy tools

Advocacy tools

Using legislative coalitions to win

Posted 9 October 2006

State veterinary medical associations (VMAs) often partner with other organizations and interest groups to support or defeat legislative or regulatory proposals. Depending on the issue, pet owners, farm producers, groomers, kennels, shelters, animal products and drug manufacturers, and even humane groups can provide support to veterinary medicine's position.

It's likely that your association has developed relationships with some of these groups over the years, and contacting them isn't very difficult. You can also ask the AVMA, which maintains contacts at the national level, or other state or allied VMAs, for suggested organizations that may be interested in your issue.

There are other ways to find potential coalition allies. One is a simple Internet search for other groups talking about a particular issue. You can also talk with legislative committee staffers to find out who else is calling them. Finally, an association directory in your state may reveal names that suggest a likely interest in your issue.

Benefits of a coalition

Associations form or join coalitions to accomplish together what they cannot do alone. Coalitions are formed in the hopes of capitalizing on strength in numbers and the strengths of each member. This applies to political clout as well as expertise, staff resources and funding.

A broad-based coalition can help small organizations reach more legislators and get the legislative leadership's attention. Reaching more legislators is easier when more organizations share the load. A coalition often creates new relationships and establishes alliances that serve various purposes. Also, the united front of a coalition is more likely to impress decision makers and the news media.

Obstacles to consider

As beneficial as coalitions can be, they are not always possible or practical. Partners may have difficulty in reaching consensus and tough compromises may be necessary. The need for approvals from individual entities on positions and strategy can slow down a group. Differences can easily appear on a range of matters, including goals, strategies and the division of responsibility. The focus must be on the group, not a single member, which may lead to loss of ownership on an issue. The large egos of those who want to be the stars can present problems too.

Some practical suggestions

Some coalitions work easily together, while others never seem to get off the ground. Below are some time-tested tips to making coalition-building a part of a successful advocacy campaign.

1. Develop a concise mission statement. A representative core group should draft a mission or consensus statement representative of the participating organizations' positions and what they hope to achieve. The statement should be brief - it is much easier for people to coalesce around a few critical issues - but broad enough to garner ample support.

2. Select the structure. Coalitions are generally temporary and loosely organized around a common goal or set of objectives. Some long-term coalitions are more formally structured by establishing bylaws and

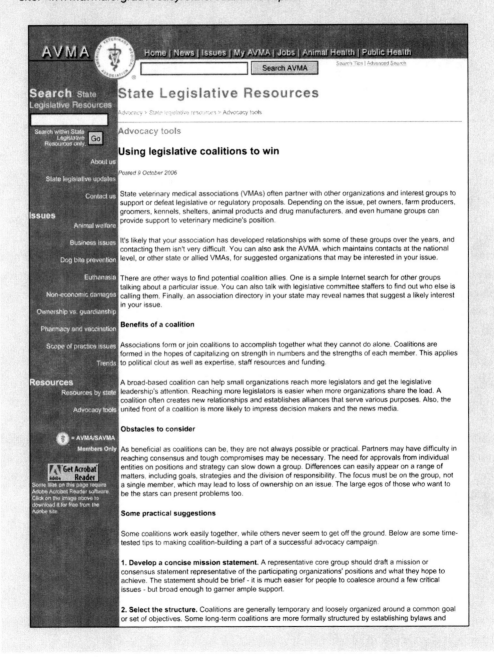

"Coming together is a beginning; keeping together is progress; working together is success."
Henry Ford

"Strength lies in differences, not in similarities."
Stephen Covey

"Synergy—the bonus that is achieved when things work together harmoniously."
Mark Twain

"Politics makes strange bedfellows."
Charles Dudley Warner

"Two heads are better than one."
Unknown

§9.14 Time Management

In a hectic legislative environment, important organizational and communication details can receive short work. However, taking time for planning, goal setting, and tracking can maximize your efforts exponentially. One success factor is effectively balancing the participants' desire to make meaningful contributions to the discussion while honoring meeting time constraints and expectations. Establishing and communicating an agenda to all participants in advance and using it as an effective tool to gracefully keep participants on track is a simple, but effective, way to maximize your meeting time and stick to the agenda to avoid tangents and unproductive diversions. A sample meeting agenda is provided in § 9.10.

§9.15 Developing Your Members and Alliances

Your members and alliances can be extremely helpful in recruiting new coalition participants. Complementary coalitions can be coordinated at the federal and state levels. National organizations frequently encourage and equip state organizations to form and run their own effective coalitions at the state and local levels. See § 9.13 for an excellent web site fact sheet from the American Veterinary Medicine Association that effectively equips state veterinary medical associations to build their own coalitions.

§9.99 Chapter Summary

- Coalitions offer strength in numbers and present a unified front, providing the opportunity to multiply resources, contacts, expertise, and intelligence. (§ 9.2)
- Most lobbyists belong to several coalitions and spend a significant amount of time on their coalition work. However, lobbyists tend to underutilize available technology tools in their work to expand their groups. (§ 9.3)

- Coalitions can vary in the degree of formality and structure ranging from short-term, unstructured efforts to more formal long-term efforts with dedicated staff, a dues structure, and office space. Your coalition organization should reflect the mission and needs of the members, sometimes requiring more structure and resources, but sometimes more informal and perhaps more transient (§ 9.3). A chart illustrating examples of coalition structure is found at § 9.12.
- Coalition leaders and members must make sure that their coalitions are properly registered at the federal or state level and abide by all legal and ethical standards, remembering that their name is associated with the coalition. The federal coalition reporting requirements include the disclosure of contributions of more than $5,000 when the contributor actively participates in the planning, supervision, or control of lobbying. Disclosure is not required if the organization lists the client on the web site as being a member of, or contributor to, the client unless the organization in whole or major part plans, supervises, or controls lobbying activities. The organization must disclose the coalition's Internet address on its registration. (§ 9.5)
- Working through coalitions presents challenges that must be overcome to maintain a united front and avoid distractions from legislative goals. (§ 9.6)
- Examples of common challenges confronting coalitions, their effects, and potential solutions are provided in the chart at § 9.7. Challenges include free-riders, ego conflicts, lack of resources, and moles.
- § 9.8 provides the following tips and resources for identifying existing efforts, opposition, and potential members:
    1. Use your networks and connections
    2. Ask established legislative leaders and experts in the area
    3. Search public records and lobbying disclosure databases
- A sample coalition agenda is provided in § 9.10.
- § 9.11 offers motivating quotes that can be used to encourage teamwork and credit sharing within coalitions.
- Time management tips are discussed in § 9.14.
- Typically, national organizations equip their state and local members and allies for effective coalition building. (§ 9.15)
- Ensure that expectations are very clearly defined among the coalition members. Much of the conflict in coalitions could be eliminated when all members are transparent regarding their level of commitment and scope of involvement. (§ 9.7)
- Finding creative ways to share the credit as well as the work among coalition members will decrease pressure for individual organizations to compete for press and attention from policymakers. (§ 9.7)

Media Engagement and Testimony:
Perfect Your Public Presence

"Public sentiment is everything. With public sentiment nothing can fail; without it nothing can succeed. He who molds public sentiment goes deeper than he who enacts statutes or decisions possible or impossible to execute."

Abraham Lincoln

Chapter 10: Media Engagement and Testimony:
Perfect Your Public Presence

§10.1 Introduction

Advocates spend countless dollars on public relations efforts designed to capture legislators' attention. Lobbyists purchase advertisements in congressional newspapers such as *CQ Today* and *Roll Call*, orchestrate rallies on the Capitol Mall, design buttons for legislative conference attendees, formulate legislative messages inscribed in chocolate (at least before the gift ban), and even arrange for trucks to drive around the Capitol area displaying signs and banners in an attempt to get their message through to busy lawmakers and the media. But do these methods actually work in connecting with legislators and changing the outcome of legislation?

While there are proven benefits to some of these methods, getting the word out to the voting public is one of the most critical parts of a successful legislative campaign. The key is to focus on the results. The media can be a powerful vehicle for informing the citizenry on upcoming policy debates and holding policymakers accountable. A guide for working with the media, media distribution resources, and tips for working with reporters are discussed in this chapter.

Lobbyists are also frequently called upon to organize media events, prepare or present congressional testimony, introduce public officials, and serve as spokespersons to the public through the media. Chapter Ten provides lobbyists with practical tools needed to effectively work with the media and participate in congressional testimony. Since congressional testimony is a major opportunity for getting your message out, this chapter provides a detailed guide to testifying before Congress or coaching a witness and includes a useful testimony preparation checklist.

§10.2 Legislative Messaging in a Crowded Environment

"Based on conservative estimates, Internet use for obtaining political information may have tripled since 2000, now nearing an estimated 60 percent of Internet users."

University of Southern California 2007 Digital Future Project, Center for the Digital Future, Internet Is Becoming Dominant Media Force in National Political Campaigns, Reports USC Digital Future Project, July 31, 2007, PRNewswire-USNewswire

In recent years, more people are vying for attention from policymakers and the media, and increased costs have presented some challenges for lobbyists in getting their message out. Your message must compete within an increasing cacophony of other messages, all vying for the attention of Congress, staffers, the media, and the public.

Advances in communications technology, the 24-hour news cycle, the influence of the Internet on politics and the media, an increase in public-policy debate programs, the rise of infotainment, and access to new media have opened relatively inexpensive venues for reaching and targeting more citizens. Simultaneously, the shrinking sound bite, the changing nature of the media, and the increased volume and complexity of legislation have all presented challenges for lobbyists as they seek to get their message heard.

"A decade ago, just one-in-fifty Americans got the news with some regularity from the internet. Today, nearly one-in-three regularly get news online."

A survey of online papers by the PEW Research Center for the People and the Press, Online Papers Modestly Boost Newspaper Readership, released July 30, 2006 <http://pewresearch.org/pubs/238/online-papers-modestly-boost-newspaper-readership>

Section I: Media Engagement

§10.3 "How-to Guide" for Working with the Media

The following ten principles provide a brief overview for lobbyists working with the media. Media training, for example, through TheCapitol.Net (<*www.TheCapitol.Net*>), is highly recommended for all government affairs professionals, since lobbying necessarily involves media relations strategies and involvement. Additionally, the *Media Relations Handbook for Agencies, Associations, Nonprofits and Congress*, by Brad Fitch, is a comprehensive treatment of the topic and is required reading for all lobbyists (<*www.MediaRelationsHandbook.com*>.)

§10.4 Media Relations Principle 1: Understand the Ultimate Goal

"Don't talk to a reporter, talk through them."
Merrie Spaeth, President Spaeth Communications, Inc.

The fundamental communications truism "know your audience" is especially applicable to influencing public policy. Never forget that the ultimate goal of legislative media coverage is to influence the public policy outcome. The goal is to reach key constituents with your message, not simply to gain media exposure or to reach elites. Consider the following observation from a congressional veteran illustrating how public opinion drives congressional decisions:

"Legislation is never passed in a vacuum, but in a cultural context. Regardless of the size of a party's majority in the Congress, certain things simply can't be done without a cultural consensus. As important as law and politics are in the immediate life of a nation, they pale in comparison to the far more powerful role played by entertainment, media, academia, and religion . . ."
Bill Wichterman, Former Chief of Staff for Two Members of Congress and Policy Advisor for the Senate Majority Leader

Lobbyists who are serious about influencing legislation recognize the need to inform the culture and to influence the public opinion that drives legislation.

§10.5 Media Relations Principle 2: Plan and Coordinate

Anticipating your public affairs activities in advance and coordinating your organization's legislative and public relations efforts are key to an effective public relations strategy. Lack of planning and coordination can lead to lost opportunities, hastily put together and ineffective events and releases, and even costly public affairs mistakes.

Lobbyists frequently seek assistance from media relations professionals within their organizations or from a consultant to connect their message to the voting public and to their members of Congress. While many lobbyists want to obtain favorable media coverage of their legislative efforts, they rarely include media relations staff in the beginning stages of the legislative campaign's planning. As a consequence of not being involved on the front end, some media relations staff feel that they are expected to fix something without adequate time to prepare to do so.

Qualified and experienced media affairs professionals can be invaluable to lobbyists in identifying holes in the press strategy or in assisting with developing new strategy ideas for spinning your legislative message. But they need sufficient lead time. Notifying an internal media relations shop the day before a hearing that you would like coverage regarding the witness is not only an inconvenience, it will result in some measure of missed opportunity. As described in Chapter Six, coordinate your efforts through effective and integrated planning, but also set up regular meetings and processes to build coordination into your legislative planning.

Regular meetings, periodic off-site brainstorming sessions, and preparing action plans will help to build coordination. To avoid miscommunication and duplication of work, establish an effective system for pulling the appropriate governmental affairs, media, and issues staff together when a legislative challenge, opportunity, or event first becomes apparent, and map out a game plan to decide who will do what. The left hand needs to know what the right hand is doing or it may inadvertently undermine or contradict it. For example, the government affairs department may be advocating a particular position on the issue while the public relations or publications department is releasing a survey or article that will unintentionally undermine or contradict the organization's position. Communication breakdowns can be especially challenging for larger organizations or during staff transitions.

See Chapter Six for a guide to developing a coordinated legislative action plan. Incorporating public affairs activities with your legislative action plan will also help you to identify areas where you may need to hire a consultant. Identifying these areas early will allow enough time for adequate coordination with an external consultant. Tips for working with consultants are provided in §10.28.

§10.6 Media Relations Principle 3: Conduct an Issue Audit

Conduct an issue audit to assess media coverage (current and anticipated) and public opinion, not only nationally, but also in key states and congressional districts.

What has been said and by whom, in the media, on homepages, and in communications to Capitol Hill?

- Legislators
- Other interests
- Administration officials (letter of intent or Statement of Administration Policy)
- Commentators in the media, such as, columnists and political pundits
- Experts, think tanks, or academics

When reviewing previous testimonies and media messages, begin building your message and refuting opposing arguments by identifying the fallacies that exist or are expected to be perpetuated.

- Questionable statistics
- Biased studies
- Biased groups
- How "problems" or "solutions" have been identified or characterized and by whom?
- Utilize the template at § 5.20 (Public Policy Research—Step 3: Study and Evaluate Existing Sources of Information) to evaluate existing arguments.
- See Ten Considerations for Lobbyists Conducting Research (§§ 5.6–5.15), especially item 4, Anticipate Scrutiny and Criticism (§ 5.9) and item 10, Opposition Research: Know Thy Enemy (and Especially Thy Enemy's Arguments) (§ 5.15).
- See § 5.16 for the Five Basic Steps of Public Policy Research.

Check public opinion polls and surveys that have been conducted and consider conducting your own. (See the recommended resources in § 10.7.)

As part of your media audit, review:

- Types of media sources.
- Who is saying it and why.
- What's being said (pros and cons).
- When it was said and whether conditions have changed.
- The effectiveness of the results.
- The strengths and weaknesses of supporting and opposing arguments up to this point.

§10.7 Recommended Resources

Conducting a Press Audit
on an Issue or Organization

- Federal News Service at: <*www.fnsg.com*> provides the following services:
  - ○ Verbatim, same-day transcripts including questions and answers, of major congressional hearings.
  - ○ Speeches, statements, and press conferences by administration leaders and spokespersons.
  - ○ Speeches, statements, and press conferences by congressional leaders and spokespersons.
  - ○ Presidential speeches, statements, and press conferences including State of the Union.
  - ○ White House briefings.
  - ○ State Department briefings.
  - ○ Defense Department briefings.
  - ○ Justice Department briefings.
  - ○ Homeland Security briefings.
  - ○ U.S. Trade Representative briefings.
  - ○ Foreign Press Center briefings.
  - ○ Speeches and press conferences by visiting international leaders.
  - ○ Political interviews on morning and weekend TV news shows.
  - ○ Key speeches at presidential political nominating conventions.
  - ○ Presidential debates.

Speeches, press conferences, interviews, and one or two hearings a day are updated the day they occur. Those not finished on the same day are completed within two business days. Price varies, depending on the type and size of client. The service provides daily or weekly reports summarizing every story concerning your interest's broadcast on networks, cable, and local news programs in more than 100 (and growing) markets. You can then order the actual video or verbatim transcript of whichever news segments you choose. You can also work with FNS to transcribe your event.

- **Check various polls:** <*www.pollingreport.com*>
- **Dictionary on polling:** <*www.pollingcompany.com*>
- **Margin of error calculator:** <*www.americanresearchgroup.com*>
- **Sample size calculator:** <*www.americanresearchgroup.com*>

Examples of resources for obtaining interest group positions on an issue:

- Search the group's web site and publications.
- Check <*www.ontheissues.org*>.
- Utilize the research chart in Chapter Five (§ 5.5).

(Continued on page 304)

§10.7 Recommended Resources (Continued)

- Check LexisNexis <*www.lexisnexis.com*> or Highbeam <*www.highbeam.com*> for media coverage.
- Check <*www.usnewswire.com*> for news releases.
- Search congressional documents including testimony at: <*www.louisdb.org*>.
- Use opposition research resources found at <*www.researchops.com*>.
- Check Congressional Research Service (CRS) issue briefs at <*www.opencrs.com*> (free) or <*www.pennyhill.com*> (subscription) for issue papers on specific topics to identify major pro and con arguments, involved parties, and potential resources.

For these resources and more, see this book's web site: <*www.LobbyingAndAdvocacy.com*>.

§10.8 Media Relations Principle 4: Select a Credible Spokesperson

Whether it's congressional testimony, a legislative press conference, a grassroots video alert, or a TV commercial, your message matters, but your messenger matters too. Who is the most credible spokesperson to communicate the most compelling part of your issue? It may or may not be the CEO or association president. It may be someone with a personal story to tell, or it may take several representatives to convey the entire message effectively.

Carefully consider who you will be putting in front of the media on behalf of your organization. The first rule is to do no harm. Be prepared and avoid unnecessary risks. One unprepared person can do significant harm to your organization's reputation in just one media appearance or in testifying before Congress. Even a short media training course can be helpful to your lobbyists at all levels as they interact with the media. Types of spokespersons can include:

- Head of organization (Association President, CEO);
- Public relations staff;
- Government relations staff;
- Chapter or state officials;
- Individual members/employees speaking on behalf of the organization;
- Individual members/employees speaking on their own behalf;
- Administration officials;
- Chairs of special efforts, such as, commissions or task forces;
- Subject-matter experts within your grassroots or client organizations; and
- Subject-matter experts on your own organization's staff.

As discussed in Chapter Six, planning ahead in this area is essential. Identify and train potential spokespersons year-round so that you have numerous options and can respond to media opportunities quickly.

§10.10 Lobby Tips

Preparing Spokespersons for Public Appearances

Give a new spokesperson adequate time to get up to speed and equipped. Provide a mock interview or testimony questioning session. Use video clips of previous debates or testimony to assist with your briefings. See § 10.61 for a step-by-step guide to preparing a congressional witness for testimony.

§10.9 Considerations for Selecting Spokespersons

Ideally, you will strike a balance between the two major types of spokespersons:

- Professional spokesperson for your organization (association or company CEO, public relations spokesperson, or lobbyist) and
- Grassroots/constituents.

The following questions may help you identify the right spokesperson in advance:

1. Is the person knowledgeable enough on the issue or can she become comfortable enough to endure detailed questioning under the time constraints? The person with the most impressive title might not make the best spokesperson. Seek opportunities to casually discuss the issue with the potential spokesperson to determine if she is equipped to undergo questioning. In the case of congressional testimony, sometimes the congressional committee may seek to have the head of the organization testify, but if that is not possible or is not the best fit for that particular hearing, you may be able to convince your principal that another individual would better help advance the specific goal of the hearing.
2. Does the person have the authority to speak on behalf of her organization, or is she able to speak on her own behalf? If organizational clearance is needed, how long will it take? Ideally, you will develop a cadre of credible spokespersons prior to press and testimony opportunities.
3. Does the person have any baggage (negative history) that could discredit her as a spokesperson for your organization? If so, what is the worst case scenario? It is a good idea to do your own research, but also ask the person directly as you help them prepare for a possible opportunity? (Under the worst case scenario, what could the opposition potentially find out about her that could discredit the testimony and your organization?)
4. Is the person's opinion on the issue consistent with your organization's position? Would she be willing to speak on behalf of your organization without reservation?
5. What is the worst thing that could happen with this person's appearance? How is the appearance likely to be characterized by opposing interests? It may be appropriate to ask the potential spokesperson this question.

§10.11 Tips for Preparing for Your Physical Presence on Television

- Define your appearance with a suit or jacket of a solid dark or primary color (not orange, pink, or purple), but not white (although white is good under a jacket).
- Avoid stripes and patterns. (The camera image jumps (moiré patterns) and viewers have a hard time focusing on the person.)
- Recognize that bright lights from the cameras will make you look more washed out, so some make up (yes, even for men) will make you look more professional, less washed out, and even your skin tone.
- If you get a raspy voice or a sore throat, use hot water with lemon.
- Turn off any electronic devices such as a cell phone or BlackBerry before you enter the studio.

Testifying before Congress is similar, especially since the hearing can be carried on C-SPAN. However, the hearing environment is slightly more conservative and your dress as a witness should be professional and not distracting. Dark colors and tailored suits are preferred to flashy or patterned dress.

§10.12 Media Relations Principle 5: Know Your Issue and Anticipate Questions

"Know your issue well enough for the toughest questions."
The 30 Laws of Lobbying (§ 8.4)

Most questions in an interview or congressional hearing can be anticipated by researching the issue, examining existing comments that have been made in the marketplace of ideas, and identifying and analyzing opposing arguments. Chapter Five provides resources for conducting issue research. Use the template at § 5.20 (Public Policy Research—Step 3: Study and Evaluate Existing Sources of Information) to evaluate existing arguments. See §§ 5.6–5.15, Ten Considerations for Lobbyists Conducting Research, especially 4, Anticipate Scrutiny and Criticism (§ 5.9) and 10, Opposition Research: Know Thy Enemy (and Especially Thy Enemy's Arguments) (§ 5.15). See § 5.16, Five Basic Steps of Public Policy Research.

- Which examples, anecdotes, and facts most effectively illustrate each message? What is the best way to make these points: a prediction or practical example of the ramifications of legislation, future trends that should be considered in determining opinion on legislation, a compelling quotation, or validation by an expert or other credible source?
- What is your bottom-line message for each targeted audience?

§10.13 Lobby Tips

Legal and Substantive Details

Identify any potential legal or technical problems. Do you need to talk to substantive experts or get your talking points, facts, or testimony reviewed by an expert or legal counsel?

§10.14 Media Relations Principle 6: Hone Your Message

"Your message must be relevant to the recipient. Numbers, statistics, or a list of dry facts do not touch people. One simple story or one relevant example can make a huge impact on the average listener and, most importantly, that listener will remember your story long afterwards and quite possibly will even share it with others."

Diane Powell, Innovative Partnerships, NASA

Carefully contemplate the best message and hone it throughout the process. This involves identifying, developing, and refining your most compelling arguments, examples, facts, and anecdotes. Consider news cycles and hot issues to find a hook that interests the media and the public at this time. Are there other themes that you can use, such as, an anniversary date or a holiday? Where's the story? Developing a motto can be extremely helpful. Your message must be interesting, so the media will include it, and relevant, so people will remember it. It also must be persuasive for those who don't yet agree with you, and be motivational for those who do.

Your message may include the following elements. (Consider scoring your message on each element to identify areas of needed focus):

- **Interesting:** Your message must be interesting for the media, who focus on public appeal and ratings, to cover it. Tell a story, include a conflict, or feature an interesting or timely perspective on an issue. Develop a hook or tie-in with a hot issue.
- **Relevant:** Why should the audience care? How does or how could your issue impact their lives? Offer a resolution or solution.
- **Persuasive:** Why is your position the correct one, and how is the opposing argument wrong or weak?
- **Motivational:** What do you expect your audience to do as a result of your message? Is it inspiring toward that end?
- **Educational:** Does your message equip your target audience with the knowledge needed to take the desired action?
- **Targeted:** Will your message find its way to your intended audience, typically your supporters and undecided constituents who care about the issue? Is it adequately targeted to avoid unnecessary distribution to great numbers of opponents?

§10.15 **Media Relations Principle 7: Consider and Coordinate Various Media**

Successful campaigns will likely mix and coordinate media in a comprehensive communications effort. Television may be the cheapest medium to reach the largest number of people, but targeting is more difficult, and someone who sees an ad on TV can't forward it to a friend. Keep in mind that broadly based media coverage can motivate your opposition as well.

Email technology firms sell voter email lists that can be selected based on demographics such as age, gender, zip code, party affiliation, and purchasing habits. Video commercials or clips from a legislative debate can be distributed to your members or clients by email as a motivator.

Lobbyists tend to underdevelop and underpromote email and web strategies for getting the word out on legislative issues to policymakers, the public, and the press. Make your web site Hill-friendly and press-friendly, and promote useful legislative web resources through your media and legislative appearances.

Consider coordinating your web and email efforts with other media:

> *"When you're thinking about message and new media, always remember people don't change when they turn the computer on. What the polling tells you is your best message is also your best message online. The most effective use of email is in conjunction with all the other mediums, for instance, sending a Paul Revere email message announcing a mailing can boost the response by 50 to 70 percent. Similarly, you will get a much higher email open and response rate during time your TV ad is up on the air. While television may be the most cost-effective means of reaching a broad audience, when you start to narrow it down, that's when the Internet and email become more cost-effective."*
> Roger Stone, President, Advocacy, Inc., Democratic technology strategy firm

Consider a variety of products including press advisories (before the event), frequently asked questions, backgrounders or issue papers (serving to educate the reader on an issue), op-eds, and letters to the editor. Do not forget the value of a picture; consider making a photo, graphic, or video clip available to the media. Many organizations include links to all of these in a "Media" or "Press" section on their web site.

Associations find good press to be an excellent way of gratifying their members, and communicating that they are making a difference on their behalf. But is your message geared for your supporters only or should your target audience include those who are not already decided on your issue? How can you best connect with all of your targeted audiences?

Think of new ways to determine the best strategies to connect with your key demographic groups for the issue. Former President Clinton's administration adopted a "Redbook" strategy because he wanted to reach the population of women who typically read *Redbook* magazine.

§10.16 Recommended Resources

Video Archives of
House and Senate Proceedings

- C-SPAN Archives will provide free access to past C-SPAN programs, including House and Senate floor proceedings. Go to C-SPAN's Congressional Chronicle at: <www.c-spanarchives.org>.

- Congressional Quarterly's Floor Video service <www.cq.com> enables you to:
  - Pinpoint and play the video of floor debate within minutes after the words are spoken.
  - View the closed-caption text of the spoken words the day before the *Congressional Record* is available.
  - Email video clips to your colleagues.
  - Search for floor debate dating to the 107th Congress in 2002.
  - Receive email alerts when there's action on your issues.

Blogs can also be effective in legislative campaigns. Not only are they used by many members of Congress on their own web sites, but bloggers are frequently engaged in legislative campaigns. For instance, in September 2006, Senate Majority Leader Bill Frist challenged bloggers to try to find out which senator had placed a confidential hold that was preventing the Senate from voting on legislation that would provide for a comprehensive database to reveal all government contracts (including earmarks). The bloggers got to work and within one day the bill was released and passed on the Senate floor. Then the House followed suit and the bill was enacted. Blogging can be yet another tool for expressing your coordinated legislative message.

All advocates must consider new media approaches, because younger citizens more frequently receive their news from cell phones, PDAs, and Podcasts. The dynamics of the younger generation also suggest that direct electronic engagement by asking them what they think through electronically based venues such as blogging can be important for their engagement.

§10.17 The Influence Model of Communications

The Influence Model below, developed by Merrie Spaeth, president of Spaeth Communications, Inc., depicts the routes of communication. A brief description of the model follows:

- The *formal* route is any information the target audience perceives that you control including marketing materials, advertising, collateral, internal publications, annual reports, and so on.

§10.18 Earned vs. Paid Media

"Earned media can benefit a campaign or further promote an issue beyond the reach of paid media because earned media provides credibility. The credibility in question is provided by a third party, the media. A candidate's position written about in print or covered in television or radio in a positive light, shows that the issue is deemed important by the media and that the media source has given authority and credibility to the candidate or the organization being covered.

"Earned media breaks all ties. When candidates or competing groups are deadlocked over ideological issues, earned media can often act as the arbiter by granting status and approval to the particular position that the media organization wishes to endorse.

"Caution: Earned media, while it can be worth millions of dollars in unpaid advertising, is not a safety net, and professional campaign organizers or organizations never rely solely on earned media to promote its positions. Earned media (by itself) will not win you a vote or an election."

—Damien Harvey, Producer, Capitol Pictures Inc.

Earned Media (PR)	Paid Media (Advertising)
Add legitimacy but you may not be able to control the content/outcome, especially if the reporter is predisposed to be against your position.	Control the content; Include your views exclusively; and Help with alerting potential allies. Ensure that your contact information is included.
Disadvantage: Risk negative portrayal since reporters try to show both sides of most issues. Reporter's ultimate objective or purpose for the piece may not be clear at the outset.	Disadvantage: Costs Can notify additional opponents of your efforts.
Just as it's always better for someone else to compliment you than for you to toot your own horn, earned media can be very flattering, but this is not always possible. While a front story above the fold highlighting your survey results before the vote will have much more credibility than a paid ad on page 23 with the same information, it is not always possible to secure that kind of coverage. Consider getting key people in the members' state/district to write op-eds and letters to the editor. Establish relationships with editorial staff writers and help them with ideas and information for editorials.	Consider taking out an ad in publications with a high readership within the Washington, DC, area if you need to bring widespread and immediate visibility to an issue with a variety of interests. Consider purchasing ads or commercials in the state or district. You might be surprised at how much bang you can get for your buck. Consider services that offer customized email outreach according to citizen demographics and based on congressional district or state (zip code).

- The *informal* routes of communication are those the target audience perceives that you do not control. The two most powerful, credible informal routes for communicating your message are through the media and through the various groups in which the target audience congregates, including person-to-person communication.
- Today, a sophisticated communication program should carefully identify the constituencies, examine the routes (formal and informal) available to reach them, and look at the vehicles currently being used and the frequency of their use. A proactive strategy using all routes will maximize the effectiveness of your communication. The idea of message alignment or consistency of communication along all three networks is crucial.
- The model has vast implications for both your professional and private worlds. If you can execute and incorporate it into your communication plan on a daily basis, you will achieve a competitive edge that few executives and companies obtain.

§10.19 Media Relations Principle 8: Get the Word Out Strategically and Target State/District Outlets

Consider your full audience, not just those in your proximity. For example, if appearing on a show, talk not only to your host or physical audience, but to everyone who will be in reach of your comments, showing particular consideration toward citizens who may be persuaded to adopt your viewpoint and weigh in with their legislative representatives.

§10.20 Press Distribution Resources for Lobbyists

- The USNewswire service at *<www.usnewswire.com>*, now combined with PRNewswire, allows you to distribute your press release to print, broadcast, and online media. Distribution can be targeted to outlets in certain states, regions, and cities. Your release can also be tailored to different types of media (talk shows and Op-Ed Pack) and to different issue groups. A blog-ready feature is also available.
- Bacon's Media Directories at *<www.bacons.com>*.
- Burrelle's Media Directory at *<www.burrelles.com>*.
- Gebbie Press at *<www.gebbieinc.com>*.
- The Capital Source (online version recommended) at *<http://nationaljournal.com>*.
- The News Media Yellow Book at *<www.leadershipdirectories.com>*.
- View recent polls at *<www.pollingreport.com>*.
- An excellent searchable media guide (by zip code) is available through the C-SPAN web site at *<http://www3.capwiz.com/c-span/dbq/media>*.
- Links to state newspapers are available at *<www.statescape.com>*.

For these resources and more, see this book's web site: *<www.LobbyingAndAdvocacy.com>*.

At the end of the day, members of Congress care more about receiving an endorsement from the newspaper in their state or district than from a major Washington, DC, newspaper. City and local media can be relatively inexpensive and extremely effective. Develop and strengthen ties with state and local groups that can help you coordinate efforts in the area. A few well-placed letters to the editor by key people can capture the attention of the government officials who regularly read their home publications.

§10.21 Media Relations Principle 9: Timing Is Everything

Often, the timing of specific events can be outside of your control, such as when you are invited to testify or appear on a show. There are times, however, when you can control the timing of your press efforts, such as when you schedule a press conference, send a release, or issue an advisory.

News cycles are not just about the time of day that you choose to have an event or issue a release, but what topics are hot. Examine national news waves, trends, and cycles as you develop and update your legislative press efforts. Certain events, deadlines, or holidays can provide a press hook that will get legislators' attention. For example, the Tax Foundation designates America's Tax Freedom Day annually to draw legislative and public attention to the number of work days it takes each year for taxpayers to fund the government. The effort also includes Tax Freedom Day by state. (See *<www.taxfoundation. org/taxfreedomday>*.)

Consider hot topics in the news as hooks and look for favorable conditions, such as, promoting conservation after a storm or toxic spill when the public has a heightened interest in the topic. The goal is to be in a position to quickly launch your media campaign when the time is right.

§10.22 Media Relations Principle 10: Follow-up

Persuasive press appearances and credible congressional testimony can be used in a variety of ways. Lobbyists typically circulate testimony and publish quotes from successful press appearances for their own interests and post them on their web sites, but there are additional methods to consider:

- Consider using particularly compelling quotes or published opinion pieces in your ads and congressional communications.
- When your organization or a compelling argument is quoted on the floor of the House or Senate, consider distributing the video via the Internet (video is available from C-SPAN's Congressional Chronicle *<www.c-spanarchives.org>* and CQ's Floor Video service *<www.cq.com>*).
- Include op-eds in letters to Capitol Hill or suggest that members of Congress circulate them in "Dear Colleague" letters. (For a sample "Dear Colleague" letter, see the *Congressional Deskbook, § 8.22.*)

§10.23 **Working with Reporters**

1. Be Honest: If You Don't Know, Say You Don't Know

"Silence is often misinterpreted, but never misquoted."
Unknown

It's a bad idea to guess during a press interview. If you don't know, say you don't know. In giving testimony, recognize that a verbatim official hearing transcript is being recorded. If you are not sure of an answer, explain that you are not sure and ask the committee chair if you can provide a written answer after the hearing to include in the hearing record. If you are testifying as part of a panel, you may wish to defer to another panelist. § 10.59 provides additional tips for answering questions during congressional testimony.

2. Remember that Everything Is on the Record

"Everything is on the record!"
The Official Rules for Lawyers, Politicians and Everyone They Torment, by Paul Dickson

When you are reluctant to speak to a reporter, he or she may offer to interview you off the record (information is not to be used publicly), on background (source may be identified generally, but not specifically), or on deep background (no identification of the source). Some media professionals recommend against ever agreeing to an off-the-record interview. While these types of interviews can help you to inform a reporter (especially reporters with whom you have worked for a number of years), they should be agreed to with caution and you should clarify what "off the record" means to the reporter.

If you're at an event with the media, talking to the media, or even socializing with reporters, assume that it's on the record.

"The credo is: 'If you don't want to read about it in the Washington
Post, *don't say or write it, and avoid thinking it, if possible.'"*
Brad Fitch, *Media Relations Handbook*, § 4.12, "Off the Record"

Recognize that the reporter can portray your comments in such a way that your identity can eventually be determined. Controversial anonymous quotes usually trigger an intense guessing game and the people who are quoted are frequently asked directly whether they made the comments. Avoid putting yourself in such an uncomfortable and potentially ethically challenging situation.

The excerpts below from the *Washington Post* illustrate how an off the record comment led to the identification of the source.

*"The candidate, immersed in one of the most competitive Senate races
in the country, sat down to lunch yesterday at a Capitol Hill steakhouse
and shared his views about this year's political currents."*
"For One Senate Candidate, The 'R' Is a 'Scarlet Letter, " by Dana Milbank,
the *Washington Post*, July 25, 2006, Page A02

"After hours of speculation, Lt. Gov. Michael Steele's campaign acknowledged yesterday afternoon that Steele was the anonymous Republican quoted in Dana Milbank's column in the Washington Post *on Tuesday.*

"The column, for those who missed it, described a Republican from a blue state declaring that his party affiliation was 'an impediment,' that the war in Iraq 'didn't work' and the response to Katrina, 'a monumental failure of government.'

"After a flurry of guessing—much of it centered on Steele—his campaign staff fessed up."

The *Washington Post* Blog, by Phyllis Jordan, July 26, 2006
<http://blog.washingtonpost.com/annapolis/2006/07>

"During the radio interview, Steele suggested that he was surprised to see his unattributed comments in print Tuesday in an article by Washington Post *reporter Dana Milbank. Steele said they represented only a portion of what he said at the luncheon—leaving out, he said, comments favorable to Bush."*

"Steele Addresses Negative Comments on Bush," by John Wagner,
The *Washington Post*, July 27, 2006, Page B01

3. Be Responsive to Reporters

Some extremely capable and knowledgeable public policy experts are reluctant to speak to reporters even when it will help their cause or inadvertently hurt it by failing to respond. While preparation is essential before speaking to reporters, recognize that they are usually looking for a credible comment to print from your organization's perspective. In most cases, you should be able to come up with something diplomatic to say, even in difficult situations. Even providing a brief explanation of why you cannot discuss the specifics of a situation or taking the extra effort to refer the reporter to people (with their direct contact information) who may be better able to comment is much better than a "no comment" in the article or a reference that the reporter's calls were not returned.

Kate Ackley, staff writer for *Roll Call* newspaper, offers lobbyists the following advice based on her work covering the lobbying beat for nearly a decade:

"I always appreciate it when lobbyists call me back and within the time frame for my deadline—which is often the same day. Even if you can't talk about your client or the issue, just connecting with the reporter, seeing what the story might be about is a good idea. That way, the lobbyist can put the reporter in touch with someone who can speak on the record.

"Stating your case is important. Sometimes I'll think I have a great story, but when I hear the other side, I realize it's not all it's cracked up to be by the initial source. But if I can't talk to all sides of a story, then I can't reflect all sides of the story, and I am left with the comments from only one side. Even if it ends up that the story isn't as compelling, I would rather hear from all sides to get the most accurate picture of what's going on.

§10.24 Lobby Tips

On the Record

Watch out for those microphones, cameras, and casual conversations in public! Reporters and their sources are everywhere. If you have any doubts, read the Heard on the Hill (HOH) gossip column in *Roll Call* at <www.rollcall.com>. An excerpt from Heard on the Hill follows:

"In a move reminiscent of the caught-on-the-microphone exchange between President Bush and Vice President Cheney that launched the phrase 'major league a—hole' into the Washington, D.C., lexicon, an agitated Rep. Ike Skelton (D-Mo.) engaged in a bit of bleep-able banter during Monday's televised hearing on the Iraq progress report.

"The highly anticipated hearing before the Armed Services and Foreign Affairs committees was marked with outbursts from CODEPINK protesters and snafus with witnesses' microphones in the committee room. Skelton, who was chairing the hearing, apparently didn't realize his own microphone was, in fact, working, and turned to Rep. Duncan Hunter (R-Calif.), the panel's ranking member. 'That really pisses me off, Duncan,' Skelton could be heard saying. When Hunter leaned in to ask who had provoked the chairman's ire, he responded by nodding in the direction of the disrupting protesters. 'Those a—holes,' Skelton said. After a few inaudible (even to HOH's well-practiced ears) words, 'g——mned' also was heard. And moments later, Rep. Ileana Ros-Lehtinen (R-Fla.) approached Skelton. 'What the hell,' Skelton could be heard saying to the Congresswoman.

"Skelton's blue streak continued when Rep. Dan Burton (R-Ind.) approached him. Burton had earlier advised Skelton on how to manage the protesters, to which Skelton responded that he didn't need the lecture. Burton told Skelton he didn't mean to lecture him. 'The hell you didn't,' Skelton snapped."

"Dropping Bombs, Caught on Tape, Heard on the Hill,"
by Emily Heil and Anna Palmer, *Roll Call*, September 11, 2007

If you keep your side silent by not calling back or saying 'no comment,' then I've done my job of trying to get your side, but the story won't reflect your side and may look like there's something to hide.

"Also, if you are pitching a story idea to a reporter, be sure to say whether you are calling just this one reporter and offering an exclusive or if you are pitching the story to other publications. That can make a huge difference in determining whether a reporter will pursue the story. The offer of an exclusive for a good story is always attractive for any reporter. Whenever pitching a story, be upfront. If you have a client that would benefit from the story, just explain your client's involvement in the story."

Kate Ackley, Staff Writer, *Roll Call*

Additional tips for working with reporters:

- When is the deadline? Time is of the essence. Recognize that the reporter is probably continuing to call other potential sources who may be helping to shape the story's direction or provide the quote from your side's perspective if you delay your response.
- Determine where the reporter is headed with the story and who else she has already interviewed. If testifying, what are the real goals of the congressional hearing, for example, how did the concept originate and are there secondary goals beyond the obvious, for example, to create a public record in support of legislation prior to moving legislation through the committee?
- Offer to assist in practical ways, and provide additional information and references. If you refer a reporter to other individuals, provide direct contact information if possible to save the reporter time.
- In rare cases when a particular person or entity is adamantly opposed to your position and you don't believe that anything you say will help, provide a brief comment and consider encouraging the reporter to consider both sides of the issue. It is useful to say something, though. Don't ever say, "No comment." "No comment" implies guilt and is not favorably received by the audience.

4. Give Credit Where Credit Is Due

Always respect copyrights and provide attribution. This is not only a legal imperative, but it protects you if there are errors in the information. For example, if you are forwarding legislative analysis to a reporter prepared by a coalition colleague, first make sure that you have the colleague's permission, and second, explain to the reporter that you did not prepare the material and have not had a chance to check it for accuracy.

5. Practice Handling Hostile Questions

See § 10.12, Media Relations Principle 5: Know Your Issue and Anticipate Questions.

6. If You Aren't Prepared or Authorized to Speak on an Issue, Don't Do It

If you are not prepared, don't agree to a press interview. Recommend someone who is. Remember that when you are representing an organization, you are not there to give your personal opinion.

7. Be Prepared to Question the Assumptions of a Fallacious Question

You might need to address the way a loaded question is framed or clarify that a question is based on a false premise, such as how often do you beat your wife?

8. Avoid Negatives and Personal Attacks

Avoid name-calling and negative phrases. Name-calling distracts from the issue at hand and lowers your esteem with your audience. If the host or moderator uses negative words in his or her phrase, refrain from repeating those words in your answer. Focus on

§10.25 Lobby Tips

Practice and Mock Interviews

Before your interview, practice communicating your points with a friend or family member who does not live inside the Washington, DC, beltway and ask him or her to point out jargon, abbreviations, or references that they do not understand. Refresh yourself on congressional terms by reviewing Appendix 4.

the positive, remembering that your quotes may be used out of context. For example, if the host asks why your organization always opposes employee benefits, don't repeat the phrase by saying, "We oppose employee benefits when they are not well crafted." A better reply is, "We support legislation that will have a positive effect on the workplace, but we recognize that legislation must be drafted well to achieve that purpose."

9. Avoid Acronyms, Abbreviations, and Jargon

Lobbyists frequently use abbreviations, legislative process terms, and jargon in their everyday conversations but should avoid this lingo when communicating with the public through the media. The general public is not going to know the meaning of a motion to recommit or an NPR (Notice of Proposed Rulemaking).

10. Use Caution in Addressing Hypothetical Situations or Unfamiliar Quotes and Studies

Commenting on situations that you do not understand fully can be risky. Responding with a caveat may be appropriate. For instance, if the reporter asks you to address a hypothetical situation that you do not fully understand, you might respond that you need more information regarding the details of the situation before responding. Similarly, if a reporter asks you to respond to a quotation of someone's comment, you might reply that you did not hear that comment and would need to look at the context in which it was said. If a reporter asks you to comment on a recently released report or study that you have not seen, you can explain that you have not yet seen it. In each situation, transition quickly to a comment that you can make on the topic, such as, I am not familiar with that particular quote and am not sure of the context, but I can say that leading policymakers have cosponsored the bill and recognize the need for it.

§10.26 Press Checklists

For good media relations tips, see *Media Relations Handbook* by Brad Fitch, specifically
- Email Press Releases, § 2.5
- Press Conference Checklist, § 2.14
- Daybooks, § 5.5

§10.27 Recommended Resources

Journalism Ethics

Society of Professional Journalists' Code of Ethics: *<www.spj.org>*

§10.28 Considerations for Consultants

You may wish to consider outsourcing certain legislative media relations efforts when you need added expertise or resources. Here are some considerations for hiring a consultant:

- Always operate with a written and signed contract;
- Get personal referrals and references;
- Hire people who know your issue;
- Do your homework. It's worth doing a little investigative work to find the best match;
- Find out who their clients are to avoid conflicts of interest (with competing organizations on your side as well as the opposition);
- Take measures to safeguard confidential information; and
- Consider a variety of options. The best fit may be a top firm or it may be an individual.

Source: Genevieve Wood, Media Consultant

Section II: Legislative Events

§10.50 Tips for Coordinating Legislative Events

- Introductions of policymakers should be brief. In an effort to provide a suitable introduction, lobbyists frequently err by speaking too long in their introductions of members of Congress. The introduction should provide essential information: the district or state represented, committee assignments, and a couple of accomplishments that the representative is especially proud of, as well as anything specific regarding the issue being discussed, for example, the senator has introduced legislation strongly supported by your members or has special insight regarding legislation of interest to your audience because of his work or previous occupation. As you prepare your introduction, remember that the audience is not there to hear you speak. You are there to provide a fitting transition so the official can speak.
- Confirm the logistics and time limits in advance with staff, but also confirm essential information, such as, the length of the speech and the presence of reporters. Work directly with the member of Congress upon his or her arrival to avoid awkward or embarrassing situations.

- Situations can become complicated when more than one member of Congress is participating in an event. Events involving more than one member of Congress or other high-ranking official, for instance, a cabinet official, should be carefully orchestrated before the event, with an understanding that all participants may need to be flexible to accommodate policymakers' varying arrival and departure times. Policymakers don't like surprises. All participants should be aware of all other participants well before the event, and kept up to date on agenda changes as the event date nears. All speakers should be made aware of the media in attendance prior to their presentation.

- Usually, senators are generally recognized before House members and members of the House leadership are generally recognized before other members; however, members of Congress can be sensitive about their order of appearance, so it is best to have them work out the speaking order among themselves if it gets complicated.

- Observe congressional ethics rules regarding sponsored activities, gifts, and meals. See § 2.3 for a comprehensive chart with web site links for keeping current on restrictions and §§ 2.34–2.39 for additional congressional rule information.

- Recognize specified rules when using a congressional facility. For example, congressional hearing rooms prohibit taping items to the walls and may limit signage. Arrive early and have multiple staff contacts in case of logistical problems, such as locked door or audio-visual equipment problems.

- Provide a sign-in table staffed by greeters to make sure that you are aware of all attendees. Have everyone in attendance sign in so you can be aware of the presence of press and follow-up with attendees.

- Post a staff person at entrance or in the lobby to intercept and escort speakers to the speaker's preparatory room or event room.

- If desired, plan specific photo opportunities before the event and notify the congressional staff arranging the appearance in advance, if possible, for example, communicate to the official's staff that following the speech, several board members would like to have their photo taken with the official if his or her schedule permits.

- Be ready to start on time and be prepared to fill time if the featured speaker is delayed, leaves abruptly to vote, or cancels immediately before the event.

- Consider visual elements. People have different learning styles. Some people tend to be visual learners and may respond strongly to a graph or other visual image, while others may respond more readily to empirical information such as numerical facts. However, avoid overusing PowerPoint, especially if television cameras are expected, and always have a back-up plan any time you are utilizing technology.

- Mind your words. Know who is in the room, but always assume the presence of the press (or someone with a good press contact) with any public presentation. Also, back entrances and staff offices adjacent to congressional meeting rooms on Capitol Hill mean that your meeting could be within earshot of individuals not invited to the meeting.

§10.52 Lobby Tips

Introducing a Member of Congress or Cabinet Official

If you are planning to introduce a member of Congress or cabinet official at an event, it is best to contact the member's press secretary in advance so that you can formulate the best introduction possible and confirm expectations. Situations with numerous VIPs can be challenging, so make sure that the protocol is worked out prior to the event. If you are uncertain who should be introduced first, ask the members or let them work it out among themselves rather than making the wrong call and offending members who can be sensitive about such matters.

Keep your introduction brief. The reality is that the audience is not there to hear you speak and anything other than a gracious and brief introduction is generally viewed as taking time away from the keynote speaker.

You should view your remarks as a brief transition into the speaker's remarks, not as an extensive speech in itself.

Specific guidelines for preparing and delivering congressional testimony are addressed in §§ 10.57–10.62.

§10.51 Addressing Elected Officials and Their Spouses: Pronunciations and Protocol

The following tips will assist you with understanding the protocol for addressing elected officials and their spouses (insert last name at X):

- You can refer to a House member as Congressman or Congresswoman. However, if the member serves as a chairman of a committee or subcommittee, they prefer to be recognized as such, for example, Chairman X or Chairwoman X.
- Unless you are aware of a specific title, a congressional spouse can normally be referred to as Mrs. X or Mr. X.
- Secretaries of executive branch agencies are referred to as Secretary, Mr. Secretary, or Madame Secretary.
- President of the United States is referred to as Mr. President or President X.
- This same format generally follows for other offices, for example, Mayor X or Mr. Mayor, Governor X or Mr. Governor, but if you are not sure, simply ask them their preference rather than risk offending them.
- Know the correct pronunciation of names of staff as well as policymakers. You can even call the congressional office to verify the pronunciation of member or staff names before the event to confirm.

§10.55 Recommended Resources

Legislative Speeches

- Toastmasters International (<*www.toastmasters.org*>): If you or your staff aim to refine your public speaking skills or improve your confidence, join a local toastmasters club (or start one at your organization). Local toastmasters groups offer a safe, practical, and non-threatening environment with excellent instruction from experts to hone your skills and increase your confidence.

- *Yale Book of Quotations*, Fred R. Shapiro, editor, available at: <*http://yalepress.yale.edu*>.

§10.53 Arrival Checklist

The following checklist is for presenters at legislative events:

- Arrive early.
- Confirm expectations with host.
- Be "presentation ready." It starts when you enter the room. Focus on the current speaker, including during your introduction, and don't fiddle with your notes.
- Consider your demeanor, eye contact, posture, tone, and pace.
- Arrange a stop signal with the host to make sure that you respect the time constraints.
- Never assume knowledge or audience composition—If in doubt, ask for a show of hands.
- Turn off cell phone, pager, BlackBerry, etc.

§10.54 What to Bring Checklist

If you are a presenter at a conference, there are essential items to bring with you:

- Business cards.
- Cell phone number, name of host/contacts (expect the unexpected).
- *Specific* address of location (with room number and phone number).
- Backup copy of PowerPoint/video on USB drive.
- Hard copy of PowerPoint.
- Adequate number of handouts or a backup copy of your original handout if sent in advance (in case the host organization encountered a problem making your copies).
- Copy of the text of legislation/analysis for the issues you discuss.

§10.56 Tips for Legislative Update Presentations

1. Determine Your Objective

- What do you want to accomplish?
- What do you want the audience to do as a result of the presentation?

2. Determine the Host's Goal

- What *type of speech* is it?
- What is the group's *true goal* for the event?
- What are the *priorities*?
  - For the host.
  - For the participants.

3. Determine Your Goals for the Speech

- Consider the long-term impact beyond the speech.
- What is the most important point that you want attendees to take away?
- What do you want them to do later, for example, call and visit their member of Congress or participate in their representative's town hall meeting?

4. Plan Your Speech

- Select your information.
- Keep it simple: Make two to four compelling points.
- The standard format is to tell them what you will tell them, tell them, and then tell them what you told them.

5. Stick to the Point

- Don't cloud the issue by going on tangents or becoming focused on irrelevant or minor issues.
- Avoid stories that aren't relevant for the listener. We tend to talk about ourselves too much.

6. Determine the Best Ways to Connect

Know the composition of your audience:

- Obtain a roster of attendees in advance if possible.
- Determine if reporters are present.
- Research the background of participants and the host, such as geographical location, job responsibilities, and hot-button issues.
- What is the level of understanding on the topic at hand?
- Avoid acronyms and lingo.
- Use compelling personal examples.
- Have an "ask." What do you want the audience to do, for example, call their members of Congress?
- Prepare in light of what you were asked to do.

- What is the group's viewpoint and history on your topic?
- Do your homework on the organization/issue/people (latest developments, press received, survey, congressional testimony, recognize a VIP, or highlight an accomplishment).

7. Prepare for Difficult Questions and Debates

- Anticipate and prepare for the most difficult questions.
- Draft a colleague, friend, or spouse to help you practice responding to anticipated questions.
- Use conflict as an opportunity to persuade.
- Separate the issue from the person and avoid name-calling.
- Address challenging questions and debate opponents with grace.

8. Questions Are Key

- Keep your participants engaged and learn from your audience through their participation.
- Leave adequate time for questions, running too long weakens message and diminishes credibility.

9. Know When to Stop

"Talk is like medicine; the right dose taken at the right time has the power to heal, but too much or at the wrong time may lead to the untimely death of a concept."
Deanna R. Gelak, *The Power of Personal Persuasion*

- More is not necessarily better.
- A short speech is preferable if you can get your point across.
- Leave audience with a point to ponder.

"We are usually convinced more easily by reasons we have found ourselves than by those which have occurred to others."
Blaise Pascal

10. Finish Strong

- Conclusion: Summarize points (tell them what you told them), give thanks, give your contact info, web site, etc. and invite specific input/action.
- Punch line: Consider ending with a quote, request, or challenge.

Follow–up

- Use the speech as a starting point for developing a stronger relationship with the group.
- Can anything from the speech be used in other communications?

"The best effect of fine persons is felt after we have left their presence."
Ralph Waldo Emerson

§10.57 Effective Congressional Testimony Strategies

" . . . [it is not far from the truth to say that] Congress in session is
Congress on public exhibition, whilst Congress in committee-rooms
is Congress at work."
President Woodrow Wilson

As discussed in Chapter Three, congressional committees play a critical role in the legislative process, and weighing in with congressional testimony can make a valuable contribution in that process. However, congressional testimony is not only important because it affords an opportunity to comment on public policy to legislators; it also is important because it is a venue to get your message out to the public through the media. Legislative testimony can be an important part of your media strategy as well as your legislative policy strategy. Since congressional hearings are a very important part of congressional deliberations, testimony is noticed by those engaged in and monitoring legislation.

Organizations frequently compete for opportunities to testify before Congress. Hearings provide advocates with valuable and visible opportunities to express their interests. Some testimony occurs in less-pleasant situations at the request of members of Congress, or even under subpoena. In 2005 alone, approximately 7,553 witnesses testified before Congress in 1,546 congressional hearings. These witnesses included CEOs, association presidents, administration officials, academicians, subject matter experts, and ordinary citizens. Each witness went through a detailed process to prepare and present his or her testimony.

Some testimony is more effective and compelling than others. What are the key success factors that distinguish testimony that communicates and makes a difference? How can testimony be used to reach beyond the few legislators in the room to also connect with the public that is so important in driving the legislators' opinions?

Having a practical guide that outlines the steps for giving testimony in a congressional hearing will not only assist you to give testimony but will help you prepare others to do so as well. General tips for testifying before Congress are provided in § 10.58; § 10.59 provides expectations for testifying before Congress; § 10.60 lists your rights while testifying before Congress; and § 10.61 provides a "Step-by-Step-Checklist for Testifying before Congress or Preparing a Witness." (Also see "Testifying Before Congress," by William LaForge (TheCapitol.Net 2010).)

§10.58 General Tips on Testifying before Congress

"It doesn't matter whether I'm talking to two people, ten people, or
thousands of people, I think as if I'm talking to just one person."
Carly Fiorina, Former CEO Hewlett Packard

Some of the most compelling testimony comes from a citizen witness or expert who shares a real-life story or provides expertise on the practical consequences of the proposed legislation. Always remember that testifying before Congress is a high honor, even for experienced lobbyists, and approach it that way. Formal business attire is appropriate unless a unique situation requires workers or professionals to dress the part of the role that they perform. The list in § 10.59 provides a summary of your rights and responsibilities during the testimony.

§10.59 Expectations for Witnesses Testifying before Congress

1. Accurately represent the constituents/members on whose behalf you have been invited to testify.

2. Be honest. Every word that you say, including your answers to unanticipated questions, will be recorded as part of a permanent public record. Some committees may swear the witnesses in at the beginning of their testimony with an oath similar to testifying in court. If you are not absolutely certain about the accuracy of a specific figure, statistic, or example, provide a caveat and offer to verify the information and submit it to the committee at a later time; for example, "I believe that a recent ABC survey revealed that 75 percent of Americans support the XWZ initiative, but I'd like to verify that exact figure and submit the survey for the committee record, if that would be acceptable."

3. Respond to all specific questions on the topic or legislation that you have been invited by the committee to address.

4. Effectively communicate your organization's position on the legislation that is the subject of the hearing.

5. Be above board and do not invent an answer on something if you aren't absolutely sure about it.

6. Be early. Sit in the front row (reserved for witnesses) and proceed to the witness table when your panel or name is called. Committee staffers need to know that the witnesses have arrived and are ready well before time for the hearing to begin.

7. Speak directly into the microphone (adjusting it if necessary) and make eye contact with the chairman upon beginning your remarks.

8. Stick strictly within the committee's time frame (which is generally five minutes) for your oral statement, while providing a more extensive written statement for the official record. You will need to practice repeatedly to be certain that you do not exceed the time limit. Be prepared to quickly summarize and conclude your statement in the event that the committee chair asks you to do so in order to wrap up the hearing or allow committee members to break from the hearing to vote on the House or Senate floor.

9. Assume that the members on the committee have personally received a copy of your full remarks that you provided to congressional committee staff, but recognize that they may not have actually read your statement. Most likely, their staff provided a brief paragraph summarizing your testimony. Therefore, you may wish to refer members to a specific page of your written testimony if you have an important graph, chart, or point that you wish to emphasize.

10. Understand that only one or two members of Congress may be physically present, and they may seem distracted during the hearing. If there are multiple panels, recognize that the first panel tends to get more attention, but be patient. Even though much of the audience may leave after the testimony of a cabinet secretary or member of Congress testifying on the first panel, the content of your testimony is being recorded by a stenographer for a full review by all committee members, their staff, the media, and many other interested parties. The committee is likely to broadcast the hearing via the web, and reporters may obtain the full text of your testimony directly from the committee without attending the hearing personally.

11. Reporters typically sit at a table designated for press. Committee staff generally have a list of all press covering the hearing. The committee's press secretary (or minority party press secretary) can be a useful resource for determining which reporters or news outlets are attending or have expressed interest in covering the event.

§10.60 **Your Rights when Testifying before Congress**

1. Ask the chair for permission to provide information to be included for the record that would back up or validate an important point that you are making.

2. Politely (and repeatedly) decline to answer questions outside the scope of your testimony, organization, or area of responsibility. You may also respectfully question the premise of loaded questions, for example, "How often do you beat your wife?"

3. You have a right not to be badgered. There is a difference between thorough questioning and badgering a witness. Members of Congress have a right to thoroughly question witnesses, and members should be treated with respect, but they should also treat witnesses with civility, recognizing that there are some questions that are off limits. When a question is clearly inappropriate, you have a right to respectfully explain why you will not answer it. Perhaps you are not the best person in your organization to answer that question, or perhaps it is beyond the scope of your organization's work. Do not let members of Congress pressure you into saying something that you really don't want to say. When in doubt, offer to respond in writing at a later time.

4. When appearing on behalf of an organization, you have a right not to be pressed to give your personal opinion. This tactic is used sometimes to emphasize divisions within organizations. When you are appearing on behalf of an organization, you have a duty to represent that organization, not just yourself, on positions that should be decided by your organization's public policy process.

5. Politely and respectfully ask if you can add an answer or clarification during questions directed to someone else on your panel of witnesses.

§10.61 Step-by-Step-Checklist for Testifying before Congress or Preparing a Witness

Stage 1 **Prior to Congressional Session—Committee Considers Agenda**	Given the priorities of your members, employer, or clients, identify relevant committees of jurisdiction and the opportunities (topics) that you will seek to advance.
	Determine the ideal witness profiles and characteristics for various topics that may arise. As you recruit, consider individuals from the districts of key congressional committee members and what aspects of the issue need highlighting.
	Determine potential hearing topics by analyzing the landscape, reviewing committee priorities, and contacting committee staff. If possible, meet with staff before the start of the congressional session to learn how you may be a resource to them and what types of witnesses they may be interested in including in their hearings.
	Develop relationships with potential witnesses. Ask members/clients to gather examples, statistics, and anecdotes to illustrate the positions that your organization is taking.
	Determine what additional information would be helpful based on anticipated opportunities/requests.
	If you may be called to testify under less than ideal situations (for example, a negative situation or subpoena), prepare for every eventuality and discuss the best responses and options under the expected circumstances.
Stage 2 **Specific Hearing Situation—Testifying is a Real Possibility**	Even when testifying is just a possibility, do what you can to foster the opportunity and prepare for the eventuality.
	If a congressional staffer mentions that a committee is considering holding a hearing on a certain topic or you see a hearing announcement, contact the relevant staffer. He may tell you the types of preferred witnesses that are under consideration and if you have any ideas to let him know.
	Once the staffer begins considering your witness, go ahead and check on the potential witnesses' availability. Put out several feelers. Discreetly

(Continued on page 328)

§10.61 Step-by-Step-Checklist for Testifying before Congress or Preparing a Witness (continued)

check with the potential witness about the possibility and consider alternative witnesses as a backup.

Conduct an informal interview to determine any negatives/risk factors, if you have not already done so.

Determine how long it would take the witness to get organizational approval to testify (if needed).

Review any press that the witness or the witness' organization has received on the issue. This can be done with a simple search. (See § 10.7.)

Get the witness to begin considering the content of her remarks. Explain the entire process to the witness. Discuss a potential time frame for travel, testimony draft, and finalization.

Explain to the witness that you don't have approval yet, but if you get it, you will need to move very quickly.

Ask the potential witness to identify who would need to authorize the testimony within the witness's organization and who would provide input if the hearing becomes a reality. What about the organization's media and government affairs departments?

Alert the chain of command in your organization and your client's organization, of the possibility. Who will need to provide input or sign off? Give them the heads-up and determine availability. Give them a general time frame of what they can expect if an invitation is extended.

Make tentative airline/hotel reservations that can be cancelled, allowing enough travel time for cancelled flights or delays. Have an out-of-town witness arrive early the evening before the hearing.

Try to get as much detail from the staff as possible, for example, starting time, other potential witnesses, concerns of the members of Congress holding the hearing and their expectations, and obtain, or begin developing, anticipated questions.

§10.61 Step-by-Step-Checklist for Testifying before Congress or Preparing a Witness (continued)

Stage 3
Witness is Invited

Receiving a confirmation from congressional staff that your witness has been officially invited is a milestone that will trigger intense witness and logistical preparation virtually around the clock until the hearing occurs. This is a good time to notify colleagues and make arrangements to put other professional and personal projects or priorities on hold until the hearing is over.

Alert the witness, confirm his availability and make sure that the witness has approval from his organization if needed. Alert all involved staff within your organization, such as, support, media, and publications.

While accepting the invitation, clarify the testimony submission expectations and details with your congressional staff contact.

Confirm as much information as possible with congressional staff upon receiving an official invitation (other invited witnesses and potential concerns from congressional committee members) since they may be unavailable immediately before the hearing.

Late testimony filed after official committee deadlines can be denied and the appearance can be cancelled. You also want to avoid embarrassing public statements from members of Congress during the hearing, such as, "Since your testimony was late, I haven't had a chance to read it." You need to know the exact time of the deadline, the format (single vs. double spaced), and the delivery method (electronic as well as number of hard copies). See the committee or subcommittee web site for instructions and confirm with congressional staff. You may need to arrange for a staff member to deliver the testimony copies personally since security concerns can hinder courier delivery of testimony.

Time is of the essence. Establish deadlines for:

• Receiving draft testimony from witness (you may be drafting some portions as well);

• Finalizing, duplicating, and submitting written testimony to Capitol Hill;

• Finalizing and issuing press release;

• Finalizing oral statement; and

(Continued on page 330)

§10.61 Step-by-Step-Checklist for Testifying before Congress or Preparing a Witness (continued)

- Finalizing witness briefing book (see Sample Briefing Book Table of Contents in § 10.68) and providing it to the witness.

Notify congressional staff if you are preparing any graphics or seeking to use any charts and would need an easel or other audio-visual equipment. Committee rules and procedures must be observed, and they vary from committee to committee. For specifics, see the committee's web site or ask your staff contact for guidance. Obtain permission in advance if you would like to bring in someone to videotape the appearance. Still photographers should check with the committee clerk upon arriving.

Confirm airline/hotel reservations (allow time for an alternative backup flight in case of flight cancellation or delay). Imagine the stress of a hearing starting and your witness not being there, or a committee staff director asking you about your witness's whereabouts fifteen minutes before the hearing begins. You want to avoid that situation.

Notify all other individuals in your organization who will be involved with various aspects of the preparation and delivery, such as a chart to attach to the testimony or to display on an easel, photocopies and delivery to Capitol Hill, photographer/videographer, internal newsletter reporter, or webmaster.

Determine if the committee will be broadcasting the hearing live from the committee/subcommittee web site and notify those whom you represent and your own staff.

Monitor the C-SPAN television, radio, and web broadcast schedules to find out if C-SPAN will be carrying the testimony live. Check periodically for rebroadcasts and web archives at *<www.cspan.org>*.

- Note: C-SPAN provides gavel to gavel coverage of the full House and Senate when they are in session, so hearings held during that time are generally broadcast later in the evening or during the next weekend.

- Confirm witness transportation from airport if needed. This will be a good time for the host to talk informally

---

§10.61 Step-by-Step-Checklist for Testifying before Congress or Preparing a Witness (continued)

	about the hearing and to assure the witness that he will do a great job.
	• Set a briefing time with witness.
	• Draft formal written testimony.
	• Obtain all necessary clearances and incorporate changes/comments.
	• Coordinate with other lobbyists/witnesses to get copies of their testimony before the hearing since your witness may be asked to respond to other statements.
	• If desired, set up a conversation with other witnesses with shared interests.
Stage 4 **Written Testimony Is Finalized and Press Release Is Issued (If Press Is Desired)**	Copies of the final statement are provided to your organization's internal staff (media and publications staff covering the hearing) and external reporters that you would like to cover the appearance.
Stage 5 **Oral Testimony Is Finalized**	No later than the day before, the content of oral testimony must be finalized so that the witness can practice delivery, eye contact and inflection and stay within the time constraints (usually five minutes). Instruct the witness about what to expect during the hearing. (See §§ 10.61–10.66.) Explain that a panel of green, yellow, and red lights will be in front of him while testifying. The green light indicates go, the yellow light is a signal to wrap up the presentation and the red light is a signal that the time limit has been reached.
Stage 6 **Briefing for Witness**	While some initial briefing can be conducted on the telephone, a formal briefing should be scheduled to walk through the testimony process with the witness, time the delivery of the oral presentation, and practice anticipated questions. It is very helpful if someone familiar with the legislation and the committee provides a mock question and answer session for the witness. This is helpful to the witness in not only reviewing potential questions, but in increasing his confidence addressing them.

(Continued on page 332)

**§10.61 Step-by-Step-Checklist for Testifying before
Congress or Preparing a Witness** (continued)

Stage 7 **Hearing**	Arrive early and inform your staff contact that you have arrived. To locate your contact, you may need to check several locations, such as, committee office and the hearing room.
	Putting together a hearing is a stressful event. Even under the best of circumstances, staff are juggling many balls at the last minute, such as, press calls and questions from members of Congress. Logistical challenges tend to arise: the committee's equipment may not be working properly or a key member, such as the chairman scheduled to preside over the event, is unavailable at the last moment.
	Bring a few backup copies of your finalized testimony and any materials referenced in your testimony, such as charts or surveys. Bring a copy of press releases that you wish to have distributed. You should notify staff before placing your material on the press table. Ideally, staff should be notified of your request to place information on the press table before the hearing date.

Stage 8 **Your Testimony**	Recognize that you may be on TV or recorded through congressional microphones and cameras at any time that you are in the hearing room. Hearing cameras and microphones are often turned on before and after the hearing. Committee web cameras may not be noticeable.
	Turn off your electronic equipment—your cell phone or BlackBerry. Show interest in all speakers throughout the event through your eye contact and body language.
	Staff typically reserve the front seat in the audience for witnesses testifying on later panels.
	You will take your seat at the witness table when the chairman calls your name. A transcriber will be positioned nearby to record the proceedings. Water will be available to you on the witness table. If you are briefing a witness, it is a good idea to remind the witness of essential points immediately before the witness is called to the table. For example, a brief reminder that permission can be requested to submit answers in writing can be useful for the witness.

§10.61 Step-by-Step-Checklist for Testifying before Congress or Preparing a Witness (continued)

Make sure that the microphone is close to your mouth each time that you speak. You may need to adjust it to make this possible. Witnesses testifying as part of a panel often share a microphone during the question-and-answer period, so the microphone may require further positioning.

If you are interrupted by the sound of buzzers during your testimony, it is most likely a signal to the members of Congress that a vote is occurring on the floor of Congress. Keep going unless the chairman interrupts the hearing so that the members can go and vote. Be prepared to quickly wrap up your testimony if a voting interruption occurs.

Stage 9 **Hearing Ends**	Listen carefully to the chairman as he or she closes the hearing. This is usually when the chairman announces any further action that is expected on the issue, such as, when the bill might be marked up. The chairman is also supposed to announce when the hearing record will close. The hearing record is typically open ten or so days after a hearing, but the time open varies by committee and situation.
	Members of Congress may ask you follow-up questions, and a formal reply is required before the deadline. If you would like to clarify or expand upon questions raised during the hearing, you might approach a committee member and discuss the possibility of responding to it.
	Attempt to determine which press were present at the event. If possible, obtain contact information of attending press so that you can track press coverage and follow up with the reporters.
	Consider having the witness drop off a copy of the testimony to his or her congressional representatives if it would be helpful.
	Your witness should thank the chairman and all congressional staff who made the appearance possible.
	Make sure that you follow up with anything that you promised to anyone during the course of the hearing.

(Continued on page 334)

---

§10.61 Step-by-Step-Checklist for Testifying before Congress or Preparing a Witness (continued)

Stage 10 **The Debrief**	A good debriefing is an essential, but often overlooked, stage of the process.
	After congratulating the witness, set up a time to review the experience. What follow-up is needed? What went right? How can you build on positive momentum?
	Are there any fires that need to be put out (controversial issues that arose during the hearing that should be addressed immediately)?
	How long is the record open? What information did you commit to send to the members as part of the hearing or to others?
Stage 11 **Communicate Testimony and Next Steps**	Who should see the testimony and associated coverage and how should it be distributed? Can material prepared for your testimony be used in other ways? A flow chart or timeline that you prepared as an attachment might make a nice feature for your web site or magazine.
Stage 12 **Follow-Up and Thank You**	Send photos, videotapes, and press clippings from the hearing, and a thank you note to your witness.
	Send a thank-you letter to members of the committee transmitting any requested material or additional information to reinforce your message.
	Make a note to follow up with congressional staff in about three months to find out if the official printed hearing record is available. Some committees post them on their web pages, but a printed copy should also be obtained.
	Send several copies of the printed hearing record to the witness and keep one for your organization's historic files. You may also want to keep one for yourself.
	Note: Even veteran lobbyists should keep a copy of everything they publish under their name and formal communications that go out under their signature. Who knows? Maybe you'll run for office or seek confirmation to a government position in the future. Better to know what is on the record than to be reminded about it during a congressional hearing at an awkward moment.

§10.62 Lobby Tips

Preparing Written Congressional Testimony

- Always check with the committee staff making the hearing arrangements to obtain the requirements for your testimony, confirm deadlines, and determine the number of copies and precise format: double- or single-spaced, margins, two-sided, etc. Generally, the cover page is one sided and the remainder of the testimony is copied two-sided on letter-sized paper. Always number your pages starting with the first page of testimony (the cover page is not numbered) and place a footer with the name of the witness and date.

- Make certain that you understand the submission deadlines. The committee may establish separate deadlines for submission of an electronic version and multiple paper copies.

- Avoid acronyms, legalese, and jargon.

- TheCapitol.Net offers training in preparing written congressional testimony: <*www.CongressionalTestimony.com*>.

§10.63 Recommended Resources

Drafting Testimony

View testimony posted on the congressional committee's web site to get an idea of the required format (but confirm the requirements with your congressional staff contact).

- Select lobbying terms, abbreviations, and acronyms are available in Appendix 4. A glossary of legislative terms is available from TheCapitol.Net at <*www.CongressionalGlossary.com*>

- The classic reference book, *The Elements of Style*, by William Strunk, Jr. provides the basic rules of usage and the composition rules most commonly violated. It is available at <*www.bartleby.com*>.

- Another essential reference book useful for lobbyists (and all writers) is *On Writing Well*, by William Zinsser.

- Before submitting your written testimony, ask a friend or family member unfamiliar with the issue at hand to read it and highlight unfamiliar lingo, jargon, abbreviations, and points that are not presented clearly. Can they recap your major two or three points after a quick read?

- TheCapitol.Net offers training in testifying before Congress: <*www.CongressionalTestimony.com*>.

§10.64 Template for
Written Congressional Testimony

A sample cover page format follows:

[LETTERHEAD/LOGO]

STATEMENT OF
[NAME]
[TITLE]

ON BEHALF OF
[ORGANIZATION]

REGARDING
[INSERT OFFICIAL SUBJECT OF HEARING, E.G., NUMBER AND NAME OF BILL)

BEFORE THE
[INSERT OFFICIAL NAME OF THE COMMITTEE OR SUBCOMMITTEE]
[INSERT DATE]
[INSERT ROOM NUMBER AND BUILDING,
E.G., 1234 RAYBURN HOUSE OFFICE BUILDING]
WASHINGTON, DC

Begin and end your statement by thanking the committee chair and committee
or subcommittee for the opportunity to testify, for example:

Mr. Chairman and Members of the Subcommittee:

My name is [insert name] and I am appearing on behalf of [insert organization].
Thank you for the opportunity to address the important issue of . . .

Sample closure:

Again, I appreciate the opportunity to appear before the subcommittee,
and I look forward to answering your questions.

A sample footer format for the testimony text (beginning on
the first page of text after the cover page) follows:

Page One
Statement of [Name]
On behalf of [Organization]
[Committee/Subcommittee Name]
[Date]

§10.65 **Preparing for Questions**

You may wish to phone the staffers of all committee/subcommittee members before the hearing to learn their areas of specific interest or concern. Intelligence garnered from pre-hearing phone calls can be extremely helpful in your efforts to anticipate questions and prepare potential responses prior to the hearing. Occasionally congressional staff members will ask lobbyists if they have any suggestions for points that should be raised during the hearing. If you are asked to suggest questions to congressional staffers, they should be offered only as general suggestions.

§10.66 **Common Witness Errors while Testifying before Congress**

- Not timing and rehearsing oral testimony, causing the chairman to interrupt the speaker at the end of the time period.
- Lack of eye contact with the committee chair, looking down and reading the testimony.
- Monotone (lack of voice inflection).
- Microphone too far away from mouth.
- Failure to rehearse hypothetical questions and answers prior to the hearing.
- Winging it on answers instead of asking permission to submit a written response at a later time.
- Failure to recognize that they may be on camera throughout the hearing, even when not testifying (such as fiddling with hair or yawning).

§10.67 **Submitting Testimony for the Record**

Even if you are not selected to testify, you may submit a statement to be included in the official hearing record. Committee rules vary, so you need to check with committee staff to make sure that you meet the format and delivery requirements for submitting a statement to be included into the record. You will need to get permission (preferably before the hearing) to place your prepared statement or any press releases on the press and congressional staff tables before the hearing begins.

§10.68 Sample Table of Contents: Briefing Book for a Congressional Witness

Place the following information on the front cover or inside front cover of the briefing book:

1. Time and location of hearing.

2. Critical and emergency contact information: cell phone of person providing transportation as well as hotel confirmation and contact information.

Contents

1. Witness List.

2. Oral Statement (unstapled and timed to be no more than five minutes, unless the committee instructs you otherwise).

3. Written Statement (unstapled for ease of reference).

4. Other Witnesses' Statements.

5. Committee Members (broken down by party and in seniority order):
   - Bios with relevant facts from the members' district/background, membership on other committees/caucuses, past occupation, and anything relevant that can affect perspective. (See "position drivers" discussion at §§ 3.2–3.12.)
   - Conservative/liberal ratings.
   - Special notes with respect to the issue: voting record on the issue, plus unique facts: cosponsored the bill; comments made or position taken on the legislation.
   - Notes on the members' positions on other issues that could come up or any relevant history that they have had with your organization, such as, spoke to your company president last week.
   - Press section of committee web site.

6. Information on Hearing Topic (legislation or subject of oversight):
   - Section-by-section (line-by-line summary of legislation).
   - Previous statements of committee members on the legislation/topic.
   - Full bill text.
   - Status: cosponsors with party, state/district identified, summary of any previous hearings or action in the other body (House or Senate).
   - If legislation has not yet been introduced, include a description of the issue, status, talking points and similar/past legislation that has been introduced if applicable.

7. Related/Opposing Legislation:
   - Text.
   - Arguments of proponents and counterarguments.
   - List of members of Congress supporting the legislation, including committee members who support it.
   - Interest groups endorsing or opposing legislation.

8. Other Issue-Related Proposals (proposals not in the form of legislation).

9. Hypothetical Questions/Answers (helpful for rehearsing).

10. Legal Cases.

11. Relevant State Laws or Bills (noting the states of committee members).

12. Administration:

   • Statement of Administration Policy (SAP).

   • Administration position/activities on issue or similar issues.

   • Letters or contacts with administration that indicate expected position.

13. Polls Taken (on the issue).

14. Press Coverage.

15. Key Players (proponents/opponents).

16. Contributors to Sponsor/Opponent Campaigns.

17. Miscellaneous/Background.

§10.69 Tips for Attending Congressional Hearings

Examples of congressional venues that can require extra early arrival:

• Appropriations Subcommittee hearing rooms on the third floor of the Rayburn House Office Building. (This is especially true for markups.)

• Markups where tables may be reconfigured taking up much of the space in the room.

• House Rules Committee (or anything else in the Capitol building). Doors open at 9:00 a.m., but there are several entrances.

Source: Chris Van Horne, Congressional Place Holding Service

Allow extra time when covering or attending hearings on controversial issues or featuring celebrity witnesses. Certain hearing rooms or locations with limited space can also require early arrival to ensure that you can get in and find a seat. Typically, you can get a good seat by arriving one hour early for a congressional hearing or markup, although some circumstances and venues require a longer waiting time to ensure getting in. There are several companies that provide placeholding (also called seat holding, line sitting, line holding, and line standing) service, including Congressional Valet, Capitol Hill Delivery Service, Congressional Services Company, linestanding.com, and others. See this book's web site for links: *<www.LobbyingAndAdvocacy.com>*.

§10.70 Diagram of a
Typical Congressional Hearing Room

Committee members' seats are typically divided by party affiliation. For example, in some cases all Democrats are seated on the right side of the chairman and in some cases it's the left. This varies by committee.

Protocol dictates that only members of Congress and congressional aides staffing the hearing are permitted on the raised dais (platform) where the member and staff are seated. As a general rule, members of Congress and staff involved in the committee meeting do not like to be interrupted from attending to last-minute details immediately before the meeting. They are busy getting ready for the meeting. After the meeting concludes, they are generally more relaxed and accessible, but be aware of dais protocol and the presence of the press. C-SPAN cameras often continue to roll after the hearing has concluded and a reporter or opposing interest may be within earshot as you share your candid take on the hearing with a member of Congress or staff. Also be aware of committee microphones that may still be turned on after the hearing has ended.

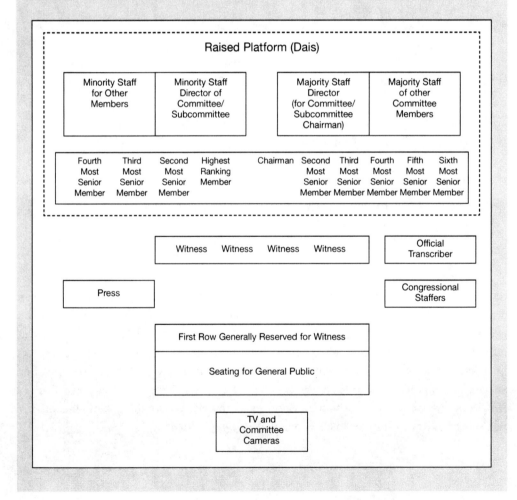

§10.99 **Chapter Summary**

- Since the media is influential in communicating with the citizenry and policymakers, lobbyists spend considerable resources on media campaigns and develop creative approaches attempting to get their message heard. (§ 10.1)
- Changes in technology and the media environment have presented both challenges and opportunities for lobbyists aiming to have their message heard through the media. (§ 10.2)
- A "How-to Guide" for working with the media is detailed in sections §§ 10.3–10.28.
- The 10 Media Relations Principles for working with the media:
    1. Understand the ultimate goal (§ 10.4)
    2. Plan and coordinate (§ 10.5)
    3. Conduct an issue audit (§ 10.6)
    4. Select a credible spokesperson (§ 10.8)
    5. Know your issue and anticipate questions (§ 10.12)
    6. Hone your message (§ 10.14)
    7. Consider and coordinate various media (§ 10.15)
    8. Get the word out strategically and target state/district outlets (§ 10.19)
    9. Timing is everything (§ 10.21)
    10. Follow-up (§ 10.22)
- § 10.7 recommends resources for conducting a press audit on an issue or organization.
- A short checklist for preparing spokespersons for interviews includes allowing adequate preparation time, providing a rehearsal, and using video clips. (§ 10.10)
- Tips for selecting spokespersons for public appearances are discussed in § 10.9, and tips for preparing for the physical aspects of a television appearance are addressed in § 10.11.
- § 10.15 discusses the need to use various media, including the new media used by the citizenry, especially younger citizens, to obtain news.
- A comparison of earned and paid media is included in § 10.18.
- Wire services allow you to distribute your press releases to various types of media and messages can be tailored to the specific mediums that you are using. Distribution of your message can be targeted to media outlets in particular states, regions, and cities. § 10.20 lists nine press distribution web site resources for lobbyists.
- The following tips for working with reporters are discussed in § 10.23:
    1. Be honest: If you don't know, say you don't know
    2. Remember that everything is on the record
    3. Be responsive to reporters
    4. Give credit where credit is due
    5. Practice handling hostile questions
    6. If you aren't prepared or authorized to speak on an issue, don't do it

7. Be prepared to question the assumptions of a fallacious question
8. Avoid negatives
9. Avoid acronyms and jargon
10. Use caution in addressing hypothetical situations or unfamiliar quotes or studies

- Resources are recommended for preparing for interviews with reporters. (§ 10.25)
- Considerations for working with consultants are provided in § 10.28.
- Tips for coordinating legislative events are provided in § 10.50, including confirming essential details directly with the speaker upon arrival, making sure that congressional introductions are brief, and working out protocol and order preferences when several policymakers are speaking.
- Tips for addressing policymakers and their spouses are discussed in §§ 10.51 and 10.52.
- A speech arrival checklist that can be used for legislative events is found at § 10.53 and a checklist of what to bring is at § 10.54.
- Resources (§ 10.55) and tips for legislative update presentations (§ 10.56) are listed.
- Congressional testimony is one of the most effective ways to weigh in on the legislative process. § 10.59 provides an overview of what is expected from a congressional witness, and § 10.60 delineates a witness's rights when testifying before Congress. Approach testifying before Congress as an honor and a responsibility. Represent your constituents well by being honest, accurate, and thorough when presenting your testimony. Recognize that some things are outside the scope of your expertise, and know the line between thorough questioning and badgering.
- Chapter Ten also includes a useful testimony preparation checklist (§ 10.61), advice for preparing for questions (§ 10.65), and typical errors while testifying (§ 10.66).
- After the hearing, debrief with the witness by reviewing the hearing, and follow up on anything that you promised to provide anyone during the course of the hearing. (§ 10.61)
- When assisting a witness with congressional testimony, clarify key issues, practice hypothetical questions and answers with the witness, and confirm as many details as possible with congressional staff. (§ 10.61)
- Even if you are not selected to testify, you may still submit a written statement, provided that you meet submission requirements. Instructions for submitting testimony for the record are summarized in § 10.67.
- Your hearing briefing book preparation will be aided by a sample table of contents provided in § 10.68.
- § 10.70 provides a diagram of a typical congressional hearing room and lists tips for covering or attending hearings.

Managing and Maintaining a High-Performance Government Affairs Program

"Talent wins games, but teamwork and intelligence wins championships."

Michael Jordan

Chapter 11: Managing and Maintaining a High-Performance Government Affairs Program

§11.1 **Introduction**

A political environment is not always conducive to exemplary management practices. Nevertheless, overcoming environmental challenges and daily pressures to invest in effective human resource management and operations is essential for achieving long-term legislative success, maximizing your effectiveness, and avoiding costly and perhaps embarrassing problems and liability exposure. Chapter Eleven provides an overview of strategies with tips and resources for establishing and maintaining a high-performance government affairs operation.

Developing, operating, and improving a government affairs program presents distinct challenges. The activities required to establish and maintain a high-performance government affairs program are frequently put on the back burner because of a work environment with intense demands and sudden public policy developments and challenges. Additionally, many government affairs managers come from Capitol Hill positions where they may not have had the benefit of direct management experience or training.

This chapter provides a walk-through of the elements essential for creating and maintaining an effective government affairs function. Practical resources and tips are provided for recruiting, interviewing, hiring, and checking references. The importance of training and developing staff is discussed, and various office organization options are explored. The chapter provides tips for staying focused on organizational goals and maximizing productivity, avoiding burnout, addressing conflict and stress, budgeting, technology management, recordkeeping, assessing risk exposure, and outsourcing. A tool that will help you assess your activities and integrate your various governmental affairs functions is also included.

Information on median lobbyist salaries is provided, and several salary surveys providing additional government affairs compensation information are recommended. Resources for conducting a job search to secure a lobbyist position are also included.

Chapter Eleven provides resources for addressing distinct government affairs challenges and issues, but it should not serve as a substitute for ongoing counsel and guidance from your qualified legal and human resource professionals.

§11.2 **Hire Qualified, Ethical, and Effective Staff**

> *"Politics is perhaps the only profession for which no preparation is thought necessary."*
> Robert Louis Stevenson

> *"It isn't the plays or the system that gets the job done, it's the quality of the people in the system."*
> Joe Paterno

Talented and ethical individuals can help you put your organization's best foot forward and represent your strongest asset: its human resources. Conversely, as discussed in

Chapter Two, inadvertently placing unethical or high-risk individuals in government affairs positions can expose the organization to reputational and legal risks.

Organizational structure, position descriptions, and goals should be coordinated and refined as part of your governmental affairs planning process. (See Chapter Six.) Information on various government affairs organizational structures is presented in § 11.13.

§11.3 Look for Legislative Experience

While subject-matter expertise is increasingly important in public policy, legislative or executive branch experience is also virtually essential to effective lobbying. This type of experience provides first-hand insights into the process that cannot be matched with a textbook understanding of how government works or even more casual interactions with the institutions. For this reason, employers recruiting lobbyists should look for legislative experience, and those pursuing lobbying as a profession should first seek it.

During the recruitment process, recognize the restrictions and requirements related to discussing employment opportunities with legislative and executive branch employees as well as post-employment (revolving door) lobbying restrictions. See § 2.3 for gift and travel restrictions applicable to job interviews, revolving door lobbying restrictions for previous congressional, executive branch, or state government employees; and requirements for government employees to recuse themselves from any issue involving future or potential employers.

§11.4 Recruit and Tap Talent

While you will need to look for talent as vacancies occur, consider yourself a talent scout year-round as you work with legislative staff and other associates. Strengthening your network on an ongoing basis will help when you need to fill a position.

In addition to personal ethics, consider the following traits when recruiting for lobbyist positions.

- Hill, state legislature, or executive branch experience
- Communication skills (obvious, but not to be underestimated)
- Emotional IQ (ability to perceive situations and read people, and handle confrontation and conflict with maturity and self-control)
- Writing/analytical skills
- Subject-matter expertise (technical, substantive, or specialized knowledge and experience)
- Ability to prioritize, maintain composure under pressure, and handle tight deadlines (ask for examples)
- Contacts on the Hill, in state legislatures, or executive branch
- Ability to work on a team and share credit
- Type and level of education (most lobbyist positions require an undergraduate degree, plus a law degree may be helpful)

§11.5 Recommended Resources

Finding Lobbyist Candidates

- *Roll Call Jobs* is the best online resource to reach potential candidates for federal government affairs positions. Go to: <*www.rcjobs.com*>.

- "Opportunities in Public Affairs," produced by Brubach Enterprises, Inc., is a bi-weekly newsletter (online only) with job listings for public and government affairs professionals. Employers can have job vacancies emailed to their database of public affairs professionals, journalists, and government affairs professionals. Go to <*www.opajobs.com*>.

- The Public Affairs Council posts job opportunities at the federal and state levels: <*www.pac.org*>.

- The American League of Lobbyists posts some jobs for its members at <*www.alldc.org*>.

- The *Washington Post* employment section is available online: <*www.washingtonpost.com*>.

- The CEO Update provides information on jobs for nonprofits and associations (3-12 month subscription) at <*www.associationjobs.com*>.

- The American Society of Association Executives (ASAE) provides jobs information at <*www.careerhq.com*>.

- To find contact information on current lobbyists by organization, client, name, and subject matters lobbied, go to <*www.lobbyists.info*> (*Washington Representatives*).

- To view lobbyists' federal registration forms (PDF), go to <*www.disclosure.senate.gov*>.

- Lobby Jobs (Influence/Legal Times): <*www.influence.biz/lobbyjobs*>.

Links to these resources are available on this book's web site: <*www.LobbyingAndAdvocacy.com*>.

 §11.6 Recommended Resources

Reference Checking

Reference checking is essential for every employer. An offer of employment can be contingent upon reference checks. Employers can be held responsible if they knew—or should have known—that someone they hired might pose an undue threat of harm to others. The following reference checking resources can be helpful to lobbyists as employers:

- *Complete Reference Checking Handbook* by Edward C. Andler and Dara Herbst
- *Legal Effective References: How to Give and Get Them* by Wendy Bliss
- *Safe Hiring*, by Lester Rosen

- Public speaking experience
- Diligence and follow-through

In addition, consider supplementing your interview questions by asking the candidate to respond to your description of hypothetical situations that involve integrity and ethics, relational skills, confrontation, and conflict.

Thorough reference checking is essential to all hiring. Several resources for recruiting and reference checking are provided in §§ 11.5–11.6.

§11.7 **Compensate Competitively**

Compensating competitively is not the only factor essential for attracting and retaining top talent with legislative experience, but it is extremely important. Resources for compensating lobbyists are provided in § 11.8. 2006 compensation surveys by the Public Affairs Council indicated that the overall median base salary (without benefits and perks) for a top corporate federal government relations position (reporting directly to the CEO) was $181,000, and the overall median base salary for a top government affairs association executive was $120,000.

§11.10 **Take Time for Training and Developing Staff**

"Leadership and learning are indispensable to each other."
John F. Kennedy

Training is not only an investment in human capital that can pay for itself many times over in future effectiveness, it is also necessary to avoid costly governmental affairs mistakes and liability exposure. Adequate training in all lobbyist competency areas is often overlooked in government affairs organizations. Consequently, many government affairs groups encounter unnecessary conflict within their organization and lack necessary focus on organizational functions.

Setting employee expectations begins in the interview process and continues throughout the employment process. Before a new hire or consultant begins representing your organization, sit down and clearly communicate your requirements for ethical conduct, integrity, and complying with lobbying laws and regulations. There is no better way to destroy your government affairs program and your own reputation, than to be tainted with a scandal or a bad reputation. Many people in Washington, DC, have lamented, "if only I had made our standards more clear to the staff." Chapter Two provides extensive guidance, tips, and resources for achieving the ethics and legal imperatives.

Common training topics include:
- Managing Multiple Priorities
- Compliance with Lobbying and Ethics Laws and Professional Standards (essential)
- How Congress Works (especially important if the staff does not have congressional experience)

§11.8 Recommended Resources

Determining Lobbyists' Salaries

- Information on the salary of specific congressional employees is available at *<www.legistorm.org>*
- Government pay scale information is available at *<www.opm.gov>*
- (The Public Affairs Council has several useful surveys on its web site (search under "Publications"): *<www.pac.org>*
  - *Association Government Relations & Public Affairs Compensation Survey*
  - *Corporate Government Relations & Public Affairs Compensation Survey*
  - *PAC Administrator Compensation Survey*
  - *Grassroots Administrator Compensation Survey*
- A table showing compensation practices for chief government affairs positions is available for purchase from the American Society of Association Executives at *<www.asaecenter.org>*.

Links to these resources are available on this book's web site: *<www.LobbyingAndAdvocacy.com>*.

§11.9 Recommended Resources

Resources for Lobbyists Seeking Employment

Lobbyists not only look for opportunities themselves, but they have many opportunities to help others seeking lobbyist positions. Most lobbyist positions are filled through personal connections and word-of-mouth. In Washington, your contacts are your best resources. The best approach is to ask people you trust for advice on your job search without giving them the impression that you are pressuring them to hire you.

Even though employers prefer to hire someone whom they trust, or someone who has worked with someone they trust personally, the following additional resources can be useful for identifying lobbying positions as well as potential employers or networking contacts:

- *Roll Call Jobs* at *<www.rcjobs.com>*.
- Opportunities in Public Affairs (online only) : *<www.opajobs.com>*.
- *Washington Representatives* (hard copy and online subscription): This book lists the contact information for all registered lobbyists and lobbying organizations by firm, name and subject area. In many cases, direct emails and phone extensions are provided. This book is worth buying for conducting a job search and can be purchased at: *<www.lobbyists.info>*.

Links to these resources are available on this book's web site: *<www.LobbyingAndAdvocacy.com>*.

§11.11 Recommended Resources

Training and Development

- TheCapitol.Net provides training on how Washington works, including many of the topics listed previously: <*www.TheCapitol.Net*>.
- Franklin Covey offers time management and priority-setting training: <*www.franklincovey.com*>.
- The Center for Creative Leadership (CCL) individual, group, team, and organizational development and resources: <*www.ccl.org*>.
- *Perfect Phrases for Building Strong Teams* by Linda Eve Diamond.
- *Working with Emotional Intelligence* by Daniel Goleman.
- The following E-Books from the Center for Creative Leadership (CCL) can be purchased online at <*www.ccl.org*>:
  - *Managing Conflict with Direct Reports* by Barbara Popejoy and Brenda J. McManigle
  - *Managing Conflict with Your Boss* by David Sharpe and Elinor Johnson
  - *Managing Difficult People* by Marilyn Pincus.

- Executive Branch Advocacy (especially important if the staff lacks executive branch experience)
- The Regulatory Process
- Media Training (essential for all lobbyists)
- Testimony Workshops
- Grassroots Development
- Public Speaking
- Legislative Research Tools and Methods (including Internet research)
- Issue or Industry specific courses and resources

Chapter Six provides guidance and resources for setting goals and communicating them to staff regularly.

§11.12 Get Your Staff on Board with Your Mission

"The most fundamental business issue facing organizations today is execution—whether or not an organization achieves its goals. There is serious misalignment between the daily activities of the front-line worker and the organizational strategy. The top priority of every executive and team leader should be to clarify, communicate and assist workers in achieving their organization's critical goals."

Stephen R. Covey, author of *The 7 Habits of Highly Effective People*

Chapter Six provides tools for developing and implementing your governmental relations plan. (§ 6.15 provides "Tips for Executing Your Plan" and § 6.11 addresses long-term goals.) Maintaining focus and perspective is a critical feature of effective advocacy over the long-term.

While lobbyists tend to live from legislative crisis to legislative crisis, successful government affairs operations involve investing in your human resources and taking a longer view. If staff members are only employed for the money, they are likely to leave when another equitable opportunity comes along. When an employee leaves, you lose someone with knowledge, invaluable skills, and contacts. New hires require time to become fully productive.

Consider the time and resources that it would take to replace a talented employee; for example, three months of a lobbyist's salary and benefits as well as time to get the next person fully trained, introduced around town at receptions, with coalitions, on the Hill and in the executive branch, and trusted and relied upon by critical legislative or executive branch contacts.

A Franklin Covey survey revealed that the majority of workers don't know their organization's most important goals. Only 48 percent of workers say their organization has a clear strategic direction and only 37 percent say they understand the reason for that strategic direction. The survey found that less than half of U.S. workers know their organization's goals or are committed to them. The study found that most organizations' goal achievement is undermined due to "execution gaps." Findings include:

- Only 44 percent of workers say their organization has clearly communicated its most important goals.
- Only 54 percent of workers say they clearly understand what they are supposed to do to help achieve their organization's goals.
- Workers identified the following as the most significant barriers to the achievement of their goals:
  - Overwhelming workload (too much to do, can't get to all my key priorities) (31 percent)
  - Lack of resources (insufficient budgets, people, tools, support) (30 percent)
  - Unclear or shifting work priorities (other people's urgencies and emergencies, conflicting demands, surprise projects) (27 percent)
  - Political issues (turf battles, rivalries, favoritism, personality clashes) (26 percent)
  - Lack of recognition or reward (credit not shared, unfair pay, rewards not tied to performance) (26 percent)
- Only 26 percent of workers say they meet at least monthly with their manager to review progress on their goals, and only 30 percent of workers say work team rewards and consequences are clearly based on performance.

Additionally, in a separate study conducted by Franklin Covey of 26,500 respondents in more than 150 companies, only 15 percent of workers could actually identify their organization's top three goals:

- Only 48 percent of workers say the goals of their work team are translated into their individual work goals
- Only 32 percent of workers say they take time each week to identify and schedule the activities around their work team's most important goals
- Only 38 percent of workers say their work team planning results in clear assignments for individuals

    Source: "Less Than Half of U.S. Workers Know or are Committed to Their Organization's Goals," Franklin Covey, PR Newswire, March 15, 2004.

    A summary of the report is available at: *<www.franklincovey.com>*.

> *"The findings confirm that most organizations suffer from major 'execution gaps,' which undermine the achievement of their most critical, strategic goals. The execution gaps result from a combination of factors and the degree to which workers understand and apply six key principles of execution at the individual, team, and organizational level—clarity, commitment, translation into action, enabling, synergy, and accountability."*
>
> Franklin Covey, PR Newswire, March 15, 2004

Mentoring

Mentoring can be particularly beneficial with government affairs staff since qualities such as discernment and judgment acquired through experience, communication, emotional intelligence, and relationships are so critical. Offer to match more junior staff with seasoned individuals in an informal mentoring relationship. Certain mentors outside of the organization can be helpful as well.

§11.13 Organize Your Team Effectively

As discussed in Chapter Six, establishing goals and tying them to individual performance are necessary for success in government affairs. The overall organizational structure of a team typically incorporates one or more of the following considerations:

- By issue: each staff person is responsible for one or more issues.
- By target: each staff person is responsible for a legislative member or public official, or a group of public officials.
- By government agency:, the House or Senate, or executive branch.
- By function: grassroots, media, tracking legislation, and advocacy.
- By operating unit: geographic location, or region.

Your government affairs organization should reflect your long-term priorities and organizational needs. No one structure is necessarily optimal. When designing or redesigning your team, consider the following factors:

- Size and resource level of your team
- Number of issues covered
- Expertise required given the complexity of your issues
- Balancing involvement with Congress, states, and the executive branch
- Organization of your grassroots or clients

The majority of corporate government affairs offices (57 percent) organize their staff according to issue expertise (§ 11.14). This reinforces the point made in Chapter One that as legislation has become more complex lobbyists have become more focused on providing issue expertise. In the long-term, lobbyists' expertise on substantive issues as well as skills assessing the issue's potential impact on specific interests will serve them and their employer well.

§11.14 Corporate Governmental Affairs Office Organization

According to a 2006 study by the Public Affairs Council of the Washington, DC, offices of corporate government affairs, the majority of these offices, 57 percent, were organized by issue.

Of the rest, 30 percent had no division of labor, 27 percent were organized by operating unit/division, 18 percent were organized by the branch of government, 7 percent by product line, 7 percent by party, 6 percent by geography, and 6 percent by other criteria.

Source: "Corporate Government Relations Washington Office Benchmarking Project," Public Affairs Council, 2006.

§11.15 Encourage Time Management and Avoid Burnout

Because of the intensity, unpredictability, and pace of the legislative environment, government affairs supervisors are challenged to manage in a way that encourages excellence and focus, yet avoids overwork, burnout, and loss of perspective. § 11.17 provides quotes on time well-kept and § 11.18 provides tips for managing workload and avoiding burnout.

Many lobbyists resign from their positions upon coming to the conclusion that they cannot balance their personal responsibilities with their work life. Some of these situations may have been avoided had their employers worked with them to address the stresses and pressures so often experienced by government affairs professionals.

Replacing lobbyist employees carries many quantifiable and non-quantifiable costs. For example, replacement costs can include:

- Quantifiable costs:
  - To calculate replacement costs for a specific position, add the salary and benefits plus the cost in time to replace the employee: if it takes you three months to recruit and hire a replacement, add the lobbyists' salary and benefits for three months plus the time it takes you to replace the employee and train the new one.

§11.16 Lobby Tips

Avoiding Burnout

- Many lobbyists increasingly expect and seek the opportunity to balance work and life responsibilities, which has been aided by technological advances and more information-based work tasks that can be structured to allow professional part-time work and flexible schedules.

- Pay special attention to team building, personal interactions, and providing ownership and recognition for certain issues or projects.

- Address workplace problems and employee concerns immediately to minimize stress, personality conflicts, and morale busters. What may seem like a minor disagreement or concern can quickly escalate into a problem that is discussed by others around town or even picked up by the media.

- Take time to celebrate successes and encourage time off for rest and regeneration after legislative votes, conferences, or other big projects or achievements.

- Intangible costs:
  - Missing important testimony or media opportunities, congressional or coalition meetings.
  - Unnecessary duplication of work.
  - Loss of supervisor's time to train the new employee.
  - Decreased responsiveness or even complaints from members, clients or Hill contacts during the transition.
  - Failure to identify substantive problems with legislation or effectively monitor legislative developments while the staff member is being replaced.
  - Since word-of-mouth is often used for lobbyists seeking employment, high turnover and stress at a particular firm can become well-known impediments to recruiting new staff.

Like all employees, most lobbyists value fulfillment and development more than money. A sense of making a meaningful contribution, professional growth, developing a respected reputation among peers, and a positive work environment where conflicts are constructively addressed are also important. Lobbyists also want to feel challenged and to understand how their work supports the organization's mission.

§11.18 Time Management Tips

Make the most of your precious minutes with a time-management system that works.

Getting your entrepreneurial tasks done in a reasonable amount of time is what time management is all about. James Clark, a time-management expert and co-founder of

---

§11.17 Quotes on Time Well-Kept

"Nine-tenths of wisdom is being wise in time."
—Theodore Roosevelt

"Do we need more time? Or do we need to be more disciplined with the time we have?"
—Kerry Johnson, author

"Time is our most precious asset; we should invest it wisely."
—Michael Levy, author

"There's a myth that time is money. In fact, time is more precious than money. It's a nonrenewable resource. Once you've spent it, and if you've spent it badly, it's gone forever."
—Neil Fiore, author

"You will never find time for anything. If you want time, you must make it."
—Charles Buxton, Member of the English Parliament

"Time and health are two precious assets that we don't recognize and appreciate until they have been depleted."
—Denis Waitley, American speaker and writer

"Those who think they have not time for bodily exercise will sooner or later have to find time for illness."
—Edward Stanley, former Prime Minister of the United Kingdom

Room 214, a marketing and communications company in Boulder, CO, provides some tips on how to fit your everyday business tasks, both large and small, into your tight schedule.

1. Get a System. Everyone works in a different way, says Clark. Whether you live by your planner, Outlook calendar, or PDA, make sure you have a system for organizing your to-do lists. "The hardest part is to dedicate yourself to a system and stick to it," he says. Clark recommends looking to *Getting Things Done: The Art of Stress-Free Productivity*, by David Allen, for a possible system of guidelines.

2. Schedule "Do Not Disturb" Time. To get any system to succeed, you'll have to make an effort—whether it's organizing your incoming emails and voice mails or clearing out your inbox into to-do files. All that takes undivided attention, notes Clark. He suggests using a block of time in the beginning of your day (say from 9:15 a.m. to 10:00 a.m.) to organize and plan your schedule. Let everyone in your office know you are unavailable during that time. "After a while, when [people] see you're really efficient, they'll start respecting that [unavailable time window]."

3. Take Action. Divide your list into action items by order of importance and the time it'll take to complete each task, says Clark. When you look at something in your email inbox, ask yourself, "Can I complete this task in two minutes?" If so, do it, because it will take you longer than two minutes to file it. If not, take that time to file it and put it on your calendar.

4. Create a Project Calendar. If a task takes more than one step, file it as a project. Divide the project into smaller tasks, and plot those on your calendar. If you want to add a blog to your web site, for example, you'll need to procure a blog server, designate an employee or employees to update the blog, meet with them to discuss size and scope, beta test, review for problems, set a start date, etc. All those smaller tasks can be plotted on your calendar. Clark also finds it helpful to work backward from a desired result to divide it up. Ask yourself, "One year into the future, what would success look like?" Defining the outcome will start driving the next action items.

5. Make Your Meetings Efficient. Meetings are often a huge waste of time, notes Clark. As the leader, you must run them smoothly—starting with defining what will be discussed. Also, have set start and end times, and stick to them. Organize what you want to discuss, keep the meeting moving, and let everyone know what needs to be accomplished by the meeting's end. Finally, notes Clark, "The worst thing about some meetings is sometimes you get out of [one] and no one understands what's happening next." Make sure there is a defined action or set of actions at the end of the meeting for you and your employees to follow."

Source: "In Good Time," by Nichole L. Torres, *Entrepreneur* magazine, December 2005, <*www.entrepreneur.com*>. Used with permission.

§11.19 Analyze Staff Activities

"There is a better way of doing it. Find it."
Thomas Edison

As discussed in Chapter Six, activity analysis can be a useful tool for government affairs evaluation and planning. Have each staff member estimate the percentage of his/her time spent on various tasks, such as, monitoring legislation, answering member questions, preparing analysis, going to Capitol Hill, and attending coalition meetings. Assess the way that time is being spent on activities. Does it reflect your organizational and government affairs priorities? Is there a better way to do it by leveraging technology, outsourcing, or hiring additional staff or interns? Has the need for some of the activities ended or do delivery methods need to be updated? Is there a better or more efficient way to accomplish your goals?

Benchmark with other government affairs shops to determine best practices, but avoid the "me-too" syndrome, for example, joining coalitions just because your colleagues are members or purchasing the latest software or gadget without a thorough evaluation.

§11.20 Worksheet: Function Resources

Use the following worksheet to discuss the performance of each function, and to evaluate the significance given to each, the resources committed, and the results.

Function	Activities	Resources (Staff, Budget, etc.)
Planning		
Ethics and Compliance		
Research		
Issue Analysis		
Grassroots Development		
Interfacing with Congressional Staff		

Developing and Training
Government Affairs Staff:

• Legislative, media, communications and public speaking training through groups such as TheCapitol.Net (<*www.TheCapitol.Net*>); and

• Professional membership through professional associations such as the American League of Lobbyists (<*www.alldc.org*>).

"The five most dangerous words in business just may be:
Everyone else is doing it."
Warren Buffett

§11.21 Measure What Matters

As discussed in Chapter Six, setting clear goals and metrics through various action plans is essential. Measuring performance accomplishes the following:

• Tracks progress against goals and planned objectives (see Chapter Six on planning)

• Provides information to present to your organization's leadership and your clients

• Supports your staff evaluations—staff performance should track with organizational performance

• Increases your reputation and credibility in promotional material, presentations in conferences, etc.

The following are examples of potential government affairs performance measures to include in your Legislative Action Plan and tie to employee performance.

- Satisfaction of grassroots with the legislative action participation program, number of members involved, numbers involved in recruitment efforts.
- Evaluations of legislative conference or Hill Day by participants.
- Number of new recruits and quality of training session to equip grassroots members.
- Number of contacts by grassroots members to members of Congress.
- Positive visibility in the public, press, on the Hill—how many hits, in what media, how positive, and feedback received.
- Friendly legislation passed or advanced.
- Stopping or slowing hostile legislation.
- Building stronger coalition relationships (meaningful contributions made and the avoidance of association with positions that do not represent your interest).
- Interfacing with Congress. This is difficult to quantify since credibility is so important, but consider evaluating relationships with members and staff. Consider not only the number of meetings and visits, but examples of key staffers seeking assistance and utilizing the organization's information and input. How effectively and credibly are you assisting congressional staffers and members with information, strategy, advice, coordination, etc.? To what extent do they use and rely on that information?
- Understanding, coordination, and engagement within your organization (or with the client organization).
- What goals can be established to improve cooperation, integration, and synergy? How much information sharing is taking place? How much buy-in are you getting from the CEO and top management? How much from other departments? How well are you coordinating in advance with other players within the organization?
- If your organization values visibility in the public policy arena, you can set a goal on the number of times that you testify before Congress or submit written testimony or comments on proposed regulations. Of course the quality of the appearance or submission is extremely important, but each appearance or submission on the record increases visibility with policymakers and the media and can lead to new opportunities.

How do you define and reward success in your organization? Periodically assess the behavior that you reward because you will get more of it. This goes for your governmental affairs staff, as well as for the interests (members, clients, and partners) with whom you work.

§11.22 **Budget for Maximum Results**

Most organizations have a fairly structured budgeting process. However, here are a few tips for budgeting a government affairs program.

- Practice zero-based budgeting, as a formal or informal approach. Step back, take a fresh approach, and objectively re-evaluate the need and effectiveness of your resources, tools, and staff capabilities.
- Assess your technology. Do you still need every technology tool? Are new or better tools available, perhaps for a more modest price (or for free)? Can you develop the technology in-house? How well do your staff skills and configuration reflect your current challenges? Talk to your information technology (IT) department, and consider customizing tools for your program. Conduct a simple cost–benefit analysis when considering whether to invest in a new technology after exploring all options.
- Set aside adequate "contingency" funds for those unanticipated demands, such as, dues for a new coalition, or consultant fees for an issue that suddenly emerges. Consider consultants in advance so that you know whom to turn to in an emergency.
- Consider savings by reducing or eliminating mailings and paper documents, although keep in mind that members or clients may appreciate receiving some regular paper publications.
- Maintain a flexible budget for public relations related to your legislative affairs, giving you the ability to respond creatively and quickly as situations develop throughout the year.

§11.23 **Effectively Leverage and Update Technology**

Keep in mind that technology offers tools to assist you in doing your job more quickly, efficiently, and effectively. Let your functional needs, customer service, and need for efficiency drive your technology decisions. Try to avoid purchases simply for impressive technology, or because someone boasts about it.

Survey what tools are available by browsing vendor booths at conferences, networking with your peers, researching through the Internet, and requesting free vendor demos, online or live. See § 7.19 for a chart of potential grassroots technology tools.

Evaluate the costs and benefits of various services. Which services are not used effectively and why? Are there new products or vendors that have emerged since you last made your decision? Are certain publications or subscriptions truly serving as a safety net or are they clutter in your government affairs information closet? Has the free daily email service resulted in any actionable item over the last year, or is it more akin to that size six dress or pants with a 32-inch waist that you unrealistically keep in your closet hoping to use? If you haven't used it in a year, it probably needs to go. Is free information or in-house technology now available that could replace subscriptions?

§11.24 Contract Cautiously

Advantages and Risks to Contracting Out Government Affairs Work

Potential Needs/Advantages	Potential Risks/Disadvantages
Short-term political expertise and contacts that you and your staff may not possess, for example, with members of Congress, congressional staffers, public officials, and media connections. Can offer a quick response and the ability to take rapid action on an unanticipated opportunity or challenge without going through an extensive recruiting process or training existing staff.	Confidentiality of information. Can this organization/person be trusted? Is confidentiality of proprietary or politically sensitive information addressed in contract?
Tracking of low priority items. May be cheaper than handling in-house.	May be more expensive than handling in-house. May lack knowledge of your organization or issues.
Help needed during staff transitions.	May be difficult to find a good fit in time for temporary situations. Confidentiality concerns.
Strategic expertise and input needed. Can provide objective perspective and benefit of a broader perspective, such as, information audit, strategic planning, process improvement and benchmarking.	Who are the other clients? What safeguards are in place to prevent potential conflicts of interest?
Auditing of compliance with legal/ethical standards.	Can be expensive, but usually worth the cost. To quote Ben Franklin, *"An ounce of prevention is worth a pound of cure."*
Added emphasis needed for a high priority issue/vote.	What are the expectations of your members/board? Is it appropriate to outsource part of the work for your most important issue, or do they expect in-house staff to take care of it? Any confidentiality or conflict of interest considerations?

Always check the capabilities and performance of an individual before deciding whether to hire her as a consultant and confirm which individuals will be working on your contract.

§11.25 Lobby Tips

Put it in Writing

"An independent lobbyist who is retained by a client should have a written agreement with the client regarding the terms and conditions for the lobbyist's services, including the amount of and basis for compensation."

—American League of Lobbyists' Code of Ethics
Article VI—Compensation and Engagement Terms

The American League of Lobbyists' Code of Ethics includes requirements for the lobbyists to always operate with a written contract, abide by all relevant laws, and avoid conflicts of interest. When contracting out, always operate with a written contract and include an expectation that the lobbyists will comply with all relevant federal, state, and local laws.

Samples of issues that you may want to consider in your contracts with lobbyists and relevant ALL Lobbyist Code of Ethics references follow (the full text of the Code is included in Appendix 6).

Conflicts of Interest

The importance of avoiding conflicts of interest is discussed in Chapter Two, and the American League of Lobbyists' language on the topic follows:

"A lobbyist should not continue or undertake representations that may create conflicts of interest without the informed consent of the client or potential client involved.

"A lobbyist should avoid advocating a position on an issue if the lobbyist is also representing another client on the same issue with a conflicting position." (4.1)

"If a lobbyist's work for one client on an issue may have a significant adverse impact on another client's interests, the lobbyist should inform and obtain consent from the other client whose interests may be affected of this fact even if the lobbyist is not representing the other client on the same issue." (4.2)

"A lobbyist should disclose all potential conflicts to the client or prospective client and discuss and resolve the conflict issues promptly." (4.3)

"A lobbyist should inform the client if any other person is receiving a direct or indirect referral or consulting fee from the lobbyist due to or in connection with the client's work and the amount of such fee or payment." (4.4)

—American League of Lobbyists, Code of Ethics,
Article IV—Conflicts of Interest

Confidentiality

"A lobbyist should not disclose confidential information without the client's or employer's informed consent.

"A lobbyist should maintain appropriate confidentiality of client or employer information." (7.1)

"A lobbyist should not use confidential client information against the interests of a client or for any purpose not contemplated by the engagement or terms of employment." (7.2)

—American League of Lobbyists, Code of Ethics,
Article VII-Confidentiality

(Continued on page 362)

§11.25 Lobby Tips (Continued)

Due Diligence and Best Efforts

"A lobbyist should vigorously and diligently advance and advocate the client's interest.

"A lobbyist should devote adequate time, attention, and resources to the client's or employer's interests." (5.1)

"A lobbyist should exercise loyalty to the client's or employer's interests." (5.2)

"A lobbyist should keep the client or employer informed regarding the work that the lobbyist is undertaking and, to the extent possible, should give the client the opportunity to choose between various options and strategies." (5.3)

—American League of Lobbyists, Code of Ethics,
Article V–Due Diligence & Best Efforts

Duty to Governmental Institutions

"In addition to fulfilling duties and responsibilities to the client or employer, a lobbyist should exhibit proper respect for the governmental institutions before which the lobbyist represents and advocates clients' interests.

"A lobbyist should not act in any manner that will undermine public confidence and trust in the democratic governmental process." (9.1)

"A lobbyist should not act in a manner that shows disrespect for government institutions." (9.2)

—American League of Lobbyists, Code of Ethics
Article IX—Duty to Governmental Institutions

§11.26 Keep a Record

In addition to legally required and human resource-related records, organizations employing lobbyists should retain the following:

- Copies of Lobbying Disclosure Act (LDA) filings and receipt confirmations as well as FEC, FARA, and relevant state filings.
- Senate and House LDA registration numbers for regular filings.
- A useful legislative archive system (with backup) that includes information on Congressional contacts from all of your staff members. See Chapter Ten for recommendations on maintaining a useful government affairs archive system.
- Copies of every formal correspondence to Capitol Hill, such as, testimony (presented and submitted), letters, one-pagers, press releases, bulk emails communicating the organization's position, and surveys.
- A video library of legislative appearances including testimony.
- Legislative position statements and the internal justification for the legislative and regulatory positions taken within your organization. You should also know the relationship history of your organization with specific members of Congress.

Commercial databases are available, or you can establish your own database updated with congressional contact information on an ongoing basis to minimize the loss of key intelligence due to staff transitions.

- Document retention/destruction policy timetable.

§11.27 Recordkeeping Time Lines Checklist, and Confidentiality

The Lobbying Disclosure Act Guidance offers the following recommendations on LDA recordkeeping and retention:

Preparing to File the Quarterly Report—Income or Expense Recording

"The LDA does not contain any special record keeping provisions, but requires, in the case of an outside lobbying firm (including self-employed individuals), a good faith estimate of all income received from the client, other than payments for matters unrelated to lobbying activities. In the case of an organization employing in-house lobbyists, the LDA requires a good faith estimate of the total expenses of its lobbying activities. As long as the registrant has a reasonable system in place and complies in good faith with that system, the requirement of reporting expenses or income would be met. Since Section 6(a)(5) requires the Secretary and Clerk to

'retain registrations for a period of at least 6 years after they are terminated and reports for a period of at least 6 years after they are filed,'

we recommend registrants retain copies of their filings and supporting documentation for the same length of time."

Source: Lobbying Disclosure Act Guidance Prepared by the Secretary of the Senate and the Clerk of the House of Representatives (Available in the *Lobbying and Advocacy Sourcebook*, 5).

A checklist for LDA records and retention follows:

- Client records must be handled in accordance with federal and state law. Particular attention must be given to the state and federal lobbying regulations.
- Records should be stored securely, and professional standards of content, legibility, and timeliness should be maintained. Periodic reports with aggregate data to management are important to maintain program accountability and support.
- Data on costs, contacts, source of referrals, disposition of matters, and conflicts of interest will prove useful in the firm's evaluative efforts. Information on source of referral and stated purpose of contact can be made during initial interviews.
- All case records must be kept absolutely confidential and located in a place where only a program coordinator has access to them. When data from case records are used for evaluation purposes, they should be presented in the aggregate with no chance for individual clients to be linked to specific information.

- Federal law requires that records be kept for six years. If your firm has attorneys their records may have to be kept for seven years depending on state law.
- In some case lawsuits may be filed six years after the event that generated the lawsuit so you may want to keep files for seven years as a general rule. Files can be stored electronically if storage space is a concern.

Source: David G. Evans, Esq., attorney at law at: <*www.davidevanslaw.com*>. Mr. Evans is a registered governmental affairs agent in New Jersey.

See also the National Association of Professional Organizers (<*www.napo.net*>); the International Association of Registered Financial Consultants (<*www.iarfc.org*>); and Wachovia Securities (<*www.wachoviasec.com*>).

§11.28 Assessing Risk Exposure

"Every decision or non-decision, every activity, every behavior, every relationship, every policy and procedure creates a risk—and an opportunity. Success is achieved through effectively managing risk and seizing opportunities."
Ronald Adler, President-CEO, Laurdan Associates, Inc.

Risks and opportunities are inherent in managing employees, and risk management is an essential function of human resource (HR) management. The importance of HR audits as a tool to manage risk and to enhance the value of an organization's human capital is now widely accepted. Consider:

- Sarbanes-Oxley requires effective internal controls . . . an evaluation of those controls should be a component of your audit activity.
- The Securities and Exchange Commission Guidelines require management to ". . . exercise reasonable management oversight" . . . HR audits can be an effective tool in ensuring organization compliance.
- The U.S. Federal Sentencing Guidelines require organizations to take reasonable steps to "monitor and audit" . . . HR audits provide management with a method of assessing the risk of noncompliance.
- The Equal Employment Opportunity Commission and Office of Federal Contract Compliance Programs considers self assessments a "best practice" . . . organizations, especially federal contractors, are strongly encouraged to conduct HR audits.

Thus your HR and lobbying internal auditing activity should assess: 1) the risk of financial and reputation loss from statutory and regulatory noncompliance; 2) the opportunities lost from misalignment of human capital management with business objectives; and 3) the liabilities created by ineffective internal controls.

Chapter 2 provides a description of key lobbying and ethics reporting requirements. See § 2.4 for information on designing an effective compliance system and § 2.5 for the seven elements of an effective government affairs compliance system. Consult legal and other professionals as needed.

§11.99 **Chapter Summary**

This chapter discusses the marks of a high-performance government affairs operation:

- Recruit effectively and hire qualified, ethical, and effective staff, which includes scouting for talent throughout the year (§ 11.2). Legislative experience should be sought (§ 11.3) and effective reference checking should be employed. Resources are provided for locating potential lobbyist candidates (§ 11.5) and checking references (§ 11.6).

- Compensating lobbyists competitively is an important factor for attracting and retaining lobbyists as employees (§ 11.7). Recommended resources on lobbyist compensation practices in corporations and associations is provided in § 11.8. Recommended resources for determining lobbyists' salaries are provided.

- Lobbyists seeking employment can use the resources in § 11.9 to assist with their job searches.

- Prioritize training and development, which is often overlooked in government affairs functions. (§ 11.10)

- Managers will find the recommended resources for effective management, development, team-building and conflict management in § 11.11.

- An essential element of a high-performance government affairs function is to make sure that staff are on board with your mission. (§ 11.12)

- Organize your team effectively (§ 11.13). Typical government affairs office structures are included at § 11.14.

- Encourage time management and avoid burnout and overwork. While this is an established management concept, it is often ignored in government affairs environments characterized by sequential and concurrent legislative battles. (§ 11.15)

- Inspirational quotes on time well-kept (§ 11.17) and time management tips (§ 11.18) help lobbyists achieve this important goal. Resources for stress and time management will help you to achieve your objectives in this area.

Analyzing activities is another mark of a high-performance government affairs function (§ 11.19). A Function Resources Worksheet (§ 11.20) will help you to evaluate and integrate your activities.

- Lobbyists should take the time and effort to develop metrics (measurement tools) that help them focus on the most important goals. (§ 11.21)

- Tips for effective budgeting are included in § 11.22 and include providing maximum flexibility to allow tailored responses for public affairs efforts.

- Effectively leveraging and updating technology (§ 11.23) involves benchmarking and re-evaluating services at least annually.

- Contract cautiously (§ 11.24). Examples of the risks and advantages of contracting government affairs work and considerations for contract language are provided.

- Keep a record of key communications, correspondence, and events. (§ 11.26)

- A recordkeeping checklist is provided. (§ 11.27)

- Assess your risk exposure. (§ 11.28)

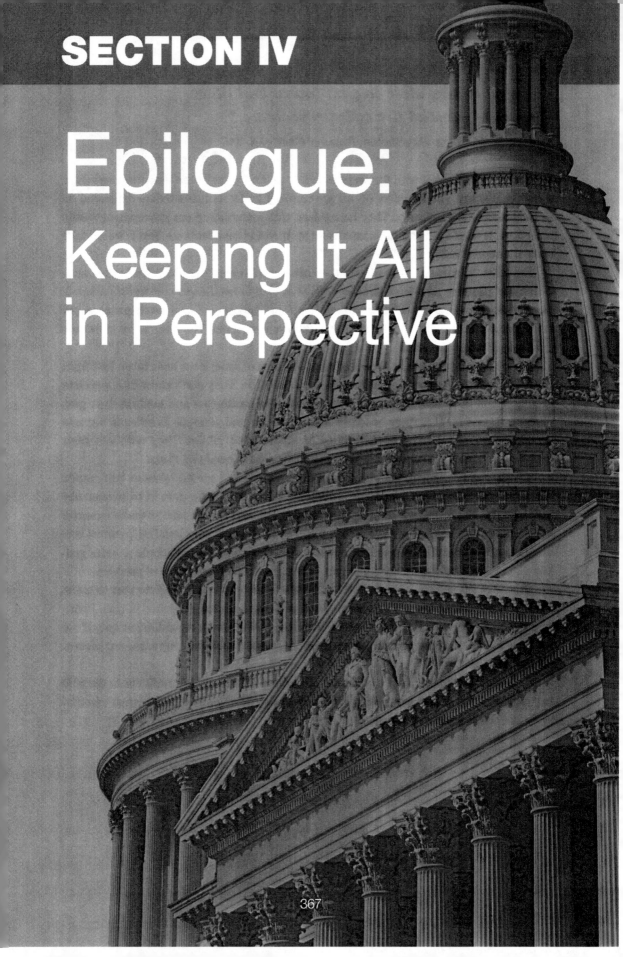

Epilogue:
Keeping It All in Perspective

"Labor to keep alive in your breast that little spark of celestial fire called conscience."

President George Washington, *Rules of Civility*, p. 115

Our nation was founded with the understanding that advocacy is an essential ingredient of our democracy. The founders of our government knew that its survival depended on the diligence of the citizenry. They recognized that maintaining our government would take effort. It would take political involvement. It would take factions. Yes, it would take "special interest" advocates.

The term "advocate" derives from the Latin word voice, "one that pleads the cause of another" (Source: *Merriam-Webster Online* at *<http://mw1.merriam-webster.com>*). The participation of many voices and their "factions" may seem like a messy process, but it's a system which is ultimately healthy and ultimately good. The alternative is to only allow select voices to speak.

Yet, we have a problem in America today. Millions of Americans have turned off from politics. They fail to connect politics with their daily life. They don't know or appreciate their right and responsibility to not only vote, but to participate and petition their government. Government service becomes less attractive and younger Americans become less interested in pursuing opportunities in government affairs. They withhold their involvement from a process that was designed for and depends on them.

It is easy to be cynical, withdraw from the process, and see the glass as half-empty. This does not take much backbone. However, what does take guts is to accept our responsibility, handed down to us by our forefathers, and do our part to make sure our nation succeeds. Factions are imperfect, but they're the best solution. Our political system isn't perfect, but it's the best in the world. America needs young people to enter government affairs who want to become part of the great American political process.

Be part of the solution. Find a teacher. Find someone to teach. Do your part to make sure that those whom Lincoln commemorated at Gettysburg have not died in vain. Politicians are imperfect people, and they can lose touch. We have a republic, but only if we can keep it. How will we do our part to keep it for our daughters, our sons, our nieces, and our nephews?

Lobbyists should not just be reluctant advocates but should be confident in the role they play and the citizen expression that they foster. They must guard against complacency and work against cynicism.

Remember Jerris Leonard

Upon becoming president of the American League of Lobbyists, I sat down with my volunteer counsel, the Honorable Jerris Leonard, to discuss how we could address the formidable challenges confronting the damaged reputation of the lobbying profession. His advice was clear: "The first thing we need to do is to convince the honest lobbyists to value the good work they are doing, and to remember that all lobbyists aren't crooks." We discussed how lobbyists need to appreciate the good in the work that they do and to value their essential role in the American political process. He provided invaluable counsel toward that end for the next two years as we worked to change the way Americans, and, yes, even lobbyists, think about lobbyists. While he passed on in 2006, the wisdom of his words lives on.

Working as a lobbyist provides intrinsic as well as extrinsic rewards. But there is much more. Whether we are paid professionally to lobby on behalf of interests or lobby directly as citizens exercising the power of the ballot box, we must value the work and necessity of citizen engagement. We must act always with the utmost integrity to earn the public trust, fairly represent our interests, and defy stereotypes through honest and ethical behavior. We must remind ourselves that it's not about us as lobbyists; it is about the interests whom we represent.

Just as this book began with the words of Abraham Lincoln, so will it end. To provide contemporary insight into the importance of promoting integrity in the lobbying profession, I've taken the liberty and replaced the terms "lawyers" and "the law" with "lobbyists" and "lobbying" in Abraham Lincoln's "Notes on the Practice of Law":

> *"There is a vague popular belief that [lobbyists] are necessarily dishonest.*
> *I say vague, because when we consider to what extent confidence and honors*
> *are reposed in and conferred upon [lobbyists] by the people, it appears*
> *improbable that their impression of dishonesty is very distinct and vivid.*
> *Yet the impression is common, almost universal. Let no young man,*
> *choosing [lobbying] for a calling for a moment yield to the popular belief.*
> *Resolve to be honest in all events; and if in your own judgment you cannot*
> *be an honest [lobbyist], resolve to be honest without being a [lobbyist]. . . ."*

I quoted Lincoln in this book's introduction as a challenge to dedicate ourselves to continue the unfinished work of the honored dead for which they gave the last full measure of devotion. Lincoln challenged the nation to a new birth of freedom through political participation. We are at a point in our nation when we need a rebirth of Lincoln's ideals and a recommitment to his timeless challenge. We need a renewed effort to value, promote, and foster citizen participation and political engagement so we can keep Lincoln's vision that "government of the people, by the people, and for the people, shall not perish from the earth."

"Deserve Victory!" Winston Churchill

Lobbying and Government Relations
Checklist of Basic Lobbying Techniques and Strategies

Checklist of Basic Lobbying Techniques and Strategies
By: Wright H. Andrews, Esq.—Partner, Butera & Andrews
<*www.butera-andrews.com*>   Reprinted with permission.

Know the Legislative Process
- Relevant Legislative History
- Budget Act and Appropriations Process
- Rules Committee
- Parliamentary Rules
- Timing

Establish and Maintain Personal Political Relationships
- Build Solid Relationships over Time
  - Political Contributions
  - Political Fundraising
  - Washington
  - Out-of-Town
  - "Meet and Greet" Events
  - Political Party Activities
  - Speeches
  - Site Visits
  - Periodic Washington Visits
  - Contacts in State/District
  - Hire Former Staff
  - Personal "Remembrances" (birthday cards)
  - Maintaining Continuing Presence
- Establish High Level of Credibility
  - Demonstrate Thorough Knowledge of Facts/Issues
  - Always Be Truthful
  - Do Not Mislead or Misinform
  - Take Reasonable Positions

Communicate Effectively
- Explain Concerns and Positions
  - Simply and Concisely
  - Exhibit Conviction
  - Substantive Knowledge
  - Pros and Cons
- Use " People Skills"
  - Exhibit Pleasant Personality
  - Be Friendly
  - Be Courteous

- Make High-Quality Educational Presentations
  - Interesting and Distinctive
  - Clear and Concise
  - Executive Summary and "Bullets"
  - Desktop Published Materials
  - Color
  - Charts/Graphs
  - Slides
- Use Special Web Site Devoted to Issue
  - Post Background and Lobbying Materials

Analyze the Specific Issues and Political Situation
- Become Well-Versed in the Substance of Issues
  - Learn Directly from Technical and Operating Personnel
  - Determine Other Parties' Positions/Actions
  - Review Legislative History
  - Carefully Analyze Pending Legislation
  - Monitor Developments Closely

Develop Strong Factual and Policy Arguments
- Cite Specific Facts and Statistics
  - Employment and Economic Impacts
  - Revenue Impact
  - Fairness
  - Discriminatory Effect
  - Competitiveness Aspects
  - Regulatory Burdens
  - Prior Legislative History for Congressional Intent
  - Legal Implications

Have a Strategic Political Plan
- Pause and Think Out an Overall Game-Plan
- Do Not Simply Charge Off without Thinking Ahead
- Give Your Plan Periodic Reality Checks/Updates

Advocate Positions
- Do Not Merely State Position—Forcefully Advocate It
- Use Direct Personal Contacts/Meetings
  - Senate and House Members
- Members' Personal and Committee Staff
- Provide Testimony, Briefings, and Presentations
- Use Calls/Letters/Emails/Record Statements/Articles
- In-House "Grassroots" Contacts

Hire Independent Lobbyists
- Valuable Experience and Know-How
- Special Contacts and Relationships

- Credibility/ Reputation
  - "Big Name" (+ and -)
- Substantive Expertise
- Join in Team Effort

Form Coalition
- Ad-Hoc Coalition
- Structured, Dues-Paying Coalition
- Comprehensive, Coordinated Efforts
- Increased Political Clout
- Activate/Energize Other Parties
  - Organizations with Similar Interests
  - Federal Agencies
  - White House and OMB
  - State and Local Officials and Agencies
  - Consumer, Minority, and Environmental Groups

Purchase "Grassroots" Contacts and/or Media/PR Capabilities
- Hire Professional Grassroots Firm
- Hire Professional Media/PR Firm
- Utilize Focus Groups and Polling

Target Efforts
- Focus on Parties Who Should Be Most Involved
- Target Key Players Who Can Make a Difference
  - Committees/Subcommittees
  - Chairman/Ranking Members
  - Members of Known or Potential Interest
  - Members with Constituent Relationships
  - Congressional Leadership
  - House Rules Committee
- Seek Bipartisan Support

Develop "Constituent" Relationships
- Educate Members/Staff on State/District Ties
  - Local Facilities and Activities
  - Number of Employees, Shareholders, and Customers
  - Investment, Taxes Paid, and Local Economic Benefits

Find Best Members to Sponsor and Advocate (Be Your "Horse")
- Should Be Interested, Committed, and Respected
- On Committee with Primary Jurisdiction
- Can Be Best "Lobbyist" with Their Colleagues
  - Introduce Legislation and Get Cosponsors
  - Arrange for Hearings
  - Write "Dear Colleague" Letters
  - Lead/Participate in "Study Group" or Caucus

Utilize "Independent" Outside Opinion
- Academic Experts and "Think Tanks"
- Opinion Polls
- GAO and CRS Studies

Use Persistence, Hard Work, and Common Sense
- Keep Pressure on
- Demonstrate High Level of Interest
  - Repeat Contacts
  - Involve CEOs
- Keep Allies Informed
- Keep Gathering Political Intelligence
- Do Not Be Caught by Surprise
- Do Not Give Up Too Easily
- Do Not Wait Too Late to Act
- Commit Adequate Resources

Consult with Another Lobbyist if Your Approach Is Not Working
- Get "Second Opinion"
- No One Is Always Right!
- No One Can Handle Many Issues in Today's Environment without Help/Team Efforts
- Different Approach Sometimes Helps You Win

Seek Strategic Delay
- Hearing
- Referral to Another Committee
- Generate Controversy
- Delay/Block via Leadership/Rules Committee

Compromise
- Posture Position as Compromise
- Do Not Compromise Too Soon
- Do Not Compromise Too Late
- Trade Off (and/or Link with) Another Issue

If you have questions or would like additional information, please contact:

Wright H. Andrews
Butera & Andrews, 1301 Penn. Ave., NW, Washington, DC 20004
Phone: 202-347-6875   Fax: 202-347-6876

Key Factors Influencing Legislative Actions

By: Wright H. Andrews, Esq.—Partner, Butera & Andrews

<www.butera-andrews.com>

Factor	Questions and Comments
Sound Technical and Policy Arguments/Solutions	Do you really know the facts and substance of the issues? Do positions ring true and make sense? Are proposed solutions understandable and logical?
Level of Congressional Understanding of Issues	Do relevant committees/members understand the issues? Does full House and Senate?
Nature and Scope of Legislation	Offense or defense (pass or stop action)? Comprehensive or narrow changes? Technical? Broad or limited industry impact?
Media Coverage	Positive or negative? Extensive or occasional articles? Balanced or one-sided coverage?
Public and Congressional Perceptions	Problem? Unfair? Abuse? Good or bad?
Strong General Grassroots Interest	Is there existing general public support or opposition on the issue? (Cut my taxes! Don't cut my Social Security!)
Impact on Local Voters	How might the issue impact on Senate/House member/local constituents? Do they and/or their voters know this?
Costs, Jobs, and Competitiveness	What budgetary/tax cost impacts are involved? Will jobs be created or lost? Does the issue impact U.S. global competitiveness positively or negatively?
Grassroots Lobbying Targeted at Key Senate/House Members	Do interested parties have significant in-house grassroots capabilities for targeted officials? Can they afford to hire grassroots firm?
Committee and/or Subcommittee Support and Interest Level	What are positions of chairmen, ranking members, other committee members? Are they really interested? What are their other priorities?
Congressional Leadership Positions	Active support or opposition? Indifference? Behind the scenes help or attack?
Administration's Position	Major presidential priority? Personal presidential involvement?

Factor	Questions and Comments
Political Strength and Level of Commitment of Leading Sponsors/Supporters ("A Good Horse")	Are sponsors powerful, capable, and committed to the issue? Real or token support?
Campaign Contributions	What past campaign contributions have interested parties made? What future contributions might they make?
Timing	Is time available in legislative schedule? Is the issue viewed as ripe for action? Might it have a significant election impact? Is a legislative vehicle available for action?
Nature and Strength of Opposition	Who are opponents and how are they perceived? Are they well-organized? Well-funded? Highly motivated?
Direct Contacts by Professional Lobbyists with Senate/House Members and Staff	Are lobbyists actively working the issue? How many lobbyists are involved and who are they? How much political clout do they have? Is the issue a priority for them? What else are they working on?
CEO Involvement	Are high-profile CEOs willing to participate in Hill visits? Will CEOs help recruit industry/coalition support? Are CEOs backing lobbying effort with substantial economic resources?
Industry Positions	Is this an issue of interest to broad industry groups? Is there an industry consensus or split?
Coalition Lobbying Efforts	Are lobbying coalitions involved? Can you form a strong, broad-based, well-managed, formal coalition? Who should be in it? Is a coalition opposing you?
Significant Economic Resource Commitment to Lobbying Program	Do you and allies understand level of economic commitment required to win or at least be competitive? Are parties willing and able to fund a credible and competitive lobbying effort?
Lobbying Strategy	What is the general lobbying strategy? Is it sound/realistic? What's the likelihood of success? Should it be changed? What are the alternatives?
Planning and Management of Lobbying Program	How can lobbying program be designed and carried out most effectively and efficiently? How will the activities be coordinated and managed?

Factor	Questions and Comments
Quality of Lobbying Materials and Presentations	Are lobbying materials clear, concise, and professional quality? Are they interesting and understandable? Do they communicate effectively?
Personal Relationships of Lobbyists and Clients with key Senate/House Members and Staff	Which of the lobbyists and/or their clients have strong personal relationships with key congressional policy makers?
Lobbyist's Judgment and Skills	Is your lobbyist an experienced professional with a proven successful track record? Does your lobbyist offer sound, reasoned judgments? Does your lobbyist understand your industry and have a good substantive knowledge of the key relevant issues?
Other Lobbying/PR Tactics	What other lobbying/PR tactics might be helpful? (trade-off or link with other issues; compromise; spotlight horror stories; raise jurisdictional or procedural concerns; etc.)

The relative importance of factors listed in this table vary from case to case; therefore, no attempt has been made here to list them in order of importance or priority. Also, no listing such as this is ever all-inclusive, and other factors not listed herein may play a significant influential role.

Appendix 2

How to Monitor and Influence Policy at the Federal Level

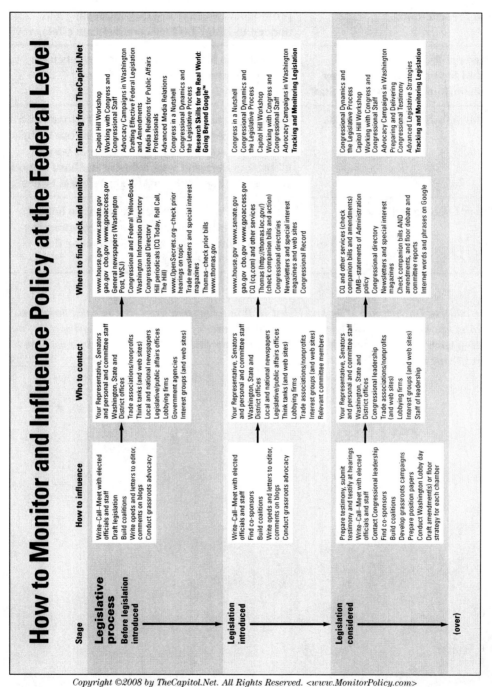

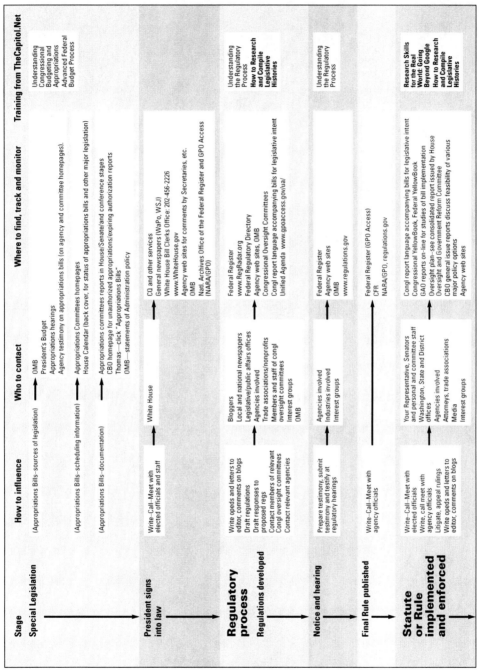

Stage	How to influence	Who to contact	Where to find, track and monitor	Training from TheCapitol.Net
Special Legislation	(Appropriations Bills - sources of legislation)	OMB President's Budget Appropriations hearings Agency testimony on appropriations bills (on agency and committee homepages).		Understanding Congressional Budgeting and Appropriations **Advanced Federal Budget Process**
	(Appropriations Bills - scheduling information)	Appropriations Committees homepages House Calendar (back cover, for status of appropriations bills and other major legislation)		
	(Appropriations Bills - documentation)	Appropriations committees reports in House/Senate/and conference stages CBO homepage for unauthorized appropriations/expiring authorization reports Thomas—click "Appropriations Bills" OMB—statements of Administration policy		
President signs into law	Write–Call–Meet with elected officials and staff	White House	CQ and other services General newspapers (WaPo, WSJ) White House Bill Clerks Office: 202-456-2226 www.WhiteHouse.gov Agency web sites for comments by Secretaries, etc. OMB Natl. Archives Office of the Federal Register and GPO Access (NARA/GPO)	
Regulatory process **Regulations developed**	Write opeds and letters to editor, comments on blogs Draft regulations Draft responses to proposed regs Contact members of relevant Congl oversight committees Contact relevant agencies	Bloggers Local and national newspapers Legislative/public affairs offices Agencies involved Trade associations/nonprofits Members and staff of congl oversight committees Interest groups OMB	Federal Register www.RegRadar.org Federal Regulatory Directory Agency web sites, OMB Congressional Oversight Committees Congl report language accompanying bills for legislative intent Unified Agenda www.gpoaccess.gov/ua/	Understanding the Regulatory Process **How to Research and Compile Legislative Histories**
Notice and hearing	Prepare testimony, submit testimony and testify at regulatory hearings	Agencies involved Industries involved Interest groups	Federal Register Agency web sites OMB www.regulations.gov	Understanding the Regulatory Process
Final Rule published	Write–Call–Meet with agency officials		Federal Register (GPO Access) CFR NARA/GPO, regulations.gov	
Statute or Rule implemented and enforced	Write–Call–Meet with elected officials Write, call meet with agency officials Litigate, appeal rulings Write opeds and letters to editor, comments on blogs	Your Representative, Senators and personal and committee staff Washington, State and District offices Agencies involved Attorneys, trade associations Media Interest groups	Congl report language accompanying bills for legislative intent Congressional YellowBook, Federal YellowBook GAO reports on-line for studies of bill implementation Oversight plan—see consolidated report issued by House Oversight and Government Reform Committee CBO general issue reports discuss feasibility of various major policy options Agency web sites	Research Skills for the Real World: Going Beyond Google **How to Research and Compile Legislative Histories**

Appendix 3

A Practical Guide to Working the Hill and Guiding Congressional Witnesses/Hill Visitors

Capitol Hill Parking Garages, Metro Stops, Restaurants, Tips for Assisting Hill Visitors, Tips for Assisting Constituents with Contacting their Legislators, and Historic Places to Take a Break

For updated information on **Capitol Hill bus drop off locations** *and official tour locations, contact the Architect of the Capitol's office at* *<www.aoc.gov/cc/visit/index.cfm>.*

Wheelchairs are available for use by visitors in the Capitol Complex. Individuals on tour or visiting the House Gallery or the Senate Gallery may borrow a wheelchair upon entering the relevant visitor facility. Constituents visiting for other purposes may request the use of a wheelchair through their senators' or representative's office.

For accessibility information, including how to arrange for sign language/ interpreting services, locations of coin-operated TTYs, and how to order Capitol Hill maps in large print, braille, ASCII disc, or audio tape form go to *<www.aoc.gov/cc/visit/accessibility.cfm>.*

Additional useful numbers are listed below:

- **Congressional Special Services Office:** *202-224-4048 (voice) or 202-224-4049 (TTY)*
- **Federal Relay Service:** *800-877-8339 (voice/TTY)*
- **Washington, DC, Relay Service:** *202-855-1000 (voice) 202-855-1234 (TTY)*

An audio CD on various constituent services available from your congressional delegation, including gallery passes, flags flown over the Capitol Building, and White House tours, is available from TheCapitol.Net: *<www.InformedCitizenSeries.com>.*

Captiol Hill Map

Parking and garage information current as of July 2008.

Metro Stations

See <wmata.com> for information.

M1 Union Station

Red Line
60 Massachusetts
Avenue NE
Washington, DC
20002

M2 Capitol South

Capitol South
Blue and
Orange Lines
355 First Street SE
Washington, DC

M3 Federal Center SW

Federal Center SW
Blue and
Orange Lines
401 3rd Street SW
Washington, DC

Street Parking

Shaded street indicates street parking. Metered and unmetered, usually 2-hour limit.

◄ **North**

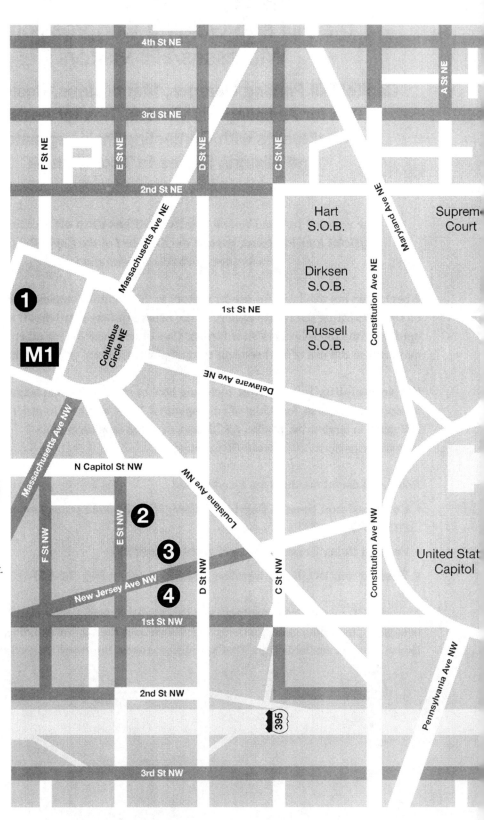

382

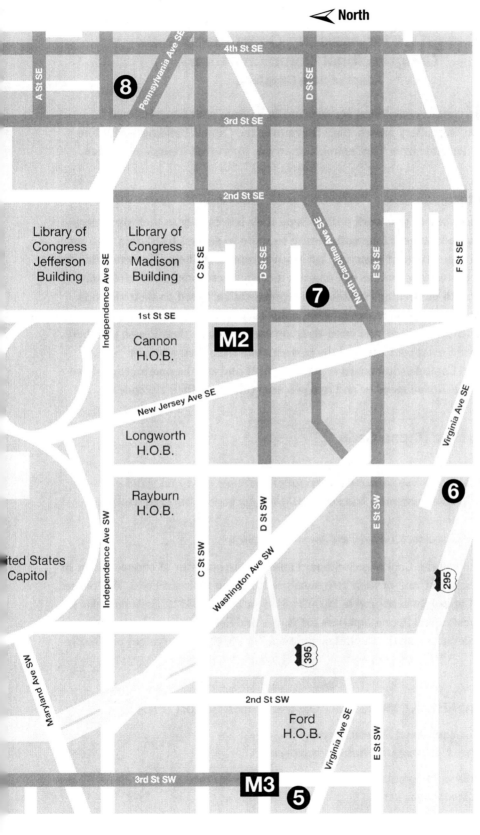

◁ **North**

Parking Garages

❶ Union Station

60 Massachusetts
Avenue NE
Washington, DC 20002

This is a large garage
with more than 1500
spaces and is open 24/7.
Enter on the right (east)
side of Union Station
and follow the signs

**❷ Hall of
the States**

444 North Capitol
Street NW
Washington, DC

Enter on E Street NW
between New Jersey
Avenue NW and North
Capitol Street

**❸ The Liaison
Capitol Hill**

415 New Jersey
Avenue NW
Washington, DC

Valet Parking

**❹ Hyatt Regency
Washington on
Capitol Hill**

400 New Jersey
Avenue NW
Washington, DC

Valet Parking

**❺ The Washington
Design Center**

300 D Street SW
Washington, DC

Garage entrance on
Virginia Avenue SW
between 3rd and
4th Streets SW

❻ Pacific Parking

Approximately 655
South Capitol Street SE

Under the railway tracks
and I-295 Overpass south
of Virginia Avenue SE
and north of Randall
Playground

Approximately 3 bllocks
south of the Rayburn HOB

**❼ Midtown
Parking Garage**

412 First Street SE
Washington, DC
South of Bullfeathers

Underground parking

**❽ National
Capitol Bank**

316 Pennsylvania
Avenue SE
Washington, DC

Enter on Independence
Avenue east of 3rd
Street SE

Basic Tips for Assisting Constituents with Congressional Communications
Adapted from Chapter 8

An audio CD on various constituent services available from your congressional delegation, including gallery passes, flags flown over the Capitol Building, and White House tours, is available from TheCapitol.Net: *<www.InformedCitizenSeries.com>*.

Tips for Letters

Advise the citizens whom you work with to send their letters only to their own elected representatives. Constituents frequently desire to write to several legislators who may have a role on their issue of concern, but do not represent them. However, due to congressional courtesies, members of Congress receiving non-constituent letters simply forward the letter to the writing constituent's representative, based on their zip code.

To determine their House representative, constituents can:

- Go to *<www.house.gov>* and enter their zip code to locate their House member;
- Go to *<www.senate.gov>* to find the two senators from their state; or
- Call the US Capitol switchboard at 202–225–3121 and ask the operator to advise them of their House member and two senators (based on their zip code).

Tips for Effective Phone Calls

"Break the barrier. When contacting a legislative office, never give a screener (a receptionist or an appointment secretary) a chance to say no. Find out which staff person currently has responsibility for your issue area and get to know him or her."

The 30 Laws of Lobbying: 26, *Lobbying and Advocacy*, Chapter 8

Constituents can call the Capitol switchboard and ask the operator to connect them to their House member or one of their two senators based on their zip code. The phone number to the Capitol Switchboard is 202–224-3121 or 202–225-3121. Calls can also be placed to the local office. Phone numbers for House and Senate offices, both voice and TTY, are available by calling the Capitol switchboard at 202-224-3121 (voice) or 202-224-3091 (TTY).

Congressional Background and District Information (Free)

1. Zoomable Congressional District Maps: *<www.govtrack.us/congress/findyourreps..xpd>*.

2. Bios (in addition to congressional bios found on *<www.house.gov>* and *<www.senate.gov>*).

- Project Vote Smart at <*www.vote-smart.org*> provides biographical information on federal and state policymakers.

3. Check a city, county, or state's official web site at <*www.governing.com/govlinks/glinks.htm*>.

4. Congressional Pictorial Directory Online (including New Member Pictorial Directory): <*www.gpoaccess.gov/pictorial/index.html*>.

The Four Cs of Congressional Calls

1. **Connect**
   To the right person
   Make your connection to the constituency clear

2. **Be Clear**
   Make a specific request (What legislation are you talking about and what is your request? For example, would you like to set up a meeting?)

3. **Be Concise**
   Recognize the time constraints and conflicting priorities

4. **Be Careful**
   Be careful what you leave on voice mail
   Use technology wisely

Tips for Hill Visits

Respect the role of staff

Don't be disappointed when you meet with the staff instead of a member of Congress. While the average age of staff is approximately 30 years old, lawmakers rely heavily on them for legislative recommendations and information. Most staff members do not have the benefit of non-governmental job experience, so they benefit greatly from receiving input from informed constituents.

Use practical examples

Practical examples can get a lot of attention on Capitol Hill because they help members of Congress to understand the real-life realities of proposals. Any effective legislative strategy should include a cadre of examples of the practical consequences of the proposal.

Respect the decision tree

Ask if a decision has been made or when one could be expected. Explain that you will be checking back to determine their position. Keep current and keep educating the legislator as well as the staff members as the vote approaches. Work to establish several contacts within the office and seek opportunities to interact directly with the member of Congress before the vote occurs.

Don't cancel

Cancel or re-schedule only as a last resort; try very hard to stick with the original schedule. Any rescheduling will result in a withdrawal of your goodwill account with congressional officials. Try to emphasize this with your visiting grassroots constituents and within your organization (or with your clients) as well.

- Phone the congressional office if an unavoidable emergency causes you to run late or cancel the visit. Canceling is bad enough, but not showing up without phoning will hurt the organization's reputation on Capitol Hill.

Dress appropriately

Wear appropriate business attire (don't dress like a tourist), but wear comfortable shoes since you will be doing a lot of walking.

Consult a map and chart your walk in advance. Become familiar with the map of Capitol Hill and the House and Senate office buildings.

Respect security concerns

- Respect Capitol Police. They will direct you if you get lost or if any type of an evacuation is required.
- Do not take: sharp objects, mace, firearms.
- Do not joke about security issues. Capitol police take all comments about threats and bombs very seriously.

Be prompt and respect their time

> *"Be respectful. Arrive at meetings on time or early. Briefings should be brief. Poor time management communicates lack of value and respect. Know when to stop. Always say thank you."*
> The 30 Laws of Lobbying: 21

Be on time, but don't be impatient if congressional staffers or members keep you waiting, which is frequently the case. Don't enter the office too early, because the rooms are cramped; usually, there is not a great place to wait. Coordinate cell phone numbers of all participants in advance so that you can make plans in case of emergency. Don't "no show" without phoning, no matter what. If you have to cancel, do it as soon as possible.

Never underestimate the role of congressional staff

> *"Be kind to everyone. The Golden Rule works on the Hill. It's not always apparent who actually wields the most influence and who might in the future. Today's receptionist may be tomorrow's chief of staff. Today, a*

congressional staff member answers the phones. Tomorrow, that staffer
may answer the senator's question on an issue important to you."
The 30 Laws of Lobbying: 11

Do not be disappointed if you meet with congressional staff. They have more power than you realize. Although typically young, these staffers have been given responsibility by the policymakers to be their eyes and ears on specific issues and to make specific recommendations. Members of Congress have so many commitments and responsibilities that they may not remember you or think to contact you for advice in the future, but the staff representative specifically charged with responsibility for your issue might, and probably represents a more realistic opportunity to establish an ongoing relationship that will eventually lead to meaningful legislative input.

Use your down time while waiting for congressional appointments to build relationships with additional staff through networking. Even entry-level staff and interns can be very helpful and frequently rise quickly within congressional ranks.

Be prepared
- Bring a concise summary of your points (one-pager/FAQ's/with useful web site URLs referenced).
- Know what you expect from the meeting. What is it you want—your "ask"? You won't get it if you don't ask for it.
- Coordinate with other attendees in advance.
- Select one issue and stick to the point.
- Be a resource (ask how you can help).
- Listen and ask thoughtful questions.
- Do not forget to say thank you.
- Follow up.
- Never assume.
- Do not threaten.
- Stick to the subject and avoid tangents.

What to bring
- One-pager/leave behind.
- Statistics or examples from the district or state.
- A copy of a letter sent by your organization to the legislator on the topic. (Most likely, staff will ask you during your meeting whether you have sent an official letter, so be sure to bring a copy with you to your lobbying meetings.)
- A web site printout if it contains useful information, that is, useful data specific to the issue under discussion.
- Your business card.

What to leave

Leave sharp objects, such as knives and scissors at home. Carrying mace and firearms is prohibited in the congressional buildings and the District of Columbia. Make sure that all meeting attendees understand that they should be prepared to go through metal detectors to enter congressional buildings.

Legislative Conference/Hill Day Checklist for Event Organizers

Provide enough time for constituents to travel between their House and Senate meetings and map out in advance the most convenient way for them to do so in light of changing security procedures.

Before the conference, verify visitor entrances and the availability of Capitol building transit passes with the House Sergeant at Arms office at 202–225–2456 and the Senate office at 202–224–2341. Depending on security procedures, constituents with appointments on both the House and Senate sides of the Capitol may be able to avoid walking around the entire Capitol block (which is under construction at the time of the writing of this book). This may be done by obtaining a transit pass from the appointment desks on the north or south side of the Capitol. The Capitol appointment desk staff will need to see the constituent's driver's license and may call the office to confirm the pending appointment.

Bring contact information regarding logistical information important in addressing problems or emergencies that may arise, for example:

- Your organization's Hill meeting coordinator (contact information should be provided to attendees in case constituents arrive and the congressional office acts as though they are unaware of the appointment).
- Bus drivers.
- Hotel reception coordinator.
- Scheduling secretaries of all speakers.
- Cell phone numbers for staff from your organization and other individuals who are essential to the program (providing speaker introductions, receiving awards).
- Information to answer constituent questions, such as, Metro stops, cab phone numbers, restaurants, etc. (see "Working the Hill" in Appendix X).
- Confirm the time/place that you will meet after the visits (bus pickup or hotel) and emergency evacuation and inclement weather contingency plans.

Tips for Sending Email

The following tips are provided to help you send effective emails that will be read and considered by legislative staff:

- Because congressional staffs are bombarded with emails, send them only what they need to know and tell them why they need to know right upfront.

- If you need to paste or include lengthy material, consider the format that will make their review of the information as efficient as possible; paste the text of the full article at the bottom of the email instead of just a link. As discussed in Chapter Six, consider transferability and where your information could end up.
- Communicate your punch line or primary point in the first one or two sentences, stick to the point, and keep the communication brief.
- Do not include congressional staff or agency officials on bulk emails that won't interest them. Blind copy staff on group emails if necessary to avoid broadcasting their email addresses to external parties.
- Use email appropriately, and don't overuse it.
- Don't rely solely on email in direct lobbying or grassroots. (See § 8.37 for a discussion on the limitations of email-only campaigns.)

"All politics is personal. Never underestimate the power of personal persuasion and the value of personal relationships. Technology will never replace the benefits of face-to-face conversations. Technology will never vote, people always will."
The 30 Laws of Lobbying, 3

- Watch what you write. Mistyping an email address by just one character or accidentally typing .org instead of .com on the end of an email address can send your candid and confidential comments to a complete stranger. Such mistakes are occasionally highlighted in the press to the great embarrassment of the sender.

". . . Apply the newspaper test: Never put anything in writing, including Email that you don't want to read on the front cover of the newspaper."
The 30 Laws of Lobbying, 8

Bells and Lights on Capitol Hill

While on Capitol Hill, you may hear bells and see lights lit or flashing around the clocks. These are signals to the members of Congress regarding the activity occurring on the House/Senate floor. The system is as follows:

U.S. Senate
Bell and Vote Signals

The number of bell rings corresponds to the number of lights around the clocks.

Rings/Lights	Meaning
🔔 ☀ 1 Ring, 1 Light	Yeas and Nays

Rings/Lights	Meaning
🔔🔔 ☼☼ **2 Rings, 2 Lights**	Quorum Call
🔔🔔🔔 ☼☼☼ **3 Rings, 3 Lights**	Call of Absentees
🔔🔔🔔🔔 ☼☼☼☼ **4 Rings, 4 Lights**	Adjournment of recess (end of a daily session)
🔔🔔🔔🔔🔔 ☼☼☼☼☼ **5 Rings, 5 Lights**	7-1/2 minutes remain on a Nay or Yea Vote
🔔🔔🔔🔔🔔🔔 ☼☼☼☼☼☼ **6 Rings, 6 Lights**	Lights cut off after 6 rings— morning business is concluded
🔔 **1 Long Ring**	Senate convenes.
☼ **A Red Light**	Stays on whenever the Senate is actually in session.

U.S. House of Representatives
Bell and Vote Signals

Rings	Lights (Around Clocks)	Meaning
🔔 -PAUSE- 🔔🔔🔔 **1 Long Ring,** **Pause, and 3 Rings** (Bells are repeated every 5 minutes unless call is vacated or converted into a regular quorum call)		Notice of quorum call (start or continuation "of a notice or short quorum call in the Committee of the Whole"). Will end when 100 members appear on the House floor.
🔔 **1 Long Ring**	✳✳✳ Extinguishing of 3 lights on the left	Short or notice quorum call vacated.

Rings	Lights (Around Clocks)	Meaning
2 Rings	2 lights on the left	15-minute recorded vote, yea-and-nay vote or automatic rollcall vote by electronic device. The bells are repeated five minutes after the first ring.
2 Rings, Pause, 2 Rings		Automatic roll call vote or yea-and-nay vote taken by a call of the roll in the House. The bells are repeated when the Clerk reaches the R's in the first call of the roll.
2 Rings, Pause, 5 Rings		First vote under Suspension of the Rules or on clustered votes. Two bells are repeated five minutes after the first ring. The first vote will take 15 minutes with successive votes at intervals of not less than five minutes. Each successive vote is signaled by five rings.
3 Rings	3 lights on the left	15-minute quorum call in either the House or in the Committee of the Whole by electronic device. The bells are repeated five minutes after the first ring.
3 Rings, Pause, 3 Rings		15-minute quorum call by a call of the roll. The bells are repeated when the Clerk reaches the R's in the first call of the roll.
3 Rings, Pause, 5 Rings		Quorum call in the Committee of the Whole that may be followed immediately by a five-minute recorded vote.
4 Rings	4 lights on the left	Adjournment of the House.

Rings	Lights (Around Clocks)	Meaning
🔔🔔🔔🔔🔔 **5 Rings**		Any five-minute vote.
🔔🔔🔔🔔🔔🔔 **6 Rings**	☼☼☼☼☼☼ 6 lights on the left	Recess of the House.
🔔🔔🔔🔔🔔🔔 🔔🔔🔔🔔🔔🔔 **12 Rings at 2-Second Intervals**	☼☼☼☼☼☼ 6 lights on the left	Civil defense warning.
	☼☼☼☼☼☼ ☼ 7th light on	House is in session.

Tips and Recommendations for Assisting Out-of-Town Visitors

See resources for getting into and out of Washington, DC by air, bus, train, and driving at *<www.thecapitol.net/VisitingDC/transportation.htm>*

See information on Capitol Hill Hotels at *<www.thecapitol.net/MapsAndDirections/capitolhillmap.htm>*

Help visitors get oriented and share some of the city's history by explaining the system of street names.

The White House was positioned in the center of the city, and the U.S. Capitol is at the center of the city's four-quadrant design (NE, NW, SE, SW) originated by Pierre Charles L'Enfant. A star in the U.S. Capitol building marks the center of where the quadrants are divided. North Capitol Street, South Capitol Street, and East Capitol Street mark three of the quadrant divisions (the National Mall takes the place of any western division). Pay special attention to the quadrant designation in any address. Accidentally going to the North East section of town instead of the North West section can cause you to miss your appointment.

Think of Washington, DC, street names in terms of two overlaid grids: the one grid has horizontal numbered lines and vertical lettered lines (First Street runs top to bottom and C Street runs left to right). Now put a diagonal grid with avenues that run at 30-degree angles over the street grid.

- Avenue names in the old part of the city were taken from the original thirteen colonies in geographic order (North is New Hampshire and South was Georgia).
- The four avenue names through the Capitol are taken from the Mid-Atlantic states: Pennsylvania, Maryland, Delaware, and New Jersey.
- Between Pennsylvania Avenue and Maryland Avenue is the National Mall, and between the Pennsylvania and Maryland border is the Mason-Dixon Line separating the old South from the Northern states.
- An interesting change occurred when the city was rebuilt. A prominent Georgia congressman didn't like the location of Georgia Avenue at the South East corner of the city, so he had Georgia Avenue changed to a major north-south route out of town from 7th Street Road to Georgia Avenue. This is why Georgia Avenue now starts at the northern end of 7th Street (and runs north).

Source: Steve Livengood, Chief Guide and Public Programs Director, U.S. Capitol Historical Society

- Additional information on the history of DC street names is available at *<http://en.wikipedia.org/wiki/Streets_and_highways_of_Washington,_D.C.>*.
- A map of the entire Washington, DC, Beltway surrounding the city is available at *<www.thecapitol.net/VisitingDC/beltway.htm>*.

Consider the Metro

Instead of trying to drive through a city with no U-turns, numerous one-way streets, and limited street parking, consider using the Metrorail System (which your tax dollars helped to fund!). The following is a list of major Metro locations for congressional visitors:

- **House side of the US Capitol**: Capitol South (First St. between C & D Street, SE)
- **Senate side of the US Capitol**: Union Station (Entrance to Amtrak Terminal), East side of First St, NW, North of Massachusetts Avenue (West side of Union Station)
- **White House**: Farragut West

A map of Metro stop locations is found at *<www.wmata.com/metrorail/systemmap.cfm>*. Metro's trip planner and alerts are found at *<www.wmata.com>*.

Recommended web sites for moving around Capitol Hill and Washington, DC (excerpted from The Top 100 Web Sites for Lobbyists).

See *<www.LobbyingResources.com>*.

- **Map and status of Capitol remodeling and construction projects**: (construction) including street closings, time of construction, public impacts, and status/timeline (Architect of the Capitol): *<www.aoc.gov/projects/project_map.cfm>*
- **Taxis/town car/limo** (any city): *<www.superpages.com>*

Parking Lots and Maps:

- **Capitol Hill map with surrounding streets**: *<www.capitolhillbid.org>*
- **Map of Georgetown with surrounding streets**: *<www.georgetowndc.com>*
- **Parking in downtown DC**: *<www.downtowndc.org>*
- **Emergency evacuation routes** (see "Emergency Preparedness" on the District Dept. of Transportation site): *<http://ddot.dc.gov>*
- **Traffic alerts**: *<http://dc.gov/closures/closures_by_type.asp?type=5>*
- **Street closures**: *<http://dc.gov/closures/closures_by_type.asp?type=4>*
- **Snow updates**: For links to WTOP's "Closings and Delays" and area school closing notifications, see *<www.SnowPolicy.com>*.

Before coming to Washington, take the following online tours to familiarize yourself with the U.S. Capitol and White House.

- **Capitol virtual tours** (U.S. Capitol Historical Society): *<www.uschs.org/04_history/tour/index.htm>*
- **White House virtual tours and videos** (White House Historical Society): General tour: *<www.whitehousehistory.org/02/subs_house/00.html>* The West Wing: *<www.whitehousehistory.org/02/subs_west/00_west.html>*
- **President's Park: gardens and grounds**: *<www.whitehousehistory.org/02/subs_grounds/index_grounds.html>*
- **White House video specific rooms** (Blue, Green, Red and State Dining Rooms): *<www.whitehousehistory.org/02/subs_house/11_video.html>*

While you're here, take a break and enjoy some of the historic sites and experiences of the Capitol complex and the Capitol city.

Enjoy sites on the Hill:

- **US Botanic Garden and National Garden** (*<www.usbg.gov>*): Conveniently located garden next to the Capitol and Rayburn House Office Building, which makes a great place to meet people or drop off friends while you take care of business on the Hill. Also available for receptions.
- **Fountains** (outside near the Rayburn House Office Building and the Russell Senate Office Building): You know it's spring in Washington when the fountains outside of the Senate Russell and House Rayburn buildings are running. An excellent location to meet a friend or enjoy an outdoor lunch.
- The **Sewall-Belmont House** is a beautiful national historic landmark right next to Hart Senate Office building (at the corner of Constitution and Second Street, NE). The house is architecturally significant as one of the oldest residences on Capitol Hill and home of the suffrage movement. Also available for receptions. See *<www.sewallbelmont.org/mainpages/museum_tours.html>*.

- **Senate Summer House**: Walk by the Summer House (open-air brick building near the north Senate Capitol entrance). The original fountain provided a place for visitors and their horses to drink.

- Have a bowl of Senate bean soup at one of the **congressional cafeterias**. Visitors can have official Senate bean soup, on the menu in the Senate for more than 100 years.

- Hear a friend's voice at the whisper chamber in the U.S. House side of the Capitol.

- When Congress is out of session, have someone take a photo of you (or take one for your guests) with the **statue of Will Rogers**, a well-known statesman. Place your forearm on his boot to follow the tradition of members of Congress who brush their forearm on the famous orator's statue's boot for good luck before entering the House floor to speak. According to House resolution and at Mr. Rogers' personal request, the statue is positioned to face the door to the U.S. House chamber so that he can keep an eye on the people spending his money.

Make it official.

Take "official" tours of the US Capitol and Washington, DC. Information on US Capitol outside walking tours, visiting inside the Capitol and sitting in on a congressional session are available at the US Capitol Historical Society at <*www.uschs.org*>. When the House is out of session, a staff member can escort family and friends onto the House floor. One interesting view is the bullet holes in the desk from the 1954 attack by Puerto Rican nationalists. Receive information on a walking tour of the city, including an outdoor White House tour (a nice alternative if you can't get an official inside tour) at <*www. washingtonwalks.com*> or 202-484-1565. Washington Walks was modeled after the venerable London Walks.

Catch a ride.

A tourmobile such as the Old Town Trolley (<*www.trolleytours.com*> or 202- 832-9800) is an efficient way to hit most DC highlights. The tourmobile stops by the various attractions periodically so that you can depart from various locations when you are ready, according to their schedule. Reservation information is available at 202-832-9800. Kids especially like the DC Ducks Tour, which takes you on a land and sea tour from the same vehicle (202-966-DUCK (3825)).

Stay at the Carriage House on Capitol Hill or host a small reception.

Beautiful bed and breakfast—amidst century-old row homes on Capitol Hill, and a perfect place to retreat after a full day of meetings or touring the city. The Carriage House is a quick walk away from the Capitol, House of Representative's buildings, Supreme Court, and the Library of Congress. Guests feel at ease and cared for and small private events can be arranged. See <*www.bedandbreakfastdc.com/properties/listingview.php?listing ID=37*>.

Get a different (aerial) perspective.

Go to the top of the Washington Monument to get a spectacular view of the city at least once in your life (Constitution Ave. & 15th St. NW 202-426-6841, September through March, daily 9:00 a.m.–5:00 p.m.)

You can also get a nice view from the Old Post Office Bell Tower (<*www.nps.gov/opot*>), home to the Bells of Congress, which were a present from England on our Nation's Bicentennial.

A trip to the National Cathedral's Observation Tower also offers a nice view from the top of the city. The National Cathedral is often overlooked on public tours because it is off the beaten path, but the cathedral is as long as the Washington Monument is high and contains beautiful architecture and much history. Many presidents' funerals have been held here. Woodrow Wilson is buried there, and Helen Keller's ashes are in the lower level.

After hours!

- **Monuments by moonlight**: Arranging your own limo with a driver is a fantastic way to see Washington in a different light, but the "Monuments by Moonlight Tour" by Old Town Trolley is also good. Reservation information is available at 202-832-9800.

- **Dance over Washington**: Go dancing in the revolving Skydome rooftop lounge, with excellent views of the capital city and the Potomac, as well as happy hour buffets and dancing. The food is average, but you won't notice with the great view. The lounge is located at the top of the Doubletree Hotel in Crystal City, near National Airport, 300 Army Navy Drive, Arlington, VA 703-416-4100.

Mark the moment.

Memorabilia, including items made from materials from the original U.S. Capitol building are available through the U.S. Capitol Historical Society at <*www.uschs.org*>. These items make wonderful presentations to honor citizens for their participation in congressional efforts. A plaque with a bronze rendering of a memorable page in the Congressional Record can be ordered from the House and Senate gift stores. They also carry excellent children's books and gifts.

Visit the White House Museum Shops (<*www.whitehousehistory.org/11/subs/11_i.html*>) located at 740 Jackson Place, NW (near the Farragut West Metro stop), and in the White House Visitor Center at 1450 Pennsylvania Avenue, NW in Washington, DC. Store hours are from Monday to Friday, 9:00 a.m. to 4:00 p.m. at the Jackson Place location (closed on holidays), and 7:30 a.m. to 4:00 p.m. seven days a week at the Visitor Center location (closed Thanksgiving, Christmas Eve, Christmas Day, and New Year's Day). Their annual White House Christmas ornaments make great gifts for those inside and outside of the DC area.

Good photos for tourists (at locations near Capitol Hill) include:

- **Moon Rock**: Touching the moon rock just inside entrance to the National Air and Space Museum.

- **Hope Diamond**: If you position yourself correctly, you can have someone take your photo while you are positioned behind the Hope Diamond, so that it appears that you are actually wearing the necklace. Best to attempt this in non-peak periods to avoid impatient glances from other tourists waiting to get their own photos of the diamond.

- The National Museum of Natural History has a vendor set up on the lower level to take your photo superimposed in various background scenes such as the museum's Wooly Mammoth, etc.

Anytime.

Watch the first seven minutes of C-SPAN's streaming video on the architecture and structure of the U.S. Capitol at: *<www.c-span.org/capitolhistory/press052406.asp>* or order the entire video at *<www.Cspan.org>*.

Some favorite Capitol Hill restaurants.

(See *<www.thecapitol.net/MapsAndDirections/capitolhillmap.htm#>* for a more expansive list of Washington, DC, restaurants):

- 701 Pennsylvania Avenue (located, guess where?). The restaurant is located on the Archives/Navy Memorial Metro Rail stop and a commercial parking lot is behind the restaurant.

- Les Halles De Paris (French), 1201 Pennsylvania Ave NW #1; 202-347-6848. A commercial parking lot is located behind the restaurant.

- The Monocle on Capitol Hill (Senate side near the Senate Hart Building, limited valet parking available or park at Union Station).

- Rooftop of the W Hotel near the White House (formerly Hotel Washington). Fantastic open view overlooking the Washington Monument and White House and the location where a scene from the movie, *No Way Out*, was filmed, at 202-661-2400. Valet parking is available and an entrance to a commercial lot is located on the side of the building. The rooftop is closed annually from October until April and will be closed until August 2009 for reconstruction.

Another great place to drop off tourists while working at the Capitol.

Air and Space Museum (Smithsonian Institution on the Mall): See the Wright Brothers' airplane and touch some moon rock. See the classic movie, *To Fly*. (I still remember it from childhood and fell in love with it again when I took my own kids.) Take a flight simulator ride. Buy tickets online in advance to avoid long lines.

Virtual map of the Capitol Mall.

- Numerous resources including excellent recommendations for touring and enjoying the entire city can be found at <*www.thecapitol.net/VisitingDC*>.

Questions to ask while approaching the Capitol building:

Q: Do you know the name of the bronze statue crowning the top of the Capitol Dome since 1863?

A: Thomas Crawford's *Statue of Freedom*, also referred to as *Armed Freedom*. The female allegorical figure stands 19 feet 6 inches. Maintenance is required on Freedom every two years to preserve the bronze.

Q: Do you wonder if the House or Senate is in session?

A: Look at the flags over the House and Senate sides of the U.S. Capitol building. If you want to see if either chamber of Congress is still meeting, look to see if the light at the top of the Capitol dome is lit.

A Select Glossary of Lobbying Terms, Abbreviations, and Acronyms

527: A political organization formed under Section 527 of the Internal Revenue Code as a party, committee, or association that is organized and operated primarily for the purpose of influencing the selection, nomination, or appointment of any individual to a public office, or office in a political organization. Not all 527 organizations must file reports with the Federal Election Commission; some file with the Internal Revenue Service. 26 U.S.C. § 527.

*Act: Legislation that has been passed by both houses of Congress and signed by the president or passed over his veto, thus becoming law. Also, parliamentary term for a measure that has been passed by one chamber and engrossed. See *Congressional Deskbook* § 11.40.

Adjourn: Close (end) a legislative meeting or day's session. See *Congressional Deskbook* § 7.20.

*Adjourn to a Day or Time Certain: Adjournment that fixes the next day and time of meeting for one or both chambers.

Administrative Procedures Act: Establishes the basic rules for federal agency procedures, including rule making, adjudications, and fact-finding. 5 U.S.C. §§ 551-559, 701-706.

Advance Notice of Proposed Rulemaking (ANPR; ANOPR; ANPRM): An optional step publishing an agency's initial proposal on a subject, generally asking for public input. Any communications on the proposal must be made available for public review.

Advice and Consent: Constitutionally based power of the Senate to consult and approve appointments made and treaties signed by the president. U.S. Constitution, Art. 2, Sec. 2.

Advisory Opinion (AO): Opinion by a government agency that merely advises on the interpretation of a law but does not have the effect of resolving a specific legal case.

Advocacy: The act of pleading the cause of another; from the Latin advocare (to call).

Affiliated Organization: For purposes of reporting federal lobbying activities pursuant to the Lobbying Disclosure Act, affiliated organization means any entity other than a client that contributes more than $5,000 toward the registrant's lobbying activities in a quarterly period, and in whole or in major part plans, supervises, or controls such lobbying activities.

Amendment: A proposal to modify or change a bill or motion by adding, striking out, or substituting language. See *Congressional Deskbook*, Ch. 8.

*Amendment between the Houses: Method for reconciling differences between the two chambers' versions of a measure by passing the measure back and forth between them until both have agreed to identical language. *Contrast to Conference Committee.* See *Congressional Deskbook*, §§ 8.70, 8.260, 8.270.

*Amendment in the Nature of a Substitute: Amendment that seeks to replace the entire text of the underlying measure. The adoption of such an amendment usually precludes any further amendment to that measure. See *Congressional Deskbook*, § 8.50.

* Indicates that the definition is taken from the Congressional Deskbook.

*Amendment Tree: A diagram showing the number and types of amendments to a measure permitted by the chamber. It also shows the relationship among the amendments, their degree or type, the order in which they may be offered, and the order in which they are voted on. See *Congressional Deskbook*, § 8.122.

Anti-Lobbying Act of 1919: See Lobbying with Appropriated Moneys Act.

*Appropriations Bill: A bill reported out of the House or Senate Appropriations Committee, which assigns government funds to spending bills. See *Congressional Deskbook*, Ch. 9.

AO: See Advisory Opinion.

Architect of the Capitol (AOC): The official responsible to the Congress for operating, developing, maintaining, and preserving the Capitol Complex. *<www.aoc.gov>*

Association or Non-profit Lobbyists: Represent members of an association or non-profit organization.

*Authorization: Provision in law that establishes or continues a program or agency and authorizes appropriations for it. See *Congressional Deskbook*, § 9.80.

Bill Number: Assigned to legislation sequentially based on the type of legislation. See the Congressional Bills Glossary at *<www.gpoaccess.gov/bills/glossary.html>* for bill types and formats. See *Congressional Deskbook*, § 11.20.

Bill Referral: The presiding officer's assignment of an introduced bill to the committees of jurisdiction consistent with House and Senate rules. See *Congressional Deskbook*, §§ 8.30, 8.31.

Bipartisan Campaign Reform Act of 2002 (also known as BCRA and McCain-Feingold): A federal law (Pub. L. 107-155, 116 Stat. 81) enacted in 2002 to regulate the financing of political campaigns by amending the Federal Election Campaign Act of 1971. Senators John McCain (R-AZ) and Russell Feingold (D-WI) were the chief sponsors of the proposal. The act was designed to address the increased role of soft money in campaign financing and the proliferation of issue ads. The law became effective on November 6, 2002, with new legal limits effective on January 1, 2003. In 2003, the Supreme Court upheld the constitutionality of most of the Bipartisan Campaign Reform Act (McConnell v. Federal Elections Commission, 540 U.S. 93), holding that not all political speech is protected by the First Amendment.

Budget of the United States Government: The president submits his budget request to Congress (typically on the first Monday in February) for the following fiscal year. House and Senate Budget committees develop budget resolutions, providing spending limits for the House and Senate Appropriations subcommittees. The subcommittees develop separate appropriations bills to fund various federal programs. Congress may also pass supplemental or emergency supplemental bills and may combine some appropriations bills into an omnibus reconciliation package. *<www.gpoaccess.gov/usbudget>*

*Budget Resolution: Concurrent resolution passed by both houses setting forth the congressional budget for budget aggregates and possibly containing reconciliation instructions.

* Indicates that the definition is taken from the Congressional Deskbook.

Bundling: The practice of one donor gathering donations from many different individuals in an organization or community and presenting the sum to a campaign.

Byrd Amendment: Prohibits lobbying with "appropriated" federal funds for any type of federal award (including any extension, continuation, renewal, amendment, or modification). Requires disclosure for using non-appropriated funds to lobby for obtaining federal contracts, loans, grants, and cooperative agreements. Promoted by Senator Robert Byrd (D-WV) in response to a West Virginia university's hiring of a lobbying firm to seek federal funds. See *Congressional Deskbook*, § 9.110.

Cannon House Office Building (CHOB): The oldest congressional office building. Situated south of the Capitol building, surrounded by Independence Avenue, First Street, New Jersey Avenue, and C Street S.E. The Cannon building was first occupied in the early 1900s and was named for former House Speaker Joseph Gurney Cannon in 1962. Rooms were added to the original structure by raising the roof and constructing a fifth floor. Designed in the Beaux Arts style, a rotunda with eighteen Corinthian columns supports a coffered dome, and twin marble staircases lead from the rotunda to the Cannon Caucus Room with a beautifully detailed ceiling and Corinthian pilasters. *<www.CapitolHillMap.net>*

Capitol: Located on top of Capitol Hill at the east end of the National Mall in Washington, DC, the U.S. Capitol building serves as the seat of government for the Congress and is arguably the most recognized building in the world. The Capitol is the point at which the district's quadrants (NE, NW, SE, SW) are divided. The west and east sides of the Capitol are referred to as fronts. *<www.CapitolHillMap.net>*

Capitol Complex: Buildings under the authority of the Architect of the Capitol and protected by the United States Capitol Police including the U.S. Capitol building and House and Senate Office buildings. The congressional office buildings are used by the Congress to augment the limited space in the U.S. Capitol building. *<www.CapitolHillMap.net>*

Capitol Hill Club: Membership club for Republicans on the House side of the Capitol, located at 300 1st Street SE (near the Library of Congress Madison Building and the Capitol South Metro station). *<www.CapitolHillMap.net>*

Capitol Police: Charged with protecting the members of Congress and the buildings used by Congress. Responsible for metal detector screening at the entrances to all congressional buildings. *<www.uscapitolpolice.gov>*

Capitol Switchboard: Switchboard for connecting to any House or Senate office from 202-225-3121 or 202-224-3121. Members of the public can call the switchboard and provide the operator with a state and zip code to determine their two senators and House representative.

Capitol Subway System: Underground subways in a tunnel system that connect congressional office buildings to the US Capitol building.

Caucus: See Congressional Caucus.

CFR: See Code of Federal Regulations.

Chairman (or Chair): Presiding officer of a committee.

* Indicates that the definition is taken from the Congressional Deskbook.

Chamber: The U.S. Congress is bicameral with two chambers: the Senate (upper house) and the House of Representatives (lower house).

Checks and Balances: Governmental system of rules that allows the three branches of government (legislative, executive, and judicial) to limit each other. A division of power also encourages them to work together. See *Congressional Deskbook*, § 10.0.

Chief of Staff: Top staff person in a congressional office (typically a political confidant of the member of Congress who is seen as a gatekeeper for allowing access to the member).

*Christmas Tree Bill: Jargon for a bill containing many amendments (see Rider) unrelated to the bill's subjects; usually refers to Senate measures. See *Congressional Deskbook*, § 8.220.

Clerk of the House (Clerk): An officer of the House and chief record-keeper. Duties include administering the Lobbying Disclosure Act's federal lobbying registration and reporting requirements and the associated House lobbyist disclosure database. *<http://clerk.house.gov>*

Client: Under the Lobbying Disclosure Act, a client is any person or entity that employs or retains another person for financial or other compensation to conduct federal lobbying activities on behalf of the person or entity. An organization employing its own lobbyists is considered its own client for reporting purposes. 2 U.S.C. § 1602(2).

Cloture: The procedure by which a Senate filibuster can be ended; requires the signatures of sixteen senators and the votes of three-fifths (sixty) of the Senate membership. See *Congressional Deskbook*, §§ 8.230-8.231.

CODEL (Congressional Delegation): A trip abroad by a group of members of Congress.

Code of Federal Regulations (CFR): The codification of the existing administrative law (permanent rules and regulations) that was published in the *Federal Register* by the federal agencies and executive departments. The CFR is published by the National Archives and Records Administration's Office of the Federal Register. *<www.gpoaccess.gov/cfr>*

Committee: Congressional entity comprised of specific members of Congress to handle a specific purpose, for example, to address legislative action in specific issue areas. Much of Congress's work occurs in the committee stage of the legislative process. The major types of committees are standing, select (special), and joint (comprised of both House and Senate members). *<www.CongressLeaders.com>*

Committee Calendar: A committee's schedule of upcoming events, such as markups and hearings.

Committee of the Whole (House on the State of the Union): A parliamentary device in which the House of Representatives is considered one large congressional committee. This is usually done to discuss and debate the details of bills and other main motions. The U.S. Senate used the Committee of the Whole until 1986. See *Congressional Deskbook*, §§ 8.90, 8.112, 8.120, 8.130.

Companion Bills: Similar (or identical) bills introduced in both the House and the Senate (typically to expedite passage).

* Indicates that the definition is taken from the Congressional Deskbook.

Comptroller General: Director of the Government Accountability Office (GAO), formerly known as the General Accounting Office. The Comptroller General is appointed by the President of the United States with the advice and consent of the Senate for a fifteen-year term. <*www.gao.gov/cghome*>

*Conferees: Representatives from each chamber who serve on a conference committee; also referred to as managers. See *Congressional Deskbook*, § 8.280.

*Conference Committee: Temporary joint committee created to resolve differences between the chambers on a measure. *Contrast to Amendment between the Houses.* See *Congressional Deskbook*, § 8.280.

Conflicts of Interest: Principle that outside activities must not conflict with official duties. Government officials may not participate in any matter in which they can use their official position to directly improve financially. Government employees may obtain prior approval for participation in certain outside employment and activities. The term also applies to lobbying and advocacy. The Lobbyists' Code of Ethics states that lobbyists should take care to avoid engaging in conflicts of interest. See Appendix 6.

Congressional Caucus: A group of members of congress formed to pursue common objectives, such as the Congressional Black Caucus or the Congressional Coalition on Adoption. See *Congressional Deskbook*, §§ 4.10, 7.40, 7.60, 7.61, 12.70.

Congressional Record: Published by the US Government Printing Office, the *Congressional Record* is the printed account of the daily proceedings of the full House and full Senate, and is published daily for the days that Congress is in session. Members may have extraneous remarks and documents printed in a section referred to as "Extension of Remarks" and Members may edit (revise and extend) their remarks. <*www.gpoaccess.gov/crecord*>

Congressional Relations Offices: Offices within each federal agency housing congressional liaison staff who are responsible for interfacing with Congress on behalf of the agency.

Congressional Review Act: Allows House and Senate to block "major" new final rules by adopting a joint resolution with presidential concurrence. Pub. L. 104-121, 5 U.S.C. §§ 801-808.

Constituent: A person who can or does elect a public official to office.

Continuing Resolution (CR): A joint (House and Senate) resolution continuing funding for the federal government, and passed when Congress has not enacted all of the necessary appropriations bills when a fiscal year begins or a previous CR expires. See *Congressional Deskbook*, §§ 9.80, 11.20.

Contract or Self-employed (Consultant) Lobbyists: Lobbyists who work on a contractual basis for client organizations who hire them with a contract or retainer.

Contribution Limit: Financial contribution limits established by federal election law and inflation indexed in odd numbered years (for 2008, individuals may give $2,300 per candidate or a candidate's committee per election). <*www.fec.gov/pages/brochures/ contriblimits.shtml*>

* Indicates that the definition is taken from the Congressional Deskbook.

Corporate lobbyists: Lobbyists employed (in-house) to work on issues that concern their companies.

C-SPAN: A cable television network devoted to airing government affairs programming including the proceedings of the US House and Senate. C-SPAN stands for the Cable-Satellite Public Affairs Network. *<www.c-span.org>*

DAEOs (pronounced Dae´ Ohs): Officials in each federal agency charged with training the agency's employees on ethics laws and rules. 5 CFR § 2638.104.

Dais: Raised platform in a congressional committee room upon which members of Congress's seats are located. Congressional protocol dictates that members of the public should not stop upon the dais unless specifically invited by a member of Congress.

Dear Colleague Letter: Letter sent by a member or several members of Congress to their House or Senate colleagues typically urging them to support a legislative position or cosponsor legislation. See *Congressional Deskbook*, §§ 8.20, 8.22.

Dirksen Senate Office Building (DSOB): The second office building constructed for senators to accommodate enlarged Senate staff located at First Street NE and Constitution Avenue. The building was first occupied in 1958 after construction delays and was named after the former Senate Minority Leader Everett Dirksen from Illinois in 1972. The Dirksen and Hart Buildings are connected, allowing one to walk between the two buildings easily. *<www.CapitolHillMap.net>*

Discharge Petition: A procedure for bringing a bill out of committee and to the House floor without a report (despite lack of support by leadership). The petition requires the signature of an absolute majority of House members (218 members) to discharge the measure to the House floor.

District: Electoral constituency that elects one member of the House based on census figures.

District Director: Top House district office staffer working in the member's congressional district.

District Offices: A House member's local offices located in the represented congressional district. Much of the district office staff work relates to constituent casework.

DOA (Dead on Arrival): A legislative proposal that does not have any political chance of moving.

Earmark: To direct approved funds to be spent on specific projects, or to direct specific exemptions from mandates or taxes. Earmarks are typically directed by a legislator toward his or her district or state. See *Congressional Deskbook*, §§ 2.10, 3.15, 4.30, 9.80, 9.81, 9.85, 10.50, 10.200.

Effective Date: The date that a law or rule becomes effective. A bill or rule may have a specific date, for example, 60 days after enactment or may specify that the provision becomes effective immediately upon enactment. Various sections within a bill or rule may have different effective dates.

* Indicates that the definition is taken from the Congressional Deskbook.

Eisenhower Executive Office Building (EEOB): Occupied by the Office of Administration/Executive Office of the President and located in Washington, DC, on 17th Street NW between Pennsylvania Avenue and New York Avenue, and West Executive Drive. Formerly known as the Old Executive Office Building, or the OEOB, and originally built as the State, War, and Navy Building. Built in the French Second Empire style of architecture.

Election Assistance Commission: See Help America Vote Act of 2002. <*www.eac.gov*>

*Engrossed Measure: Official copy of a measure as passed by one chamber, including the text as amended by floor action. Measure is certified by the clerk of the House or the secretary of the Senate. See *Congressional Deskbook*, §§ 8.260, 8.270.

*Enrolled Measure: Final official copy of a measure as passed in identical form by both chambers and then printed on parchment. Measure is certified by the house of origin and signed by the Speaker of the House and the president pro tempore of the Senate before it is sent to the president. See *Congressional Deskbook*, §§ 8.290, 15.22.

Executive Office of the President: Includes the White House offices, the Office of the Vice President, the Cabinet, and fifteen additional offices that develop the president's policy and programs. In addition to the cabinet-level executive departments, the executive branch includes independent agencies, government corporations, boards, commissions, committees, and quasi-official agencies.

Executive Order (EO): A directive issued by the President of the United States.

Executive Session: A closed House or Senate committee meeting. See *Congressional Deskbook*, §§ 7.20, 8.190, 10.81, 10.150, 14.20.

Ex-Officio: When a public official, such as a member of Congress, holds one position by virtue of another position or office. For example, congressional committee chairs and ranking members are typically ex-officio members of all of the committee's subcommittees. The term comes from the Latin phrase meaning "from the office."

Express Advocacy: Communication that can be interpreted by a reasonable person as advocating the election or defeat of one or more clearly identified candidates (uses words such as vote for, defeat, elect). See Federal Election Commission. 2 U.S.C. § 431(17), 11 CFR § 100.22.

Factions: Various and interfering interests referred to by James Madison that are a necessary part of the U.S. competitive system of checks and balances.

FARA: See Foreign Agents Registration Act of 1938.

FEC: See Federal Election Commission.

Federal Corrupt Practices Act: Repealed with the passage of the Federal Election Campaign Act (FECA) and no longer in effect on April 8, 1972.

Federal Election Campaign Act (FECA): The statute that governs the financing of federal elections. Passed by Congress in 1971 to increase disclosure of federal campaign contributions. Pub.L. 92-225, 86 Stat. 3, 2 U.S.C. § 431 et seq.

* *Indicates that the definition is taken from the* Congressional Deskbook.

Federal Election Commission (FEC): The independent regulatory agency created in a 1975 amendment to the Federal Election Campaign Act that administers federal campaign finance laws. The agency discloses campaign finance information, enforces limits and prohibitions on contributions, and oversees the public funding of presidential elections. The FEC maintains a database, going back to 1980, that lists how much congressional and presidential campaigns have raised and spent, and publishes a list of all donors over $200, along with each donor's home address, employer, and job title. *<www.fec.gov>*

Federal Register: Published by the Office of the Federal Register of the National Archives and Records Administration (NARA), it is the official daily publication for proposed rule, rules, and notices of federal agencies, as well as executive orders and other presidential documents. *<www.gpoaccess.gov/fr>*

*Filibuster: Unlimited debate in the Senate designed to delay or kill a bill by talking it to death. A filibuster can be ended by a process called cloture. Senate Rule 22.

Final Rule: After a proposed regulatory rule is finalized, the final rule is published in the Federal Register and codified into the Code of Federal Regulations.

First Amendment (to the US Constitution): Provides the constitutional basis for lobbying:

> *". . . Congress shall make no law . . . or abridging the freedom of speech, or of the press; or the right of the people peaceably to assemble, and to **petition the Government for a redress of grievances**."* [Emphasis added.]

Fiscal Year (FY): Twelve-month period of government financial operations (beginning on October 1 and ending on September 30 of the following year). Carries the date of the calendar year in which it ends. (FY 2010 is October 1, 2009 to September 20, 2010.) See *Congressional Deskbook*, § 9.20.

Floor: Area in the Capitol building where the full House or Senate meets, debates, and votes on legislation. Floor action is aired on television by C-SPAN. *<www.c-span.org>*

Floor Manager: The member of Congress designated to manage the time and speakers from his or her political party during the floor debate. See *Congressional Deskbook*, §§ 8.80, 8.100, 8.110, 14.20, 15.06.

Floor Speech: A speech delivered by a member of Congress on the floor of the U.S. House or Senate chamber.

Ford House Office Building: A fourth House office building located several blocks southwest of the other three House office buildings (Cannon, Longworth, and Rayburn) at 416 3rd Street SW. The building previously housed the FBI's fingerprint records and took on the name House Annex-2 after its purchase by the Architect of the Capitol. It is the only House Office Building that is not connected underground to the Capitol. The building is named after former U.S. President and House Minority Leader Gerald Ford, and houses congressional committee offices and congressional support offices, such as the Congressional Budget Office and the Architect of the Capitol. *<www.CapitolHillMap.net>*

---

* Indicates that the definition is taken from the Congressional Deskbook.

Foreign Agent: Anyone who acts within the U.S. for, or in the interests of, a foreign principal:

1. On political activities or as a political consultant;
2. As a public relations counsel or a publicity agent; to solicit or disburse funding; or,
3. To represent the interest before any U.S. government official or agency.

22 U.S.C. § 611 (c). See Foreign Agents Registration Act for registration requirements.

Foreign Agents Registration Act of 1938 (FARA): A disclosure statute with criminal penalties that requires persons acting as agents of foreign principals in a political or quasi-political capacity to make periodic public disclosure of their relationship with the foreign principal, as well as activities, receipts, and disbursements in support of those activities. 22 U.S.C. § 611 et seq. The law is enforced by the FARA Registration Unit of the Counterespionage Section in the National Security Division of the Department of Justice. *<www.usdoj.gov/criminal/fara>*

Foreign Principal: Foreign governments, foreign political parties, foreign individuals, foreign non-governmental organizations, or foreign businesses. 22 U.S.C. § 611 (b).

FR: See Federal Register.

Gallery: Observation area above the House or Senate chamber with seats to view the deliberations. Visitors must have a gallery pass, which may be obtained from the individual's member of Congress. (See Capitol Switchboard.)

*General Debate: Term for period of time at the beginning of proceedings in the Committee of the Whole to debate a measure. The time is generally divided equally between majority and minority floor managers. See *Congressional Deskbook*, §§ 8.80, 8.90, 8.110, 14.10.

Germane: Relating to the purpose of the bill under discussion or debate. See *Congressional Deskbook*, §§ 8.50, 8.90, 8.120, 8.220.

Government Accountability Office (GAO): Known as the investigative arm of Congress, the GAO helps Congress improve the performance and ensure the accountability of the federal government and meet its constitutional responsibilities. GAO issues reports, legal decisions, and opinions and frequently testifies before Congress. The Honest Leadership and Open Government Act (HLOGA) requires the GAO to audit randomly selected federal lobbying registrations and reports. HLOGA also authorized the GAO to notify Congress of any person who does not comply with the agency's requests for information related to the lobbying disclosure filings. *<www.gao.gov>*

Grassroots: Constituents of a community.

Grasstops: Constituent leaders of a community.

Hard Money: Regulated contributions to candidate campaigns from individuals or Political Action Committees.

Hart Senate Office Building (HSOB): The largest Senate office building, first occupied in 1982, built well after the other (Russell and Dirksen) Senate office buildings, and displaying a distinctly contemporary appearance, is located at 2nd Street NE and

* Indicates that the definition is taken from the Congressional Deskbook.

Constitution Avenue. The building is named for Senator Philip A. Hart, who served seventeen years as a U.S. senator from Michigan. The Hart Building is situated farthest from the Capitol. The Hart and Dirksen Buildings are connected, allowing one to walk between the two buildings easily. The atrium's centerpiece is Alexander Calder's structure, "Mountains and Clouds," featuring black aluminum clouds suspended above black steel mountains, with the tallest peak being fifty-one feet high. A large central hearing facility is located on the second floor that is frequently shown on television during high-profile confirmation hearings and investigations. *<www.CapitolHillMap.net>*

Hatch Act of 1939: A federal law that prohibits federal employees from engaging in partisan political activity. Named after Senator Carl Hatch of New Mexico and originally known as An Act to Prevent Pernicious Political Activities. 5 U.S.C. §§ 7321-7326.

Hearing: Congressional committee meeting held to review the merits and details of a proposal and hear the testimony of witnesses. Field hearings are held at a location outside of congressional buildings relevant to the issue at hand. See *Congressional Deskbook*, §§ 8.40, 8.41, 8.44, 10.70, 15.0.

Help America Vote Act of 2002 (HAVA): The Election Assistance Commission, created by the Help America Vote Act of 2002, provides information concerning the administration of federal elections. Pub. L. 107-252, 116 Stat. 1666, 42 U.S.C. §§ 15301-15545.

Honest Leadership and Open Government Act of 2007 (HLOGA, pronounced, Ha' low-gah): Sweeping lobbying and Congressional ethics reform enacted in 2007 in large part as a response to a scandal involving infamous lobbyist, Jack Abramoff. HLOGA provides numerous reporting and disclosure requirements and potential criminal penalties for lobbyists. Pub. L. 110-81, 121 Stat. 769. Available in *Lobbying and Advocacy Sourcebook*, 2.

House Office Buildings (HOB): Located on the South side of the Capitol building and containing various congressional offices. See Cannon House Office Building (CHOB), Longworth House Office Building (LHOB), Rayburn House Office Building (RHOB), and Ford House Office Building (FHOB). *<www.CapitolHillMap.net>*

Houses of Congress: The two chambers of the federal legislative branch, the House and the Senate.

In-house Lobbyist: Employed by an organization, such as a company or association, to represent its interests.

Interest Group Rating: A percentage score assigned to a member of Congress by an interest group reflecting the number of times that the member of Congress voted in support of that interest group's position, for example, a member of Congress with a 100 percent rating voted with the group in all instances that it rated.

Joint Committee: A committee comprised of both House and Senate members.

Judicial Review: Review by the courts of improper rulemaking pursuant to a lawsuit by regulated parties or members of the public.

K Street (Crowd): Colloquialism for Washington, DC, lobbyists. The name is taken from K Street NW in Washington, DC, where many lobbying firms are located.

* Indicates that the definition is taken from the Congressional Deskbook.

Lame Duck Session: House or Senate session held after the general elections and before the next Congress's inauguration. See *Congressional Deskbook*, §§ 7.20, 7.22.

LD-1 Form: Initial Lobbying Disclosure (LD) registration required under the Lobbying Disclosure Act to be submitted to the Clerk of the House and the Secretary of the Senate within 45 days of meeting threshold requirements. *<http://lobbyingdisclosure.house.gov>*

LD-2 Form: Periodic or regular Lobbying Disclosure (LD) forms required after initial (LD-1) registration as a federal lobbyist. Once registered, federal lobbyists are required to file periodic LD-2 reports until a termination report is filed, even if there is not any lobbying activity during that period. Reporting periods and deadlines for submitting forms are established by Congress and periodically changed pursuant to lobbying reform legislation. The Honest Leadership and Open Government Act of 2007 (Pub. L.110-81) replaced semi-annual reporting with quarterly periods. Quarterly reports are due within twenty days of the end of the quarter (or the first business day after the twentieth day if that day is not a business day). *<http://lobbyingdisclosure.house.gov>*

LD-203 Form: Pursuant to the Honest Leadership and Open Government Act (HLOGA), registered federal lobbyists must submit a LD-203 Form to the Clerk of the House and the Secretary of the Senate certifying, under penalty of perjury, that they have read and abided by the gift and travel rules pertaining to House and Senate officials (Rule 35 of the Standing Rules of the Senate or Rule 25 of the Rules of the House of Representatives). The form receives its name from the HLOGA section number (203) that created the reporting requirement. *<http://lobbyingdisclosure.house.gov>*

LDA: See Lobbying Disclosure Act

Legislative Assistant: Congressional staff person with responsibility for handling one or more issue areas for a member of Congress, but generally without managerial responsibility.

Legislative Correspondent: Congressional staff charged with the task of preparing answers to large volumes of constituent mail, including form emails received from constituents.

Legislative Day: In the Senate, means the period of time from when the Senate adjourns until the next time the Senate adjourns. See *Congressional Deskbook*, § 8.170.

Legislative Director: Congressional staff person in charge of managing several legislative staff people and overseeing several (if not all) legislative issue areas within the congressional office.

Lobbying Activities (reportable under the Lobbying Disclosure Act): Lobbying contacts and any efforts in support of such contacts, including preparation or planning activities, research and other background work that is intended, at the time of its preparation, for use in contacts and coordination with the lobbying activities of others. 2 U.S.C. § 1602(7).

Lobbying Code of Ethics: Professional code of conduct developed by the American League of Lobbyists. See Appendix 6.

Lobbying Disclosure Act of 1995: Federal law requiring federal lobbyists who are paid or otherwise compensated to register and report on lobbying activities. 2 U.S.C. § 1601 et seq.

* Indicates that the definition is taken from the Congressional Deskbook.

Lobbying Firm: For purposes of registration and reporting under the Lobbying Disclosure Act, a person or entity consisting of one or more individuals who meet the definition of a lobbyist with respect to a client other than that person or entity. The definition includes a self-employed lobbyist. 2 U.S.C. § 1602(9).

Lobbying with Appropriated Moneys Act (Commonly referred to as the Anti-Lobbying Act of 1919): Pertains to executive branch employees' lobbying of Congress and other government officials. The Anti-Lobbying Act aims to addresses concerns regarding the use of lobbying with appropriated funds. 18 U.S.C. § 1913.

Lobbyist: One who attempts to influence the decisions of government through public officials. The right to petition the government for redress of grievances is grounded in the First Amendment to the U.S. Constitution.

Longworth House Office Building (LHOB): The second and smallest House office building completed in 1933 and located between South Capitol Street and New Jersey Avenue in Southwest DC. The building was named in honor of former Speaker of the House, Nicholas Longworth of Ohio, in 1962. The former speaker was married to Alice Roosevelt, Theodore Roosevelt's daughter. The Longworth building includes the hearing room used by the Ways and Means Committee. The Longworth Building is one of Washington's best examples of the Neo-classical Revival architectural style that is also seen in the Jefferson Memorial. *<www.CapitolHillMap.net>*

Majority Leader: Partisan political leader in the House or Senate assisted by whips, who enforce discipline on votes important to the party. See *Congressional Deskbook*, §§ 7.40, 7.42. *<www.congressleaders.com>*

*Managers: Representatives from a chamber to a conference committee; also called conferees.

*Markup: Meeting by a committee or subcommittee during which members offer, debate, and vote on amendments to a measure. See *Congressional Deskbook*, §§ 8.50, 8.51, 8.52, 8.60, 8.61.

McCain-Feingold: See Bipartisan Campaign Reform Act of 2002.

*Morning Business: In the Senate, routine business transacted at the beginning of the Morning Hour, or by unanimous consent throughout the day. See *Congressional Deskbook*, §§ 8.20, 8.170, 8.190, 14.20.

*Motion to Recommit: See Recommit.

National Democratic Club: Membership club for Democrats on the House side of the Capitol building at 30 Ivy Street SE, Washington, DC 20003. *<www.CapitolHillMap.net>*

Negotiated Rulemaking: A bargaining process during rulemaking by a specific board of parties potentially affected by the proposal.

Oath of Office: Oath taken by officials, including members of Congress and executive branch officials, as they are sworn into office; includes a pledge to defend the U.S. Constitution.

* Indicates that the definition is taken from the Congressional Deskbook.

OEOB: See Eisenhower Executive Office Building.

Office of the Federal Register: Federal agency within the National Archives and Records Administration that publishes the Federal Register (FR) and the Code of Federal Regulations (CFR). *<www.archives.gov/federal-register>*

Office of Government Ethics (OGE): Federal agency that oversees federal ethics efforts and trains the various designated agency (ethics) officials (DAEOs). *<www.oge.gov>*

Office of Information and Regulatory Affairs (OIRA): Established by Congress by the 1980 Paperwork Reduction Act, this federal office is part of the Office of Management and Budget. The office reviews draft regulations and develops and oversees the implementation of government-wide polices in the areas of information technology, information policy, privacy, and statistical policy. *<www.whitehouse.gov/OMB/inforeg>*

Office of Management and Budget (OMB): The policymaking arm of the executive branch located in the Executive Office of the President. *<www.omb.gov>*

Office of Personnel Management (OPM): Federal agency that manages the civil service and coordinates hiring for the federal agencies. *<www.opm.gov>*

Office of Public Records: Department within the Secretary of the Senate's office responsible for administering the Lobbying Disclosure Act's federal lobbying registration and reporting requirements and the associated forms.

Office of Special Counsel: An independent federal agency charged with protecting federal employees from prohibited personnel practices under the Hatch Act, the Whistleblower Protection Act, and the Civil Service Reform Act. *<www.osc.gov>*

OGE: See Office of Government Ethics.

OIRA: See Office of Information and Regulatory Affairs.

Old Executive Office Building (OEOB): See Eisenhower Executive Office Building.

OMB: See Office of Management and Budget.

One-Minute Speech: A short speech on any topic, timed at one minute in length, and delivered by a member of the House on the floor. See *Congressional Deskbook*, § 14.10.

One-Pager: An issue paper, one page in length, provided to congressional representatives by lobbyists/constituents, typically during a Hill meeting. In light of the time and space constraints confronted by congressional officials, lobbyists work to effectively summarize the best and most relevant information on the issue at stake.

O'Neill House Office Building (Former): The building was demolished in 2002 and a parking lot is currently on the site. The building was referred to as House Annex-1 until it was renamed the O'Neill House Office Building after former Speaker of the House Tip O'Neill. Located on C Street, it was originally the Congressional Hotel and also previously included residences for House pages.

OPM: See Office of Personnel Management.

OSC: See Office of Special Counsel.

* Indicates that the definition is taken from the Congressional Deskbook.

Override (Veto): Enactment of a bill into law despite the president's veto. Requires a two-thirds majority vote in both the Senate and the House. Pocket vetoes may not be overridden. See *Congressional Deskbook*, §§ 8.290, 8.291.

Paperwork Reduction Act: Creates standards for agency imposition of information-collection burdens on the public. 44 U.S.C. § 3501 et seq.

*PAYGO (Pay-As-You-Go): Process by which direct spending or revenue legislation must be offset so that a surplus is not reduced or a deficit increased. See *Congressional Deskbook*, §§ 9.10, 9.11, 9.30, 9.50.

Person or Entity (Lobbying Disclosure Act): Any individual, corporation, company, foundation, association, labor organization, firm, partnership, society, joint stock company, group of organizations, or state or local government. 2 U.S.C. § 1602(14).

Pocket Veto: Process by which a veto occurs when the president ignores a bill between congressional sessions. May not be overridden. See *Congressional Deskbook*, § 8.290.

Poison Pill: Amendment specifically designed to be politically attractive enough to pass yet be so unattractive to the bill's supporters that it results in the bill's withdrawal or death.

Political Action Committee (PAC): A private group organized to elect or defeat government officials or to promote or defeat legislation. PACs are defined and regulated by state and federal law. A leadership PAC is a political action committee established by a congressional member to support other candidates. *<www.fec.gov>*

Political Appointee: Appointed by the president and serving at his pleasure.

Post-Employment Restrictions: The restrictions, applicable to certain federal government employees, including congressional employees, prohibit lobbying under certain circumstances for a specific period of time after leaving public service and are designed to provide a cooling-off period to prevent undue influence. Also known as Revolving Door Restrictions.

POTUS (pronounced "Poe´ tus): Acronym for President of the United States.

*President Pro Tempore: Presiding officer of the Senate in the absence of the vice president; usually the majority-party senator with the longest period of continuous service. See *Congressional Deskbook*, §§ 5.120, 7.70, 8.20, 8.210, 8.290, 10.90, 10.92, 14.22.

Presidential Appointment (PA): Executive-level position in the federal executive branch established by statute.

Presidential Appointment with Senate Confirmation (PAS): High-level executive branch position established by statute and requiring confirmation by the Senate.

Presser: Colloquial expression for press conference.

*Previous Question: Nondebatable House (or House committee) motion, which, when agreed to, cuts off further debate, prevents the offering of additional amendments, and brings the pending matter to an immediate vote. See *Congressional Deskbook*, §§ 8.50, 8.80, 8.100, 8,120.

* Indicates that the definition is taken from the Congressional Deskbook.

Proposed Rule: Proposed regulatory language published in the Federal Register by an agency justifying and analyzing the rule and responding to public comments on any advance notice.

Public Comment: A specified period of time (typically ranging from 30 to 180 days) when the public is allowed to submit written comments to an agency on a proposed rule that has been published in the Federal Register.

*Public Law (P.L. or Pub. L.): Act of Congress that has been signed by the president or passed over his veto. It is designated by the letters P.L. and numbers noting the Congress and the numerical sequence in which the measure was signed; for example, P.L. 107-111 was an act of Congress in the 107th Congress and was the 111th measure signed by the president (or passed over his veto) during the 107th Congress.

Quid Pro Quo: A legal term describing the illegal act of a public official receiving something of value such as a campaign contribution in exchange for an official act (or inaction). The term comes from the Latin phrase which means "something for something"; a bribe.

*Quorum: Minimum number of members required for the transaction of business. See *Congressional Deskbook*, §§ 8.100, 8.110, 8.250.

*Quorum Call: A procedure for determining whether a quorum is present—218 in the House and 100 in the Committee of the Whole House on the State of the Union; a quorum in the Senate is 51.

*Ramseyer Rule: House rule that requires a committee report to show changes the reported measure would make in current law. See *Congressional Deskbook*, § 8.60.

Ranking Member (Highest): Minority party leader on a congressional committee and frequently the minority committee member with the most seniority. The ranking member often serves, along with the chairman, as an ex officio member of all of the committee's subcommittees. Some Senate committees refer to their highest ranking minority members as vice-chairman.

Rayburn House Office Building (RHOB): The Rayburn House Office Building is the newest and largest House building and is located between South Capitol and First Streets, and is named after former Speaker of the House Sam Rayburn of Texas. The classical building reflects some 1960s-era style and contains a statue of Sam Rayburn near the ground-level courtyard. The main entrance is on Independence Avenue, with pedestrian entrances located on South Capitol Street, C Street, and First Street Southwest. One of the pedestrian entrances, known as the Rayburn Horseshoe, is located on the South Capitol Street of the Rayburn office building facing Longworth House Office Building. The building was fully occupied in 1965. The sub-basement contains a gymnasium with a swimming pool and basketball court. The Rayburn building is connected to the Capitol building by the underground Capitol subway system. Pedestrian tunnels connect the Rayburn building to two other House office buildings as well as the Capitol. *<www.CapitolHillMap.net>*

*Recede: Motion by one chamber to withdraw from its previous position during amendments between the chambers.

* Indicates that the definition is taken from the Congressional Deskbook.

*Recess: Temporary interruption or suspension of a committee or chamber meeting. In the House, the Speaker is authorized to declare recess. In the Senate, the chamber normally recesses rather than adjourns at the end of the day so as not to trigger a new legislative day. See *Congressional Deskbook*, § 7.20.

*Recommit: To send a measure back to the committee that reported it. A motion to recommit without instructions kills a measure; a motion to recommit with instructions proposes to amend a measure. In the House, the motion may be offered just before vote on final passage. In the Senate, the motion may be offered at any time before a measure's passage. See *Congressional Deskbook*, §§ 8.90, 8.100, 8.140, 14.10.

*Reconciliation: Process by which Congress changes existing laws to conform revenue and spending levels to the limits set in a budget resolution. See *Congressional Deskbook*, Ch. 9.

Regulation: A measure developed by an agency in the executive branch to implement the details of legislation passed by Congress. See Administrative Procedures Act.

Regulatory Flexibility Act: Creates procedures for agencies to consider the impact or burden of new rules on small businesses. Pub. L. 96-354, 5 U.S.C. §§ 601-612.

Report (Lobbying Report): A quarterly report on Form LD-2 filed pursuant to Section 5 of the Lobbying Disclosure Act (2 U.S.C. § 1604). *<www.disclosure.senate.gov>*

*Report/Reported: Formal submission of a measure by a committee to its parent chamber.

Revolving Door Restrictions: See Post-Employment Restrictions.

*Rider: Colloquialism for an amendment unrelated to the subject matter of the measure to which it was attached.

*Roll-Call (Record) Vote: A vote in which members are recorded by name for or against a measure.

Russell Senate Office Building (RSOB): The oldest of the three Senate office buildings, built in the early 1900s and named for former Senator Richard Brevard Russell, Jr., of Georgia in 1972. The Russell Building is situated on a site north of the Capitol surrounded by Constitution Avenue, First Street, Delaware Avenue, and C Street NE. The Russell Caucus Room has been used for many hearings on subjects of national significance, including the Senate hearings on Watergate and Iran-Contra. The building displays the Beaux-Arts architectural style. *<www.CapitolHillMap.net>*

SAP: See Statement of Administration Policy.

Secretary of the Senate: The officer of the Senate who is charged with administering lobbying disclosure and reporting requirements. The secretary's office includes the Office of Public Records that administers (along with the Clerk of the House) reporting and disclosure requirements under the Lobbying Disclosure Act of 1995. See *Congressional Deskbook*, §§ 5.40, 5.120.

* Indicates that the definition is taken from the Congressional Deskbook.

Section 501 (c)(3) organizations: May not engage in significant lobbying activities, subject to the "election" exemption. Specifically, nonprofits that receive significant public support may file an "election" with the IRS that permits more substantial lobbying activities. Election requires substantial record-keeping, but may be well worth it nonetheless. 26 U.S.C. § 501(c)(3).

Section 501 (c)(4) organizations: Permitted to lobby without the restrictions placed on Section 501 (c)(3) organizations. 26 U.S.C. § 501(c)(4).

Semiannual Regulatory Agenda: See Unified Agenda.

Sen.: Abbreviation for Senate.

Senate Office Buildings: The three Senate office buildings north of the Capitol on Constitution Avenue. See Russell Senate Office Building, Dirksen Senate Office Building, and Hart Senate Office Building. <*www.CapitolHillMap.net*>

Sessions of Congress: Each elected "Congress" is numbered and comprised of two one-year sessions; for example, a vote taken in 2008 was held in the second session of the 110th Congress. A new congressional session begins each January and continues until Sine Die adjournment. See *Congressional Deskbook*, § 7.20.

Sewall-Belmont House: Historic museum for the suffrage movement situated next to the Hart Senate Office Building. The house is frequently rented for congressional events. <*www.sewallbelmont.org*>

Sic: Latin for "thus." Used in drafting legislative language.

Sine Die (Adjournment): The final adjournment of a session of Congress requiring bills not already enacted to die and be reintroduced in the next session. See *Congressional Deskbook*, § 7.20.

*Slip Law: First official publication of a law, published in unbound single sheets or pamphlet form. See *Congressional Deskbook*, § 8.300.

Soft Money: Funds spent by organizations such as 527 groups that are not contributed to political campaigns directly and do not "expressly advocate" a candidate's election or defeat.

Speaker of the House: The top presiding officer of the U.S. House of Representatives, a member of the majority party, and elected by the full House. <*www.speaker.gov*>

Staff Assistant: Congressional staff person frequently charged with supporting the more senior congressional staff.

State Director: Top Senate state office staffer based in the member's state.

State of the Union: Address provided annually by the president to a joint session of Congress (usually the third Monday evening in January). Members of Congress are afforded press opportunities to comment on the event in Statutary Hall immediately after the address. Typically, a transcript of the address is available at <*www.whitehouse.gov*>.

* Indicates that the definition is taken from the Congressional Deskbook.

Statement of Administration Policy (SAP): Official administration position on legislation issued prior to a congressional vote and available from the Office of Management and Budget *<www.omb.gov>* by date and bill number. SAPs frequently state whether the president's senior advisors would recommend that he sign or veto the legislation.

Statue of Freedom: Bronze statue crowning the top of the U.S. Capitol dome since 1863. Also called "Armed Freedom" or "Freedom." *<www.aoc.gov/cc/art/freedom.cfm>*

*Suspend the Rules: Expeditious procedure for passing noncontroversial measures in the House. Requires a two-thirds vote of those present and voting, after forty minutes of debate, and does not allow floor amendments. See *Congressional Deskbook*, §§ 8.70, 8.80.

Swamp Site: Area located on the grass across the drive from the east Senate steps near the corner of Constitution and Delaware Avenues NE used by Senators for press events.

*Table/Lay on the Table: Prevents further consideration of a measure, amendment, or motion, thus killing it. See *Congressional Deskbook*, § 8.140.

Target List: A list of the most crucial members of Congress on a specific issue that a lobbyist uses to focus lobbying activities during a legislative campaign.

THOMAS: Internet-accessible legislative database of the U.S. Congress named after President Thomas Jefferson. The database provides information on congressional activities including the text and status of bills and the voting records of members of Congress. *<www.thomas.gov>*

Time Limitation Agreement/Unanimous Consent Agreement (Time Agreement): Device in the Senate to expedite legislation by spelling out the process for considering a proposal. See *Congressional Deskbook*, §§ 8.190, 8.200, 8.201.

Town Hall Meeting: Public meetings held by members of Congress in their home state/district, typically during congressional recesses.

UC, Unanimous Consent: See Time Limitation Agreement.

Unified Agenda (Semiannual Regulatory Agenda): Published in the Federal Register semiannually (usually in April and October). An official list of anticipated regulatory actions that each federal agency expects to issue during the next six months. Agenda is published by the Office of Federal Register National Archives and Records Administration (NARA). *<www.gpoaccess.gov/ua/>*

*Veto: Disapproval by the president of a bill or joint resolution (other than a joint resolution proposing a constitutional amendment). See *Congressional Deskbook*, § 8.290.

Veto Message: Official statement by the president providing comment on the reason for the veto.

* Indicates that the definition is taken from the Congressional Deskbook.

Appendix 5
The Lobbyist's Annual Calendar:
Key Dates and Activities Template
With Annual Schedule Highlights

Note: These dates should be periodically updated with information from the current Congressional calendars which may be found at <http://www.thecapitol.net/FAQ/cong_schedule.html> and on the House and Senate web sites.

Although House and Senate schedules vary and can be changed by Congress at any time, session schedules typically conform to a pattern, as reflected in the following template. Also, note that lobbying filing and disclosure deadlines and methods should be verified directly with the Clerk of the House (<*http://lobbyingdisclosure.house.gov*> or 202–225–7000), the Secretary of the Senate (<*www.disclosure.senate.gov*> or 202–224-0758), the Federal Election Commission (<*www.fec.gov*> or 202–694–1000) and, in the case of foreign agents, the U.S. Department of Justice (<*www.fara.gov*> or 202–514–1145) well before filing deadlines. See *Lobbying and Advocacy*, Chapter Two, for additional information on maintaining an effective compliance program. Additional references to relevant chapters of *Lobbying and Advocacy* are provided in bold.

Date/Time Period	Legislative/Executive Branch Activity and Deadlines
January	New session starts. Members of Congress are in town briefly as Congress officially opens and then typically recesses until the State of the Union Address.
	Note the following lobbying reporting and disclosure deadlines, recognizing that the dates are subject to change. For example, lobbying reform legislation (HLOGA) contained a recommendation that Congress change the Contribution Reports (LD-203) from a semiannual to a quarterly basis.
	On Jan. 1, recordkeeping begins for various Lobbying Disclosure Act (LDA) reports.
	Lobbying Disclosure Act lobbying reporting deadlines as of April 1, 2007:
	Quarterly Activity Reports (LD-2 Forms) April 20: First Quarter (January 1–March 31) July 20: Second Quarter (April 1–June 30) October 20: Third Quarter (July 1–September 30) January 20: Fourth Quarter (October 1–December 31)
	Contribution Reports (LD-203 Forms) July 30: Mid Year (January 1–June 30) January 30: Year End (July 1–December 31)

Note: Sign up with the Clerk of the House for House lobbying registration Email updates, by selecting the Subscribe option at *<http://lobbyingdisclosure.house.gov>*. Obtain a Senate password for electronic filing via *<lobby@sec.senate.gov>* or *<www.disclosure.senate.gov>*.

FARA
Review and note Foreign Agents Registration Act (FARA) requirements and deadlines at *<www.fara.gov>*.

Suggested Government Affairs Activities

Per the Lobbying Disclosure Act, read House and Senate gift, travel, and ethics rules (including political convention restrictions) at *<www.house.gov/ethics>* and *<http://ethics.senate.gov>* and establish a system to make sure that all of your organization's activities fall within these guidelines. **See Chapter 2 for additional information on establishing and maintaining an effective government affairs compliance program.**

Review executive branch ethics rules at *<www.usoge.gov>*. Review any relevant state and local ethics rules at *<http://www.ncsl.org/programs/ethics/lawsforlobbyists.htm>*. Review the Lobbyists' Code of Ethics (American League of Lobbyists): *<http://www.alldc.org/ethicscode.htm>*

Review and note on your calendars the current *Federal Election Commission reporting requirements and deadlines* and sign up for email updates on FEC reporting developments at *<http://www.fec.gov/info/report_dates.shtml>* or *<www.fec.gov>*.

Review your information collection procedures in light of any lobbying reporting and disclosure requirements as well as data collection procedures for election and campaign activities. (**See Chapter 2 for compliance resources.**) For nonprofit organizations: Review your IRS lobbying regulations and procedures for filing IRS Form 990. For organizations with government contracts, cooperative agreements and grants: Review your Byrd Amendment certifications and government contract cost recoveries.

Typically, most members of Congress are out of town during most of the month of January. This is a good time to sit down with legislative staff. **See Chapter 2 on meal and gift prohibitions and Chapter 8 on presenting your message through effective meetings.** This is also an ideal time to update your goals and provide training for lobbyists. **See Chapter on 6 for planning guidelines and Chapter 11 for training resources.**

Read the 30 Laws of Lobbying at *<www.lobbyingandadvocacy.com>*.

Date/Time Period	Legislative/Executive Branch Activity and Deadlines
Usually the third Monday evening in January	State of the Union Address (Joint Meeting of Congress).

Congressional party planning retreats are generally held in late January and early February as priorities for the session are finalized. |

Suggested Government Affairs Activities

Members of Congress are available to reporters following the State of the Union. The media is heavily focused on Congress's agenda and the president's priorities before and after the State of the Union address. Members of Congress are afforded press opportunities to comment on the event in Statutary Hall immediately after the address. Typically, a transcript of the address is available at *<www.whitehouse.gov>*.

Update your regulatory action plan as needed. **See Chapter 6 for tips on building and maintaining your Regulatory Action Plan.**

Date/Time Period	Legislative/Executive Branch Activity and Deadlines
Third Monday in January	Martin Luther King's Birthday (federal holiday).

Suggested Government Affairs Activities

The congressional recess is an excellent time for constituents to participate in town hall meetings with their members back in the state/district. Constituents can contact their congressional office prior to the recess to determine the legislator's public appearances and town hall meeting schedule. **See Chapter 8 for information on advising constituents on their meetings with legislators and Chapter 7 (§ 7.17) for a checklist for planning a site visit.**

Date/Time Period	Legislative/Executive Branch Activity and Deadlines
First Monday in February	President submits the budget to Congress. Six weeks after the budget is submitted, House and Senate Committees submit reports on views and estimates to their respective congressional budget committees.

Suggested Government Affairs Activities

Review the president's budget online at <*www.budget.gov*> and determine the implications for your interests, updating your legislative or regulatory action plan as needed. **See Chapter 6 for tips on updating your legislative and regulatory action plans.**

Date/Time Period	Suggested Government Affairs Activities
February	The House and Senate floor action is usually relatively slow during this time because committees haven't had time to hold hearings and pass legislation.

Date/Time Period	Legislative/Executive Branch Activity and Deadlines
Week of February 19	President's Day District Work Period (recess).

Suggested Government Affairs Activities

The congressional recess is an excellent time for constituents to participate in town hall meetings with their members back in the state/district. Constituents can contact their congressional office prior to the recess to determine the legislator's public appearances and town hall meeting schedule. **See Chapter 7 for tips on educating, informing, and energizing constituents.**

Date/Time Period	Legislative/Executive Branch Activity and Deadlines
March 11	Daylight Savings Time begins (spring forward).

Date/Time Period	Legislative/Executive Branch Activity and Deadlines
April 2: Passover begins at sundown	April 1, recordkeeping begins for second quarter Lobbying Disclosure Act (LDA) reports to be filed July 20th.
	Generally in April, the administration releases the Semiannual Regulatory (Unified) Agenda.
April 6: Good Friday	
April 8: Easter	**Suggested Government Affairs Activities**
	Spring congressional district work period.

The Administration's Regulatory Agenda, also referred to as the Unified Agenda, is published by the Office of the Federal Register National Archives and Records Administration (NARA). Current and previous issues may be searched at *<www.gpoaccess.gov/ua/index.html>*. **See Chapter 6 for tips on building and maintaining your Regulatory Action Plan.**

Date/Time Period	
May 15, 2008 (or the 15th day of the fifth month following the end of your fiscal year)	

Date/Time Period	Legislative/Executive Branch Activity and Deadlines
May	Memorial Day Recess.

Suggested Government Affairs Activities

Constituents participate in town hall meetings back in the state/district. **See Chapter 7 for tips on educating, informing, and energizing constituents.**

Date/Time Period	Legislative/Executive Branch Activity and Deadlines
July	On July 1, recordkeeping begins for third quarter Lobbying Disclosure Act (LDA) quarterly reports to be filed August 20 as well as the second semiannual period for LDA contribution reports for each individual lobbyist (certain campaign contribution disclosures and attesting to having read and abided by the gift and travel rules).

Date/Time Period	Legislative/Executive Branch Activity and Deadlines
Around July 4	Independence Day Recess.

Suggested Government Affairs Activities

Constituents participate in Fourth of July celebrations and town hall meetings back in the state/district.

Date/Time Period	Legislative/Executive Branch Activity and Deadlines
July 30	LDA Contribution (LD–203) Reports due on July 30 covering the first semiannual period (January 1–June 30).

Suggested Government Affairs Activities

Each federal lobbyist must submit semiannual political contribution reports detailing certain political contributions and attesting that he or she has read and abided by the House and Senate gift and travel rules.

Date/Time Period	Legislative/Executive Branch Activity and Deadlines
August	August Recess.
	August 1, recordkeeping begins for fourth quarter LDA (LD–2) Report tracking.

Suggested Government Affairs Activities

Update staff, grassroots or clients on legislative and regulatory projections and priorities for the remainder of the session. Send correspondence and hold meetings with congressional staff. **See Chapter 8 for tips on communicating effectively, making and keeping the right connections, and developing and maintaining a target list.**

Clarify priorities for the final days of the congressional session, when much work is done and appropriations bills are finalized. This is a critical time when much unanticipated legislative activity occurs. Review your media strategy (**see Chapter 10**) and update your Legislative Action Plan and Regulatory Action Plan (**recommendations are provided in Chapter 6**).

Finalize information needed for remainder of session (work on charts studies and research, develop grassroots, evaluate technology and information resources). **See Chapter 5 for tips on updating your facts, data, and arguments.**

Check your technology (delete unnecessary electronic clutter and confirm back-up procedures).

Evaluate staff professional development and resource needs. Schedule training and events to occur after adjournment.

Date/Time Period	Legislative/Executive Branch Activity and Deadlines
September 4	House and Senate expected to reconvene after Labor Day.

Suggested Government Affairs Activities

Prepare for intense fall schedule.

Date/Time Period	Legislative/Executive Branch Activity and Deadlines
September 17	Constitution Day (commemorates Constitution signing on September 17, 1787).

Suggested Government Affairs Activities

Resources: Pocket Edition of the Constitution of the United States of America Online and instructions on ordering bulk copies: *<http://frwebgate.access.gpo.gov/cgi-bin/getdoc.cgi?dbname= 108_cong_documents&docid=f:hd096.108>*.

Date/Time Period	Legislative/Executive Branch Activity and Deadlines
October 1	Beginning of fiscal year.

Suggested Government Affairs Activities

Legislative appropriations must be enacted to avoid closing the government. In the absence of passage of the various appropriations bills, Congress often passes a temporary stop-gap measure to prevent government closure. This is a busy season for those tracking and influencing legislation since unrelated provisions are often added to funding bills without hearings or debate.

Date/Time Period	Legislative/Executive Branch Activity and Deadlines
October	Administration's Semiannual Regulatory (Unified) Agenda Released in the Federal Register.

Suggested Government Affairs Activities

The agenda is published by the Office of the Federal Register National Archives and Records Administration (NARA). Current and previous issues may be searched at *<www.gpoaccess.gov/ua/index.html>*.

Date/Time Period	Legislative/Executive Branch Activity and Deadlines
November	This is a time of turnover on Capitol Hill and elsewhere even during non-election years.
November 4: Daylight Savings Time (fall back)	

Suggested Government Affairs Activities

Update your legislative action plan, resources, staff assignments and contacts to reflect new leadership, agenda, member, staff, and committee changes. (**See Chapter 6.**)

November 6: Election Day

Provide information to and make contact with or strengthen relationships with new members, new chairmen, and new leaders.

November 12: Veterans Day Observed

Consider new member meetings, briefings and site visits. (**See § 7.15 for a site visit checklist.**) Congressional rosters for mailing labels are available through <*www.house.gov*> and <*www.senate.gov*>. A number of commercial providers also offer updated congressional directory information online, which can be accessed through a BlackBerry.

Examples of directory services are included in Chapter 7 (§ 7.35). A list of senators up for reelection is available at <*www.thecapitol.net/FAQ/termsofcongress.html*>.

Tip: To locate a new member during the transition period, you may want to contact the member's campaign headquarters before it is closed. You may wish to coordinate this with any contacts in the home state or district that have been made with the campaign prior to the election.

New members will receive their phone numbers, emails and room assignments based on a lottery system that will be held later in the year. Have a system in place for making contact with new members of Congress who are elected or appointed throughout the year due to resignations, death, etc.

Also during this time, returning members hold town hall meetings back in the state/district.

Date/Time Period	Legislative/Executive Branch Activity and Deadlines
After Session	Ten days after session ends, the Congressional Budget Office issues final sequestration report.
Sine die (final for the year) adjournment	Fifteen days after session ends, OMB issues final sequestration report.

Thanksgiving Recess

December 4 Hanukkah begins at sundown

December 25 Christmas

January 1: New Years Day

Suggested Government Affairs Activities

See Chapter 6 for planning tips. Review strategic goals and legislative action plans in light of upcoming congressional agenda. Evaluate and strengthen coordination of key functions (media, issues management, technology, and government affairs). Evaluate resource allocation. Set aside time to update archives (electronic and paper), check back up systems and eliminate extraneous information (paper as well as electronic clutter).

Establish and strengthen relationships with your grassroots and with your DC contacts on and off the Hill. **See Chapter 8 for tips on communicating effectively, making and keeping the right connections, and developing and maintaining a target list.**

Develop your grassroots. **See Chapter 7 for grassroots training and development suggestions.** Update those you represent on your accomplishments for the year and receive input and direction for the upcoming session. Provide a prognosis of what they can expect to hear from you throughout the year and what types of input and activities would help throughout the year to advance their cause.

Prepare materials for the Hill and the media for the next session. Develop charts, studies and research. **See Chapter 5 for special considerations for legislative research.**

Evaluate staff professional development needs and clarify or update performance measures if needed. This is an ongoing process. **See Chapter 11 for resources on staff development (including *<www.TheCapitol.Net>*) and performance measures.**

Monitor reporting and disclosure requirement changes to the Lobbying Disclosure Act. (Congress is studying the feasibility of making the Section 203 semiannual reports due on a quarterly basis.) **See Chapter 2 for tips on keeping current with lobbying reporting and disclosure requirements.**

Appendix 6
Lobbyists' Code of Ethics

Source: The American League of Lobbyists at: <*http://www.alldc.org/ethicscode.cfm*>

*"An important document which recognizes the
critical need for ethical behavior in public affairs."*

Pat Roberts, Former Chairman, Senate Select Committee on Ethics

**The ALL Code of Ethics is utilized as a model by various organizations and
serves to strengthen our image and enhance our role as a vital and respected
link in the democratic process.**

Lobbying is an integral part of our nation's democratic process and is a constitutionally guaranteed right. Government officials are continuously making public policy decisions that affect the vital interests of individuals, corporations, labor organizations, religious groups, charitable institutions and other entities. Public officials need to receive
factual information from affected interests and to know such parties' views in order to
make informed policy judgments. In exercising their rights to try to influence public policy, interests often choose to employ professional representatives to monitor developments and advocate their positions, or to use lobbyists through their membership in
trade associations and other membership organizations. Tens of thousands of men and
women now are professional lobbyists and represent virtually every type of interest.

To help preserve and advance public trust and confidence in our democratic institutions and the public policy advocacy process, professional lobbyists have a strong obligation to act always in the highest ethical and moral manner in their dealings with all
parties. Lobbyists also have a duty to advance public understanding of the lobbying profession. The American League of Lobbyists ("ALL"), accordingly, has adopted the following "Code of Lobbying Ethics" to provide basic guidelines and standards for lobbyists'
conduct. In general, this Code is intended to apply to independent lobbyists who are
retained to represent third party clients' interests and to lobbyists employed on the staff
of corporations, labor organizations, associations and other entities where their employer is in effect their "client." Lobbyists are strongly urged to comply with this Code and to
seek always to practice the highest ethical conduct in their lobbying endeavors. Individual members of American League of Lobbyists affirm their commitment to abide by this
code.

Article I – Honesty & Integrity

A lobbyist should conduct lobbying activities with honesty and integrity.

1.1. A lobbyist should be truthful in communicating with public officials and with
other interested persons and should seek to provide factually correct, current
and accurate information.

1.2. If a lobbyist determines that the lobbyist has provided a public official or other interested person with factually inaccurate information of a significant, relevant, and material nature, the lobbyist should promptly provide the factually accurate information to the interested person.

1.3. If a material change in factual information that the lobbyist provided previously to a public official causes the information to become inaccurate and the lobbyist knows the public official may still be relying upon the information, the lobbyist should provide accurate and updated information to the public official.

Article II – Compliance With Applicable Laws, Regulations & Rules

A lobbyist should seek to comply fully with all laws, regulations and rules applicable to the lobbyist.

2.1. A lobbyist should be familiar with laws, regulations and rules applicable to the lobbying profession and should not engage in any violation of such laws, regulations and rules.

2.2. A lobbyist should not cause a public official to violate any law, regulation or rule applicable to such public official.

Article III – Professionalism

A lobbyist should conduct lobbying activities in a fair and professional manner.

3.1. A lobbyist should have a basic understanding of the legislative and governmental process and such specialized knowledge as is necessary to represent clients or an employer in a competent, professional manner.

3.2. A lobbyist should maintain the lobbyist's understanding of governmental processes and specialized knowledge through appropriate methods such as continuing study, seminars and similar sessions in order to represent clients or an employer in a competent, professional manner.

3.3. A lobbyist should treat others—both allies and adversaries—with respect and civility.

Article IV – Conflicts Of Interest

A lobbyist should not continue or undertake representations that may create conflicts of interest without the informed consent of the client or potential client involved.

4.1. A lobbyist should avoid advocating a position on an issue if the lobbyist is also representing another client on the same issue with a conflicting position.

4.2. If a lobbyist's work for one client on an issue may have a significant adverse impact on another client's interests, the lobbyist should inform and obtain consent from the other client whose interests may be affected of this fact even if the lobbyist is not representing the other client on the same issue.

4.3. A lobbyist should disclose all potential conflicts to the client or prospective client and discuss and resolve the conflict issues promptly.

4.4. A lobbyist should inform the client if any other person is receiving a direct or indirect referral or consulting fee from the lobbyist due to or in connection with the client's work and the amount of such fee or payment.

Article V – Due Diligence & Best Efforts

A lobbyist should vigorously and diligently advance and advocate the client's or employer's interests.

5.1. A lobbyist should devote adequate time, attention, and resources to the client's or employer's interests.

5.2. A lobbyist should exercise loyalty to the client's or employer's interests.

5.3. A lobbyist should keep the client or employer informed regarding the work that the lobbyist is undertaking and, to the extent possible, should give the client the opportunity to choose between various options and strategies.

Article VI – Compensation And Engagement Terms

An independent lobbyist who is retained by a client should have a written agreement with the client regarding the terms and conditions for the lobbyist's services, including the amount of and basis for compensation.

Article VII – Confidentiality

A lobbyist should maintain appropriate confidentiality of client or employer information.

7.1. A lobbyist should not disclose confidential information without the client's or employer's informed consent.

7.2 .A lobbyist should not use confidential client information against the interests of a client or employer or for any purpose not contemplated by the engagement or terms of employment.

Article VIII – Public Education

A lobbyist should seek to ensure better public understanding and appreciation of the nature, legitimacy and necessity of lobbying in our democratic governmental process. This includes the First Amendment right to "petition the government for redress of grievances."

Article IX – Duty To Governmental Institutions

In addition to fulfilling duties and responsibilities to the client or employer, a lobbyist should exhibit proper respect for the governmental institutions before which the lobbyist represents and advocates clients' interests.

9.1. A lobbyist should not act in any manner that will undermine public confidence and trust in the democratic governmental process.

9.2. A lobbyist should not act in a manner that shows disrespect for government institutions.

Approved by the Board February 28, 2000.
Copyright © 1999-2008, American League of Lobbyists
Reprinted with permission.

Amendments to the Lobbying Disclosure Act, the Foreign Agents Registration Act, and the Federal Election Campaign Act, by Showing Changes to Previous Law made by The Honest Leadership and Open Government Act of 2007 [HLOGA].

Title II—The Honest Leadership and Open Government Act of 2007[HLOGA]

Prepared by William Luneburg, Professor of Law, University of Pittsburgh School of Law

This is available online on the American Bar Association's Wed page for
The Lobbying Manual at: *<www.abanet.org/abapubs/lobbyingmanual>*

Changes made by HLOGA: Amendments to The Lobbying Disclosure Act,
the Foreign Agents Registration Act, and the Federal Election Campaign Act

Changes to existing law <u>underlined</u>; replaced language is ~~strike through~~; other new provisions **<u>bold underlined</u>**.

The Lobbying Disclosure Act As Amended

Sec. 1. Short title

This act may be cited as the "Lobbying Disclosure Act of 1995".

Sec. 2 (2 U.S.C. §1601). Findings

The Congress finds that—
(1) responsible representative Government requires public awareness of the efforts of paid lobbyists to influence the public decisionmaking process in both the legislative and executive branches of the Federal Government;
(2) existing lobbying disclosure statutes have been ineffective because of unclear statutory language, weak administrative and enforcement provisions, and an absence of clear guidance as to who is required to register and what they are required to disclose; and
(3) the effective public disclosure of the identity and extent of the efforts of paid lobbyists to influence Federal officials in the conduct of Government actions will increase public confidence in the integrity of Government.

Sec. 3 (2 U.S.C. § 1602). Definitions

As used in this chapter:

(1) Agency
The term "agency" has the meaning given that term in section 551 (1) of title 5.

Changes made by HLOGA: Amendments to The Lobbying Disclosure Act,
the Foreign Agents Registration Act, and the Federal Election Campaign Act

Changes to existing law underlined; replaced language is ~~strike-through~~; other new provisions **bold underlined**.

(2) Client

The term "client" means any person or entity that employs or retains another person for financial or other compensation to conduct lobbying activities on behalf of that person or entity. A person or entity whose employees act as lobbyists on its own behalf is both a client and an employer of such employees. In the case of a coalition or association that employs or retains other persons to conduct lobbying activities, the client is the coalition or association and not its individual members.

(3) Covered executive branch official

The term "covered executive branch official" means—

(A) the President;

(B) the Vice President;

(C) any officer or employee, or any other individual functioning in the capacity of such an officer or employee, in the Executive Office of the President;

(D) any officer or employee serving in a position in level I, II, III, IV, or V of the Executive Schedule, as designated by statute or Executive order;

(E) any member of the uniformed services whose pay grade is at or above O–7 under section 201 of title 37, United States Code; and

(F) any officer or employee serving in a position of a confidential, policy-determining, policy-making, or policy-advocating character described in section 7511 (b)(2)(B) of title 5.

(4) Covered legislative branch official

The term "covered legislative branch official" means—

(A) a Member of Congress;

(B) an elected officer of either House of Congress;

(C) any employee of, or any other individual functioning in the capacity of an employee of—

(i) a Member of Congress;

(ii) a committee of either House of Congress;

(iii) the leadership staff of the House of Representatives or the leadership staff of the Senate;

(iv) a joint committee of Congress; and

(v) a working group or caucus organized to provide legislative services or other assistance to Members of Congress; and

(D) any other legislative branch employee serving in a position described under section 109(13) of the Ethics in Government Act of 1978 (5 U.S.C. App.).

(5) Employee

The term "employee" means any individual who is an officer, employee, partner, director, or proprietor of a person or entity, but does not include—

(A) independent contractors; or

Changes made by HLOGA: Amendments to The Lobbying Disclosure Act,
the Foreign Agents Registration Act, and the Federal Election Campaign Act

Changes to existing law underlined; replaced language is ~~strike-through~~; other new provisions **bold underlined**.

(B) volunteers who receive no financial or other compensation from the person or entity for their services.

(6) Foreign entity

The term "foreign entity" means a foreign principal (as defined in section 1(b) of the Foreign Agents Registration Act of 1938 (22 U.S.C. 611 (b)).

(7) Lobbying activities

The term "lobbying activities" means lobbying contacts and efforts in support of such contacts, including preparation and planning activities, research and other background work that is intended, at the time it is performed, for use in contacts, and coordination with the lobbying activities of others.

(8) Lobbying contact

(A) Definition

The term "lobbying contact" means any oral or written communication (including an electronic communication) to a covered executive branch official or a covered legislative branch official that is made on behalf of a client with regard to—

(i) the formulation, modification, or adoption of Federal legislation (including legislative proposals);

(ii) the formulation, modification, or adoption of a Federal rule, regulation, Executive order, or any other program, policy, or position of the United States Government;

(iii) the administration or execution of a Federal program or policy (including the negotiation, award, or administration of a Federal contract, grant, loan, permit, or license); or

(iv) the nomination or confirmation of a person for a position subject to confirmation by the Senate.

(B) Exceptions

The term "lobbying contact" does not include a communication that is—

(i) made by a public official acting in the public official's official capacity;

(ii) made by a representative of a media organization if the purpose of the communication is gathering and disseminating news and information to the public;

(iii) made in a speech, article, publication or other material that is distributed and made available to the public, or through radio, television, cable television, or other medium of mass communication;

(iv) made on behalf of a government of a foreign country or a foreign political party and disclosed under the Foreign Agents Registration Act of 1938 (22 U.S.C. 611 et seq.);

(v) a request for a meeting, a request for the status of an action, or any other similar administrative request, if the request does not include an attempt to influence a covered executive branch official or a covered legislative branch official;

Changes made by HLOGA: Amendments to The Lobbying Disclosure Act,
the Foreign Agents Registration Act, and the Federal Election Campaign Act
Changes to existing law underlined; replaced language is ~~strike-through~~; other new provisions **bold underlined**.

(**vi**) made in the course of participation in an advisory committee subject to the Federal Advisory Committee Act;

(**vii**) testimony given before a committee, subcommittee, or task force of the Congress, or submitted for inclusion in the public record of a hearing conducted by such committee, subcommittee, or task force;

(**viii**) information provided in writing in response to an oral or written request by a covered executive branch official or a covered legislative branch official for specific information;

(**ix**) required by subpoena, civil investigative demand, or otherwise compelled by statute, regulation, or other action of the Congress or an agency, including any communication compelled by a Federal contract, grant, loan, permit, or license;

(**x**) made in response to a notice in the Federal Register, Commerce Business Daily, or other similar publication soliciting communications from the public and directed to the agency official specifically designated in the notice to receive such communications;

(**xi**) not possible to report without disclosing information, the unauthorized disclosure of which is prohibited by law;

(**xii**) made to an official in an agency with regard to—

(**I**) a judicial proceeding or a criminal or civil law enforcement inquiry, investigation, or proceeding; or

(**II**) a filing or proceeding that the Government is specifically required by statute or regulation to maintain or conduct on a confidential basis,
if that agency is charged with responsibility for such proceeding, inquiry, investigation, or filing;

(**xiii**) made in compliance with written agency procedures regarding an adjudication conducted by the agency under section 554 of title 5 or substantially similar provisions;

(**xiv**) a written comment filed in the course of a public proceeding or any other communication that is made on the record in a public proceeding;

(**xv**) a petition for agency action made in writing and required to be a matter of public record pursuant to established agency procedures;

(**xvi**) made on behalf of an individual with regard to that individual's benefits, employment, or other personal matters involving only that individual, except that this clause does not apply to any communication with—

(**I**) a covered executive branch official, or

(**II**) a covered legislative branch official (other than the individual's elected Members of Congress or employees who work under such Members' direct supervision),

with respect to the formulation, modification, or adoption of private legislation for the relief of that individual;

Changes made by HLOGA: Amendments to The Lobbying Disclosure Act,
the Foreign Agents Registration Act, and the Federal Election Campaign Act

Changes to existing law underlined; replaced language is ~~strike through~~; other new provisions **bold underlined**.

(**xvii**) a disclosure by an individual that is protected under the amendments made by the Whistleblower Protection Act of 1989, under the Inspector General Act of 1978, or under another provision of law;

(**xviii**) made by—

    (**I**) a church, its integrated auxiliary, or a convention or association of churches that is exempt from filing a Federal income tax return under paragraph 2(A)(i) of section 6033 (a) of title 26, or

    (**II**) a religious order that is exempt from filing a Federal income tax return under paragraph (2)(A)(iii) of such section 6033 (a); and

(**xix**) between—

    (**I**) officials of a self-regulatory organization (as defined in section 3(a)(26) of the Securities Exchange Act [15 U.S.C. 78c (a)(26)]) that is registered with or established by the Securities and Exchange Commission as required by that Act [15 U.S.C. 78a et seq.] or a similar organization that is designated by or registered with the Commodities Future Trading Commission as provided under the Commodity Exchange Act [7 U.S.C. 1 et seq.]; and

    (**II**) the Securities and Exchange Commission or the Commodities Future Trading Commission, respectively; relating to the regulatory responsibilities of such organization under that Act.

(9) Lobbying firm

The term "lobbying firm" means a person or entity that has 1 or more employees who are lobbyists on behalf of a client other than that person or entity. The term also includes a self-employed individual who is a lobbyist.

(10) Lobbyist

The term "lobbyist" means any individual who is employed or retained by a client for financial or other compensation for services that include more than one lobbying contact, other than an individual whose lobbying activities constitute less than 20 percent of the time engaged in the services provided by such individual to that client over a ~~six month period~~ 3-month period.

(11) Media organization

The term "media organization" means a person or entity engaged in disseminating information to the general public through a newspaper, magazine, other publication, radio, television, cable television, or other medium of mass communication.

(12) Member of Congress

The term "Member of Congress" means a Senator or a Representative in, or Delegate or Resident Commissioner to, the Congress.

(13) Organization

The term "organization" means a person or entity other than an individual.

Changes made by HLOGA: Amendments to The Lobbying Disclosure Act,
the Foreign Agents Registration Act, and the Federal Election Campaign Act

Changes to existing law underlined; replaced language is ~~strike-through~~; other new provisions **bold underlined**.

(14) Person or entity

The term "person or entity" means any individual, corporation, company, foundation, association, labor organization, firm, partnership, society, joint stock company, group of organizations, or State or local government.

(15) Public official

The term "public official" means any elected official, appointed official, or employee of—
  (A) a Federal, State, or local unit of government in the United States other than—
      (i) a college or university;
      (ii) a government-sponsored enterprise (as defined in section 622(8) of this title);
      (iii) a public utility that provides gas, electricity, water, or communications;
      (iv) a guaranty agency (as defined in section 1085(j) of title 20), including any affiliate of such an agency; or
      (v) an agency of any State functioning as a student loan secondary market pursuant to section 1085 (d)(1)(F) of title 20;
  (B) a Government corporation (as defined in section 9101 of title 31);
  (C) an organization of State or local elected or appointed officials other than officials of an entity described in clause (i), (ii), (iii), (iv), or (v) of subparagraph (A);
  (D) an Indian tribe (as defined in section 450b(e) of title 25);
  (E) a national or State political party or any organizational unit thereof; or
  (F) a national, regional, or local unit of any foreign government, or a group of governments acting together as an international organization.

(16) State

The term "State" means each of the several States, the District of Columbia, and any commonwealth, territory, or possession of the United States.

Sec. 4 (2. U.S.C. § 1603). Registration of lobbyists

(a) Registration

(1) General rule

No later than 45 days after a lobbyist first makes a lobbying contact or is employed or retained to make a lobbying contact, whichever is earlier, or on the first business day after such 45th day if the 45th day is not a business day such lobbyist (or, as provided under paragraph (2), the organization employing such lobbyist), shall register with the Secretary of the Senate and the Clerk of the House of Representatives.

(2) Employer filing

Any organization that has 1 or more employees who are lobbyists shall file a single registration under this section on behalf of such employees for each client on whose behalf the employees act as lobbyists.

Changes made by HLOGA: Amendments to The Lobbying Disclosure Act,
the Foreign Agents Registration Act, and the Federal Election Campaign Act

Changes to existing law underlined; replaced language is ~~strike through~~; other new provisions **bold underlined**.

(3) Exemption

(A) General rule

Notwithstanding paragraphs (1) and (2), a person or entity whose—

(i) total income for matters related to lobbying activities on behalf of a particular client (in the case of a lobbying firm) does not exceed and is not expected to exceed ~~$5,000~~ $2,500; or

(ii) total expenses in connection with lobbying activities (in the case of an organization whose employees engage in lobbying activities on its own behalf) do not exceed or are not expected to exceed ~~$20,000~~ $10,000, (as estimated under section 1604 of this title) in the ~~semiannual period~~ quarterly period described in section 1604(a) of this title during which the registration would be made is not required to register under this subsection with respect to such client.

(B) Adjustment

The dollar amounts in subparagraph (A) shall be adjusted—

(i) on January 1, 1997, to reflect changes in the Consumer Price Index (as determined by the Secretary of Labor) since December 19, 1995; and

(ii) on January 1 of each fourth year occurring after January 1, 1997, to reflect changes in the Consumer Price Index (as determined by the Secretary of Labor) during the preceding 4-year period, rounded to the nearest $500.

(b) Contents of registration

Each registration under this section shall contain—

(1) the name, address, business telephone number, and principal place of business of the registrant, and a general description of its business or activities;

(2) the name, address, and principal place of business of the registrant's client, and a general description of its business or activities (if different from paragraph (1));

(3) the name, address, and principal place of business of any organization, other than the client, that—

(A) ~~contributes more than $10,000 towards the lobbying activities of a registrant in a semiannual period described in section 5(a)~~ contributes more than $5,000 to the registrant or the client in the quarterly period to fund the lobbying activities of the registrant; and

(B) ~~in whole or in major part plans, supervises, or controls such lobbying activities~~ actively participates in the planning, supervision, or control of such lobbying activities;

(4) the name, address, principal place of business, amount of any contribution of more than ~~$10,000~~ $5,000 to the lobbying activities of the registrant, and approximate percentage of equitable ownership in the client (if any) of any foreign entity that—

(A) holds at least 20 percent equitable ownership in the client or any organization identified under paragraph (3);

Changes made by HLOGA: Amendments to The Lobbying Disclosure Act,
the Foreign Agents Registration Act, and the Federal Election Campaign Act
Changes to existing law underlined; replaced language is ~~strike through~~; other new provisions **bold underlined**.

(B) directly or indirectly, in whole or in major part, plans, supervises, controls, directs, finances, or subsidizes the activities of the client or any organization identified under paragraph (3); or

(C) is an affiliate of the client or any organization identified under paragraph (3) and has a direct interest in the outcome of the lobbying activity;

(5) a statement of—

(A) the general issue areas in which the registrant expects to engage in lobbying activities on behalf of the client; and

(B) to the extent practicable, specific issues that have (as of the date of the registration) already been addressed or are likely to be addressed in lobbying activities; and

(6) the name of each employee of the registrant who has acted or whom the registrant expects to act as a lobbyist on behalf of the client and, if any such employee has served as a covered executive branch official or a covered legislative branch official ~~in the 2 years before the date on which such employee first acted (after the date of enactment of this Act [enacted Dec. 19, 1995])~~ in the 20 years before the date on which the employee first acted as a lobbyist on behalf of the client, the position in which such employee served.

No disclosure is required under paragraph (3)(B) if the organization that would be identified as affiliated with the client is listed on the client's publicly accessible Internet website as being a member of or contributor to the client, unless the organization in whole or in major part plans, supervises, or controls such lobbying activities. If a registrant relies upon the preceding sentence, the registrant must disclose the specific Internet address of the web page containing the information relied upon. Nothing in paragraph (3)(B) shall be construed to require the disclosure of any information about individuals who are members of, or donors to, an entity treated as a client by this Act or an organization identified under that paragraph.

(c) Guidelines for registration

(1) Multiple clients
In the case of a registrant making lobbying contacts on behalf of more than 1 client, a separate registration under this section shall be filed for each such client.

(2) Multiple contacts
A registrant who makes more than 1 lobbying contact for the same client shall file a single registration covering all such lobbying contacts.

(d) Termination of registration
A registrant who after registration—
(1) is no longer employed or retained by a client to conduct lobbying activities, and

Changes made by HLOGA: Amendments to The Lobbying Disclosure Act,
the Foreign Agents Registration Act, and the Federal Election Campaign Act

Changes to existing law underlined; replaced language is ~~strike through~~; other new provisions **bold underlined**.

---

(2) does not anticipate any additional lobbying activities for such client, may so notify the Secretary of the Senate and the Clerk of the House of Representatives and terminate its registration.

Sec. 5 (2 U.S.C. § 1604). Reports by registered lobbyists

(a) ~~Semiannual~~ Quarterly report

~~No later than 45 days after the end of the semiannual period beginning on the first day of each January and the first day of July of each year in which a registrant is registered under section 4,~~ No later than 20 days after the end of the quarterly period beginning on the first day of January, April, July, and October of each year in which a registrant is registered under section 4, or on the first business day after such 20th day if the 20th day is not a business day, each registrant shall file a report with the Secretary of the Senate and the Clerk of the House of Representatives on its lobbying activities during ~~such semiannual period~~ such quarterly period. A separate report shall be filed for each client of the registrant.

(b) Contents of report

Each ~~semiannual~~ quarterly report filed under subsection (a) of this section shall contain—
(1) the name of the registrant, the name of the client, and any changes or updates to the information provided in the initial registration, including information under section 4(b)(3);
(2) for each general issue area in which the registrant engaged in lobbying activities on behalf of the client during the ~~semiannual~~ quarterly period—

   (A) a list of the specific issues upon which a lobbyist employed by the registrant engaged in lobbying activities, including, to the maximum extent practicable, a list of bill numbers and references to specific executive branch actions;

   (B) a statement of the Houses of Congress and the Federal agencies contacted by lobbyists employed by the registrant on behalf of the client;

   (C) a list of the employees of the registrant who acted as lobbyists on behalf of the client; and

   (D) a description of the interest, if any, of any foreign entity identified under section 1603(b)(4) of this title in the specific issues listed under subparagraph (A);

(3) in the case of a lobbying firm, a good faith estimate of the total amount of all income from the client (including any payments to the registrant by any other person for lobbying activities on behalf of the client) during the ~~semiannual~~ quarterly period, other than income for matters that are unrelated to lobbying activities;
(4) in the case of a registrant engaged in lobbying activities on its own behalf, a good faith estimate of the total expenses that the registrant and its employees incurred in connection with lobbying activities during the ~~semiannual filing period~~ quarterly period; and
(5) for each client, immediately after listing the client, an identification of whether the client is a State or local government or a department, agency, special purpose district, or other instrumentality controlled by one or more State or local governments.

Changes made by HLOGA: Amendments to The Lobbying Disclosure Act,
the Foreign Agents Registration Act, and the Federal Election Campaign Act

Changes to existing law underlined; replaced language is ~~strike through~~; other new provisions **bold underlined**.

(c) Estimates of income or expenses
For purposes of this section, estimates of income or expenses shall be made as follows:
(1) Estimates of amounts in excess ~~$10,000~~ $5,000 shall be rounded to the nearest ~~$20,000~~ $10,000.
(2) In the event income or expenses do not exceed ~~$10,000~~ $5,000, the registrant shall include a statement that income or expenses totaled less than ~~$10,000~~ $5,000 for the reporting period.

(d) Semiannual Reports on Certain Contributions—
(1) IN GENERAL—Not later than 30 days after the end of the semiannual period beginning on the first day of January and July of each year, or on the first business day after such 30th day if the 30th day is not a business day, each person or organization who is registered or is required to register under paragraph (1) or (2) of section 4(a), and each employee who is or is required to be listed as a lobbyist under section 4(b)(6) or subsection (b)(2)(C) of this section, shall file a report with the Secretary of the Senate and the Clerk of the House of Representatives containing—
    (A) the name of the person or organization;
    (B) in the case of an employee, his or her employer;
    (C) the names of all political committees established or controlled by the person or organization;
    (D) the name of each Federal candidate or officeholder, leadership PAC, or political party committee, to whom aggregate contributions equal to or exceeding $200 were made by the person or organization, or a political committee established or controlled by the person or organization within the semiannual period, and the date and amount of each such contribution made within the semiannual period;
    (E) the date, recipient, and amount of funds contributed or disbursed during the semiannual period by the person or organization or a political committee established or controlled by the person or organization—
        (i) to pay the cost of an event to honor or recognize a covered legislative branch official or covered executive branch official;
        (ii) to an entity that is named for a covered legislative branch official, or to a person or entity in recognition of such official;
        (iii) to an entity established, financed, maintained, or controlled by a covered legislative branch official or covered executive branch official, or an entity designated by such official; or
        (iv) to pay the costs of a meeting, retreat, conference, or other similar event held by, or in the name of, 1 or more covered legislative branch officials or covered executive branch officials,
    except that this subparagraph shall not apply if the funds are provided to a person who is required to report the receipt of the funds under section 304 of the Federal Election Campaign Act of 1971 (2 U.S.C. 434);

Changes made by HLOGA: Amendments to The Lobbying Disclosure Act,
the Foreign Agents Registration Act, and the Federal Election Campaign Act

Changes to existing law underlined; replaced language is ~~strike through~~; other new provisions **bold underlined**.

(F) the name of each Presidential library foundation, and each Presidential inaugural committee, to whom contributions equal to or exceeding $200 were made by the person or organization, or a political committee established or controlled by the person or organization, within the semiannual period, and the date and amount of each such contribution within the semiannual period; and

(G) a certification by the person or organization filing the report that the person or organization—

    (i) has read and is familiar with those provisions of the Standing Rules of the Senate and the Rules of the House of Representatives relating to the provision of gifts and travel; and

    (ii) has not provided, requested, or directed a gift, including travel, to a Member of Congress or an officer or employee of either House of Congress with knowledge that receipt of the gift would violate rule XXXV of the Standing Rules of the Senate or rule XXV of the Rules of the House of Representatives.

(2) DEFINITION—In this subsection, the term 'leadership PAC' has the meaning given such term in section 304(i)(8)(B) of the Federal Election Campaign Act of 1971.

[SECTION 203 (b) [HLOGA] Effective Date—The amendment made by subsection (a)[that is, new Section 5(d) of the LDA] shall apply with respect to the first semiannual period described in section 5(d)(1) of the Lobbying Disclosure Act of 1995 (as added by this section) that begins after the date of the enactment of this Act and each succeeding semiannual period.

(c) Report on Requiring Quarterly Reports—The Clerk of the House of Representatives and the Secretary of the Senate shall submit a report to the Congress, not later than 1 year after the date on which the first reports are required to be made under section 5(d) of the Lobbying Disclosure Act of 1995 (as added by this section), on the feasibility of requiring the reports under such section 5(d) to be made on a quarterly, rather than a semiannual, basis.

(d) Sense of Congress—It is the sense of the Congress that after the end of the 2-year period beginning on the day on which the amendment made by subsection (a) of this section first applies, the reports required under section 5(d) of the Lobbying Disclosure Act of 1995 (as added by this section) should be made on a quarterly basis if it is practicably feasible to do so.]

(e) Electronic Filing Required—A report required to be filed under this section shall be filed in electronic form, in addition to any other form that the Secretary of the Senate or the Clerk of the House of Representatives may require or allow. The Secretary of the Senate and the Clerk of the House of Representatives shall use the same electronic software for receipt and recording of filings under this Act.

Changes made by HLOGA: Amendments to The Lobbying Disclosure Act,
the Foreign Agents Registration Act, and the Federal Election Campaign Act

Changes to existing law underlined; replaced language is ~~strike through~~; other new provisions **bold underlined**.

Sec. 6 (2 U.S.C. § 1605). Disclosure and enforcement

(a) In General—The Secretary of the Senate and the Clerk of the House of Representatives shall—

(1) provide guidance and assistance on the registration and reporting requirements of this chapter and develop common standards, rules, and procedures for compliance with this chapter;

(2) review, and, where necessary, verify and inquire to ensure the accuracy, completeness, and timeliness of registration and reports;

(3) develop filing, coding, and cross-indexing systems to carry out the purpose of this chapter, including—

(A) a publicly available list of all registered lobbyists, lobbying firms, and their clients; and

(B) computerized systems designed to minimize the burden of filing and maximize public access to materials filed under this chapter;

(4) make available for public inspection and copying at reasonable times the registrations and reports filed under this chapter and, in the case of a report filed in electronic form under section 5(e), make such report available for public inspection over the Internet as soon as technically practicable after the report is so filed;

(5) retain registrations for a period of at least 6 years after they are terminated and reports for a period of at least 6 years after they are filed;

(6) compile and summarize, with respect to each ~~semiannual~~ quarterly period, the information contained in registrations and reports filed with respect to such period in a clear and complete manner;

(7) notify any lobbyist or lobbying firm in writing that may be in noncompliance with this chapter;

(8) notify the United States Attorney for the District of Columbia that a lobbyist or lobbying firm may be in noncompliance with this chapter, if the registrant has been notified in writing and has failed to provide an appropriate response within 60 days after notice was given under paragraph (7);

(9) maintain all registrations and reports filed under this Act, and make them available to the public over the Internet, without a fee or other access charge, in a searchable, sortable, and downloadable manner, to the extent technically practicable, that—

(A) includes the information contained in the registrations and reports;

(B) is searchable and sortable to the maximum extent practicable, including searchable and sortable by each of the categories of information described in section 4(b) or 5(b); and

(C) provides electronic links or other appropriate mechanisms to allow users to obtain relevant information in the database of the Federal Election Commission;

(10) retain the information contained in a registration or report filed under this Act for a period of 6 years after the registration or report (as the case may be) is filed; and

Changes made by HLOGA: Amendments to The Lobbying Disclosure Act,
the Foreign Agents Registration Act, and the Federal Election Campaign Act

Changes to existing law underlined; replaced language is ~~strike-through~~; other new provisions **bold underlined**.

---

(11) make publicly available, on a semiannual basis, the aggregate number of registrants referred to the United States Attorney for the District of Columbia for noncompliance as required by paragraph (8).

(b) Enforcement Report-
(1) REPORT—The Attorney General shall report to the congressional committees referred to in paragraph (2), after the end of each semiannual period beginning on January 1 and July 1, the aggregate number of enforcement actions taken by the Department of Justice under this Act during that semiannual period and, by case, any sentences imposed, except that such report shall not include the names of individuals, or personally identifiable information, that is not already a matter of public record.
(2) COMMITTEES—The congressional committees referred to in paragraph (1) are the Committee on Homeland Security and Governmental Affairs and the Committee on the Judiciary of the Senate and the Committee on the Judiciary of the House of Representatives.

[Section 209 (c)[HLOGA]: Authorization of Appropriations—There are authorized to be appropriated such sums as may be necessary to carry out paragraph (9) of section 6 of the Lobbying Disclosure Act of 1995 (2 U.S.C. 1605), as added by subsection (a) of this section.]

Sec. 7 (2 U.S.C. § 1606). Penalties

(a) Civil Penalty—Whoever knowingly fails to—
(1) remedy a defective filing within 60 days after notice of such a defect by the Secretary of the Senate or the Clerk of the House of Representatives; or
(2) comply with any other provision of this Act;
shall, upon proof of such knowing violation by a preponderance of the evidence, be subject to a civil fine of not more than ~~$50,000~~ $200,000, depending on the extent and gravity of the violation.

(b) Criminal Penalty—Whoever knowingly and corruptly fails to comply with any provision of this Act shall be imprisoned for not more than 5 years or fined under title 18, United States Code, or both.

[Section 211(b)[HLOGA] Effective Date—The amendments made by subsection (a)[increased civil and added criminal penalties] shall apply to any violation committed on or after the date of the enactment of this Act.]

Changes made by HLOGA: Amendments to The Lobbying Disclosure Act,
the Foreign Agents Registration Act, and the Federal Election Campaign Act

Changes to existing law underlined; replaced language is ~~strike through~~; other new provisions **bold underlined**.

Sec. 8 (2 U.S.C. § 1607). Rules of Construction

(a) Constitutional rights
Nothing in this chapter shall be construed to prohibit or interfere with—
(1) the right to petition the Government for the redress of grievances;
(2) the right to express a personal opinion; or
(3) the right of association, protected by the first amendment to the Constitution.

(b) Prohibition of activities
Nothing in this chapter shall be construed to prohibit, or to authorize any court to prohibit, lobbying activities or lobbying contacts by any person or entity, regardless of whether such person or entity is in compliance with the requirements of this chapter.

(c) Audit and investigations
Nothing in this chapter shall be construed to grant general audit or investigative authority to the Secretary of the Senate or the Clerk of the House of Representatives.

Sec. 13 (2 U.S.C. § 1608). Severability

If any provision of this chapter, or the application thereof, is held invalid, the validity of the remainder of this chapter and the application of such provision to other persons and circumstances shall not be affected thereby.

Sec. 14 (2 U.S.C. 1609). Identification of clients and covered officials

(a) Oral lobbying contacts
Any person or entity that makes an oral lobbying contact with a covered legislative branch official or a covered executive branch official shall, on the request of the official at the time of the lobbying contact—
(1) state whether the person or entity is registered under this chapter and identify the client on whose behalf the lobbying contact is made; and
(2) state whether such client is a foreign entity and identify any foreign entity required to be disclosed under section 1603 (b)(4) of this title that has a direct interest in the outcome of the lobbying activity.

(b) Written lobbying contacts
Any person or entity registered under this chapter that makes a written lobbying contact (including an electronic communication) with a covered legislative branch official or a covered executive branch official shall—
(1) if the client on whose behalf the lobbying contact was made is a foreign entity, identify such client, state that the client is considered a foreign entity under this chapter, and state

Changes made by HLOGA: Amendments to The Lobbying Disclosure Act,
the Foreign Agents Registration Act, and the Federal Election Campaign Act

Changes to existing law underlined; replaced language is ~~strike through~~; other new provisions **bold underlined**.

whether the person making the lobbying contact is registered on behalf of that client under section 1603 of this title; and

(2) identify any other foreign entity identified pursuant to section 1603 (b)(4) of this title that has a direct interest in the outcome of the lobbying activity.

(c) Identification as covered official

Upon request by a person or entity making a lobbying contact, the individual who is contacted or the office employing that individual shall indicate whether or not the individual is a covered legislative branch official or a covered executive branch official.

Sec. 15 (2 U.S.C. § 1610). Estimates based on tax reporting system

(a) Entities covered by section 6033 (b) of title 26-

A person, other than a lobbying firm, that is required to report and does report lobbying expenditures pursuant to section 6033 (b)(8) of title 26 may—

(1) make a good faith estimate (by category of dollar value) of applicable amounts that would be required to be disclosed under such section for the appropriate ~~semiannual~~ quarterly period to meet the requirements of sections 1603 (a)(3) and 1604 (b)(4) of this title; and

(2) for all other purposes consider as lobbying contacts and lobbying activities only—

(A) lobbying contacts with covered legislative branch officials (as defined in section 1602 (4) of this title) and lobbying activities in support of such contacts; and

(B) lobbying of Federal executive branch officials to the extent that such activities are influencing legislation as defined in section 4911 (d) of title 26.

(b) Entities covered by section 162 (e) of title 26

A person, other than a lobbying firm, who is required to account and does account for lobbying expenditures pursuant to section 162 (e) of title 26 may—

(1) make a good faith estimate (by category of dollar value) of applicable amounts that would not be deductible pursuant to such section for the appropriate ~~semiannual~~ quarterly period to meet the requirements of sections 1603 (a)(3) and 1604 (b)(4) of this title; and

(2) for all other purposes consider as lobbying contacts and lobbying activities only—

(A) lobbying contacts with covered legislative branch officials (as defined in section 1602 (4) of this title) and lobbying activities in support of such contacts; and

(B) lobbying of Federal executive branch officials to the extent that amounts paid or costs incurred in connection with such activities are not deductible pursuant to section 162 (e) of title 26.

(c) Disclosure of estimate

Any registrant that elects to make estimates required by this chapter under the procedures authorized by subsection (a) or (b) of this section for reporting or threshold purposes shall—

Changes made by HLOGA: Amendments to The Lobbying Disclosure Act,
the Foreign Agents Registration Act, and the Federal Election Campaign Act

Changes to existing law underlined; replaced language is ~~strike through~~; other new provisions **bold underlined**.

(1) inform the Secretary of the Senate and the Clerk of the House of Representatives that the registrant has elected to make its estimates under such procedures; and

(2) make all such estimates, in a given calendar year, under such procedures.

(d) Study

Not later than March 31, 1997, the Comptroller General of the United States shall review reporting by registrants under subsections (a) and (b) of this section and report to the Congress—

(1) the differences between the definition of "lobbying activities" in section 1602 (7) of this title and the definitions of "lobbying expenditures", "influencing legislation", and related terms in sections 162 (e) and 4911 of title 26, as each are implemented by regulations;

(2) the impact that any such differences may have on filing and reporting under this chapter pursuant to this subsection; and

(3) any changes to this chapter or to the appropriate sections of title 26 that the Comptroller General may recommend to harmonize the definitions.

Sec. 18 (2 U.S.C. § 1611). Exempt organizations

An organization described in section 501 (c)(4) of title 26 which engages in lobbying activities shall not be eligible for the receipt of Federal funds constituting an award, grant, or loan.

Sec. 23 (2 U.S.C.§ 1612). Sense of the Senate that lobbying expenses should remain nondeductible

(a) Findings

The Senate finds that ordinary Americans generally are not allowed to deduct the costs of communicating with their elected representatives.

(b) Sense of Senate

It is the sense of the Senate that lobbying expenses should not be tax deductible

Sec. 25. Prohibition on provision of gifts or travel by registered lobbyists to members of Congress and the Congressional employees

(a) Prohibition—Any person described in subsection (b) may not make a gift or provide travel to a covered legislative branch official if the person has knowledge that the gift or travel may not be accepted by that covered legislative branch official under the Rules of the House of Representatives or the Standing Rules of the Senate (as the case may be).

(b) Persons Subject to Prohibition—The persons subject to the prohibition under subsection (a) are any lobbyist that is registered or is required to register under section

Changes made by HLOGA: Amendments to The Lobbying Disclosure Act,
the Foreign Agents Registration Act, and the Federal Election Campaign Act

Changes to existing law underlined; replaced language is ~~strike through~~; other new provisions **bold underlined**.

4(a)(1), any organization that employs 1 or more lobbyists and is registered or is required to register under section 4(a)(2), and any employee listed or required to be listed as a lobbyist by a registrant under section 4(b)(6) or 5(b)(2)(C).

[Section 206(b) [HLOGA] Effective Date—The amendment made by this section shall take effect on the date of the enactment of this Act.]

Sec. 26. Annual audits and reports by Comptroller General

(a) Audit—On an annual basis, the Comptroller General shall audit the extent of compliance or noncompliance with the requirements of this Act by lobbyists, lobbying firms, and registrants through a random sampling of publicly available lobbying registrations and reports filed under this Act during each calendar year.

(b) Reports to Congress-
(1) ANNUAL REPORTS—Not later than April 1 of each year, the Comptroller General shall submit to the Congress a report on the review required by subsection (a) for the preceding calendar year. The report shall include the Comptroller General's assessment of the matters required to be emphasized by that subsection and any recommendations of the Comptroller General to—
  (A) improve the compliance by lobbyists, lobbying firms, and registrants with the requirements of this Act; and
  (B) provide the Department of Justice with the resources and authorities needed for the effective enforcement of this Act.
(2) ASSESSMENT OF COMPLIANCE—The annual report under paragraph (1) shall include an assessment of compliance by registrants with the requirements of section 4(b)(3).

(c) Access to Information—The Comptroller General may, in carrying out this section, request information from and access to any relevant documents from any person registered under paragraph (1) or (2) of section 4(a) and each employee who is listed as a lobbyist under section 4(b)(6) or section 5(b)(2)(C) if the material requested relates to the purposes of this section. The Comptroller General may request such person to submit in writing such information as the Comptroller General may prescribe. The Comptroller General may notify the Congress in writing if a person from whom information has been requested under this subsection refuses to comply with the request within 45 days after the request is made.

[Section 213(b) [HLOGA] Initial Audit and Report—The initial audit under subsection (a) of section 26 of the Lobbying Disclosure Act of 1995 (as added by subsection (a) of this section) shall be made with respect to lobbying registrations and reports filed during the first calendar quarter of 2008,

Changes made by HLOGA: Amendments to The Lobbying Disclosure Act,
the Foreign Agents Registration Act, and the Federal Election Campaign Act

Changes to existing law underlined; replaced language is ~~strike through~~; other new provisions **bold underlined**.

and the initial report under subsection (b) of such section shall be filed, with respect to those registrations and reports, not later than 6 months after the end of that calendar quarter.]

SEC. 214 [HLOGA] SENSE OF CONGRESS.
It is the sense of the Congress that—
(1) the use of a family relationship by a lobbyist who is an immediate family member of a Member of Congress to gain special advantages over other lobbyists is inappropriate; and
(2) the lobbying community should develop proposals for multiple self-regulatory organizations which could—
    (A) provide for the creation of standards for the organizations appropriate to the type of lobbying and individuals to be served;
    (B) provide training for the lobbying community on law, ethics, reporting requirements, and disclosure requirements;
    (C) provide for the development of educational materials for the public on how to responsibly hire a lobbyist or lobby firm;
    (D) provide standards regarding reasonable fees charged to clients;
    (E) provide for the creation of a third-party certification program that includes ethics training; and
    (F) provide for disclosure of requirements to clients regarding fee schedules and conflict of interest rules.

SEC. 215 [HLOGA] EFFECTIVE DATE.
Except as otherwise provided in sections 203, 204, 206, 211, 212, and 213, the amendments made by this title shall apply with respect to registrations under the Lobbying Disclosure Act of 1995 having an effective date of January 1, 2008, or later and with respect to quarterly reports under that Act covering calendar quarters beginning on or after January 1, 2008.

Changes made by HLOGA: Amendments to The Lobbying Disclosure Act,
the Foreign Agents Registration Act, and the Federal Election Campaign Act

Changes to existing law underlined; replaced language is ~~strike through~~; other new provisions **bold underlined**.

Amendment to the FARA

Underlined sections indicate additions pursuant to HLOGA

FARA sec. 2 (22 U.S.C. § 612)—Registration statement

(a) Filing; contents. No person shall act as an agent of a foreign principal unless he has
filed with the Attorney General a true and complete registration statement and supplements
thereto as required by subsections (a) and (b)of this section or unless he is exempt from
registration under the provisions of this subchapter. Except as hereinafter provided, every
person who becomes an agent of a foreign principal shall, within ten days thereafter, file
with the Attorney General, in duplicate, a registration statement, under oath on a form
prescribed by the Attorney General. The obligation of an agent of a foreign principal to file
a registration statement shall, after the tenth day of his becoming such agent, continue from
day to day, and termination of such status shall not relieve such agent from his obligation
to file a registration statement for the period during which he was an agent of a foreign
principal. The registration statement shall include the following, which shall be regarded
as material for the purposes of this subchapter:

(1) Registrant's name, principal business address, and all other business addresses
in the United States or elsewhere, and all residence addresses, if any;

(2) Status of the registrant; if an individual, nationality; if a partnership, name,
residence addresses, and nationality of each partner and a true and complete copy of
its articles of copartnership; if an association, corporation, organization, or any other
combination of individuals, the name, residence addresses, and nationality of each
director and officer and of each person performing the functions of a director
or officer and a true and complete copy of its charter, articles of incorporation,
association, constitution, and bylaws, and amendments thereto; a copy of every other
instrument or document and a statement of the terms and conditions of every oral
agreement relating to its organization, powers, and purposes; and a statement of its
ownership and control;

(3) A comprehensive statement of the nature of registrant's business; a complete list
of registrant's employees and a statement of the nature of the work of each; the name
and address of every foreign principal for whom the registrant is acting, assuming or
purporting to act or has agreed to act; the character of the business or other activities
of every such foreign principal, and, if any such foreign principal be other than a
natural person, a statement of the ownership and control of each; and the extent, if
any, to which each such foreign principal is supervised, directed, owned, controlled,
financed, or subsidized, in whole or in part, by any government of a foreign country
or foreign political party, or by any other foreign principal;

(4) Copies of each written agreement and the terms and conditions of each oral
agreement, including all modifications of such agreements, or, where no contract

Changes made by HLOGA: Amendments to The Lobbying Disclosure Act,
the Foreign Agents Registration Act, and the Federal Election Campaign Act

Changes to existing law underlined; replaced language is ~~strike through~~; other new provisions **bold underlined**.

exists, a full statement of all the circumstances, by reason of which the registrant is an agent of a foreign principal; a comprehensive statement of the nature and method of performance of each such contract, and of the existing and proposed activity or activities engaged in or to be engaged in by the registrant as agent of a foreign principal for each such foreign principal, including a detailed statement of any such activity which is a political activity;

(5) The nature and amount of contributions, income, money, or thing of value, if any, that the registrant has received within the preceding sixty days from each such foreign principal, either as compensation or for disbursement or otherwise, and the form and time of each such payment and from whom received;

(6) A detailed statement of every activity which the registrant is performing or is assuming or purporting or has agreed to perform for himself or any other person other than a foreign principal and which requires his registration hereunder;

(7) The name, business, and residence addresses, and if an individual, the nationality, of any person other than a foreign principal for whom the registrant is acting, assuming or purporting to act or has agreed to act under such circumstances as require his registration hereunder; the extent to which each such person is supervised, directed, owned, controlled, financed, or subsidized, in whole or in part, by any government of a foreign country or foreign political party or by any other foreign principal; and the nature and amount of contributions, income, money, or thing of value, if any, that the registrant has received during the preceding sixty days from each such person in connection with any of the activities referred to in clause (6) of this subsection, either as compensation or for disbursement or otherwise, and the form and time of each such payment and from whom received;

(8) A detailed statement of the money and other things of value spent or disposed of by the registrant during the preceding sixty days in furtherance of or in connection with activities which require his registration hereunder and which have been undertaken by him either as an agent of a foreign principal or for himself or any other person or in connection with any activities relating to his becoming an agent of such principal, and a detailed statement of any contributions of money or other things of value made by him during the preceding sixty days (other than contributions the making of which is prohibited under the terms of section 613 of title 18, United States Code) in connection with an election to any political office or in connection with any primary election, convention, or caucus held to select candidates for any political office;

(9) Copies of each written agreement and the terms and conditions of each oral agreement, including all modifications of such agreements, or, where no contract exists, a full statement of all the circumstances, by reason of which the registrant is performing or assuming or purporting or has agreed to perform for himself or for a foreign principal or for any person other than a foreign principal any activities which require his registration hereunder;

Changes made by HLOGA: Amendments to The Lobbying Disclosure Act,
the Foreign Agents Registration Act, and the Federal Election Campaign Act

Changes to existing law underlined; replaced language is ~~strike through~~; other new provisions **bold underlined**.

(10) Such other statements, information, or documents pertinent to the purposes of this Act as the Attorney General, having due regard for the national security and the public interest, may from time to time require;

(11) Such further statements and such further copies of documents as are necessary to make the statements made in the registration statement and supplements thereto, and the copies of documents furnished therewith, not misleading.

(b) Supplements; filing period. Every agent of a foreign principal who has filed a registration statement required by subsection (a) of this section shall, within thirty days after the expiration of each period of six months succeeding such filing, file with the Attorney General a supplement thereto, under oath, on a form prescribed by the Attorney General, which shall set forth with respect to such preceding six months' period such facts as the Attorney General, having due regard for the national security and the public interest, may deem necessary to make the information required under this section accurate, complete, and current with respect to such period. In connection with the information furnished under clauses (3), (4), (6), and (9) of subsection (a) of this section, the registrant shall give notice to the Attorney General of any changes therein within ten days after such changes occur. If the Attorney General, having due regard for the national security and the public interest, determines that it is necessary to carry out the purposes of this Act, he may, in any particular case, require supplements to the registration statement to be filed at more frequent intervals in respect to all or particular items of information to be furnished.

(c) Execution of statement under oath. The registration statement and supplement thereto shall be executed under oath as follows: If the registrant is an individual, by him; if the registrant is a partnership, by the majority of the members thereof; if the registrant is a person other than an individual or a partnership, by a majority of the officers thereof or persons performing the functions of officers or by a majority of the board of directors thereof or persons performing the functions of directors, if any.

(d) Filing of statement not deemed full compliance nor as preclusion from prosecution. The fact that a registration statement or supplement thereto has been filed shall not necessarily be deemed a full compliance with this Act and the regulations thereunder on the part of the registrant; nor shall it indicate that the Attorney General has in any way passed upon the merits of such registration statement or supplement thereto; nor shall it preclude prosecution, as provided for in this Act, for willful failure to file a registration statement or supplement thereto when due or for a willful false statement of a material fact therein or the willful omission of a material fact required to be stated therein or the willful omission of a material fact or copy of a material document necessary to make the statements made in a registration statement and supplements thereto, and the copies of documents furnished therewith, not misleading.

Changes made by HLOGA: Amendments to The Lobbying Disclosure Act,
the Foreign Agents Registration Act, and the Federal Election Campaign Act

Changes to existing law underlined; replaced language is ~~strike through~~; other new provisions **bold underlined**.

(e) Incorporation of previous statement by reference. If any agent of a foreign principal, required to register under the provisions of this Act, has previously thereto registered with the Attorney General under the provisions of the Act of October 17, 1940 (54 Stat. 1201), the Attorney General, in order to eliminate inappropriate duplication, may permit the incorporation by reference in the registration statement or supplements thereto filed hereunder of any information or documents previously filed by such agent of a foreign principal under the provisions of the Act of October 17, 1940 (54 Stat. 1201).

(f) Exemption by Attorney General. The Attorney General may, by regulation, provide for the exemption—

(1) from registration, or from the requirement of furnishing any of the information required by this section, of any person who is listed as a partner, officer, director, or employee in the registration statement filed by an agent of a foreign principal under this Act, and

(2) from the requirement of furnishing any of the information required by this section of any agent of a foreign principal, where by reason of the nature of the functions or activities of such person the Attorney General, having due regard for the national security and the public interest, determines that such registration, or the furnishing of such information, as the case may be, is not necessary to carry out the purposes of this Act.

(g) Electronic filing of registration statements and supplements *[Caution: This subsection takes effect on the 90th day after enactment, as provided by § 212(c) of such Act Sept. 15, 2007, P.L. 110-81, which appears as a note to this section.].* A registration statement or supplement required to be filed under this section shall be filed in electronic form, in addition to any other form that may be required by the Attorney General.

FARA sec. 6 (22 U.S.C. § 616)—Public examination of official records; transmittal of records and information

(a) Permanent copy of statement; inspection; withdrawal. The Attorney General shall retain in permanent form one copy of all registration statements furnished under this Act, and the same shall be public records and open to public examination and inspection at such reasonable hours, under such regulations, as the Attorney General may prescribe, and copies of the same shall be furnished to every applicant at such reasonable fee as the Attorney General may prescribe. The Attorney General may withdraw from public examination the registration statement and other statements of any agent of a foreign principal whose activities have ceased to be of a character which requires registration under the provisions of this Act.

Changes made by HLOGA: Amendments to The Lobbying Disclosure Act,
the Foreign Agents Registration Act, and the Federal Election Campaign Act

Changes to existing law underlined; replaced language is ~~strike through~~; other new provisions **bold underlined**.

(**b**) Secretary of State. The Attorney General shall, promptly upon receipt, transmit one copy of every registration statement filed hereunder and one copy of every amendment or supplement thereto filed hereunder, to the Secretary of State for such comment and use as the Secretary of State may determine to be appropriate from the point of view of the foreign relations of the United States. Failure of the Attorney General so to transmit such copy shall not be a bar to prosecution under this Act.

(**c**) Executive departments and agencies; congressional committees. The Attorney General is authorized to furnish to departments and agencies in the executive branch and committees of the Congress such information obtained by him in the administration of this Act, including the names of registrants under this Act, copies of registration statements, or parts thereof, or other documents or information filed under this Act, as may be appropriate in the light of the purposes of this Act.

(**d**) Public database of registration statements and updates *[Caution: This subsection takes effect on the 90th day after enactment, as provided by § 212(c) of such Act Sept. 14, 2007, P.L. 110-81, which appears as 22 USCS § 612 note.]*.

   (**1**) In general. The Attorney General shall maintain, and make available to the public over the Internet, without a fee or other access charge, in a searchable, sortable, and downloadable manner, to the extent technically practicable, an electronic database that—
      (**A**) includes the information contained in registration statements and updates filed under this Act; and
      (**B**) is searchable and sortable, at a minimum, by each of the categories of information described in section 2(a) [22 USCS § 612(a)].
   (**2**) Accountability. The Attorney General shall make each registration statement and update filed in electronic form pursuant to section 2(g) [22 USCS § 612(g)] available for public inspection over the Internet as soon as technically practicable after the registration statement or update is filed.

[Effective Date—The amendments made by this section shall take effect on the 90th day after the date of the enactment of this Act.]

Changes made by HLOGA: Amendments to The Lobbying Disclosure Act,
the Foreign Agents Registration Act, and the Federal Election Campaign Act

Changes to existing law underlined; replaced language is ~~strike-through~~; other new provisions **bold underlined**.

Amendment to the Federal Election Campaign Act

Underlined sections indicate amendments pursuant to HLOGA sec. 204

FECA sec. 304 (2 U.S.C. 434)

(a) Receipts and disbursements by treasurers of political committees; filing requirements

(1) Each treasurer of a political committee shall file reports of receipts and disbursements in accordance with the provisions of this subsection. The treasurer shall sign each such report.

(2) If the political committee is the principal campaign committee of a candidate for the House of Representatives or for the Senate—

(A) in any calendar year during which there is [1] regularly scheduled election for which such candidate is seeking election, or nomination for election, the treasurer shall file the following reports:

(i) a pre-election report, which shall be filed no later than the 12th day before (or posted by any of the following: registered mail, certified mail, priority mail having a delivery confirmation, or express mail having a delivery confirmation, or delivered to an overnight delivery service with an on-line tracking system, if posted or delivered no later than the 15th day before) any election in which such candidate is seeking election, or nomination for election, and which shall be complete as of the 20th day before such election;

(ii) a post-general election report, which shall be filed no later than the 30th day after any general election in which such candidate has sought election, and which shall be complete as of the 20th day after such general election; and

(iii) additional quarterly reports, which shall be filed no later than the 15th day after the last day of each calendar quarter, and which shall be complete as of the last day of each calendar quarter: except that the report for the quarter ending December 31 shall be filed no later than January 31 of the following calendar year; and

(B) in any other calendar year the treasurer shall file quarterly reports, which shall be filed not later than the 15th day after the last day of each calendar quarter, and which shall be complete as of the last day of each calendar quarter, except that the report for the quarter ending December 31 shall be filed not later than January 31 of the following calendar year.

(3) If the committee is the principal campaign committee of a candidate for the office of President—

(A) in any calendar year during which a general election is held to fill such office—

(i) the treasurer shall file monthly reports if such committee has on January 1 of such year, received contributions aggregating $100,000 or made expenditures

Changes made by HLOGA: Amendments to The Lobbying Disclosure Act,
the Foreign Agents Registration Act, and the Federal Election Campaign Act
Changes to existing law underlined; replaced language is ~~strike through~~; other new provisions **bold underlined**.

aggregating $100,000 or anticipates receiving contributions aggregating $100,000 or more or making expenditures aggregating $100,000 or more during such year: such monthly reports shall be filed no later than the 20th day after the last day of each month and shall be complete as of the last day of the month, except that, in lieu of filing the report otherwise due in November and December, a pre-general election report shall be filed in accordance with paragraph (2)(A)(i), a post-general election report shall be filed in accordance with paragraph (2)(A)(ii), and a year end report shall be filed no later than January 31 of the following calendar year;

(ii) the treasurer of the other principal campaign committees of a candidate for the office of President shall file a pre-election report or reports in accordance with paragraph (2)(A)(i), a post-general election report in accordance with paragraph (2)(A)(ii), and quarterly reports in accordance with paragraph (2)(A)(iii); and

(iii) if at any time during the election year a committee filing under paragraph (3)(A)(ii) receives contributions in excess of $100,000 or makes expenditures in excess of $100,000, the treasurer shall begin filing monthly reports under paragraph (3)(A)(i) at the next reporting period; and

(B) in any other calendar year, the treasurer shall file either—

(i) monthly reports, which shall be filed no later than the 20th day after the last day of each month and shall be complete as of the last day of the month; or

(ii) quarterly reports, which shall be filed no later than the 15th day after the last day of each calendar quarter and which shall be complete as of the last day of each calendar quarter.

(4) All political committees other than authorized committees of a candidate shall file either—

(A)

(i) quarterly reports, in a calendar year in which a regularly scheduled general election is held, which shall be filed no later than the 15th day after the last day of each calendar quarter: except that the report for the quarter ending on December 31 of such calendar year shall be filed no later than January 31 of the following calendar year;

(ii) a pre-election report, which shall be filed no later than the 12th day before (or posted by any of the following: registered mail, certified mail, priority mail having a delivery confirmation, or express mail having a delivery confirmation, or delivered to an overnight delivery service with an on-line tracking system, if posted or delivered no later than the 15th day before) any election in which the committee makes a contribution to or expenditure on behalf of a candidate in such election, and which shall be complete as of the 20th day before the election;

(iii) a post-general election report, which shall be filed no later than the 30th day after the general election and which shall be complete as of the 20th day after such general election; and

Changes made by HLOGA: Amendments to The Lobbying Disclosure Act,
the Foreign Agents Registration Act, and the Federal Election Campaign Act

Changes to existing law underlined; replaced language is ~~strike-through~~; other new provisions **bold underlined**.

(iv) in any other calendar year, a report covering the period beginning January 1 and ending June 30, which shall be filed no later than July 31 and a report covering the period beginning July 1 and ending December 31, which shall be filed no later than January 31 of the following calendar year; or

(B) monthly reports in all calendar years which shall be filed no later than the 20th day after the last day of the month and shall be complete as of the last day of the month, except that, in lieu of filing the reports otherwise due in November and December of any year in which a regularly scheduled general election is held, a pre-general election report shall be filed in accordance with paragraph (2)(A)(i), a post-general election report shall be filed in accordance with paragraph (2)(A)(ii), and a year end report shall be filed no later than January 31 of the following calendar year. Notwithstanding the preceding sentence, a national committee of a political party shall file the reports required under subparagraph (B).

(5) If a designation, report, or statement filed pursuant to this Act (other than under paragraph (2)(A)(i) or (4)(A)(ii) or subsection (g)(1) of this section) is sent by registered mail, certified mail, priority mail having a delivery confirmation, or express mail having a delivery confirmation, the United States postmark shall be considered the date of filing the designation, report or statement. If a designation, report or statement filed pursuant to this Act (other than under paragraph (2)(A)(i) or (4)(A)(ii), or subsection (g)(1) of this section) is sent by an overnight delivery service with an on-line tracking system, the date on the proof of delivery to the delivery service shall be considered the date of filing of the designation, report, or statement.

(6)

(A) The principal campaign committee of a candidate shall notify the Secretary or the Commission, and the Secretary of State, as appropriate, in writing, of any contribution of $1,000 or more received by any authorized committee of such candidate after the 20th day, but more than 48 hours before, any election. This notification shall be made within 48 hours after the receipt of such contribution and shall include the name of the candidate and the office sought by the candidate, the identification of the contributor, and the date of receipt and amount of the contribution.

(B) Notification of expenditure from personal funds.—

(i) Definition of expenditure from personal funds.—In this subparagraph, the term "expenditure from personal funds" means—

(I) an expenditure made by a candidate using personal funds; and

(II) a contribution or loan made by a candidate using personal funds or a loan secured using such funds to the candidate's authorized committee.

(ii) Declaration of intent.—Not later than the date that is 15 days after the date on which an individual becomes a candidate for the office of Senator, the candidate shall file a declaration stating the total amount of expenditures from personal funds that the candidate intends to make, or to obligate to make, with

Changes made by HLOGA: Amendments to The Lobbying Disclosure Act,
the Foreign Agents Registration Act, and the Federal Election Campaign Act

Changes to existing law underlined; replaced language is ~~strike-through~~; other new provisions **bold underlined**.

respect to the election that will exceed the State-by-State competitive and fair campaign formula with—

(I) the Commission; and

(II) each candidate in the same election.

(iii) Initial notification.—Not later than 24 hours after a candidate described in clause (ii) makes or obligates to make an aggregate amount of expenditures from personal funds in excess of 2 times the threshold amount in connection with any election, the candidate shall file a notification with—

(I) the Commission; and

(II) each candidate in the same election.

(iv) Additional notification.—After a candidate files an initial notification under clause (iii), the candidate shall file an additional notification each time expenditures from personal funds are made or obligated to be made in an aggregate amount that exceed [2] $10,000 with—

(I) the Commission; and

(II) each candidate in the same election.

Such notification shall be filed not later than 24 hours after the expenditure is made.

(v) Contents.—A notification under clause (iii) or (iv) shall include—

(I) the name of the candidate and the office sought by the candidate;

(II) the date and amount of each expenditure; and

(III) the total amount of expenditures from personal funds that the candidate has made, or obligated to make, with respect to an election as of the date of the expenditure that is the subject of the notification.

(C) Notification of disposal of excess contributions.—In the next regularly scheduled report after the date of the election for which a candidate seeks nomination for election to, or election to, Federal office, the candidate or the candidate's authorized committee shall submit to the Commission a report indicating the source and amount of any excess contributions (as determined under paragraph (1) of section 441a (i) of this title) and the manner in which the candidate or the candidate's authorized committee used such funds.

(D) Enforcement.—For provisions providing for the enforcement of the reporting requirements under this paragraph, see section 437g of this title.

(E) The notification required under this paragraph shall be in addition to all other reporting requirements under this Act.

(7) The reports required to be filed by this subsection shall be cumulative during the calendar year to which they relate, but where there has been no change in an item reported in a previous report during such year, only the amount need be carried forward.

(8) The requirement for a political committee to file a quarterly report under paragraph (2)(A)(iii) or paragraph (4)(A)(i) shall be waived if such committee is required to file a

Changes made by HLOGA: Amendments to The Lobbying Disclosure Act,
the Foreign Agents Registration Act, and the Federal Election Campaign Act

Changes to existing law underlined; replaced language is ~~strike-through~~; other new provisions **bold underlined**.

pre-election report under paragraph (2)(A)(i), or paragraph (4)(A)(ii) during the period beginning on the 5th day after the close of the calendar quarter and ending on the 15th day after the close of the calendar quarter.

(9) The Commission shall set filing dates for reports to be filed by principal campaign committees of candidates seeking election, or nomination for election, in special elections and political committees filing under paragraph (4)(A) which make contributions to or expenditures on behalf of a candidate or candidates in special elections. The Commission shall require no more than one pre-election report for each election and one post-election report for the election which fills the vacancy. The Commission may waive any reporting obligation of committees required to file for special elections if any report required by paragraph (2) or (4) is required to be filed within 10 days of a report required under this subsection. The Commission shall establish the reporting dates within 5 days of the setting of such election and shall publish such dates and notify the principal campaign committees of all candidates in such election of the reporting dates.

(10) The treasurer of a committee supporting a candidate for the office of Vice President (other than the nominee of a political party) shall file reports in accordance with paragraph (3).

(11)

    (A) The Commission shall promulgate a regulation under which a person required to file a designation, statement, or report under this Act—

        (i) is required to maintain and file a designation, statement, or report for any calendar year in electronic form accessible by computers if the person has, or has reason to expect to have, aggregate contributions or expenditures in excess of a threshold amount determined by the Commission; and

        (ii) may maintain and file a designation, statement, or report in electronic form or an alternative form if not required to do so under the regulation promulgated under clause (i).

    (B) The Commission shall make a designation, statement, report, or notification that is filed with the Commission under this Act available for inspection by the public in the offices of the Commission and accessible to the public on the Internet not later than 48 hours (or not later than 24 hours in the case of a designation, statement, report, or notification filed electronically) after receipt by the Commission.

    (C) In promulgating a regulation under this paragraph, the Commission shall provide methods (other than requiring a signature on the document being filed) for verifying designations, statements, and reports covered by the regulation. Any document verified under any of the methods shall be treated for all purposes (including penalties for perjury) in the same manner as a document verified by signature.

    (D) As used in this paragraph, the term "report" means, with respect to the Commission, a report, designation, or statement required by this Act to be filed with the Commission.

Changes made by HLOGA: Amendments to The Lobbying Disclosure Act,
the Foreign Agents Registration Act, and the Federal Election Campaign Act

Changes to existing law underlined; replaced language is ~~strike-through~~; other new provisions **bold underlined**.

(12) Software for filing of reports.—
    (A) In general.—The Commission shall—
        (i) promulgate standards to be used by vendors to develop software that—
            (I) permits candidates to easily record information concerning receipts and disbursements required to be reported under this Act at the time of the receipt or disbursement;
            (II) allows the information recorded under subclause (I) to be transmitted immediately to the Commission; and
            (III) allows the Commission to post the information on the Internet immediately upon receipt; and
        (ii) make a copy of software that meets the standards promulgated under clause (i) available to each person required to file a designation, statement, or report in electronic form under this Act.
    (B) Additional information.—To the extent feasible, the Commission shall require vendors to include in the software developed under the standards under subparagraph (A) the ability for any person to file any designation, statement, or report required under this Act in electronic form.
    (C) Required use.—Notwithstanding any provision of this Act relating to times for filing reports, each candidate for Federal office (or that candidate's authorized committee) shall use software that meets the standards promulgated under this paragraph once such software is made available to such candidate.
    (D) Required posting.—The Commission shall, as soon as practicable, post on the Internet any information received under this paragraph.

(b) Contents of reports
Each report under this section shall disclose—
(1) the amount of cash on hand at the beginning of the reporting period;
(2) for the reporting period and the calendar year (or election cycle, in the case of an authorized committee of a candidate for Federal office), the total amount of all receipts, and the total amount of all receipts in the following categories:
    (A) contributions from persons other than political committees;
    (B) for an authorized committee, contributions from the candidate;
    (C) contributions from political party committees;
    (D) contributions from other political committees;
    (E) for an authorized committee, transfers from other authorized committees of the same candidate;
    (F) transfers from affiliated committees and, where the reporting committee is a political party committee, transfers from other political party committees, regardless of whether such committees are affiliated;
    (G) for an authorized committee, loans made by or guaranteed by the candidate;

Changes made by HLOGA: Amendments to The Lobbying Disclosure Act,
the Foreign Agents Registration Act, and the Federal Election Campaign Act
Changes to existing law underlined; replaced language is strike-through; other new provisions **bold underlined**.

(H) all other loans;

(I) rebates, refunds, and other offsets to operating expenditures;

(J) dividends, interest, and other forms of receipts; and

(K) for an authorized committee of a candidate for the office of President, Federal funds received under chapter 95 and chapter 96 of title 26;

(3) the identification of each—

(A) person (other than a political committee) who makes a contribution to the reporting committee during the reporting period, whose contribution or contributions have an aggregate amount or value in excess of $200 within the calendar year (or election cycle, in the case of an authorized committee of a candidate for Federal office), or in any lesser amount if the reporting committee should so elect, together with the date and amount of any such contribution;

(B) political committee which makes a contribution to the reporting committee during the reporting period, together with the date and amount of any such contribution;

(C) authorized committee which makes a transfer to the reporting committee;

(D) affiliated committee which makes a transfer to the reporting committee during the reporting period and, where the reporting committee is a political party committee, each transfer of funds to the reporting committee from another political party committee, regardless of whether such committees are affiliated, together with the date and amount of such transfer;

(E) person who makes a loan to the reporting committee during the reporting period, together with the identification of any endorser or guarantor of such loan, and the date and amount or value of such loan;

(F) person who provides a rebate, refund, or other offset to operating expenditures to the reporting committee in an aggregate amount or value in excess of $200 within the calendar year (or election cycle, in the case of an authorized committee of a candidate for Federal office), together with the date and amount of such receipt; and

(G) person who provides any dividend, interest, or other receipt to the reporting committee in an aggregate value or amount in excess of $200 within the calendar year (or election cycle, in the case of an authorized committee of a candidate for Federal office), together with the date and amount of any such receipt;

(4) for the reporting period and the calendar year (or election cycle, in the case of an authorized committee of a candidate for Federal office), the total amount of all disbursements, and all disbursements in the following categories:

(A) expenditures made to meet candidate or committee operating expenses;

(B) for authorized committees, transfers to other committees authorized by the same candidate;

(C) transfers to affiliated committees and, where the reporting committee is a political party committee, transfers to other political party committees, regardless of whether they are affiliated;

Changes made by HLOGA: Amendments to The Lobbying Disclosure Act,
the Foreign Agents Registration Act, and the Federal Election Campaign Act

Changes to existing law underlined; replaced language is ~~strike-through~~; other new provisions **bold underlined**.

(D) for an authorized committee, repayment of loans made by or guaranteed by the candidate;

(E) repayment of all other loans;

(F) contribution refunds and other offsets to contributions;

(G) for an authorized committee, any other disbursements;

(H) for any political committee other than an authorized committee—

    (i) contributions made to other political committees;

    (ii) loans made by the reporting committees;

    (iii) independent expenditures;

    (iv) expenditures made under section 441a (d) of this title; and

    (v) any other disbursements; and

        (I) for an authorized committee of a candidate for the office of President, disbursements not subject to the limitation of section 441a (b) of this title;

(5) the name and address of each—

(A) person to whom an expenditure in an aggregate amount or value in excess of $200 within the calendar year is made by the reporting committee to meet a candidate or committee operating expense, together with the date, amount, and purpose of such operating expenditure;

(B) authorized committee to which a transfer is made by the reporting committee;

(C) affiliated committee to which a transfer is made by the reporting committee during the reporting period and, where the reporting committee is a political party committee, each transfer of funds by the reporting committee to another political party committee, regardless of whether such committees are affiliated, together with the date and amount of such transfers;

(D) person who receives a loan repayment from the reporting committee during the reporting period, together with the date and amount of such loan repayment; and

(E) person who receives a contribution refund or other offset to contributions from the reporting committee where such contribution was reported under paragraph (3)(A) of this subsection, together with the date and amount of such disbursement;

(6)

(A) for an authorized committee, the name and address of each person who has received any disbursement not disclosed under paragraph (5) in an aggregate amount or value in excess of $200 within the calendar year (or election cycle, in the case of an authorized committee of a candidate for Federal office), together with the date and amount of any such disbursement;

(B) for any other political committee, the name and address of each—

    (i) political committee which has received a contribution from the reporting committee during the reporting period, together with the date and amount of any such contribution;

Changes made by HLOGA: Amendments to The Lobbying Disclosure Act,
the Foreign Agents Registration Act, and the Federal Election Campaign Act

Changes to existing law underlined; replaced language is ~~strike through~~; other new provisions **bold underlined**.

(ii) person who has received a loan from the reporting committee during the reporting period, together with the date and amount of such loan;

(iii) person who receives any disbursement during the reporting period in an aggregate amount or value in excess of $200 within the calendar year (or election cycle, in the case of an authorized committee of a candidate for Federal office), in connection with an independent expenditure by the reporting committee, together with the date, amount, and purpose of any such independent expenditure and a statement which indicates whether such independent expenditure is in support of, or in opposition to, a candidate, as well as the name and office sought by such candidate, and a certification, under penalty of perjury, whether such independent expenditure is made in cooperation, consultation, or concert, with, or at the request or suggestion of, any candidate or any authorized committee or agent of such committee;

(iv) person who receives any expenditure from the reporting committee during the reporting period in connection with an expenditure under section 441a (d) of this title, together with the date, amount, and purpose of any such expenditure as well as the name of, and office sought by, the candidate on whose behalf the expenditure is made; and

(v) person who has received any disbursement not otherwise disclosed in this paragraph or paragraph (5) in an aggregate amount or value in excess of $200 within the calendar year (or election cycle, in the case of an authorized committee of a candidate for Federal office), from the reporting committee within the reporting period, together with the date, amount, and purpose of any such disbursement;

(7) the total sum of all contributions to such political committee, together with the total contributions less offsets to contributions and the total sum of all operating expenditures made by such political committee, together with total operating expenditures less offsets to operating expenditures, for both the reporting period and the calendar year (or election cycle, in the case of an authorized committee of a candidate for Federal office); and

(8) the amount and nature of outstanding debts and obligations owed by or to such political committee; and where such debts and obligations are settled for less than their reported amount or value, a statement as to the circumstances and conditions under which such debts or obligations were extinguished and the consideration therefor.

(c) Statements by other than political committees; filing; contents; indices of expenditures

(1) Every person (other than a political committee) who makes independent expenditures in an aggregate amount or value in excess of $250 during a calendar year shall file a statement containing the information required under subsection (b)(3)(A) of this section for all contributions received by such person.

Changes made by HLOGA: Amendments to The Lobbying Disclosure Act,
the Foreign Agents Registration Act, and the Federal Election Campaign Act

Changes to existing law underlined; replaced language is ~~strike through~~; other new provisions **bold underlined**.

(**2**) Statements required to be filed by this subsection shall be filed in accordance with subsection (a)(2) of this section, and shall include—

(**A**) the information required by subsection (b)(6)(B)(iii) of this section, indicating whether the independent expenditure is in support of, or in opposition to, the candidate involved;

(**B**) under penalty of perjury, a certification whether or not such independent expenditure is made in cooperation, consultation, or concert, with, or at the request or suggestion of, any candidate or any authorized committee or agent of such candidate; and

(**C**) the identification of each person who made a contribution in excess of $200 to the person filing such statement which was made for the purpose of furthering an independent expenditure.

(**3**) The Commission shall be responsible for expeditiously preparing indices which set forth, on a candidate-by-candidate basis, all independent expenditures separately, including those reported under subsection (b)(6)(B)(iii) of this section, made by or for each candidate, as reported under this subsection, and for periodically publishing such indices on a timely pre-election basis.

(**d**) **Filing by facsimile device or electronic mail**

(**1**) Any person who is required to file a statement under subsection (c) or (g) of this section, except statements required to be filed electronically pursuant to subsection (a)(11)(A)(i) of this section may file the statement by facsimile device or electronic mail, in accordance with such regulations as the Commission may promulgate.

(**2**) The Commission shall make a document which is filed electronically with the Commission pursuant to this paragraph accessible to the public on the Internet not later than 24 hours after the document is received by the Commission.

(**3**) In promulgating a regulation under this paragraph, the Commission shall provide methods (other than requiring a signature on the document being filed) for verifying the documents covered by the regulation. Any document verified under any of the methods shall be treated for all purposes (including penalties for perjury) in the same manner as a document verified by signature.

(**e**) **Political committees**

(**1**) **National and congressional political committees**

The national committee of a political party, any national congressional campaign committee of a political party, and any subordinate committee of either, shall report all receipts and disbursements during the reporting period.

(**2**) **Other political committees to which section 441i applies**

(**A**) **In general**

In addition to any other reporting requirements applicable under this Act, a political committee (not described in paragraph (1)) to which section 441i (b)(1) of this title

Changes made by HLOGA: Amendments to The Lobbying Disclosure Act,
the Foreign Agents Registration Act, and the Federal Election Campaign Act

Changes to existing law underlined; replaced language is ~~strike through~~; other new provisions **bold underlined**.

applies shall report all receipts and disbursements made for activities described in section 431 (20)(A) of this title, unless the aggregate amount of such receipts and disbursements during the calendar year is less than $5,000.

(B) Specific disclosure by State and local parties of certain non-Federal amounts permitted to be spent on Federal election activity

Each report by a political committee under subparagraph (A) of receipts and disbursements made for activities described in section 431 (20)(A) of this title shall include a disclosure of all receipts and disbursements described in section 441i (b)(2)(A) and (B) of this title.

(3) Itemization

If a political committee has receipts or disbursements to which this subsection applies from or to any person aggregating in excess of $200 for any calendar year, the political committee shall separately itemize its reporting for such person in the same manner as required in paragraphs (3)(A), (5), and (6) of subsection (b) of this section.

(4) Reporting periods

Reports required to be filed under this subsection shall be filed for the same time periods required for political committees under subsection (a)(4)(B) of this section.

(f) Disclosure of electioneering communications

(1) Statement required

Every person who makes a disbursement for the direct costs of producing and airing electioneering communications in an aggregate amount in excess of $10,000 during any calendar year shall, within 24 hours of each disclosure date, file with the Commission a statement containing the information described in paragraph (2).

(2) Contents of statement

Each statement required to be filed under this subsection shall be made under penalty of perjury and shall contain the following information:

(A) The identification of the person making the disbursement, of any person sharing or exercising direction or control over the activities of such person, and of the custodian of the books and accounts of the person making the disbursement.

(B) The principal place of business of the person making the disbursement, if not an individual.

(C) The amount of each disbursement of more than $200 during the period covered by the statement and the identification of the person to whom the disbursement was made.

(D) The elections to which the electioneering communications pertain and the names (if known) of the candidates identified or to be identified.

(E) If the disbursements were paid out of a segregated bank account which consists of funds contributed solely by individuals who are United States citizens or nationals or lawfully admitted for permanent residence (as defined in section 1101 (a)(20) of

Changes made by HLOGA: Amendments to The Lobbying Disclosure Act,
the Foreign Agents Registration Act, and the Federal Election Campaign Act

Changes to existing law underlined; replaced language is ~~strike through~~; other new provisions **bold underlined**.

title 8) directly to this account for electioneering communications, the names and addresses of all contributors who contributed an aggregate amount of $1,000 or more to that account during the period beginning on the first day of the preceding calendar year and ending on the disclosure date. Nothing in this subparagraph is to be construed as a prohibition on the use of funds in such a segregated account for a purpose other than electioneering communications.

(F) If the disbursements were paid out of funds not described in subparagraph (E), the names and addresses of all contributors who contributed an aggregate amount of $1,000 or more to the person making the disbursement during the period beginning on the first day of the preceding calendar year and ending on the disclosure date.

(3) Electioneering communication

For purposes of this subsection—

(A) In general

(i) The term "electioneering communication" means any broadcast, cable, or satellite communication which—

(I) refers to a clearly identified candidate for Federal office;

(II) is made within—

(aa) 60 days before a general, special, or runoff election for the office sought by the candidate; or

(bb) 30 days before a primary or preference election, or a convention or caucus of a political party that has authority to nominate a candidate, for the office sought by the candidate; and

(III) in the case of a communication which refers to a candidate for an office other than President or Vice President, is targeted to the relevant electorate.

(ii) If clause (i) is held to be constitutionally insufficient by final judicial decision to support the regulation provided herein, then the term "electioneering communication" means any broadcast, cable, or satellite communication which promotes or supports a candidate for that office, or attacks or opposes a candidate for that office (regardless of whether the communication expressly advocates a vote for or against a candidate) and which also is suggestive of no plausible meaning other than an exhortation to vote for or against a specific candidate. Nothing in this subparagraph shall be construed to affect the interpretation or application of section 100.22(b) of title 11, Code of Federal Regulations.

(B) Exceptions

The term "electioneering communication" does not include—

(i) a communication appearing in a news story, commentary, or editorial distributed through the facilities of any broadcasting station, unless such facilities are owned or controlled by any political party, political committee, or candidate;

(ii) a communication which constitutes an expenditure or an independent expenditure under this Act;

Changes made by HLOGA: Amendments to The Lobbying Disclosure Act,
the Foreign Agents Registration Act, and the Federal Election Campaign Act
Changes to existing law underlined; replaced language is ~~strike through~~; other new provisions **bold underlined**.

> **(iii)** a communication which constitutes a candidate debate or forum conducted pursuant to regulations adopted by the Commission, or which solely promotes such a debate or forum and is made by or on behalf of the person sponsoring the debate or forum; or
>
> **(iv)** any other communication exempted under such regulations as the Commission may promulgate (consistent with the requirements of this paragraph) to ensure the appropriate implementation of this paragraph, except that under any such regulation a communication may not be exempted if it meets the requirements of this paragraph and is described in section 431 (20)(A)(iii) of this title.

(C) Targeting to relevant electorate

For purposes of this paragraph, a communication which refers to a clearly identified candidate for Federal office is "targeted to the relevant electorate" if the communication can be received by 50,000 or more persons—

> **(i)** in the district the candidate seeks to represent, in the case of a candidate for Representative in, or Delegate or Resident Commissioner to, the Congress; or
>
> **(ii)** in the State the candidate seeks to represent, in the case of a candidate for Senator.

(4) Disclosure date

For purposes of this subsection, the term "disclosure date" means—

> **(A)** the first date during any calendar year by which a person has made disbursements for the direct costs of producing or airing electioneering communications aggregating in excess of $10,000; and
>
> **(B)** any other date during such calendar year by which a person has made disbursements for the direct costs of producing or airing electioneering communications aggregating in excess of $10,000 since the most recent disclosure date for such calendar year.

(5) Contracts to disburse

For purposes of this subsection, a person shall be treated as having made a disbursement if the person has executed a contract to make the disbursement.

(6) Coordination with other requirements

Any requirement to report under this subsection shall be in addition to any other reporting requirement under this Act.

(7) Coordination with title 26

Nothing in this subsection may be construed to establish, modify, or otherwise affect the definition of political activities or electioneering activities (including the definition of participating in, intervening in, or influencing or attempting to influence a political campaign on behalf of or in opposition to any candidate for public office) for purposes of title 26.

Changes made by HLOGA: Amendments to The Lobbying Disclosure Act,
the Foreign Agents Registration Act, and the Federal Election Campaign Act

Changes to existing law underlined; replaced language is ~~strike through~~; other new provisions **bold underlined**.

(g) Time for reporting certain expenditures

(1) Expenditures aggregating $1,000

(A) Initial report

A person (including a political committee) that makes or contracts to make independent expenditures aggregating $1,000 or more after the 20th day, but more than 24 hours, before the date of an election shall file a report describing the expenditures within 24 hours.

(B) Additional reports

After a person files a report under subparagraph (A), the person shall file an additional report within 24 hours after each time the person makes or contracts to make independent expenditures aggregating an additional $1,000 with respect to the same election as that to which the initial report relates.

(2) Expenditures aggregating $10,000

(A) Initial report

A person (including a political committee) that makes or contracts to make independent expenditures aggregating $10,000 or more at any time up to and including the 20th day before the date of an election shall file a report describing the expenditures within 48 hours.

(B) Additional reports

After a person files a report under subparagraph (A), the person shall file an additional report within 48 hours after each time the person makes or contracts to make independent expenditures aggregating an additional $10,000 with respect to the same election as that to which the initial report relates.

(3) Place of filing; contents

A report under this subsection—

(A) shall be filed with the Commission; and

(B) shall contain the information required by subsection (b)(6)(B)(iii) of this section, including the name of each candidate whom an expenditure is intended to support or oppose.

(4) Time of filing for expenditures aggregating $1,000

Notwithstanding subsection (a)(5) of this section, the time at which the statement under paragraph (1) is received by the Commission or any other recipient to whom the notification is required to be sent shall be considered the time of filing of the statement with the recipient.

(h) Reports from Inaugural Committees

The Federal Election Commission shall make any report filed by an Inaugural Committee under section 510 of title 36 accessible to the public at the offices of the Commission and on the Internet not later than 48 hours after the report is received by the Commission.

Changes made by HLOGA: Amendments to The Lobbying Disclosure Act,
the Foreign Agents Registration Act, and the Federal Election Campaign Act

Changes to existing law underlined; replaced language is ~~strike through~~; other new provisions **bold underlined**.

(i) Disclosure of Bundled Contributions-

(1) REQUIRED DISCLOSURE—Each committee described in paragraph (6) shall include in the first report required to be filed under this section after each covered period (as defined in paragraph (2)) a separate schedule setting forth the name, address, and employer of each person reasonably known by the committee to be a person described in paragraph (7) who provided 2 or more bundled contributions to the committee in an aggregate amount greater than the applicable threshold (as defined in paragraph (3)) during the covered period, and the aggregate amount of the bundled contributions provided by each such person during the covered period.

(2) COVERED PERIOD—In this subsection, a 'covered period' means, with respect to a committee—

(A) the period beginning January 1 and ending June 30 of each year;

(B) the period beginning July 1 and ending December 31 of each year; and

(C) any reporting period applicable to the committee under this section during which any person described in paragraph (7) provided 2 or more bundled contributions to the committee in an aggregate amount greater than the applicable threshold.

(3) APPLICABLE THRESHOLD—

(A) IN GENERAL—In this subsection, the 'applicable threshold' is $15,000, except that in determining whether the amount of bundled contributions provided to a committee by a person described in paragraph (7) exceeds the applicable threshold, there shall be excluded any contribution made to the committee by the person or the person's spouse.

(B) INDEXING—In any calendar year after 2007, section 315(c)(1)(B) shall apply to the amount applicable under subparagraph (A) in the same manner as such section applies to the limitations established under subsections (a)(1)(A), (a)(1)(B), (a)(3), and (h) of such section, except that for purposes of applying such section to the amount applicable under subparagraph (A), the 'base period' shall be 2006.

(4) PUBLIC AVAILABILITY—The Commission shall ensure that, to the greatest extent practicable—

(A) information required to be disclosed under this subsection is publicly available through the Commission website in a manner that is searchable, sortable, and downloadable; and

(B) the Commission's public database containing information disclosed under this subsection is linked electronically to the websites maintained by the Secretary of the Senate and the Clerk of the House of Representatives containing information filed pursuant to the Lobbying Disclosure Act of 1995.

(5) REGULATIONS—Not later than 6 months after the date of enactment of the Honest Leadership and Open Government Act of 2007, the Commission shall promulgate regulations to implement this subsection. Under such regulations, the Commission—

(A) may, notwithstanding paragraphs (1) and (2), provide for quarterly filing of the

Changes made by HLOGA: Amendments to The Lobbying Disclosure Act,
the Foreign Agents Registration Act, and the Federal Election Campaign Act

Changes to existing law underlined; replaced language is ~~strike through~~; other new provisions **bold underlined**.

schedule described in paragraph (1) by a committee which files reports under this section more frequently than on a quarterly basis;

(B) shall provide guidance to committees with respect to whether a person is reasonably known by a committee to be a person described in paragraph (7), which shall include a requirement that committees consult the websites maintained by the Secretary of the Senate and the Clerk of the House of Representatives containing information filed pursuant to the Lobbying Disclosure Act of 1995;

(C) may not exempt the activity of a person described in paragraph (7) from disclosure under this subsection on the grounds that the person is authorized to engage in fundraising for the committee or any other similar grounds; and

(D) shall provide for the broadest possible disclosure of activities described in this subsection by persons described in paragraph (7) that is consistent with this subsection.

(6) COMMITTEES DESCRIBED—A committee described in this paragraph is an authorized committee of a candidate, a leadership PAC, or a political party committee.

(7) PERSONS DESCRIBED—A person described in this paragraph is any person, who, at the time a contribution is forwarded to a committee as described in paragraph (8)(A)(i) or is received by a committee as described in paragraph (8)(A)(ii), is—

(A) a current registrant under section 4(a) of the Lobbying Disclosure Act of 1995;

(B) an individual who is listed on a current registration filed under section 4(b)(6) of such Act or a current report under section 5(b)(2)(C) of such Act; or

(C) a political committee established or controlled by such a registrant or individual.

(8) DEFINITIONS—For purposes of this subsection, the following definitions apply:

(A) BUNDLED CONTRIBUTION—The term 'bundled contribution' means, with respect to a committee described in paragraph (6) and a person described in paragraph (7), a contribution (subject to the applicable threshold) which is—

(i) forwarded from the contributor or contributors to the committee by the person; or

(ii) received by the committee from a contributor or contributors, but credited by the committee or candidate involved (or, in the case of a leadership PAC, by the individual referred to in subparagraph (B) involved) to the person through records, designations, or other means of recognizing that a certain amount of money has been raised by the person.

(B) LEADERSHIP PAC—The term 'leadership PAC' means, with respect to a candidate for election to Federal office or an individual holding Federal office, a political committee that is directly or indirectly established, financed, maintained or controlled by the candidate or the individual but which is not an authorized committee of the candidate or individual and which is not affiliated with an authorized committee of the candidate or individual, except that such term does not include a political committee of a political party.

Changes made by HLOGA: Amendments to The Lobbying Disclosure Act,
the Foreign Agents Registration Act, and the Federal Election Campaign Act

Changes to existing law underlined; replaced language is ~~strike through~~; other new provisions **bold underlined**.

*[**Section 204(b) Effective Date—The amendment made by subsection (a) shall apply with respect to reports filed under section 304 of the Federal Election Campaign Act after the expiration of the 3-month period which begins on the date that the regulations required to be promulgated by the Federal Election Commission under section 304(i)(5) of such Act (as added by subsection (a)) become final.]**

Index

The index is in letter-by-letter order.
For example, "Congress Plus" follows "Congressional Valet."

O

Oath of office, congressional, 2.36

Obstacles, overcoming, 6.16

Office of Federal Contract Compliance Programs, 11.28

Office of Government Ethics (OGE), 2.3, 2.29–2.33, 2.37

Office of Information and Regulatory Affairs (OIRA), 4.53, 8.50

Office of Management and Budget (OMB), 3.8, 4.53, 8.15, 8.44

Office of Public Records, 2.3, 2.9, 4.52

Office of Special Counsel, 2.29, 2.30, 2.32

Office of the Federal Register, 3.8

Off the record, 10.23

"Off to the Races," 3.9

OGE. *See* Office of Government Ethics

OIRA (Office of Information and Regulatory Affairs), 4.53, 8.50

Old Executive Office Building, Appendix 4

OMB. *See* Office of Management and Budget

OMBWatch, 3.6

Omnibus measures, 4.10

O'Neill, Tip, 3.2, 7.2, 8.2

One-pager, sample, 8.30

Online services, 5.5

Online tours, Capitol and White House, Appendix 3

On the record, 10.23

Open hearings, 3.11

Open Secrets campaign contributions database, 2.3, 3.12

Opposition arguments, 5.15, 8.4

Opposition Research, 5.5, 10.7

Orfalea, Paul, 8.49

Outside/contract lobbyists, 1.15, 1.19 (table), 2.9

Override votes, 4.33

Overstreet, Harry A., 8.2

P

PACs (Political Action Committees), 2.26, 7.16

Paine, Thomas, Ch. 2 (title page)

Paperwork Reduction Act of 1980, 4.53, 4.54

Parking map of Capitol Hill, Appendix 3

Parliamentary procedure, 4.2, 4.26–4.28

Partisan discipline as position driver, 3.18

Partisan politics prohibition for federal employees. *See* Hatch Act of 1939

Partners. *See* Coalitions

Pascal, Blaise, 8.5, 10.56

Paterno, Joe, 5.2, 11.2

Patten, John W., Ch. 6 (title page)

Penalties, 2.8

Pendleton, Ronald K., Ch. 5 (title page)

Personal attacks, 8.2, 8.4

Personal experience as position driver, 3.5, 3.12

Personal qualities of lobbyists, 1.21

Petitioners and colonial agents, 1.6

Pet projects, 4.29

PEW Research Center for the People and the Press, 10.2

Phone calls, 8.24, Appendix 3

Planning strategies, government affairs, 6.2

Plum Book, 3.6

Plurality of interests, 1.4

Pocket veto, 4.33

Political Action Committees (PACs), 2.26, 7.16

Political appointees, turnover rate, 8.54

Political campaigns. *See* Campaign contributions; Campaigns

Politics in America (CQ Press), 3.6, 5.5

Polling resources, 10.7

"Pork," 4.29

Position drivers, Ch. 3
    benefits of study of, 3.3
    caucuses and specialized groups, 3.21
    chart of Seven P's, 3.6

U

Unanimous consent, 4.9, 4.23

Unified agenda, 3.8, 4.53

United States Government Policy and Supporting Positions (Plum Book), 3.6

U.S. Attorneys' Manual, 2.3

U.S. Attorneys' Offices, 2.30

U.S. Capitol Historical Society, 7.13, Appendix 3

U.S. Chamber of Commerce, 3.8

U.S. Conference of Mayors, 9.8

U.S. House of Representatives Committee on Standards of Official Conduct, 2.3

U.S. Senate Select Committee on Ethics, 2.3

USNewswire/PRNewswire, 3.6, 3.9, 10.20

V

Van Horne, Chris, 10.69

Vetoes, 4.7, 4.33

Visitors to D.C., how to assist, Appendix 3

Voice mail, 8.24

vos Savant, Marilyn, 6.16

W

Wachovia Securities, 11.27

Wagner, John, 10.23

Waitley, Denis, 11.17

Warner, Charles Dudley, 9.11

Washington, George, 2.34, 4.5

Washington Post, 10.23

Washington Representatives (Columbia Books), 1.27, 11.9

Web search engines, 5.5

Web sites, 5.5

Webster, Daniel, 1.7

Weekly radio addresses, 3.8, 3.16

West, Jade, 3.27

Whistleblowing, 2.5, 2.32

White House
  Comment Line, 8.51
  email updates, 3.8
  executive branch lobbyists, 1.22
  priorities, determination of, 3.26
  switchboard, 8.51
  tours, online, Appendix 3
  Visitors Office, 8.51
  web site, 3.8

Wichterman, Bill, 4.45, 10.4

Willard Hotel (Washington, DC), 1.5

Williams, Marmaduke, 2.34

Wilson, Harold, 3.1

Wilson, Woodrow, Ch. 4 (title page), 4.19, 10.57

Witnesses. *See* Testimony

Wood, Genevieve, 10.28

Wooden, John, 9.2, 9.11

Woodstock Theological Center, Forum on Lobbying Ethics held at, 2.3

Work experience of lobbyists, 1.17

Written testimony, 10.62, 10.64

CPSIA information can be obtained at www.ICGtesting.com
Printed in the USA
BVOW01s1324150614

356340BV00014B/257/P